The Next 10 Actual, Official

LSAT
PrepTests™

A Publication of the Law School Admission Council
Newtown, PA

The Law School Admission Council (LSAC) is a nonprofit corporation whose members are more than 200 law schools in the United States and Canada. It was founded in 1947 to coordinate, facilitate, and enhance the law school admission process. The organization also provides programs and services related to legal education. All law schools approved by the American Bar Association (ABA) are LSAC members. Canadian law schools recognized by a provincial or territorial law society or government agency are also included in the voting membership of the Council.

The services provided by LSAC include the Law School Admission Test (LSAT); the Law School Data Assembly Service (LSDAS); the Candidate Referral Service (CRS); software, including ADMIT-M admission office software; and various publications and LSAT preparation tools. The LSAT, LSDAS, and CRS are provided to assist law schools in serving and evaluating applicants. LSAC does not engage in assessing an applicant's chances for admission to any law school; all admission decisions are made by individual law schools.

LSAT, *The Official LSAT PrepTest, The Official LSAT SuperPrep, ADMIT-M*, and LSAC are registered marks of the Law School Admission Council, Inc. Law School Forums is a service mark of the Law School Admission Council, Inc. *10 Actual, Official LSAT PrepTests; 10 More Actual, Official LSAT PrepTests; The Next 10 Actual, Official LSAT PrepTests; The New Whole Law School Package; ABA-LSAC Official Guide to ABA-Approved Law Schools;* and LSDAS are trademarks of Law School Admission Council, Inc.

Law School Admission Council fees, policies, and procedures relating to, but not limited to, test registration, test administration, test score reporting, misconduct and irregularities, and other matters may change without notice at any time. Up-to-date Law School Admission Council policies and procedures are available at *www.LSAC.org*, or you may contact our candidate service representatives.

ISBN 0-942639-89-8

The 10 PrepTests in this book are disclosed Law School Admission Tests (LSATs) that were administered between October 1999 and October 2002. Each test in this volume includes actual logical reasoning, reading comprehension, and analytical reasoning items followed by the writing sample, score computation table, and answer key for that test. This publication is designed to be an inexpensive way for you to gain practice and better prepare yourself for taking the LSAT.

The LSAT is a half-day standardized test required for admission to all LSAC-member law schools. It consists of five 35-minute sections of multiple-choice questions. Four of the five sections contribute to the test taker's score. These sections include one reading comprehension section, one analytical reasoning section, and two logical reasoning sections. The unscored section typically is used to pretest new test items and to preequate new test forms. The placement of this section, which is commonly referred to as the variable section, is varied for each administration of the test. A 30-minute writing sample is administered at the end of the test. The writing sample is not scored by LSAC, but copies are sent to all law schools to which you apply. The score scale for the LSAT is 120 to 180.

The LSAT is designed to measure skills that are considered essential for success in law school: the reading and comprehension of complex texts with accuracy and insight; the organization and management of information and the ability to draw reasonable inferences from it; the ability to think critically; and the analysis and evaluation of the reasoning and arguments of others.

The LSAT provides a standard measure of acquired reading and verbal reasoning skills that law schools can use as one of several factors in assessing applicants.

For up-to-date information about LSAC's services, go to our website, *www.LSAC.org*, or pick up a current *LSAT & LSDAS Information Book*.

Scoring

Your LSAT score is based on the number of questions you answer correctly (the raw score). There is no deduction for incorrect answers, and all questions count equally. In other words, there is no penalty for guessing.

■ Test Score Accuracy—Reliability and Standard Error of Measurement

Candidates perform at different levels on different occasions for reasons quite unrelated to the characteristics of a test itself. The accuracy of test scores is best described by the use of two related statistical terms, reliability and standard error of measurement.

Reliability is a measure of how consistently a test measures the skills being assessed. The higher the reliability coefficient for a test, the more certain we can be that test takers would get very similar scores if they took the test again.

LSAC reports an internal consistency measure of reliability for every test form. Reliability can vary from 0.00 to 1.00, and a test with no measurement error would have a reliability coefficient of 1.00 (never attained in practice). Reliability coefficients for past LSAT forms have ranged from .90 to .95, indicating a high degree of consistency for these tests. LSAC expects the reliability of the LSAT to continue to fall within the same range.

LSAC also reports the amount of measurement error associated with each test form, a concept known as the standard error of measurement (SEM). The SEM, which is usually about 2.6 points, indicates how close a test taker's observed score is likely to be to his or her true score. True scores are theoretical scores that would be obtained from perfectly reliable tests with no measurement error—scores never known in practice.

Score bands, or ranges of scores that contain a test taker's true score a certain percentage of the time, can be derived using the SEM. LSAT score bands are constructed by adding and subtracting the (rounded) SEM to and from an actual LSAT score (e.g., the LSAT score, plus or minus 3 points). Scores near 120 or 180 have asymmetrical bands. Score bands constructed in this manner will contain an individual's true score approximately 68 percent of the time.

Measurement error also must be taken into account when comparing LSAT scores of two test takers. It is likely that small differences in scores are due to measurement error rather than to meaningful differences in ability. The standard error of score differences provides some guidance as to the importance of differences between two scores. The standard error of score differences is approximately 1.4 times larger than the standard error of measurement for the individual scores.

Thus, a test score should be regarded as a useful but approximate measure of a test taker's abilities as measured by the test, not as an exact determination of his or her abilities. LSAC encourages law schools to examine the range of scores within the interval that probably contains the test taker's true score (e.g., the test taker's score band) rather than solely interpret the reported score alone.

Adjustments for Variation in Test Difficulty

All test forms of the LSAT reported on the same score scale are designed to measure the same abilities, but one test form may be slightly easier or more difficult than another. The scores from different test forms are made comparable through a statistical procedure known as equating. As a result of equating, a given scaled score earned on different test forms reflects the same level of ability.

Research on the LSAT

Summaries of LSAT validity studies and other LSAT research can be found in member law school libraries.

To Inquire About Test Questions

If you find what you believe to be an error or ambiguity in a test question that affects your response to the question contact LSAC by e-mail: *LSATTS@LSAC.org*, or write to Law School Admission Council, Test Development Group, 662 Penn Street, Box 40, Newtown, PA 18940-0040.

How These PrepTests Differ From an Actual LSAT

These PrepTests are made up of the scored sections and writing samples from the actual disclosed LSATs administered from October 1999 through October 2002. However, they do not contain the extra, variable section that is used to pretest new test items of one of the three question types. The three LSAT question types may be in a different order in an actual LSAT than in these PrepTests. This is because the order of the question types is intentionally varied for each administration of the test.

The Question Types

The multiple-choice questions that make up most of the LSAT reflect a broad range of academic disciplines and are intended to give no advantage to candidates from a particular academic background.

The five sections of the test contain three different question types. The following material presents a general discussion of the nature of each question type and some strategies that can be used in answering them.

Reading Comprehension Questions

The purpose of reading comprehension questions is to measure your ability to read, with understanding and insight, examples of lengthy and complex materials similar to those commonly encountered in law school work. The reading comprehension section of the test consists of four passages, each approximately 450 words long, followed by five to eight questions that test your reading and reasoning abilities. Passages for reading comprehension items are drawn from subjects such as the humanities, the social sciences, the biological and physical sciences, and issues related to the law.

Reading comprehension questions require you to read carefully and accurately, to determine the relationships among the various parts of the passage, and to draw reasonable inferences from the material in the passage. The questions may ask about:

- the main idea or primary purpose of the passage;

- the meaning or purpose of words or phrases used in the passage;

- information explicitly stated in the passage;

- information or ideas that can be inferred from the passage;

- the organization of the passage;

- the application of information in the passage to a new context; and

- the tone of the passage or the author's attitude as it is revealed in the language used.

Suggested Approach

Since passages are drawn from many different disciplines and sources, you should not be discouraged if you encounter material with which you are not familiar. It is important to remember that questions are to be answered exclusively on the basis of the information provided in the passage. There is no particular knowledge that you are expected to bring to the test, and you should not make inferences based on any prior knowledge of a subject that you may have. You may, however, wish to defer working on a passage that seems particularly difficult or unfamiliar until after you have dealt with passages you find easier.

Strategies. In preparing for the test, you should experiment with different strategies, and decide which work most effectively for you. These include:

- Reading the passage very closely and then answering the questions;

- Reading the questions first, reading the passage closely, and then returning to the questions; and

- Skimming the passage and questions very quickly, then rereading the passage closely and answering the questions.

Remember that your strategy must be effective under timed conditions.

Reading the passage. Whatever strategy you choose, you should give the passage at least one careful reading before answering the questions. Separate main ideas from supporting ideas and the author's own ideas or attitudes from factual, objective information. Note transitions from one idea to the next and examine the relationships among the different ideas or parts of the passage. For example, are they contrasting or complementary? Consider how and why the author makes points and draws conclusions. Be sensitive to the implications of what the passage says.

You may find it helpful to mark key parts of the passage. For example, you might underline main ideas or important arguments, and you might circle transitional words—'although,' 'nevertheless,' 'correspondingly,' and the like—that will help you map the structure of the passage. Moreover, you might note descriptive words that will help you identify the author's attitude toward a particular idea or person.

Answering the Questions

- Always read all the answer choices before selecting the best answer. The best answer choice is the one that most accurately and completely answers the question being posed.

- Respond to the specific question being asked. Do not pick an answer choice simply because it is a true statement. For example, picking a true statement might yield an incorrect answer to a question in which you are asked to identify the author's position on an issue, since here you are not being asked to evaluate the truth of the author's position, but only to correctly identify what that position is.

- Answer the questions only on the basis of the information provided in the passage. Your own views, interpretations, or opinions, and those you have heard from others, may sometimes conflict with those expressed in the passage; however, you are expected to work within the context provided by the passage. You should not expect to agree with everything you encounter in reading comprehension passages.

■ Analytical Reasoning Questions

Analytical reasoning items are designed to measure the ability to understand a structure of relationships and to draw logical conclusions about the structure. You are asked to make deductions from a set of statements, rules, or conditions that describe relationships among entities such as persons, places, things, or events. They simulate the kinds of detailed analyses of relationships that a law student must perform in solving legal problems. For example, a passage might describe four diplomats sitting around a table, following certain rules of protocol as to who can sit where. You must answer questions about the implications of the given information, for example, who is sitting between diplomats X and Y.

The passage used for each group of questions describes a common relationship such as the following:

- Assignment: Two parents, P and O, and their children, R and S, must go to the dentist on four consecutive days, designated 1, 2, 3, and 4;

- Ordering: X arrived before Y but after Z;

- Grouping: A manager is trying to form a project team from seven staff members—R,S,T,U,V,W, and X. Each staff member has a particular strength—writing, planning, or facilitating;

- Spatial: A certain country contains six cities and each city is connected to at least one other city by a system of roads, some of which are one-way.

Careful reading and analysis are necessary to determine the exact nature of the relationships involved. Some relationships are fixed (e.g., P and R always sit at the same table). Other relationships are variable (e.g., Q must be assigned to either table 1 or table 3). Some relationships that are not stated in the conditions are implied by and can be deduced from those that are stated. (e.g., If one condition about books on a shelf specifies that Book L is to the left of Book Y, and another specifies that Book P is to the left of Book L, then it can be deduced that Book P is to the left of Book Y.)

No formal training in logic is required to answer these questions correctly. Analytical reasoning questions are intended to be answered using knowledge, skills, and reasoning ability generally expected of college students and graduates.

Suggested Approach

Some people may prefer to answer first those questions about a passage that seem less difficult and then those that seem more difficult. In general, it is best not to start another passage before finishing one begun earlier, because much time can be lost in returning to a passage and reestablishing familiarity with its relationships. Do not assume that, because the conditions for a set of questions look long or complicated, the questions based on those conditions will necessarily be especially difficult.

Reading the passage. In reading the conditions, do not introduce unwarranted assumptions. For instance, in a set establishing relationships of height and weight among the members of a team, do not assume that a person who is taller than another person must weigh more than that person. All the information needed to answer each question is provided in the passage and the question itself.

The conditions are designed to be as clear as possible; do not interpret them as if they were intended to trick you. For example, if a question asks how many people could be eligible to serve on a committee, consider only those people named in the passage unless directed otherwise. When in doubt, read the conditions in their most obvious sense. Remember, however, that the language in the conditions is intended to be read for precise meaning. It is essential to pay particular attention to words that describe or limit relationships, such as 'only,' 'exactly,' 'never,' 'always,' 'must be,' 'cannot be,' and the like.

The result of this careful reading will be a clear picture of the structure of the relationships involved, including the kinds of relationships permitted, the participants in the relationships, and the range of actions or attributes allowed by the relationships for these participants.

Questions are independent. Each question should be considered separately from the other questions in its set; no information, except what is given in the original conditions, should be carried over from one question to another. In some cases a question will simply ask for conclusions to be drawn from the conditions as originally given. Some questions may, however, add information to the original conditions or temporarily suspend one of the original conditions for the purpose of that question only. For example, if Question 1 adds the information "if P is sitting at table 2...," this information should NOT be carried over to any other question in the group.

Highlighting the text; using diagrams. Many people find it useful to underline key points in the passage and in each question. In addition, it may prove very helpful to draw a diagram to assist you in finding the solution to the problem.

In preparing for the test, you may wish to experiment with different types of diagrams. For a scheduling problem, a calendar-like diagram may be helpful. For a spatial relationship problem, a simple map can be a useful device.

Even though some people find diagrams to be very helpful, other people seldom use them. And among those who do regularly use diagrams in solving these problems, there is by no means universal agreement on which kind of diagram is best for which problem or in which cases a diagram is most useful. Do not be concerned if a particular problem in the test seems to be best approached without the use of a diagram.

■ Logical Reasoning Questions

Logical reasoning questions evaluate your ability to understand, analyze, criticize, and complete a variety of arguments. The arguments are contained in short passages taken from a variety of sources, including letters to the editor, speeches, advertisements, newspaper articles and editorials, informal discussions and conversations, as well as articles in the humanities, the social sciences, and the natural sciences.

Each logical reasoning question requires you to read and comprehend a short passage, then answer one or two questions about it. The questions test a variety of abilities involved in reasoning logically and thinking critically. These include:

- recognizing the point or issue of an argument or dispute;

- detecting the assumptions involved in an argumentation or chain of reasoning;

- drawing reasonable conclusions from given evidence or premises;

- identifying and applying principles;

- identifying the method or structure of an argument or chain of reasoning;

- detecting reasoning errors and misinterpretations;

- determining how additional evidence or argumentation affects an argument or conclusion; and

- identifying explanations and recognizing resolutions of conflicting facts or arguments.

The questions do not presuppose knowledge of the terminology of formal logic. For example, you will not be expected to know the meaning of specialized terms such as "ad hominem" or "syllogism." On the other hand, you will be expected to understand and critique the reasoning contained in arguments. This requires that you possess, at a minimum, a college-level understanding of widely used concepts such as argument, premise, assumption, and conclusion.

Suggested Approach

Read each question carefully. Make sure that you understand the meaning of each part of the question. Make

sure that you understand the meaning of each answer choice and the ways in which it may or may not relate to the question posed.

Do not pick a response simply because it is a true statement. Although true, it may not answer the question posed.

Answer each question on the basis of the information that is given, even if you do not agree with it. Work within the context provided by the passage. LSAT questions do not involve any tricks or hidden meanings.

The Writing Sample

On the day of the test, you are required to write one sample essay. LSAC does not score the writing sample, but copies are sent to all law schools to which you apply. During the 2005-2006 testing year, you will be randomly assigned one of two different kinds of writing prompt—decision or argument. In both cases the task is to deal with argument, either by constructing an argument for deciding in a certain way or by evaluating a given argument. You will have 35 minutes in which to plan and write an essay on the individual topic you receive. Current information can be found at *www.LSAC.org* and in the appropriate edition of the *LSAT & LSDAS Information Book.*

Read the topic and the accompanying directions carefully. You will probably find it best to spend a few minutes considering the topic and organizing your thoughts before you begin writing. In your essay, be sure to develop your ideas fully, leaving time, if possible, to review what you have written. **Do not write on a topic other than the one specified. Writing on a topic of your own choice is not acceptable.**

No special knowledge is required or expected for this writing exercise. Law schools are interested in the reasoning, clarity, organization, language usage, and writing mechanics displayed in your essay. How well you write is more important than how much you write. Confine your essay to the blocked, lined area on the front and back of the separate writing sample response sheet. Only that area will be reproduced for law schools. Be sure that your writing is legible. The LSAT Writing Sample Topic Sheet contains two areas as scratch paper.

Notes made on the scratch paper will not be reproduced for law schools.

Note: Please note that LSAC's LSAT preparation books contain only the actual writing prompts administered with the LSATs included in the book. Only one kind of writing prompt was administered prior to June 2005.

The Decision Prompt

This kind of writing prompt presents a decision problem. You are asked to make a choice between two positions or courses of action. Both of the choices are defensible, and you are given criteria and facts on which to base your decision. There is no "right" or "wrong" position to take on the topic, so the quality of each test taker's response is a function not of which choice is made, but of how well or poorly the choice is supported and how well or poorly the other choice is criticized.

The Argument Prompt

This kind of writing prompt is designed to assess your ability to understand, analyze, and evaluate arguments and to clearly convey your evaluation in writing. The prompt consists of a brief passage in which the author makes a case for some course of action or interpretation of events by presenting claims backed by reasons and evidence. Your task is to discuss the cogency of the author's case by critically examining its line of reasoning and use of evidence.

Taking the PrepTests Under Simulated LSAT Conditions

One important way to prepare for the LSAT is to take a sample test under the same requirements and time limits you will encounter in taking an actual LSAT. This helps you to estimate the amount of time you can afford to spend on each question in a section and to determine the question types on which you may need additional practice.

Since the LSAT is a timed test, it is important to use your allotted time wisely. During the test, you may work only on the section designated by the test supervisor. You cannot devote extra time to a difficult section and make up that time on a section you find easier. In pacing yourself, and checking your answers, you should think of each section of the test as a separate minitest.

Be sure that you answer every question on the test. When you do not know the correct answer to a question, first eliminate the responses that you know are incorrect, then make your best guess among the remaining choices. Do not be afraid to guess, as there is no penalty for incorrect answers.

When you take a sample test, abide by all the requirements specified in the directions and keep strictly within the specified time limits. Work without a rest period. When you take an actual test you will have only a short break—usually 10–15 minutes—after SECTION III. When taken under conditions as much like actual testing conditions as possible, a sample test provides very useful preparation for taking the LSAT.

Official directions for the four multiple-choice sections and the writing sample are included in these PrepTests so that you can approximate actual testing conditions as you practice.

To take a test:

- Set a timer for 35 minutes. Answer all the questions in SECTION I of a PrepTest. Stop working on that section when the 35 minutes have elapsed.

- Repeat, allowing yourself 35 minutes for each of the other three sections.

- Set the timer for 30 minutes, then prepare your response to the writing sample for the PrepTest. (**Note:** The PrepTests in this book were published prior to the timing change in June 2005)

- Refer to "Computing Your Score" for the PrepTest for instruction on evaluating your performance. An answer key is provided for that purpose.

The Official LSAT PrepTest

29

- October 1999
  PrepTest 29

- Form 9LSS44

SECTION I

Time—35 minutes

25 Questions

Directions: The questions in this section are based on the reasoning contained in brief statements or passages. For some questions, more than one of the choices could conceivably answer the question. However, you are to choose the best answer; that is, the response that most accurately and completely answers the question. You should not make assumptions that are by commonsense standards implausible, superfluous, or incompatible with the passage. After you have chosen the best answer, blacken the corresponding space on your answer sheet.

Questions 1–2

Politician: The funding for the new nationwide health-awareness campaign should come from an increase in taxes on cigarettes. It is well established that cigarette smoking causes many serious health problems, and it is only reasonable that people whose unhealthful habits cause so many health problems should bear the costs of that campaign.

Smoker: But it is equally well established that regularly eating high-fat, high-cholesterol foods causes as many serious health problems as does smoking, yet it would be manifestly unreasonable to force those who purchase such foods to bear the burden of financing this campaign.

1. Which one of the following is the point at issue between the politician and the smoker?

    (A)   whether the politician's proposal for financing the health-awareness campaign is an unreasonable one
    (B)   whether smokers are more aware of the harmful effects of their habit than are people who regularly eat high-fat, high-cholesterol foods
    (C)   whether the effects of smoking constitute a greater health hazard than do the effects of regularly eating high-fat, high-cholesterol foods
    (D)   whether it is unreasonable to require people who do not benefit from certain governmental programs to share the costs of those programs
    (E)   whether the proposed increase on cigarette taxes is an efficient means of financing the health-awareness campaign

2. The smoker's response to the politician's argument

    (A)   offers a counterexample that calls into question the politician's reasoning
    (B)   presents an alternative solution to that proposed by the politician
    (C)   argues that the method proposed by the politician would be inadequate for its intended purpose
    (D)   questions the accuracy of the information cited by the politician in reaching a conclusion
    (E)   illustrates how the politician's proposal could aggravate the problem it is intended to solve

3. There should be a greater use of gasohol. Gasohol is a mixture of alcohol and gasoline, and has a higher octane rating and fewer carbon monoxide emissions than straight gasoline. Burning gasohol adds no more carbon dioxide to the atmosphere than plants remove by photosynthesis.

    Each of the following, if true, strengthens the argument above EXCEPT:

    (A)   Cars run less well on gasoline than they do on gasohol.
    (B)   Since less gasoline is needed with the use of gasohol, an energy shortage is less likely.
    (C)   Cars burn on the average slightly more gasohol per kilometer than they do gasoline.
    (D)   Gasohol is cheaper to produce and hence costs less at the pump than gasoline.
    (E)   Burning gasoline adds more carbon dioxide to the atmosphere than plants can remove.

4. Cats spend much of their time sleeping; they seem to awaken only to stretch and yawn. Yet they have a strong, agile musculature that most animals would have to exercise strenuously to acquire.

    Which one of the following, if true, most helps to resolve the apparent paradox described above?

    (A)   Cats have a greater physiological need for sleep than other animals.
    (B)   Many other animals also spend much of their time sleeping yet have a strong, agile musculature.
    (C)   Cats are able to sleep in apparently uncomfortable positions.
    (D)   Cats derive ample exercise from frequent stretching.
    (E)   Cats require strength and agility in order to be effective predators.

GO ON TO THE NEXT PAGE.

5. Barnes: The two newest employees at this company have salaries that are too high for the simple tasks normally assigned to new employees and duties that are too complex for inexperienced workers. Hence, the salaries and the complexity of the duties of these two newest employees should be reduced.

Which one of the following is an assumption on which Barnes's argument depends?

(A) The duties of the two newest employees are not less complex than any others in the company.
(B) It is because of the complex duties assigned that the two newest employees are being paid more than is usually paid to newly hired employees.
(C) The two newest employees are not experienced at their occupations.
(D) Barnes was not hired at a higher-than-average starting salary.
(E) The salaries of the two newest employees are no higher than the salaries that other companies pay for workers with a similar level of experience.

6. These days, drug companies and health professionals alike are focusing their attention on cholesterol in the blood. The more cholesterol we have in our blood, the higher the risk that we shall die of a heart attack. The issue is pertinent since heart disease kills more North Americans every year than any other single cause. At least three factors—smoking, drinking, and exercise—can each influence levels of cholesterol in the blood.

Which one of the following can be properly concluded from the passage?

(A) If a person has low blood cholesterol, then that person's risk of fatal heart disease is low.
(B) Smoking in moderation can entail as great a risk of fatal heart disease as does heavy smoking.
(C) A high-cholesterol diet is the principal cause of death in North America.
(D) The only way that smoking increases one's risk of fatal heart disease is by influencing the levels of cholesterol in the blood.
(E) The risk of fatal heart disease can be altered by certain changes in lifestyle.

7. In Debbie's magic act, a volunteer supposedly selects a card in a random fashion, looks at it without showing it to her, and replaces it in the deck. After several shuffles, Debbie cuts the deck and supposedly reveals the same selected card. A skeptic conducted three trials. In the first, Debbie was videotaped, and no sleight of hand was found. In the second, the skeptic instead supplied a standard deck of cards. For the third trial, the skeptic selected the card. Each time, Debbie apparently revealed the selected card. The skeptic concluded that Debbie uses neither sleight of hand, nor a trick deck, nor a planted "volunteer" to achieve her effect.

Which one of the following most accurately describes a flaw in the skeptic's reasoning?

(A) The skeptic failed to consider the possibility that Debbie did not always use the same method to achieve her effect.
(B) The skeptic failed to consider the possibility that sleight of hand could also be detected by some means other than videotaping.
(C) The skeptic failed to consider the possibility that Debbie requires both sleight of hand and a trick deck to achieve her effect.
(D) The skeptic failed to consider the possibility that Debbie used something other than sleight of hand, a trick deck, or a planted "volunteer" to achieve her effect.
(E) The skeptic failed to consider the possibility that Debbie's success in the three trials was something other than a coincidence.

GO ON TO THE NEXT PAGE.

8. Nutritionist: Many people claim that simple carbohydrates are a reasonable caloric replacement for the fatty foods forbidden to those on low-fat diets. This is now in doubt. New studies show that, for many people, a high intake of simple carbohydrates stimulates an overproduction of insulin, a hormone that is involved in processing sugars and starches to create energy when the body requires energy, or, when energy is not required, to store the resulting by-products as fat.

Which one of the following is most strongly supported by the nutritionist's statements?

(A) People on low-fat diets should avoid consumption of simple carbohydrates if they wish to maintain the energy that their bodies require.

(B) People who produce enough insulin to process their intake of simple carbohydrates should not feel compelled to adopt low-fat diets.

(C) People who consume simple carbohydrates should limit their intake of foods high in fat.

(D) People who wish to avoid gaining body fat should limit their intake of foods high in simple carbohydrates.

(E) People who do not produce an excessive amount of insulin when they consume foods high in simple carbohydrates will not lose weight if they restrict only their intake of these foods.

9. Jean: Our navigational equipment sells for $1,100 and dominates the high end of the market, but more units are sold by our competitors in the $700 to $800 range. We should add a low-cost model, which would allow us to increase our overall sales while continuing to dominate the high end.

Tracy: I disagree. Our equipment sells to consumers who associate our company with quality. Moving into the low-cost market would put our competitors in the high-cost market on an equal footing with us, which could hurt our overall sales.

Jean's and Tracy's statements most strongly suggest that they disagree over which one of the following propositions?

(A) There is a greater potential for profits in the low-cost market than there is in the high-cost market.

(B) The proposed cheaper model, if it were made available, would sell to customers who would otherwise be buying the company's present model.

(C) The company could dominate the low-cost market in the same way it has dominated the high-cost market.

(D) The company would no longer dominate the high-cost market if it began selling a low-cost model.

(E) Decreased sales of the high-cost model would result in poor sales for the proposed low-cost model.

10. The symptoms of hepatitis A appear no earlier than 60 days after a person has been infected. In a test of a hepatitis A vaccine, 50 people received the vaccine and 50 people received a harmless placebo. Although some people from each group eventually exhibited symptoms of hepatitis A, the vaccine as used in the test is completely effective in preventing infection with the hepatitis A virus.

Which one of the following, if true, most helps resolve the apparent discrepancy in the information above?

(A) The placebo did not produce any side effects that resembled any of the symptoms of hepatitis A.

(B) More members of the group that had received the placebo recognized their symptoms as symptoms of hepatitis A than did members of the group that had received the vaccine.

(C) The people who received the placebo were in better overall physical condition than were the people who received the vaccine.

(D) The vaccinated people who exhibited symptoms of hepatitis A were infected with the hepatitis A virus before being vaccinated.

(E) Of the people who developed symptoms of hepatitis A, those who received the vaccine recovered more quickly, on average, than those who did not.

GO ON TO THE NEXT PAGE.

Questions 11–12

It is well known that many species adapt to their environment, but it is usually assumed that only the most highly evolved species alter their environment in ways that aid their own survival. However, this characteristic is actually quite common. Certain species of plankton, for example, generate a gas that is converted in the atmosphere into particles of sulfate. These particles cause water vapor to condense, thus forming clouds. Indeed, the formation of clouds over the ocean largely depends on the presence of these particles. More cloud cover means more sunlight is reflected, and so the Earth absorbs less heat. Thus plankton cause the surface of the Earth to be cooler and this benefits the plankton.

11. Of the following, which one most accurately expresses the main point of the argument?

   (A)   The Earth would be far warmer than it is now if certain species of plankton became extinct.

   (B)   By altering their environment in ways that improve their chances of survival, certain species of plankton benefit the Earth as a whole.

   (C)   Improving their own chances of survival by altering the environment is not limited to the most highly evolved species.

   (D)   The extent of the cloud cover over the oceans is largely determined by the quantity of plankton in those oceans.

   (E)   Species such as plankton alter the environment in ways that are less detrimental to the well-being of other species than are the alterations to the environment made by more highly evolved species.

12. Which one of the following accurately describes the argumentative strategy employed?

   (A)   A general principle is used to justify a claim made about a particular case to which that principle has been shown to apply.

   (B)   An explanation of how a controversial phenomenon could have come about is given in order to support the claim that this phenomenon did in fact come about.

   (C)   A generalization about the conditions under which a certain process can occur is advanced on the basis of an examination of certain cases in which that process did occur.

   (D)   A counterexample to a position being challenged is presented in order to show that this position is incorrect.

   (E)   A detailed example is used to illustrate the advantage of one strategy over another.

13. The top priority of the school administration should be student attendance. No matter how good the teachers, texts, and facilities are, none of these does any good if few students come to school.

The pattern of reasoning in the argument above is LEAST similar to that in which one of the following?

   (A)   The top priority of a salesperson should be not to alienate customers. Honesty and a good knowledge of the product line are useful to a salesperson only if the customer feels at ease.

   (B)   The top priority of a person lost in the wilderness should be food-gathering. Knowing how to find one's way back or how to build a comfortable shelter does one no good if one does not have enough food to survive.

   (C)   The top priority of a detective should be to gather physical evidence. High-tech crime lab equipment and the most sophisticated criminological analysis are of no use if crucial clues are not gathered.

   (D)   The top priority of a library should be to maintain its collection of books. A knowledgeable staff and beautiful facilities are of no value if there is an inadequate supply of books to lend.

   (E)   The top priority of a criminal defense lawyer should be to ensure that innocent clients are found not guilty. Such clients can justly be released from jail and resume their normal lives if they are found not guilty.

GO ON TO THE NEXT PAGE.

14. Prosecutor: Dr. Yuge has testified that, had the robbery occurred after 1:50 A.M., then, the moon having set at 1:45 A.M., it would have been too dark for Klein to recognize the perpetrator. But Yuge acknowledged that the moon was full enough to provide considerable light before it set. And we have conclusively shown that the robbery occurred between 1:15 and 1:30 A.M. So there was enough light for Klein to make a reliable identification.

The prosecutor's reasoning is most vulnerable to criticism because it overlooks which one of the following possibilities?

(A) Klein may be mistaken about the time of the robbery and so it may have taken place after the moon had set.
(B) The perpetrator may closely resemble someone who was not involved in the robbery.
(C) Klein may have been too upset to make a reliable identification even in good light.
(D) Without having been there, Dr. Yuge has no way of knowing whether the light was sufficient.
(E) During the robbery the moon's light may have been interfered with by conditions such as cloud cover.

15. Ordinary mountain sickness, a common condition among mountain climbers, and one from which most people can recover, is caused by the characteristic shortage of oxygen in the atmosphere at high altitudes. Cerebral edema, a rarer disruption of blood circulation in the brain that quickly becomes life-threatening if not correctly treated from its onset, can also be caused by a shortage of oxygen. Since the symptoms of cerebral edema resemble those of ordinary mountain sickness, cerebral edema is especially dangerous at high altitudes.

Which one of the following is an assumption on which the argument depends?

(A) The treatment for ordinary mountain sickness differs from the treatment for cerebral edema.
(B) Cerebral edema can cause those who suffer from it to slip into a coma within a few hours.
(C) Unlike cerebral edema, ordinary mountain sickness involves no disruption of blood circulation in the brain.
(D) Shortage of oxygen at extremely high altitudes is likely to affect thinking processes and cause errors of judgment.
(E) Most people who suffer from ordinary mountain sickness recover without any special treatment.

16. We can learn about the living conditions of a vanished culture by examining its language. Thus, it is likely that the people who spoke Proto-Indo-European, the language from which all Indo-European languages descended, lived in a cold climate, isolated from ocean or sea, because Proto-Indo-European lacks a word for "sea," yet contains words for "winter," "snow," and "wolf."

Which one of the following, if true, most seriously weakens the argument?

(A) A word meaning "fish" was used by the people who spoke Proto-Indo-European.
(B) Some languages lack words for prominent elements of the environments of their speakers.
(C) There are no known languages today that lack a word for "sea."
(D) Proto-Indo-European possesses words for "heat."
(E) The people who spoke Proto-Indo-European were nomadic.

17. Columnist: It is impossible for there to be real evidence that lax radiation standards that were once in effect at nuclear reactors actually contributed to the increase in cancer rates near such sites. The point is a familiar one: who can say if a particular case of cancer is due to radiation, exposure to environmental toxins, smoking, poor diet, or genetic factors.

The argument's reasoning is most vulnerable to criticism on which one of the following grounds?

(A) The argument fails to recognize that there may be convincing statistical evidence even if individual causes cannot be known.
(B) The argument inappropriately presupposes that what follows a certain phenomenon was caused by that phenomenon.
(C) The argument inappropriately draws a conclusion about causes of cancer in general from evidence drawn from a particular case of cancer.
(D) The argument ignores other possible causes of the increase in cancer rates near the nuclear reactor complexes.
(E) The argument concludes that a claim about a causal connection is false on the basis of a lack of evidence for the claim.

GO ON TO THE NEXT PAGE.

18. Some planning committee members—those representing the construction industry—have significant financial interests in the committee's decisions. No one who is on the planning committee lives in the suburbs, although many of them work there.

If the statements above are true, which one of the following must also be true?

(A) No persons with significant financial interests in the planning committee's decisions are not in the construction industry.

(B) No person who has a significant financial interest in the planning committee's decisions lives in the suburbs.

(C) Some persons with significant financial interests in the planning committee's decisions work in the suburbs.

(D) Some planning committee members who represent the construction industry do not work in the suburbs.

(E) Some persons with significant financial interests in the planning committee's decisions do not live in the suburbs.

19. Arbitrator: The shipping manager admits that he decided to close the old facility on October 14 and to schedule the new facility's opening for October 17, the following Monday. But he also claims that he is not responsible for the business that was lost due to the new facility's failing to open as scheduled. He blames the contractor for not finishing on time, but he, too, is to blame, for he was aware of the contractor's typical delays and should have planned for this contingency.

Which one of the following principles underlies the arbitrator's argument?

(A) A manager should take foreseeable problems into account when making decisions.

(B) A manager should be able to depend on contractors to do their jobs promptly.

(C) A manager should see to it that contractors do their jobs promptly.

(D) A manager should be held responsible for mistakes made by those whom the manager directly supervises.

(E) A manager, and only a manager, should be held responsible for a project's failure.

20. The price of a full-fare coach ticket from Toronto to Dallas on Breezeway Airlines is the same today as it was a year ago, if inflation is taken into account by calculating prices in constant dollars. However, today 90 percent of the Toronto-to-Dallas coach tickets that Breezeway sells are discount tickets and only 10 percent are full-fare tickets, whereas a year ago half were discount tickets and half were full-fare tickets. Therefore, on average, people pay less today in constant dollars for a Breezeway Toronto-to-Dallas coach ticket than they did a year ago.

Which one of the following, if assumed, would allow the conclusion above to be properly drawn?

(A) A Toronto-to-Dallas full-fare coach ticket on Breezeway Airlines provides ticket-holders with a lower level of service today than such a ticket provided a year ago.

(B) A Toronto-to-Dallas discount coach ticket on Breezeway Airlines costs about the same amount in constant dollars today as it did a year ago.

(C) All full-fare coach tickets on Breezeway Airlines cost the same in constant dollars as they did a year ago.

(D) The average number of coach passengers per flight that Breezeway Airlines carries from Toronto to Dallas today is higher than the average number per flight a year ago.

(E) The criteria that Breezeway Airlines uses for permitting passengers to buy discount coach tickets on the Toronto-to-Dallas route are different today than they were a year ago.

GO ON TO THE NEXT PAGE.

Questions 21–22

Editorial: The government claims that the country's nuclear power plants are entirely safe and hence that the public's fear of nuclear accidents at these plants is groundless. The government also contends that its recent action to limit the nuclear industry's financial liability in the case of nuclear accidents at power plants is justified by the need to protect the nuclear industry from the threat of bankruptcy. But even the government says that unlimited liability poses such a threat only if injury claims can be sustained against the industry; and the government admits that for such claims to be sustained, injury must result from a nuclear accident. The public's fear, therefore, is well founded.

21.   If all of the statements offered in support of the editorial's conclusion correctly describe the government's position, which one of the following must also be true on the basis of those statements?

(A)   The government's claim about the safety of the country's nuclear power plants is false.
(B)   The government's position on nuclear power plants is inconsistent.
(C)   The government misrepresented its reasons for acting to limit the nuclear industry's liability.
(D)   Unlimited financial liability in the case of nuclear accidents poses no threat to the financial security of the country's nuclear industry.
(E)   The only serious threat posed by a nuclear accident would be to the financial security of the nuclear industry.

22.   Which one of the following principles, if valid, most helps to justify the editorial's argumentation?

(A)   If the government claims that something is unsafe then, in the absence of overwhelming evidence to the contrary, that thing should be assumed to be unsafe.
(B)   Fear that a certain kind of event will occur is well founded if those who have control over the occurrence of events of that kind stand to benefit financially from such an occurrence.
(C)   If a potentially dangerous thing is safe only because the financial security of those responsible for its operation depends on its being safe, then eliminating that dependence is not in the best interests of the public.
(D)   The government sometimes makes unsupported claims about what situations will arise, but it does not act to prevent a certain kind of situation from arising unless there is a real danger that such a situation will arise.
(E)   If a real financial threat to a major industry exists, then government action to limit that threat is justified.

23.   Linda says that, as a scientist, she knows that no scientist appreciates poetry. And, since most scientists are logical, at least some of the people who appreciate poetry are illogical.

Which one of the following is most parallel in its reasoning to the flawed reasoning above?

(A)   Ralph says that, as an expert in biology, he knows that no marsupial lays eggs. And, since most marsupials are native to Australia, at least some of the animals native to Australia do not lay eggs.
(B)   Franz says that, as a father of four children, he knows that no father wants children to eat candy at bedtime. And, since most fathers are adults, at least some of the people who want children to eat candy at bedtime are children.
(C)   Yuri says that, as a wine connoisseur, he knows that no wine aged in metal containers is equal in quality to the best wine aged in oak. And, since most California wine is aged in metal containers, California wine is inferior to at least the best French wine aged in oak.
(D)   Xi says that, as an experienced photographer, she knows that no color film produces images as sharp as the best black-and-white film. And, since most instant film is color film, at least some instant film produces images less sharp than the best black-and-white film.
(E)   Betty says that, as a corporate executive, she knows that no corporate executives like to pay taxes. And, since most corporate executives are honest people, at least some people who like to pay taxes are honest people.

GO ON TO THE NEXT PAGE.

24. Automobile-emission standards are enforced through annual inspection. At those inspections cars are tested while idling; that is, standing still with their engines running. Testing devices measure the levels of various pollutants as exhaust gases leave the tail pipe.

Which one of the following, if true, most strongly indicates that current enforcement of automobile-emission standards might be ineffective in controlling overall pollutant levels?

(A) As an emission-control technology approaches its limits, any additional gains in effectiveness become progressively more expensive.

(B) The testing devices used must be recalibrated frequently to measure pollutant levels with acceptable accuracy.

(C) The adjustments needed to make a car idle cleanly make it likely that the car will emit high levels of pollutants when moving at highway speeds.

(D) Most car owners ask their mechanics to make sure that their cars are in compliance with emission standards.

(E) When emission standards are set, no allowances are made for older cars.

25. The indigenous people of Tasmania are clearly related to the indigenous people of Australia, but were separated from them when the land bridge between Australia and Tasmania disappeared approximately 10,000 years ago. Two thousand years after the disappearance of the land bridge, however, there were major differences between the culture and technology of the indigenous Tasmanians and those of the indigenous Australians. The indigenous Tasmanians, unlike their Australian relatives, had no domesticated dogs, fishing nets, polished stone tools, or hunting implements like the boomerang and the spear-thrower.

Each of the following, if true, would contribute to an explanation of differences described above EXCEPT:

(A) After the disappearance of the land bridge the indigenous Tasmanians simply abandoned certain practices and technologies that they had originally shared with their Australian relatives.

(B) Devices such as the spear-thrower and the boomerang were developed by the indigenous Tasmanians more than 10,000 years ago.

(C) Technological innovations such as fishing nets, polished stone tools, and so on, were imported to Australia by Polynesian explorers more recently than 10,000 years ago.

(D) Indigenous people of Australia developed hunting implements like the boomerang and the spear-thrower after the disappearance of the land bridge.

(E) Although the technological and cultural innovations were developed in Australia more than 10,000 years ago, they were developed by groups in northern Australia with whom the indigenous Tasmanians had no contact prior to the disappearance of the land bridge.

S T O P

IF YOU FINISH BEFORE TIME IS CALLED, YOU MAY CHECK YOUR WORK ON THIS SECTION ONLY.
DO NOT WORK ON ANY OTHER SECTION IN THE TEST.

SECTION II

Time—35 minutes

27 Questions

<u>Directions</u>: Each passage in this section is followed by a group of questions to be answered on the basis of what is <u>stated</u> or <u>implied</u> in the passage. For some of the questions, more than one of the choices could conceivably answer the question. However, you are to choose the <u>best</u> answer; that is, the response that most accurately and completely answers the question, and blacken the corresponding space on your answer sheet.

For some years before the outbreak of World War I, a number of painters in different European countries developed works of art that some have described as prophetic: paintings that by challenging
(5) viewers' habitual ways of perceiving the world of the present are thus said to anticipate a future world that would be very different. The artistic styles that they brought into being varied widely, but all these styles had in common a very important break with traditions
(10) of representational art that stretched back to the Renaissance.

So fundamental is this break with tradition that it is not surprising to discover that these artists—among them Picasso and Braque in France, Kandinsky in
(15) Germany, and Malevich in Russia—are often credited with having anticipated not just subsequent developments in the arts, but also the political and social disruptions and upheavals of the modern world that came into being during and after the war. One art
(20) critic even goes so far as to claim that it is the very prophetic power of these artworks, and not their break with traditional artistic techniques, that constitutes their chief interest and value.

No one will deny that an artist may, just as much as
(25) a writer or a politician, speculate about the future and then try to express a vision of that future through making use of a particular style or choice of imagery; speculation about the possibility of war in Europe was certainly widespread during the early years of the
(30) twentieth century. But the forward-looking quality attributed to these artists should instead be credited to their exceptional aesthetic innovations rather than to any power to make clever guesses about political or social trends. For example, the clear impression we get
(35) of Picasso and Braque, the joint founders of cubism, from their contemporaries as well as from later statements made by the artists themselves, is that they were primarily concerned with problems of representation and form and with efforts to create a far
(40) more "real" reality than the one that was accessible only to the eye. The reformation of society was of no interest to them as artists.

It is also important to remember that not all decisive changes in art are quickly followed by
(45) dramatic events in the world outside art. The case of Delacroix, the nineteenth-century French painter, is revealing. His stylistic innovations startled his contemporaries—and still retain that power over modern viewers—but most art historians have decided
(50) that Delacroix adjusted himself to new social

conditions that were already coming into being as a result of political upheavals that had occurred in 1830, as opposed to other artists who supposedly told of changes still to come.

1. Which one of the following most accurately states the main idea of the passage?

(A)   Although they flourished independently, the pre–World War I European painters who developed new ways of looking at the world shared a common desire to break with the traditions of representational art.

(B)   The work of the pre–World War I European painters who developed new ways of looking at the world cannot be said to have intentionally predicted social changes but only to have anticipated new directions in artistic perception and expression.

(C)   The work of the pre–World War I European painters who developed new ways of looking at the world was important for its ability to predict social changes and its anticipation of new directions in artistic expression.

(D)   Art critics who believe that the work of some pre–World War I European painters foretold imminent social changes are mistaken because art is incapable of expressing a vision of the future.

(E)   Art critics who believe that the work of some pre–World War I European painters foretold imminent social changes are mistaken because the social upheavals that followed World War I were impossible to predict.

GO ON TO THE NEXT PAGE.

2. The art critic mentioned in lines 19–20 would be most likely to agree with which one of the following statements?

    (A) The supposed innovations of Picasso, Braque, Kandinsky, and Malevich were based on stylistic discoveries that had been made in the Renaissance but went unexplored for centuries.
    (B) The work of Picasso, Braque, Kandinsky, and Malevich possessed prophetic power because these artists employed the traditional techniques of representational art with unusual skill.
    (C) The importance of the work of Picasso, Braque, Kandinsky, and Malevich is due largely to the fact that the work was stylistically ahead of its time.
    (D) The prophecies embodied in the work of Picasso, Braque, Kandinsky, and Malevich were shrewd predictions based on insights into the European political situation.
    (E) The artistic styles brought into being by Picasso, Braque, Kandinsky, and Malevich, while stylistically innovative, were of little significance to the history of post–World War I art.

3. According to the passage, the statements of Picasso and Braque indicate that

    (A) they had a long-standing interest in politics
    (B) they worked actively to bring about social change
    (C) their formal innovations were actually the result of chance
    (D) their work was a deliberate attempt to transcend visual reality
    (E) the formal aspects of their work were of little interest to them

4. The author presents the example of Delacroix in order to illustrate which one of the following claims?

    (A) Social or political changes usually lead to important artistic innovations.
    (B) Artistic innovations do not necessarily anticipate social or political upheavals.
    (C) Some European painters have used art to predict social or political changes.
    (D) Important stylistic innovations are best achieved by abandoning past traditions.
    (E) Innovative artists can adapt themselves to social or political changes.

5. Which one of the following most accurately describes the contents of the passage?

    (A) The author describes an artistic phenomenon; introduces one interpretation of this phenomenon; proposes an alternative interpretation and then supports this alternative by criticizing the original interpretation.
    (B) The author describes an artistic phenomenon; identifies the causes of that phenomenon; illustrates some of the consequences of the phenomenon and then speculates about the significance of these consequences.
    (C) The author describes an artistic phenomenon; articulates the traditional interpretation of this phenomenon; identifies two common criticisms of this view and then dismisses each of these criticisms by appeal to an example.
    (D) The author describes an artistic phenomenon; presents two competing interpretations of the phenomenon; dismisses both interpretations by appeal to an example and then introduces an alternative interpretation.
    (E) The author describes an artistic phenomenon; identifies the causes of the phenomenon; presents an argument for the importance of the phenomenon and then advocates an attempt to recreate the phenomenon.

6. According to the author, the work of the pre–World War I painters described in the passage contains an example of each of the following EXCEPT:

    (A) an interest in issues of representation and form
    (B) a stylistic break with traditional art
    (C) the introduction of new artistic techniques
    (D) the ability to anticipate later artists
    (E) the power to predict social changes

7. Which one of the following characteristics of the painters discussed in the second paragraph does the author of the passage appear to value most highly?

    (A) their insights into pre–World War I politics
    (B) the visionary nature of their social views
    (C) their mastery of the techniques of representational art
    (D) their ability to adjust to changing social conditions
    (E) their stylistic and aesthetic accomplishments

GO ON TO THE NEXT PAGE.

Tribal communities in North America believe that their traditional languages are valuable resources that must be maintained. However, these traditional languages can fall into disuse when some of the effects
(5) of the majority culture on tribal life serve as barriers between a community and its traditional forms of social, economic, or spiritual interaction. In some communities the barrier has been overcome because people have recognized that language loss is serious
(10) and have taken action to prevent it, primarily through community self-teaching.

Before any community can systematically and formally teach a traditional language to its younger members, it must first document the language's
(15) grammar; for example, a group of Northern Utes spent two years conducting a thorough analysis and classification of Northern Ute linguistic structures. The grammatical information is then arranged in sequence from the simpler to the more complex types of usage,
(20) and methods are devised to present the sequence in ways that will be most useful and appropriate to the culture.

Certain obstacles can stand in the way of developing these teaching methods. One is the
(25) difficulty a community may encounter when it attempts to write down elements (particularly the spellings of words) of a language that has been primarily oral for centuries, as is often the case with traditional languages. Sometimes this difficulty can simply be a
(30) matter of the lack of acceptable written equivalents for certain sounds in the traditional language: problems arise because of an insistence that every sound in the language have a unique written equivalent—a desirable but ultimately frustrating condition that no written
(35) language has ever fully satisfied.

Another obstacle is dialect. There may be many language traditions in a particular community; which one is to be written down and taught? The Northern Utes decided not to standardize their language,
(40) agreeing that various phonetic spellings of words would be accepted as long as their meanings were clear. Although this troubled some community members who favored Western notions of standard language writing or whose training in Western-style
(45) linguistics was especially rigid, the lack of standard orthography made sense in the context of the community's needs. Within a year after the adoption of instruction in the Northern Ute language, even elementary school children could write and speak it
(50) effectively.

It has been argued that the attempt to write down traditional languages is misguided and unnecessary; after all, in many cases these languages have been transmitted in their oral form since their origins.
(55) Defenders of the practice counter that they are writing down their languages precisely because of a general decline in oral traditions, but they concede that languages could be preserved in their oral form if a community made every effort to eschew aspects of the
(60) majority culture that make this preservation difficult.

8. Which one of the following most accurately states the main idea of the passage?

(A) In the face of the pervasive influences of the majority culture, some tribes are having difficulty teaching their traditional languages to younger tribe members.

(B) If tribes are to continue to hold on to their cultures in the face of majority culture influences, it is necessary for them to first teach their traditional languages to younger tribe members.

(C) Responding to doubts about the value of preserving oral forms of culture, some tribes, using techniques of Western-style linguistics, have taught their traditional languages to younger tribe members.

(D) Recognizing the value of their traditional languages, some tribes, despite the difficulties involved, have developed programs to teach their traditional languages to younger tribe members.

(E) Sidestepping the inherent contradiction of preserving oral forms of culture in writing, some tribes are attempting, eschewing the influences of the majority culture, to teach their traditional languages to younger tribe members.

9. According to the passage, the first step in preparing to formally teach a traditional language is to

(A) analyze and classify its linguistic structures

(B) develop a hierarchy of its grammatical information

(C) determine appropriate methods for its presentation

(D) search for written equivalents for each of its sounds

(E) decide whether its syntax and spelling will be standardized

10. Based on the passage, those who hold the view described in lines 51–54 would be most likely to agree with which one of the following statements?

(A) Even if left exclusively in oral form, traditional languages are likely to survive.

(B) There has been a decline in communication among tribal members in general.

(C) Some oral customs do not need to be preserved orally.

(D) External influences have little effect on tribal customs.

(E) Tribes must focus on establishing a written tradition.

GO ON TO THE NEXT PAGE.

11. Which one of the following scenarios is LEAST compatible with aspects of traditional-language preservation discussed in the passage?

    (A) A community decides that the best way to maintain its traditional language is to rejuvenate its oral culture.

    (B) A community arranges the grammatical structures of its traditional language sequentially according to the degree of their complexity.

    (C) A community agrees to incorporate words from the majority culture in its traditional language to make it easier to teach.

    (D) A community determines the most appropriate methods for presenting its traditional language to students.

    (E) A community deliberates about which dialect of its traditional language should be taught to students.

12. Which one of the following most accurately describes the organization of the passage?

    (A) A problem is identified, followed by a list of obstacles to its solution; examples of the obstacles are discussed; a solution is proposed; methods of implementing the solution are described; an alternative to the solution is introduced and endorsed.

    (B) A problem is identified, followed by solutions to the problem; methods of implementing the solutions are discussed; obstacles to implementing the solutions are described; an alternative method of implementing one of the solutions is proposed.

    (C) A problem is identified, followed by a solution to the problem; a method of implementing the solution is discussed; obstacles to implementing the solution are described; a challenge to the solution is introduced and countered.

    (D) A problem is identified, followed by examples of the problem; a solution is proposed; a method for implementing the solution is described; examples of successful implementation are discussed; the solution is applied to other similar problems.

    (E) A problem is identified, followed by a proposal for solving the problem; benefits and drawbacks of the proposal are discussed; examples of the benefits and drawbacks are described; a challenge to the proposal is introduced and the proposal is rejected.

13. Based on the passage, the group of Northern Utes mentioned in lines 38–42 would be likely to believe each of the following statements EXCEPT:

    (A) Standardizing traditional languages requires arbitrary choices and is sometimes unnecessary.

    (B) Written languages should reflect one standard dialect rather than several dialects.

    (C) Traditional languages can be taught even if they are not rigorously standardized.

    (D) Variant spellings of words are acceptable in a language if their meanings are clear.

    (E) The extent to which a language should be standardized depends upon a community's needs.

14. Which one of the following most accurately describes the author's attitude toward the goal of having a written language exactly match its oral equivalent?

    (A) conviction that an exact match is all but impossible to achieve

    (B) doubt that an exact match is worthy of consideration even in principle

    (C) faith that an exact match is attainable if certain obstacles are eliminated

    (D) confidence that an exact match can easily be accomplished in most languages

    (E) suspicion that the motives behind the attempts to achieve the goal are not entirely benevolent

15. Based on the passage, which one of the following appears to be a principle guiding the actions of those attempting to preserve their traditional languages?

    (A) In writing down an oral language, one should always be concerned primarily with the degree of correspondence between spoken sounds and written symbols.

    (B) In deciding whether and how to standardize and teach a primarily oral language, one should always keep the needs of the community and the culture foremost.

    (C) In determining whether to preserve a language orally or preserve it in writing, one should always strive to ignore the influences of the majority culture and focus on which method is most effective.

    (D) In considering how to present the grammar of a primarily oral language to students, one should always employ a sequence that tackles more difficult concepts first.

    (E) In adjudicating among variant spellings of words from different language traditions, one should always favor the spelling preferred by the majority of the community.

GO ON TO THE NEXT PAGE.

Scientists have long known that the soft surface of the bill of the platypus is perforated with openings that contain sensitive nerve endings. Only recently, however, have biologists concluded on the basis of new

(5) evidence that the animal uses its bill to locate its prey while underwater, a conclusion suggested by the fact that the animal's eyes, ears, and nostrils are sealed when it is submerged. The new evidence comes from neurophysiological studies, which have recently

(10) revealed that within the pores on the bill there are two kinds of sensory receptors: mechanoreceptors, which are tiny pushrods that respond to tactile pressure, and electroreceptors, which respond to weak electrical fields. Having discovered that tactile stimulation of the

(15) pushrods sends nerve impulses to the brain, where they evoke an electric potential over an area of the neocortex much larger than the one stimulated by input from the limbs, eyes, and ears, Bohringer concluded that the bill must be the primary sensory organ for the

(20) platypus. Her finding was supported by studies showing that the bill is extraordinarily sensitive to tactile stimulation: stimulation with a fine glass stylus sent a signal by way of the fifth cranial nerve to the neocortex and from there to the motor cortex.

(25) Presumably nerve impulses from the motor cortex then induced a snapping movement of the bill. But Bohringer's investigations did not explain how the animal locates its prey at a distance.

Scheich's neurophysiological studies contribute to

(30) solving this mystery. His initial work showed that when a platypus feeds, it swims along, steadily wagging its bill from side to side until prey is encountered. It thereupon switches to searching behavior, characterized by erratic movements of the

(35) bill over a small area at the bottom of a body of water, which is followed by homing in on the object and seizing it. In order to determine how the animal senses prey and then distinguishes it from other objects on the bottom, Scheich hypothesized that a sensory system

(40) based on electroreception similar to that found in sharks might exist in the platypus. In further experiments he found he could trigger the switch from patrolling to searching behavior in the platypus by creating a dipole electric field in the water with the aid

(45) of a small 1.5-volt battery. The platypus, sensitive to the weak electric current that was created, rapidly oriented toward the battery at a distance of 10 centimeters and sometimes as much as 30 centimeters. Once the battery was detected, the

(50) platypus would inevitably attack it as if it were food. Scheich then discovered that the tail flicks of freshwater shrimp, a common prey of the platypus, also produce weak electric fields and elicit an identical response. Scheich and his colleagues believe that it is

(55) reasonable to assume that all the invertebrates on which the platypus feeds must produce electric fields.

16. The primary purpose of the passage is to

(A) explain how the platypus locates prey at a distance

(B) present some recent scientific research on the function of the platypus's bill

(C) assess the results of Bohringer's experimental work about the platypus

(D) present Scheich's contributions to scientific work about the platypus

(E) describe two different kinds of pores on the platypus's bill

17. Which one of the following statements best expresses the main idea of the passage?

(A) Neurophysiological studies have established that the bill of the platypus is one of its primary sensory organs.

(B) Neurophysiological studies have established that the platypus uses its bill to locate its prey underwater.

(C) Bohringer's neurophysiological studies have established that sensory receptors in the bill of the platypus respond to electrical stimulation.

(D) Biologists have concluded that the surface of the bill of the platypus is perforated with openings that contain sensitive nerve endings.

(E) Biologists have concluded that the hunting platypus responds to weak electric fields emitted by freshwater invertebrates.

GO ON TO THE NEXT PAGE.

18. During the studies supporting Bohringer's finding, as they are described in the passage, which one of the following occurred before a nerve impulse reached the motor cortex of the platypus?

   (A)   The electroreceptors sent the nerve impulse to the fifth cranial nerve.
   (B)   The neocortex induced a snapping movement of the bill.
   (C)   The mechanoreceptors sent the nerve impulse via the fifth cranial nerve to the electroreceptors.
   (D)   The platypus opened the pores on its bill.
   (E)   The fifth cranial nerve carried the nerve impulse to the neocortex.

19. Which one of the following strategies is most similar to Scheich's experimental strategy as it is described in the passage?

   (A)   To determine the mating habits of birds, a biologist places decoys near the birds' nests that resemble the birds and emit bird calls.
   (B)   To determine whether certain animals find their way by listening for echoes to their cries, a biologist plays a tape of the animals' cries in their vicinity.
   (C)   To determine whether an animal uses heat sensitivity to detect prey, a biologist places a heat-generating object near the animal's home.
   (D)   A fisherman catches fish by dangling in the water rubber replicas of the fishes' prey that have been scented with fish oil.
   (E)   A game warden captures an animal by baiting a cage with a piece of meat that the animal will want to eat.

20. It can be inferred from the passage that during patrolling behavior, the platypus is attempting to

   (A)   capture prey that it has detected
   (B)   distinguish one kind of prey from another
   (C)   detect electric fields produced by potential prey
   (D)   stimulate its mechanoreceptors
   (E)   pick up the scent of its prey

21. Which one of the following best describes the organization of the passage?

   (A)   A hypothesis is presented and defended with supporting examples.
   (B)   A conclusion is presented and the information supporting it is provided.
   (C)   A thesis is presented and defended with an argument.
   (D)   Opposing views are presented, discussed, and then reconciled.
   (E)   A theory is proposed, considered, and then amended.

GO ON TO THE NEXT PAGE.

Until about 1970, anyone who wanted to write a comprehensive history of medieval English law as it actually affected women would have found a dearth of published books or articles concerned with specific
(5) legal topics relating to women and derived from extensive research in actual court records. This is a serious deficiency, since court records are of vital importance in discovering how the law actually affected women, as opposed to how the law was
(10) intended to affect them or thought to affect them. These latter questions can be answered by consulting such sources as treatises, commentaries, and statutes; such texts were what most scholars of the nineteenth and early twentieth centuries concentrated on whenever
(15) they did write about medieval law. But these sources are of little help in determining, for example, how often women's special statutory privileges were thwarted by intimidation or harassment, or how often women managed to evade special statutory limitations. And,
(20) quite apart from provisions designed to apply only, or especially, to women, they cannot tell us how general law affected the female half of the population—how women defendants and plaintiffs were treated in the courts in practice when they tried to exercise the rights
(25) they shared with men. Only quantitative studies of large numbers of cases would allow even a guess at the answers to these questions, and this scholarly work has been attempted by few.

One can easily imagine why. Most medieval
(30) English court records are written in Latin or Anglo-Norman French and have never been published. The sheer volume of material to be sifted is daunting: there are over 27,500 parchment pages in the common plea rolls of the thirteenth century alone, every page nearly
(35) three feet long, and written often front and back in highly stylized court hand. But the difficulty of the sources, while it might appear to explain why the relevant scholarship has not been undertaken, seems actually to have deterred few: the fact is that few
(40) historians have wanted to write anything approaching women's legal history in the first place. Most modern legal historians who have written on one aspect or another of special laws pertaining to women have begun with an interest in a legal idea or event or
(45) institution, not with a concern for how it affected women. Very few legal historians have started with an interest in women's history that they might have elected to pursue through various areas of general law. And the result of all this is that the current state of our
(50) scholarly knowledge relating to law and the medieval Englishwoman is still fragmentary at best, though the situation is slowly improving.

22. It can be inferred from the passage that the author believes which one of the following to be true of the sources consulted by nineteenth-century historians of medieval law?

(A) They are adequate to the research needs of a modern legal historian wishing to investigate medieval law.

(B) They are to be preferred to medieval legal sources, which are cumbersome and difficult to use.

(C) They lack fundamental relevance to the history of modern legal institutions and ideas.

(D) They provide relatively little information relevant to the issues with which writers of women's legal history ought most to concern themselves.

(E) They are valuable primarily because of the answers they can provide to some of the questions that have most interested writers of women's legal history.

23. Which one of the following best describes the organization of the first paragraph of the passage?

(A) The preparations necessary for the production of a particular kind of study are discussed, and reasons are given for why such preparations have not been undertaken until recently.

(B) A problem is described, a taxonomy of various kinds of questions relevant to its solution is proposed, and an evaluation regarding which of those questions would be most useful to answer is made.

(C) An example suggesting the nature of present conditions in a discipline is given, past conditions in that discipline are described, and a prediction is made regarding the future of the discipline.

(D) A deficiency is described, the specific nature of the deficiency is discussed, and a particular kind of remedy is asserted to be the sole possible means of correcting that deficiency.

(E) The resources necessary to the carrying out of a task are described, the inherent limitations of those resources are suggested by means of a list of questions, and a suggestion is made for overcoming these limitations.

GO ON TO THE NEXT PAGE.

24. According to the passage, quantitative studies of the kind referred to in line 25 can aid in determining

    (A) what were the stated intentions of those who wrote medieval statutes
    (B) what were the unconscious or hidden motives of medieval lawmakers with regard to women
    (C) what was the impact of medieval legal thought concerning women on the development of important modern legal ideas and institutions
    (D) how medieval women's lives were really affected by medieval laws
    (E) how best to categorize the masses of medieval documents relating to women

25. According to the passage, the sources consulted by legal scholars of the nineteenth and early twentieth centuries provided adequate information concerning which one of the following topics?

    (A) the intent of medieval English laws regarding women and the opinions of commentators concerning how those laws affected women
    (B) the overall effectiveness of English law in the medieval period and some aspects of the special statutes that applied to women only
    (C) the degree of probability that a woman defendant or plaintiff would win a legal case in medieval England
    (D) the degree to which the male relatives of medieval Englishwomen could succeed in preventing those women from exercising their legal rights
    (E) which of the legal rights theoretically shared by men and women were, in practice, guaranteed only to men

26. As used in lines 37–38, the phrase "the relevant scholarship" can best be understood as referring to which one of the following kinds of scholarly work?

    (A) linguistic studies of Anglo-Norman French and Latin undertaken in order to prepare for further study of medieval legal history
    (B) the editing and publication of medieval court records undertaken in order to facilitate the work of legal and other historians
    (C) quantitative studies of large numbers of medieval court cases undertaken in order to discover the actual effects of law on medieval women's lives
    (D) comparative studies of medieval statutes, treatises, and commentaries undertaken in order to discover the views and intentions of medieval legislators
    (E) reviews of the existing scholarly literature concerning women and medieval law undertaken as groundwork for the writing of a comprehensive history of medieval law as it applied to women

27. It can be inferred from the passage that, in the author's view, which one of the following factors is most responsible for the current deficiencies in our knowledge of women's legal history?

    (A) most modern legal historians' relative lack of interest in pursuing the subject
    (B) the linguistic and practical difficulties inherent in pursuing research relevant to such knowledge
    (C) a tendency on the part of most modern legal historians to rely too heavily on sources such as commentaries and treatises
    (D) the mistaken view that the field of women's legal history should be defined as the study of laws that apply only, or especially, to women
    (E) the relative scarcity of studies providing a comprehensive overview of women's legal history

S T O P

IF YOU FINISH BEFORE TIME IS CALLED, YOU MAY CHECK YOUR WORK ON THIS SECTION ONLY.
DO NOT WORK ON ANY OTHER SECTION IN THE TEST.

SECTION III

Time—35 minutes

24 Questions

Directions: Each group of questions in this section is based on a set of conditions. In answering some of the questions, it may be useful to draw a rough diagram. Choose the response that most accurately and completely answers each question and blacken the corresponding space on your answer sheet.

Questions 1–6

On a Tuesday, an accountant has exactly seven bills— numbered 1 through 7—to pay by Thursday of the same week. The accountant will pay each bill only once according to the following rules:

    Either three or four of the seven bills must be paid on Wednesday, the rest on Thursday.

    Bill 1 cannot be paid on the same day as bill 5.

    Bill 2 must be paid on Thursday.

    Bill 4 must be paid on the same day as bill 7.

    If bill 6 is paid on Wednesday, bill 7 must be paid on Thursday.

1. If exactly four bills are paid on Wednesday, then those four bills could be

    (A)   1, 3, 4, and 6
    (B)   1, 3, 5, and 6
    (C)   2, 4, 5, and 7
    (D)   3, 4, 5, and 7
    (E)   3, 4, 6, and 7

2. Which one of the following is a complete and accurate list of the bills any one of which could be among the bills paid on Wednesday?

    (A)   3, 5, and 6
    (B)   1, 3, 4, 6, and 7
    (C)   1, 3, 4, 5, 6, and 7
    (D)   2, 3, 4, 5, 6, and 7
    (E)   1, 2, 3, 4, 5, 6, and 7

3. If bill 2 and bill 6 are paid on different days from each other, which one of the following must be true?

    (A)   Exactly three bills are paid on Wednesday.
    (B)   Exactly three bills are paid on Thursday.
    (C)   Bill 1 is paid on the same day as bill 4.
    (D)   Bill 2 is paid on the same day as bill 3.
    (E)   Bill 5 is paid on the same day as bill 7.

4. If bill 6 is paid on Wednesday, which one of the following bills must also be paid on Wednesday?

    (A)   1
    (B)   3
    (C)   4
    (D)   5
    (E)   7

5. If bill 4 is paid on Thursday, which one of the following is a pair of bills that could also be paid on Thursday?

    (A)   1 and 5
    (B)   1 and 7
    (C)   3 and 5
    (D)   3 and 6
    (E)   6 and 7

6. Which one of the following statements must be true?

    (A)   If bill 2 is paid on Thursday, bill 3 is paid on Wednesday.
    (B)   If bill 4 is paid on Thursday, bill 1 is paid on Wednesday.
    (C)   If bill 4 is paid on Thursday, bill 3 is paid on Wednesday.
    (D)   If bill 6 is paid on Thursday, bill 3 is also paid on Thursday.
    (E)   If bill 6 is paid on Thursday, bill 4 is also paid on Thursday.

GO ON TO THE NEXT PAGE.

Questions 7–13

Two mannequins—1 and 2—will be dressed for display in outfits chosen from ten articles of clothing. Each article is in exactly one of three colors: navy, red, or yellow. There are three hats—one in each color; three jackets—one in each color; three skirts—one in each color; and one red tie. Each mannequin wears exactly one of the hats, one of the jackets, and one of the skirts. Furthermore, their outfits must meet the following restrictions:

  Neither mannequin wears all three colors.
  Each mannequin wears a hat in a different color from the
   jacket it wears.
  Mannequin 2 wears the navy skirt.
  Mannequin 1 wears the tie.

7. Which one of the following could be complete outfits for the two mannequins?

   (A) mannequin 1: navy hat, red jacket, yellow skirt,
        red tie
        mannequin 2: red hat, navy jacket, navy skirt
   (B) mannequin 1: red hat, red jacket, yellow skirt, red
        tie
        mannequin 2: yellow hat, navy jacket, navy skirt
   (C) mannequin 1: red hat, yellow jacket, red skirt, red
        tie
        mannequin 2: yellow hat, navy jacket, yellow
        skirt
   (D) mannequin 1: yellow hat, red jacket, yellow skirt,
        red tie
        mannequin 2: red hat, navy jacket, navy skirt
   (E) mannequin 1: yellow hat, yellow jacket, red skirt
        mannequin 2: red hat, navy jacket, navy skirt

8. Which one of the following could be true of the mannequins' outfits?

   (A) Mannequin 1 wears the navy jacket and the
        yellow skirt.
   (B) Mannequin 2 wears the red hat and the red jacket.
   (C) Mannequin 1 wears exactly one red article of
        clothing.
   (D) Mannequin 1 wears exactly three yellow articles
        of clothing.
   (E) Mannequin 2 wears no red articles of clothing.

9. If mannequin 1 wears the navy jacket, which one of the following could be true?

   (A) Mannequin 1 wears the yellow hat.
   (B) Mannequin 1 wears the yellow skirt.
   (C) Mannequin 2 wears the red hat.
   (D) Mannequin 2 wears the yellow hat.
   (E) Mannequin 2 wears the yellow jacket.

10. If all four of the red articles of clothing are included in the two mannequins' outfits, which one of the following must be true?

   (A) Mannequin 1 wears the red hat.
   (B) Mannequin 1 wears the yellow jacket.
   (C) Mannequin 2 wears the navy jacket.
   (D) Mannequin 1 wears no navy articles of clothing.
   (E) Mannequin 2 wears no yellow articles of clothing.

11. If mannequin 2 wears the red jacket, then mannequin 1 must wear the

   (A) navy hat
   (B) red hat
   (C) yellow hat
   (D) red skirt
   (E) yellow skirt

12. If all three of the yellow articles of clothing are included in the two mannequins' outfits, which one of the following could be true?

   (A) Mannequin 1 wears the navy jacket.
   (B) Mannequin 1 wears the yellow jacket.
   (C) Mannequin 1 wears the red skirt.
   (D) Mannequin 2 wears the red hat.
   (E) Mannequin 2 wears the red jacket.

13. If mannequin 1 wears the skirt that is the same color as the jacket that mannequin 2 wears, which one of the following must be true?

   (A) Mannequin 1 wears the yellow hat.
   (B) Mannequin 1 wears the yellow jacket.
   (C) Mannequin 2 wears the navy hat.
   (D) Mannequin 2 wears the red hat.
   (E) Mannequin 2 wears the red jacket.

GO ON TO THE NEXT PAGE.

Questions 14–19

A college dean will present seven awards for outstanding language research. The awards—one for French, one for German, one for Hebrew, one for Japanese, one for Korean, one for Latin, and one for Swahili—must be presented consecutively, one at a time, in conformity with the following constraints:

The German award is not presented first.
The Hebrew award is presented at some time before the Korean award is presented.
The Latin award is presented at some time before the Japanese award is presented.
The French award is presented either immediately before or immediately after the Hebrew award is presented.
The Korean award is presented either immediately before or immediately after the Latin award is presented.

14. Which one of the following must be true?

  (A) The French award is presented at some time before the Japanese award is presented.
  (B) The French award is presented at some time before the Swahili award is presented.
  (C) The German award is presented at some time before the Korean award is presented.
  (D) The German award is presented at some time before the Swahili award is presented.
  (E) The Swahili award is presented at some time before the Hebrew award is presented.

15. If the Hebrew award is presented fourth, which one of the following must be true?

  (A) The French award is presented fifth.
  (B) The German award is presented third.
  (C) The Japanese award is presented sixth.
  (D) The Korean award is presented fifth.
  (E) The Swahili award is presented first.

16. If the German award is presented third, which one of the following could be true?

  (A) The French award is presented fourth.
  (B) The Japanese award is presented fifth.
  (C) The Japanese award is presented sixth.
  (D) The Korean award is presented second.
  (E) The Swahili award is presented fifth.

17. The earliest that the Japanese award could be presented is

  (A) third
  (B) fourth
  (C) fifth
  (D) sixth
  (E) seventh

18. If the Japanese award is presented at some time before the Swahili award is presented, any of the following could be true EXCEPT:

  (A) The German award is presented immediately before the French award is presented.
  (B) The German award is presented immediately before the Japanese award is presented.
  (C) The Hebrew award is presented immediately before the Latin award is presented.
  (D) The Korean award is presented immediately before the Japanese award is presented.
  (E) The Swahili award is presented immediately before the German award is presented.

19. The order in which the awards are presented is completely determined if which one of the following is true?

  (A) The French award is presented immediately before the German award is presented, and the Korean award is presented immediately before the Latin award is presented.
  (B) The French award is presented immediately before the Hebrew award is presented, and the Hebrew award is presented immediately before the Korean award is presented.
  (C) The French award is presented immediately before the Latin award is presented, and the Korean award is presented immediately before the Japanese award is presented.
  (D) The German award is presented immediately before the French award is presented, and the Latin award is presented immediately before the Japanese award is presented.
  (E) The German award is presented immediately before the Korean award is presented, and the Hebrew award is presented immediately before the French award is presented.

GO ON TO THE NEXT PAGE.

Questions 20–24

Exactly six piano classes are given sequentially on Monday: two with more than one student and four with exactly one student. Exactly four females—Gimena, Holly, Iyanna, and Kate—and five males—Leung, Nate, Oscar, Pedro, and Saul—attend these classes. Each student attends exactly one class. The following must obtain:

  Iyanna and Leung together constitute one class.
  Pedro and exactly two others together constitute one class.
  Kate is the first female, but not the first student, to attend a class.
  Gimena's class is at some time after Iyanna's but at some time before Pedro's.
  Oscar's class is at some time after Gimena's.

20. Which one of the following students could attend the first class?

    (A)   Holly
    (B)   Leung
    (C)   Oscar
    (D)   Pedro
    (E)   Saul

21. Which one of the following is a complete and accurate list of classes any one of which could be the class Gimena attends?

    (A)   the fourth, the fifth
    (B)   the fourth, the sixth
    (C)   the second, the fourth, the fifth
    (D)   the third, the fifth, the sixth
    (E)   the second, the third, the fourth

22. Which one of the following pairs of students could be in the class with Pedro?

    (A)   Gimena and Holly
    (B)   Holly and Saul
    (C)   Kate and Nate
    (D)   Leung and Oscar
    (E)   Nate and Saul

23. If Oscar and Pedro do not attend the same class as each other, then which one of the following could be true?

    (A)   Gimena attends the fifth class.
    (B)   Holly attends the third class.
    (C)   Iyanna attends the fourth class.
    (D)   Nate attends the fifth class.
    (E)   Saul attends the second class.

24. Suppose the condition that Oscar attends a class after Gimena is replaced with the condition that Oscar attends a class before Gimena and after Kate. If all the other conditions remain the same, then which class must Holly attend?

    (A)   the second
    (B)   the third
    (C)   the fourth
    (D)   the fifth
    (E)   the sixth

S T O P

IF YOU FINISH BEFORE TIME IS CALLED, YOU MAY CHECK YOUR WORK ON THIS SECTION ONLY.
DO NOT WORK ON ANY OTHER SECTION IN THE TEST.

SECTION IV
Time—35 minutes
25 Questions

Directions: The questions in this section are based on the reasoning contained in brief statements or passages. For some questions, more than one of the choices could conceivably answer the question. However, you are to choose the best answer; that is, the response that most accurately and completely answers the question. You should not make assumptions that are by commonsense standards implausible, superfluous, or incompatible with the passage. After you have chosen the best answer, blacken the corresponding space on your answer sheet.

1. Combustion of gasoline in automobile engines produces benzene, a known carcinogen. Environmentalists propose replacing gasoline with methanol, which does not produce significant quantities of benzene when burned. However, combustion of methanol produces formaldehyde, also a known carcinogen. Therefore the environmentalists' proposal has little merit.

   Which one of the following, if true, most supports the environmentalists' proposal?

   (A)   The engines of some automobiles now on the road burn diesel fuel rather than gasoline.
   (B)   Several large research efforts are under way to formulate cleaner-burning types of gasoline.
   (C)   In some regions, the local economy is largely dependent on industries devoted to the production and distribution of automobile fuel.
   (D)   Formaldehyde is a less potent carcinogen than benzene.
   (E)   Since methanol is water soluble, methanol spills are more damaging to the environment than gasoline spills.

2. Economist: To the extent that homelessness arises from a lack of available housing, it should not be assumed that the profit motive is at fault. Private investors will, in general, provide housing if the market allows them to make a profit; it is unrealistic to expect investors to take risks with their property unless they get some benefit in return.

   Which one of the following most accurately describes the role played in the economist's argument by the phrase "To the extent that homelessness arises from a lack of available housing"?

   (A)   It limits the application of the argument to a part of the problem.
   (B)   It suggests that the primary cause of homelessness is lack of available housing.
   (C)   It is offered as evidence crucial to the conclusion.
   (D)   It expresses the conclusion to be argued for.
   (E)   It suggests a possible solution to the problem of homelessness.

3. Physical education should teach people to pursue healthy, active lifestyles as they grow older. But the focus on competitive sports in most schools causes most of the less competitive students to turn away from sports. Having learned to think of themselves as unathletic, they do not exercise enough to stay healthy.

   Which one of the following is most strongly supported by the statements above, if they are true?

   (A)   Physical education should include noncompetitive activities.
   (B)   Competition causes most students to turn away from sports.
   (C)   People who are talented at competitive physical endeavors exercise regularly.
   (D)   The mental aspects of exercise are as important as the physical ones.
   (E)   Children should be taught the dangers of a sedentary lifestyle.

GO ON TO THE NEXT PAGE.

<u>Questions 4–5</u>

Political opinion and analysis outside the mainstream rarely are found on television talk shows, and it might be thought that this state of affairs is a product of the political agenda of the television stations themselves. In fact, television stations are driven by the same economic forces as sellers of more tangible goods. Because they must attempt to capture the largest possible share of the television audience for their shows, they air only those shows that will appeal to large numbers of people. As a result, political opinions and analyses aired on television talk shows are typically bland and innocuous.

4. An assumption made in the explanation offered by the author of the passage is that

   (A)   most television viewers cannot agree on which elements of a particular opinion or analysis are most disturbing
   (B)   there are television viewers who might refuse to watch television talk shows that they knew would be controversial and disturbing
   (C)   each television viewer holds some opinion that is outside the political mainstream, but those opinions are not the same for everyone
   (D)   there are television shows on which economic forces have an even greater impact than they do on television talk shows
   (E)   the television talk shows of different stations resemble one another in most respects

5. The explanation offered by the author of the passage makes the assumption that

   (A)   television station executives usually lack a political agenda of their own
   (B)   bland and innocuous political opinions and analyses are generally in the mainstream
   (C)   political analysts outside the mainstream are relatively indifferent to the effect their analyses have on television viewers
   (D)   most television viewers are prepared to argue against allowing the expression of political opinions and analyses with which they disagree
   (E)   the political opinions of television station executives are not often reflected in the television shows their stations produce

6. Some judges complain about statutes that specify mandatory minimum sentences for criminal offenses. These legal restrictions, they complain, are too mechanical and prevent judges from deciding when a given individual can or cannot be rehabilitated. But that is precisely why mandatory minimum sentences are necessary. History amply demonstrates that when people are free to use their own judgment they invariably believe themselves to act wisely when in fact they are often arbitrary and irrational. There is no reason to think that judges are an exception to this rule.

Which one of the following sentences most accurately expresses the main point of the passage?

   (A)   People believe that they have good judgment but never do.
   (B)   Mandatory minimum sentences are too mechanical and reduce judicial discretion.
   (C)   Judges should be free to exercise their own judgment.
   (D)   Judges are often arbitrary and irrational.
   (E)   Mandatory minimum sentences are needed to help prevent judicial arbitrariness.

GO ON TO THE NEXT PAGE.

Questions 7–8

Conservationist: The population of a certain wildflower is so small that the species is headed for extinction. However, this wildflower can cross-pollinate with a closely related domesticated daisy, producing viable seeds. Such cross-pollination could result in a significant population of wildflower-daisy hybrids. The daisy should therefore be introduced into the wildflower's range, since although the hybrid would differ markedly from the wildflower, hybridization is the only means of preventing total loss of the wildflower in its range.

7. Which one of the following principles, if valid, most helps to justify the conservationist's reasoning?

(A) It is better to take measures to preserve a valued type of organism, even if those measures are drastic, than to accept a less valuable substitute for the organism.

(B) It is better to preserve a type of organism that is in danger of extinction, even if surviving organisms of that type are not vigorous, than to allow something more vigorous to replace it.

(C) It is better to change a type of organism that would otherwise be lost, even if the changes are radical, than to lose it entirely.

(D) It is better to destroy one of two competing types of organisms, even if both are irreplaceable, than to allow both of them to be lost.

(E) It is better to protect an endangered type of organism, even if doing so has some negative effects on another type of organism, than to do nothing at all.

8. Which one of the following is an assumption on which the conservationist's reasoning depends?

(A) The wildflower currently reproduces only by forming seeds.

(B) The domesticated daisy was bred from wild plants that once grew in the wildflower's range.

(C) Increasing the population of the wildflower will also expand its range.

(D) Wildflower-daisy hybrids will be able to reproduce.

(E) The domesticated daisy will cross-pollinate with any daisylike plant.

9. Because of increases in the price of oil and because of government policies promoting energy conservation, the use of oil to heat homes fell by 40 percent from 1970 to the present, and many homeowners switched to natural gas for heating. Because switching to natural gas involved investing in equipment, a significant switch back to oil in the near future is unlikely.

The prediction that ends the passage would be most seriously called into question if it were true that in the last few years

(A) the price of natural gas to heat homes has remained constant, while the cost of equipment to heat homes with natural gas has fallen sharply

(B) the price of home heating oil has remained constant, while the cost of equipment to heat homes with natural gas has risen sharply

(C) the cost of equipment to heat homes with natural gas has fallen sharply, while the price of home heating oil has fallen to 1970 levels

(D) the cost of equipment to heat homes with oil has fallen sharply, while the price of heating with oil has fallen below the price of heating with natural gas

(E) the use of oil to heat homes has continued to decline, while the price of heating oil has fallen to 1970 levels

10. Parents should not necessarily raise their children in the ways experts recommend, even if some of those experts are themselves parents. After all, parents are the ones who directly experience which methods are successful in raising their own children.

Which one of the following most closely conforms to the principle that the passage above illustrates?

(A) Although music theory is intrinsically interesting and may be helpful to certain musicians, it does not distinguish good music from bad: that is a matter of taste and not of theory.

(B) One need not pay much attention to the advice of automotive experts when buying a car if those experts are not interested in the mundane factors that concern the average consumer.

(C) In deciding the best way to proceed, a climber familiar with a mountain might do well to ignore the advice of mountain climbing experts unfamiliar with that mountain.

(D) A typical farmer is less likely to know what types of soil are most productive than is someone with an advanced degree in agricultural science.

(E) Unlike society, one's own conscience speaks with a single voice; it is better to follow the advice of one's own conscience than the advice of society.

GO ON TO THE NEXT PAGE.

11. Sometimes when their trainer gives the hand signal for "Do something creative together," two dolphins circle a pool in tandem and then leap through the air simultaneously. On other occasions the same signal elicits synchronized backward swims or tail-waving. These behaviors are not simply learned responses to a given stimulus. Rather, dolphins are capable of higher cognitive functions that may include the use of language and forethought.

Which one of the following, if true, most strengthens the argument?

(A) Mammals have some resemblance to one another with respect to bodily function and brain structure.

(B) The dolphins often exhibit complex new responses to the hand signal.

(C) The dolphins are given food incentives as part of their training.

(D) Dolphins do not interact with humans the way they interact with one another.

(E) Some of the behaviors mentioned are exhibited by dolphins in their natural habitat.

12. Editorialist: Drivers with a large number of demerit points who additionally have been convicted of a serious driving-related offense should either be sentenced to jail or be forced to receive driver re-education, since to do otherwise would be to allow a crime to go unpunished. Only if such drivers are likely to be made more responsible drivers should driver re-education be recommended for them. Unfortunately, it is always almost impossible to make drivers with a large number of demerit points more responsible drivers.

If the editorialist's statements are true, they provide the most support for which one of the following?

(A) Drivers with a large number of demerit points who have been convicted of a serious driving-related offense should be sent to jail.

(B) Driver re-education offers the best chance of making drivers with a large number of demerit points responsible drivers.

(C) Driver re-education is not a harsh enough punishment for anyone convicted of a serious driving-related offense who has also accumulated a large number of demerit points.

(D) Driver re-education should not be recommended for those who have committed no serious driving-related offenses.

(E) Drivers with a large number of demerit points but no conviction for a serious driving-related offense should receive driver re-education rather than jail.

Questions 13–14

Plant manager: We could greatly reduce the amount of sulfur dioxide our copper-smelting plant releases into the atmosphere by using a new process. The new process requires replacing our open furnaces with closed ones and moving the copper from one furnace to the next in solid, not molten, form. However, not only is the new equipment expensive to buy and install, but the new process also costs more to run than the current process, because the copper must be reheated after it has cooled. So overall, adopting the new process will cost much but bring the company no profit.

Supervisor: I agree with your overall conclusion, but disagree about one point you make, since the latest closed furnaces are extremely fuel-efficient.

13. The point about which the supervisor expresses disagreement with the plant manager is

(A) whether the new copper-smelting process releases less sulfur dioxide gas into the atmosphere than the current process

(B) whether the new copper-smelting process is more expensive to run than the current process

(C) whether the new process should be adopted in the copper-smelting plant

(D) whether closed copper-smelting furnaces are more fuel-efficient than open furnaces

(E) whether cooling and reheating the copper will cost more than moving it in molten form

14. The plant manager's argument is most vulnerable to criticism on which one of the following grounds?

(A) The overall conclusion is about a net effect but is based solely on evidence about only some of the factors that contribute to the effect.

(B) The support for the overall conclusion is the authority of the plant manager rather than any independently verifiable evidence.

(C) The overall conclusion reached merely repeats the evidence offered.

(D) Evidence that is taken to be only probably true is used as the basis for a claim that something is definitely true.

(E) Facts that are not directly relevant to the argument are treated as if they supported the overall conclusion.

GO ON TO THE NEXT PAGE.

15. Ambiguity inspires interpretation. The saying "We are the measure of all things," for instance, has been interpreted by some people to imply that humans are centrally important in the universe, while others have interpreted it to mean simply that, since all knowledge is human knowledge, humans must rely on themselves to find the truth.

The claim that ambiguity inspires interpretation figures in the argument in which one of the following ways?

(A) It is used to support the argument's conclusion.
(B) It is an illustration of the claim that we are the measure of all things.
(C) It is compatible with either accepting or rejecting the argument's conclusion.
(D) It is a view that other statements in the argument are intended to support.
(E) It sets out a difficulty the argument is intended to solve.

16. Franklin: It is inconsistent to pay sports celebrities ten times what Nobel laureates are paid. Both have rare talents and work hard.

Tomeka: What you've neglected to consider is that unlike Nobel laureates, sports celebrities earn millions of dollars for their employers in the form of gate receipts and TV rights.

Franklin's and Tomeka's statements provide the most support for holding that they disagree about the truth of which one of the following?

(A) Nobel laureates should be taken more seriously.
(B) Nobel laureates should be paid more than sports celebrities.
(C) Sports celebrities and Nobel laureates work equally hard for their employers.
(D) There is no rational basis for the salary difference between sports celebrities and Nobel laureates.
(E) The social contributions made by sports celebrities should be greater than they currently are.

17. Studies of the reliability of eyewitness identifications show little correlation between the accuracy of a witness's account and the confidence the witness has in the account. Certain factors can increase or undermine a witness's confidence without altering the accuracy of the identification. Therefore, police officers are advised to disallow suspect lineups in which witnesses can hear one another identifying suspects.

Which one of the following is a principle underlying the advice given to police officers?

(A) The confidence people have in what they remember having seen is affected by their awareness of what other people claim to have seen.
(B) Unless an eyewitness is confronted with more than one suspect at a time, the accuracy of his or her statements cannot be trusted.
(C) If several eyewitnesses all identify the same suspect in a lineup, it is more likely that the suspect committed the crime than if only one eyewitness identifies the suspect.
(D) Police officers are more interested in the confidence witnesses have when testifying than in the accuracy of that testimony.
(E) The accuracy of an eyewitness account is doubtful if the eyewitness contradicts what other eyewitnesses claim to have seen.

GO ON TO THE NEXT PAGE.

18. All actions are motivated by self-interest, since any action that is apparently altruistic can be described in terms of self-interest. For example, helping someone can be described in terms of self-interest: the motivation is hope for a reward or other personal benefit to be bestowed as a result of the helping action.

Which one of the following most accurately describes an error in the argument's reasoning?

(A) The term "self-interest" is allowed to shift in meaning over the course of the argument.

(B) The argument takes evidence showing merely that its conclusion could be true to constitute evidence showing that the conclusion is in fact true.

(C) The argument does not explain what is meant by "reward" and "personal benefit."

(D) The argument ignores the possibility that what is taken to be necessary for a certain interest to be a motivation actually suffices to show that that interest is a motivation.

(E) The argument depends for its appeal only on the emotional content of the example cited.

19. In the decade from the mid-1980s to the mid-1990s, large corporations were rocked by mergers, reengineering, and downsizing. These events significantly undermined employees' job security. Surprisingly, however, employees' perception of their own job security hardly changed over that period. Fifty-eight percent of employees surveyed in 1984 and 55 percent surveyed in 1994 stated that their own jobs were very secure.

Each of the following contributes to an explanation of the surprising survey results described above EXCEPT:

(A) A large number of the people in both surveys work in small companies that were not affected by mergers, reengineering, and downsizing.

(B) Employees who feel secure in their jobs tend to think that the jobs of others are secure.

(C) The corporate downsizing that took place during this period had been widely anticipated for several years before the mid-1980s.

(D) Most of the major downsizing during this period was completed within a year after the first survey.

(E) In the mid-1990s, people were generally more optimistic about their lives, even in the face of hardship, than they were a decade before.

20. Amphibian populations are declining in numbers worldwide. Not coincidentally, the earth's ozone layer has been continuously depleted throughout the last 50 years. Atmospheric ozone blocks UV-B, a type of ultraviolet radiation that is continuously produced by the sun, and which can damage genes. Because amphibians lack hair, hide, or feathers to shield them, they are particularly vulnerable to UV-B radiation. In addition, their gelatinous eggs lack the protection of leathery or hard shells. Thus, the primary cause of the declining amphibian population is the depletion of the ozone layer.

Each of the following, if true, would strengthen the argument EXCEPT:

(A) Of the various types of radiation blocked by atmospheric ozone, UV-B is the only type that can damage genes.

(B) Amphibian populations are declining far more rapidly than are the populations of nonamphibian species whose tissues and eggs have more natural protection from UV-B.

(C) Atmospheric ozone has been significantly depleted above all the areas of the world in which amphibian populations are declining.

(D) The natural habitat of amphibians has not become smaller over the past century.

(E) Amphibian populations have declined continuously for the last 50 years.

GO ON TO THE NEXT PAGE.

21. All too many weaklings are also cowards, and few cowards fail to be fools. Thus there must be at least one person who is both a weakling and a fool.

    The flawed pattern of reasoning in the argument above is most similar to that in which one of the following?

    (A) All weasels are carnivores and no carnivores fail to be nonherbivores, so some weasels are nonherbivores.
    (B) Few moralists have the courage to act according to the principles they profess, and few saints have the ability to articulate the principles by which they live, so it follows that few people can both act like saints and speak like moralists.
    (C) Some painters are dancers, since some painters are musicians, and some musicians are dancers.
    (D) If an act is virtuous, then it is autonomous, for acts are not virtuous unless they are free, and acts are not free unless they are autonomous.
    (E) A majority of the voting population favors a total ban, but no one who favors a total ban is opposed to stiffer tariffs, so at least one voter is not opposed to stiffer tariffs.

22. Critic: Most chorale preludes were written for the organ, and most great chorale preludes written for the organ were written by J. S. Bach. One of Bach's chorale preludes dramatizes one hymn's perspective on the year's end. This prelude is agonizing and fixed on the passing of the old year, with its dashed hopes and lost opportunities. It does not necessarily reveal Bach's own attitude toward the change of the year, but does reflect the tone of the hymn's text. People often think that artists create in order to express their own feelings. Some artists do. Master artists never do, and Bach was a master artist.

    If the critic's statements are true, then on the basis of them which one of the following CANNOT be true?

    (A) Bach believed that the close of the year was not a time for optimism and joyous celebration.
    (B) In composing music about a particular subject, Bach did not write the music in order to express his own attitude toward the subject.
    (C) In compositions other than chorale preludes, Bach wrote music in order to express his feelings toward various subjects.
    (D) Most of Bach's chorale preludes were written for instruments other than the organ.
    (E) Most of the great chorale preludes were written for instruments other than the organ.

23. Quasars—celestial objects so far away that their light takes at least 500 million years to reach Earth—have been seen since 1963. For anything that far away to appear from Earth the way quasars do, it would have to burn steadily at a rate that produces more light than 90 billion suns would produce. But nothing that burns at a rate that produces that much light could exist for more than about 100 million years.

    If the statements above are true, which one of the following must also be true on the basis of them?

    (A) Instruments in use before 1963 were not sensitive enough to permit quasars to be seen.
    (B) Light from quasars first began reaching Earth in 1963.
    (C) Anything that from Earth appears as bright as a quasar does must produce more light than would be produced by 90 billion suns.
    (D) Nothing that is as far from Earth as quasars are can continue to exist for more than about 100 million years.
    (E) No quasar that has ever been seen from Earth exists any longer.

GO ON TO THE NEXT PAGE.

24. Medical researcher: As expected, records covering the last four years of ten major hospitals indicate that babies born prematurely were more likely to have low birth weights and to suffer from health problems than were babies not born prematurely. These records also indicate that mothers who had received adequate prenatal care were less likely to have low birth weight babies than were mothers who had received inadequate prenatal care. Adequate prenatal care, therefore, significantly decreases the risk of low birth weight babies.

Which one of the following, if true, most weakens the medical researcher's argument?

(A)   The hospital records indicate that many babies that are born with normal birth weights are born to mothers who had inadequate prenatal care.

(B)   Mothers giving birth prematurely are routinely classified by hospitals as having received inadequate prenatal care when the record of that care is not available.

(C)   The hospital records indicate that low birth weight babies were routinely classified as having been born prematurely.

(D)   Some babies not born prematurely, whose mothers received adequate prenatal care, have low birth weights.

(E)   Women who receive adequate prenatal care are less likely to give birth prematurely than are women who do not receive adequate prenatal care.

25. Formal performance evaluations in the professional world are conducted using realistic situations. Physicians are allowed to consult medical texts freely, attorneys may refer to law books and case records, and physicists and engineers have their manuals at hand for ready reference. Students, then, should likewise have access to their textbooks whenever they take examinations.

The reasoning in the argument is questionable because the argument

(A)   cites examples that are insufficient to support the generalization that performance evaluations in the professional world are conducted in realistic situations

(B)   fails to consider the possibility that adopting its recommendation will not significantly increase most students' test scores

(C)   neglects to take into account the fact that professionals were once students who also did not have access to textbooks during examinations

(D)   neglects to take into account the fact that, unlike students, professionals have devoted many years of study to one subject

(E)   fails to consider the possibility that the purposes of evaluation in the professional world and in school situations are quite dissimilar

S T O P

IF YOU FINISH BEFORE TIME IS CALLED, YOU MAY CHECK YOUR WORK ON THIS SECTION ONLY.
DO NOT WORK ON ANY OTHER SECTION IN THE TEST.

Acknowledgment is made to the following sources from which material has been adapted for use in this test booklet:

Paul Boyer and Bill Leap, "Culture with Literacy." ©1993 by Tribal College.

Francis Haskell, "Art & the Apocalypse." ©1993 by NYREV, Inc.

Eugene Linden, "Can Animals Think?" ©1993 by Time Inc.

LSAT WRITING SAMPLE TOPIC

Janet and Joe Wilson want to open a restaurant in Clearmont, a city of about a million people. The restaurant would feature country French cooking. The Wilsons are considering the two locations described below. Using the following guidelines, write an argument in favor of one of the locations.

- The Wilsons have only a modest amount of capital to start their restaurant and therefore need to generate income fairly quickly.
- The Wilsons want the restaurant to be distinctive enough to attract a steady clientele.

The Wilsons could take a 5-year lease, at $1200 per month, on a storefront property on Main Street in Clearmont's theater district. Within ten blocks of this location are four theaters, three movie houses, and ten other restaurants. Only one of the ten restaurants serves French food. The Wilsons have spoken with the owner of the French restaurant and the restaurant appears to be doing well financially. The space they are considering has an exterior like any other plate-glass storefront and an interior of one large room. The Wilsons would like to have an outdoor café, and the sidewalk is wide enough to accommodate a dozen outside tables. Parking is a problem, but there is plenty of public transportation. Because of its downtown location, the restaurant should have no trouble attracting a first-class kitchen and serving staff.

The Wilsons could also take a three-year lease, at $900 per month, on a charming farmhouse; the lease would include an option to buy the property at the end of those three years. The farmhouse, which is about fifteen minutes from downtown Clearmont, has lovely views and adequate parking, but no area available for outdoor tables. During peak rush hours, getting from Clearmont to the expressway that goes near the farmhouse can be slow, but at other times it is a quick and direct drive to this location. The area around the farmhouse is largely undeveloped, but it is beginning to attract antique and specialty craft shops. There is only one other nearby restaurant and it caters to vegetarians. The Wilsons could have a large garden and grow their own herbs, vegetables, and flowers. If the Wilsons choose this site, a local food critic, who writes a weekly column in the newspaper, is interested in joining them in a partnership.

Directions:

1. Use the Answer Key on the next page to check your answers.

2. Use the Scoring Worksheet below to compute your raw score.

3. Use the Score Conversion Chart to convert your raw score into the 120-180 scale.

Scoring Worksheet

1. Enter the number of questions you answered correctly in each section.

	Number Correct
SECTION I.	———
SECTION II	———
SECTION III.	———
SECTION IV.	———

2. Enter the sum here: ———
   This is your Raw Score.

Conversion Chart

For Converting Raw Score to the 120-180 LSAT Scaled Score
LSAT Form 9LSS44

Reported Score	Raw Score Lowest	Raw Score Highest
180	99	101
179	98	98
178	97	97
177	96	96
176	95	95
175	94	94
174	93	93
173	92	92
172	91	91
171	90	90
170	89	89
169	87	88
168	86	86
167	85	85
166	83	84
165	82	82
164	80	81
163	78	79
162	77	77
161	75	76
160	73	74
159	72	72
158	70	71
157	68	69
156	67	67
155	65	66
154	63	64
153	61	62
152	60	60
151	58	59
150	56	57
149	55	55
148	53	54
147	51	52
146	50	50
145	48	49
144	46	47
143	45	45
142	43	44
141	42	42
140	40	41
139	39	39
138	37	38
137	36	36
136	34	35
135	33	33
134	32	32
133	30	31
132	29	29
131	28	28
130	27	27
129	25	26
128	24	24
127	23	23
126	22	22
125	21	21
124	19	20
123	18	18
122	17	17
121	16	16
120	0	15

SECTION I

1.	A	8.	D	15.	A	22.	D
2.	A	9.	D	16.	B	23.	B
3.	C	10.	D	17.	A	24.	C
4.	D	11.	C	18.	E	25.	B
5.	C	12.	D	19.	A		
6.	E	13.	E	20.	B		
7.	A	14.	E	21.	B		

SECTION II

1.	B	8.	D	15.	B	22.	D
2.	D	9.	A	16.	B	23.	D
3.	D	10.	A	17.	B	24.	D
4.	B	11.	C	18.	E	25.	A
5.	A	12.	C	19.	C	26.	C
6.	E	13.	B	20.	C	27.	A
7.	E	14.	A	21.	B		

SECTION III

1.	D	8.	E	15.	E	22.	B
2.	C	9.	E	16.	C	23.	D
3.	A	10.	E	17.	C	24.	E
4.	B	11.	B	18.	A		
5.	B	12.	B	19.	D		
6.	C	13.	C	20.	E		
7.	D	14.	A	21.	A		

SECTION IV

1.	D	8.	D	15.	D	22.	C
2.	A	9.	D	16.	D	23.	E
3.	A	10.	C	17.	A	24.	B
4.	B	11.	B	18.	B	25.	E
5.	B	12.	A	19.	B		
6.	E	13.	B	20.	A		
7.	C	14.	A	21.	C		

The Official LSAT PrepTest

30

- December 1999
  PrepTest 30

- Form 9LSS43

SECTION I

Time—35 minutes

23 Questions

Directions: Each group of questions in this section is based on a set of conditions. In answering some of the questions, it may be useful to draw a rough diagram. Choose the response that most accurately and completely answers each question and blacken the corresponding space on your answer sheet.

Questions 1–5

This morning, a bakery makes exactly one delivery, consisting of exactly six loaves of bread. Each of the loaves is exactly one of three kinds: oatmeal, rye, or wheat, and each is either sliced or unsliced. The loaves that the bakery delivers this morning must be consistent with the following:

There are at least two kinds of loaves.
There are no more than three rye loaves.
There is no unsliced wheat loaf.
There is at least one unsliced oatmeal loaf.
If two or more of the loaves are unsliced, then at least one of the unsliced loaves is rye.

1. Which one of the following could be a complete and accurate list of the loaves that the bakery delivers?

(A) six unsliced oatmeal loaves
(B) five unsliced oatmeal loaves, one sliced rye loaf
(C) five unsliced oatmeal loaves, one unsliced wheat loaf
(D) four unsliced oatmeal loaves, two unsliced rye loaves
(E) four unsliced oatmeal loaves, two sliced wheat loaves

2. Each of the following could be a complete and accurate list of the unsliced loaves that the bakery delivers EXCEPT:

(A) three oatmeal loaves
(B) three oatmeal loaves, one rye loaf
(C) two oatmeal loaves, two rye loaves
(D) two oatmeal loaves, three rye loaves
(E) one oatmeal loaf, one rye loaf

3. Which one of the following statements CANNOT be true?

(A) The only unsliced loaves are oatmeal loaves.
(B) The only sliced loaves are rye loaves.
(C) The only unsliced loaves are rye loaves.
(D) The number of sliced loaves is exactly one greater than the number of sliced oatmeal loaves.
(E) The number of unsliced loaves is exactly one greater than the number of unsliced oatmeal loaves.

4. Which one of the following statements must be true?

(A) At least one of the loaves is rye.
(B) At least one of the loaves is wheat.
(C) At least one of the loaves is sliced.
(D) No more than four oatmeal loaves are sliced.
(E) No more than four wheat loaves are sliced.

5. If the bakery delivers exactly four wheat loaves, then the bakery could also deliver

(A) one sliced rye loaf and one unsliced rye loaf
(B) one sliced oatmeal loaf and one unsliced oatmeal loaf
(C) two unsliced rye loaves
(D) two unsliced oatmeal loaves
(E) two sliced oatmeal loaves

GO ON TO THE NEXT PAGE.

Questions 6–10

The six messages on an answering machine were each left by one of Fleure, Greta, Hildy, Liam, Pasquale, or Theodore, consistent with the following:

At most one person left more than one message.
No person left more than three messages.
If the first message is Hildy's, the last is Pasquale's.
If Greta left any message, Fleure and Pasquale did also.
If Fleure left any message, Pasquale and Theodore did also, all of Pasquale's preceding any of Theodore's.
If Pasquale left any message, Hildy and Liam did also, all of Hildy's preceding any of Liam's.

6. Which one of the following could be a complete and accurate list of the messages left on the answering machine, from first to last?

(A) Fleure's, Pasquale's, Theodore's, Hildy's, Pasquale's, Liam's
(B) Greta's, Pasquale's, Theodore's, Theodore's, Hildy's, Liam's
(C) Hildy's, Hildy's, Hildy's, Liam's, Pasquale's, Theodore's
(D) Pasquale's, Hildy's, Fleure's, Liam's, Theodore's, Theodore's
(E) Pasquale's, Hildy's, Theodore's, Hildy's, Liam's, Liam's

7. The first and last messages on the answering machine could be the first and second messages left by which one of the following?

(A) Fleure
(B) Hildy
(C) Liam
(D) Pasquale
(E) Theodore

8. If Greta left the fifth message, then which one of the following messages CANNOT have been left by Theodore?

(A) the first message
(B) the second message
(C) the third message
(D) the fourth message
(E) the sixth message

9. Each of the following must be true EXCEPT:

(A) Liam left at least one message.
(B) Theodore left at least one message.
(C) Hildy left at least one message.
(D) Exactly one person left at least two messages.
(E) At least four people left messages.

10. If the only message Pasquale left is the fifth message, then which one of the following could be true?

(A) Hildy left the first message.
(B) Theodore left exactly two messages.
(C) Liam left exactly two messages.
(D) Liam left the second message.
(E) Fleure left the third and fourth messages.

GO ON TO THE NEXT PAGE.

Questions 11–16

Exactly five cars—Frank's, Marquitta's, Orlando's, Taishah's, and Vinquetta's—are washed, each exactly once. The cars are washed one at a time, with each receiving exactly one kind of wash: regular, super, or premium. The following conditions must apply:

The first car washed does not receive a super wash, though at least one car does.

Exactly one car receives a premium wash.

The second and third cars washed receive the same kind of wash as each other.

Neither Orlando's nor Taishah's is washed before Vinquetta's.

Marquitta's is washed before Frank's, but after Orlando's.

Marquitta's and the car washed immediately before Marquitta's receive regular washes.

11. Which one of the following could be an accurate list of the cars in the order in which they are washed, matched with type of wash received?

   (A)   Orlando's: premium; Vinquetta's: regular; Taishah's: regular; Marquitta's: regular; Frank's: super
   (B)   Vinquetta's: premium; Orlando's: regular; Taishah's: regular; Marquitta's: regular; Frank's: super
   (C)   Vinquetta's: regular; Marquitta's: regular; Taishah's: regular; Orlando's: super; Frank's: premium
   (D)   Vinquetta's: super; Orlando's: regular; Marquitta's: regular; Frank's: regular; Taishah's: super
   (E)   Vinquetta's: premium; Orlando's: regular; Marquitta's: regular; Frank's: regular; Taishah's: regular

12. If Vinquetta's car does not receive a premium wash, which one of the following must be true?

   (A)   Orlando's and Vinquetta's cars receive the same kind of wash as each other.
   (B)   Marquitta's and Taishah's cars receive the same kind of wash as each other.
   (C)   The fourth car washed receives a premium wash.
   (D)   Orlando's car is washed third.
   (E)   Marquitta's car is washed fourth.

13. If the last two cars washed receive the same kind of wash as each other, then which one of the following could be true?

   (A)   Orlando's car is washed third.
   (B)   Taishah's car is washed fifth.
   (C)   Taishah's car is washed before Marquitta's car.
   (D)   Vinquetta's car receives a regular wash.
   (E)   Exactly one car receives a super wash.

14. Which one of the following must be true?

   (A)   Vinquetta's car receives a premium wash.
   (B)   Exactly two cars receive a super wash.
   (C)   The fifth car washed receives a super wash.
   (D)   The fourth car washed receives a super wash.
   (E)   The second car washed receives a regular wash.

15. Which one of the following is a complete and accurate list of the cars that must receive a regular wash?

   (A)   Frank's, Marquitta's
   (B)   Marquitta's, Orlando's
   (C)   Marquitta's, Orlando's, Taishah's
   (D)   Marquitta's, Taishah's
   (E)   Marquitta's, Vinquetta's

16. Suppose that in addition to the original five cars Jabrohn's car is also washed. If all the other conditions hold as given, which one of the following CANNOT be true?

   (A)   Orlando's car receives a premium wash.
   (B)   Vinquetta's car receives a super wash.
   (C)   Four cars receive a regular wash.
   (D)   Only the second and third cars washed receive a regular wash.
   (E)   Jabrohn's car is washed after Frank's car.

GO ON TO THE NEXT PAGE.

Questions 17–23

Exactly seven toy-truck models—F, G, H, J, K, M, and S—are assembled on seven assembly lines, exactly one model to a line. The seven lines are arranged side by side and numbered consecutively 1 through 7. Assignment of models to lines must meet the following conditions:

F is assembled on a lower-numbered line than J.
M is assembled on the line numbered one lower than the line on which G is assembled.
H is assembled on line 1 or else line 7.
S is assembled on line 4.

17. Which one of the following is an acceptable assignment of toy-truck models to lines, in order from line 1 through line 7 ?

   (A)   F, J, K, S, H, M, G
   (B)   F, K, J, S, M, G, H
   (C)   F, M, K, S, G, J, H
   (D)   H, K, S, M, G, F, J
   (E)   H, M, G, S, J, F, K

18. It must be true that the lowest-numbered line on which

   (A)   F can be assembled is line 2
   (B)   G can be assembled is line 3
   (C)   J can be assembled is line 2
   (D)   K can be assembled is line 3
   (E)   M can be assembled is line 2

19. If K is assembled on line 5, which one of the following is a pair of models that could be assembled, not necessarily in the order given, on lines whose numbers are consecutive to each other?

   (A)   G, H
   (B)   G, J
   (C)   H, J
   (D)   J, M
   (E)   M, S

20. There can be at most how many lines between the line on which F is assembled and the line on which J is assembled?

   (A)   one
   (B)   two
   (C)   three
   (D)   four
   (E)   five

21. If K is assembled on line 2, which one of the following must be true?

   (A)   F is assembled on a lower-numbered line than S.
   (B)   H is assembled on a lower-numbered line than G.
   (C)   J is assembled on a lower-numbered line than H.
   (D)   M is assembled on a lower-numbered line than J.
   (E)   S is assembled on a lower-numbered line than J.

22. If G is assembled on the line numbered one less than the line on which F is assembled, then which one of the following must be true?

   (A)   F is assembled on line 3.
   (B)   G is assembled on line 5.
   (C)   H is assembled on line 1.
   (D)   K is assembled on line 5.
   (E)   M is assembled on line 6.

23. If M is assembled on line 1, which one of the following could be true?

   (A)   F is assembled on a line numbered one lower than the line on which H is assembled.
   (B)   F is assembled on a line numbered one lower than the line on which K is assembled.
   (C)   G is assembled on a line numbered one lower than the line on which J is assembled.
   (D)   G is assembled on a line numbered one lower than the line on which K is assembled.
   (E)   K is assembled on a line numbered one lower than the line on which G is assembled.

S T O P

IF YOU FINISH BEFORE TIME IS CALLED, YOU MAY CHECK YOUR WORK ON THIS SECTION ONLY.
DO NOT WORK ON ANY OTHER SECTION IN THE TEST.

SECTION II

Time—35 minutes

26 Questions

<u>Directions:</u> The questions in this section are based on the reasoning contained in brief statements or passages. For some questions, more than one of the choices could conceivably answer the question. However, you are to choose the <u>best</u> answer; that is, the response that most accurately and completely answers the question. You should not make assumptions that are by commonsense standards implausible, superfluous, or incompatible with the passage. After you have chosen the best answer, blacken the corresponding space on your answer sheet.

1. More and more computer programs that provide solutions to mathematical problems in engineering are being produced, and it is thus increasingly unnecessary for practicing engineers to have a thorough understanding of fundamental mathematical principles. Consequently, in training engineers who will work in industry, less emphasis should be placed on mathematical principles, so that space in the engineering curriculum will be available for other important subjects.

   Which one of the following, if true, most seriously weakens the argument given for the recommendation above?

   (A) The effective use of computer programs that provide solutions to mathematical problems in engineering requires an understanding of mathematical principles.

   (B) Many of the computer programs that provide solutions to mathematical problems in engineering are already in routine use.

   (C) Development of composites and other such new materials has meant that the curriculum for engineers who will work in industry must allow time for teaching the properties of these materials.

   (D) Most of the computer programs that provide solutions to mathematical problems in engineering can be run on the types of computers available to most engineering firms.

   (E) The engineering curriculum already requires that engineering students be familiar with and able to use a variety of computer programs.

2. Raymond Burr played the role of lawyer Perry Mason on television. Burr's death in 1993 prompted a prominent lawyer to say "Although not a lawyer, Mr. Burr strove for such authenticity that we feel as if we lost one of our own." This comment from a prestigious attorney provides appalling evidence that, in the face of television, even some legal professionals are losing their ability to distinguish fiction from reality.

   The reasoning in the argument is flawed because the argument

   (A) takes the views of one lawyer to represent the views of all lawyers

   (B) criticizes the lawyer rather than the lawyer's statement

   (C) presumes that the lawyer is qualified to evaluate the performance of an actor

   (D) focuses on a famous actor's portrayal of a lawyer rather than on the usual way in which lawyers are portrayed on television

   (E) ignores the part of the lawyer's remark that indicates an awareness of the difference between reality and fiction

GO ON TO THE NEXT PAGE.

3. Opponents of peat harvesting in this country argue that it would alter the ecological balance of our peat-rich wetlands and that, as a direct consequence of this, much of the country's water supply would be threatened with contamination. But this cannot be true, for in Ireland, where peat has been harvested for centuries, the water supply is not contaminated. We can safely proceed with the harvesting of peat.

Which one of the following, if true, most strengthens the argument?

(A) Over hundreds of years, the ecological balance of all areas changes slowly but significantly, sometimes to the advantage of certain flora and fauna.

(B) The original ecology of the peat-harvesting areas of Ireland was virtually identical to that of the undisturbed wetlands of this country.

(C) The activities of other industries in coming years are likely to have adverse effects on the water supply of this country.

(D) The peat resources of this country are far larger than those of some countries that successfully harvest peat.

(E) The peat-harvesting industry of Ireland has been able to supply most of that country's fuel for generations.

4. For next year, the Chefs' Union has requested a 10 percent salary increase for each of its members, whereas the Hotel Managers' Union has requested only an 8 percent salary increase for each of its members. These facts demonstrate that the average dollar amount of the raises that the Chefs' Union has requested for next year is greater than that of the raises requested by the Hotel Managers' Union.

Which one of the following, if true, most strengthens the argument?

(A) The Chefs' Union has many more members than does the Hotel Managers' Union.

(B) The Chefs' Union is a more powerful union than is the Hotel Managers' Union and is therefore more likely to obtain the salary increases it requests.

(C) The current salaries of the members of the Chefs' Union are, on average, higher than the current salaries of the members of the Hotel Managers' Union.

(D) The average dollar amount of the raises that the members of the Chefs' Union received last year was equal to the average dollar amount of the raises that the members of the Hotel Managers' Union received.

(E) The members of the Chefs' Union received salary increases of 10 percent in each of the last two years, while the members of the Hotel Managers' Union received salary increases of only 8 percent in each of the last two years.

5. Parent: I had tried without success to get my young child to brush her teeth. I had hoped that she would imitate me, or that she would be persuaded by reason to brush her teeth. Then, I made a point of brushing her teeth for her immediately before reading her a story before her naps and at night. After several weeks, when I would pick up a storybook at these times, she began automatically to retrieve her toothbrush and brush her teeth herself.

The parent's experience with the child most closely conforms to which one of the following generalizations?

(A) Children are most effectively taught to do something by someone's setting an example.

(B) Children more readily adopt a behavior through habit and repetition than through other means.

(C) Children are too young to understand rational arguments for adopting a behavior.

(D) Children often imitate the behavior of others rather than listening to reason.

(E) Children ordinarily act contrary to their parents' expectations in order to get more attention.

6. The student body at this university takes courses in a wide range of disciplines. Miriam is a student at this university, so she takes courses in a wide range of disciplines.

Which one of the following arguments exhibits flawed reasoning most similar to that exhibited by the argument above?

(A) The students at this school take mathematics. Miguel is a student at this school, so he takes mathematics.

(B) The editorial board of this law journal has written on many legal issues. Louise is on the editorial board, so she has written on many legal issues.

(C) The component parts of bulldozers are heavy. This machine is a bulldozer, so it is heavy.

(D) All older automobiles need frequent oil changes. This car is new, so its oil need not be changed as frequently.

(E) The individual cells of the brain are incapable of thinking. Therefore, the brain as a whole is incapable of thinking.

GO ON TO THE NEXT PAGE.

Questions 7–8

Opponent of offshore oil drilling: The projected benefits of drilling new oil wells in certain areas in the outer continental shelf are not worth the risk of environmental disaster. The oil already being extracted from these areas currently provides only 4 percent of our country's daily oil requirement, and the new wells would only add one-half of 1 percent.

Proponent of offshore oil drilling: Don't be ridiculous! You might just as well argue that new farms should not be allowed, since no new farm could supply the total food needs of our country for more than a few minutes.

7. The drilling proponent's reply to the drilling opponent proceeds by

   (A)   offering evidence in support of drilling that is more decisive than is the evidence offered by the drilling opponent

   (B)   claiming that the statistics cited as evidence by the drilling opponent are factually inaccurate

   (C)   pointing out that the drilling opponent's argument is a misapplication of a frequently legitimate way of arguing

   (D)   citing as parallel to the argument made by the drilling opponent an argument in which the conclusion is strikingly unsupported

   (E)   proposing a conclusion that is more strongly supported by the drilling opponent's evidence than is the conclusion offered by the drilling opponent

8. Which one of the following, if true, most weakens the drilling proponent's reply?

   (A)   New farms do not involve a risk analogous to that run by new offshore oil drilling.

   (B)   Many of the largest oil deposits are located under land that is unsuitable for farming.

   (C)   Unlike oil, common agricultural products fulfill nutritional needs rather than fuel requirements.

   (D)   Legislation governing new oil drilling has been much more thoroughly articulated than has that governing new farms.

   (E)   The country under discussion imports a higher proportion of the farm products it needs than it does of the oil it needs.

9. A running track with a hard surface makes for greater running speed than a soft one, at least under dry conditions, because even though step length is shorter on a hard surface, the time the runner's foot remains in contact with the running surface is less with a hard surface.

Which one of the following, if true, is evidence that the explanation given above is only a partial one?

   (A)   Dry running conditions can be guaranteed for indoor track races only.

   (B)   In general, taller runners have greater average step length than shorter runners do.

   (C)   Hard tracks enhance a runner's speed by making it easier for the runner to maintain a posture that minimizes wind resistance.

   (D)   The tracks at which the world's fastest running times have been recorded are located well above sea level, where the air is relatively thin.

   (E)   To remain in top condition, a soft track surface requires different maintenance procedures than does a hard one.

10. Goswami: I support the striking workers at Ergon Foods. They are underpaid. The majority of them make less than $20,000 per year.

   Nordecki: If pay is the issue, I must disagree. The average annual salary of the striking workers at Ergon Foods is over $29,000.

Goswami and Nordecki disagree over the truth of which one of the following statements?

   (A)   The average annual salary at Ergon Foods is over $29,000.

   (B)   Pay is the primary issue over which the workers are striking at Ergon Foods.

   (C)   It is reasonable to support striking workers who are underpaid.

   (D)   The striking workers at Ergon Foods are underpaid.

   (E)   It was unreasonable for the workers at Ergon Foods to go on strike.

GO ON TO THE NEXT PAGE.

11. Teacher to a student: You agree that it is bad to break promises. But when we speak to each other we all make an implicit promise to tell the truth, and lying is the breaking of that promise. So even if you promised Jeanne that you would tell me she is home sick, you should not tell me that, if you know that she is well.

Which one of the following is an assumption on which the teacher's argument depends?

(A) Most people always tell the truth.
(B) It is sometimes better to act in a friend's best interests than to keep a promise to that friend.
(C) Breaking a promise leads to worse consequences than does telling a lie.
(D) Some implicit promises are worse to break than some explicit ones.
(E) One should never break a promise.

12. Despite the fact that antilock brakes are designed to make driving safer, research suggests that people who drive cars equipped with antilock brakes have more accidents than those who drive cars not equipped with antilock brakes.

Each of the following, if true, would help resolve the apparent discrepancy described above EXCEPT:

(A) Most cars equipped with antilock brakes are, on average, driven more carelessly than cars not equipped with antilock brakes.
(B) Antilock brakes malfunction more often than regular brakes.
(C) Antilock brakes require expensive specialized maintenance to be even as effective as unmaintained regular brakes.
(D) Most people who drive cars equipped with antilock brakes do not know how to use those brakes properly.
(E) Antilock brakes were designed for safety in congested urban driving, but accidents of the most serious nature take place on highways.

13. President of the Regional Chamber of Commerce: We are all aware of the painful fact that almost no new businesses have moved into our region or started up here over the last ten years. But the Planning Board is obviously guilty of a gross exaggeration in its recent estimate that businesses are leaving the region at the rate of about four a week. After all, there were never more than about one thousand businesses in the region, so if they were really leaving at such a rate, they would all have been gone long ago.

The argument is most vulnerable to criticism on the ground that it

(A) focuses on what is going out of a system while ignoring the issue of what is coming into the system
(B) confuses a claim about a rate of change within a system with a claim about the absolute size of the system
(C) argues against a position simply by showing that the position serves the interest of the Planning Board
(D) treats a claim about what is currently the case as if it were a claim about what has been the case for an extended period
(E) attacks what was offered as an estimate on the ground that it is not precise

GO ON TO THE NEXT PAGE.

14. It is inaccurate to say that a diet high in refined sugar cannot cause adult-onset diabetes, since a diet high in refined sugar can make a person overweight, and being overweight can predispose a person to adult-onset diabetes.

The argument is most parallel, in its logical structure, to which one of the following?

(A) It is inaccurate to say that being in cold air can cause a person to catch a cold, since colds are caused by viruses, and viruses flourish in warm, crowded places.

(B) It is accurate to say that no airline flies from Halifax to Washington. No airline offers a direct flight, although some airlines have flights from Halifax to Boston and others have flights from Boston to Washington.

(C) It is correct to say that overfertilization is the primary cause of lawn disease, since fertilizer causes lawn grass to grow rapidly and rapidly growing grass has little resistance to disease.

(D) It is incorrect to say that inferior motor oil cannot cause a car to get poorer gasoline mileage, since inferior motor oil can cause engine valve deterioration, and engine valve deterioration can lead to poorer gasoline mileage.

(E) It is inaccurate to say that Alexander the Great was a student of Plato; Alexander was a student of Aristotle and Aristotle was a student of Plato.

15. During the recent economic downturn, banks contributed to the decline by loaning less money. Prior to the downturn, regulatory standards for loanmaking by banks were tightened. Clearly, therefore, banks will lend more money if those standards are relaxed.

The argument assumes that

(A) the downturn did not cause a significant decrease in the total amount of money on deposit with banks which is the source of funds for banks to lend

(B) the imposition of the tighter regulatory standards was not a cause of the economic downturn

(C) the reason for tightening the regulatory standards was not arbitrary

(D) no economic downturn is accompanied by a significant decrease in the amount of money loaned out by banks to individual borrowers and to businesses

(E) no relaxation of standards for loanmaking by banks would compensate for the effects of the downturn

16. Zoos have served both as educational resources and as entertainment. Unfortunately, removing animals from their natural habitats to stock the earliest zoos reduced certain species' populations, endangering their survival. Today most new zoo animals are obtained from captive breeding programs, and many zoos now maintain breeding stocks for continued propagation of various species. This makes possible efforts to reestablish endangered species in the wild.

Which one of the following statements is most strongly supported by the information above?

(A) Zoos have played an essential role in educating the public about endangered species.

(B) Some specimens of endangered species are born and bred in zoos.

(C) No zoos exploit wild animals or endanger the survival of species.

(D) Nearly all of the animals in zoos today were born in captivity.

(E) The main purpose of zoos has shifted from entertainment to education.

GO ON TO THE NEXT PAGE.

17. Only a very small percentage of people from the service professions ever become board members of the 600 largest North American corporations. This shows that people from the service professions are underrepresented in the most important corporate boardrooms in North America.

Which one of the following points out a flaw committed in the argument?

(A) Six hundred is too small a sample on which to base so sweeping a conclusion about the representation of people from the service professions.

(B) The percentage of people from the service professions who serve on the boards of the 600 largest North American corporations reveals little about the percentage of the members of these boards who are from the service professions.

(C) It is a mistake to take the 600 largest North American corporations to be typical of corporate boardrooms generally.

(D) It is irrelevant to smaller corporations whether the largest corporations in North America would agree to have significant numbers of workers from the service professions on the boards of the largest corporations.

(E) The presence of people from the service professions on a corporate board does not necessarily imply that that corporation will be more socially responsible than it has been in the past.

18. If there are any inspired musical performances in the concert, the audience will be treated to a good show. But there will not be a good show unless there are sophisticated listeners in the audience, and to be a sophisticated listener one must understand one's musical roots.

If all of the statements above are true, which one of the following must also be true?

(A) If there are no sophisticated listeners in the audience, then there will be no inspired musical performances in the concert.

(B) No people who understand their musical roots will be in the audience if the audience will not be treated to a good show.

(C) If there will be people in the audience who understand their musical roots, then at least one musical performance in the concert will be inspired.

(D) The audience will be treated to a good show unless there are people in the audience who do not understand their musical roots.

(E) If there are sophisticated listeners in the audience, then there will be inspired musical performances in the concert.

19. Columnist: A recent study suggests that living with a parrot increases one's risk of lung cancer. But no one thinks the government should impose financial impediments on the owning of parrots because of this apparent danger. So by the same token, the government should not levy analogous special taxes on hunting gear, snow skis, recreational parachutes, or motorcycles.

Each of the following principles is logically consistent with the columnist's conclusion EXCEPT:

(A) The government should fund education by taxing nonessential sports equipment and recreational gear.

(B) The government should not tax those who avoid dangerous activities and adopt healthy lifestyles.

(C) The government should create financial disincentives to deter participation in activities it deems dangerous.

(D) The government should not create financial disincentives for people to race cars or climb mountains, even though these are dangerous activities.

(E) The government would be justified in levying taxes to provide food and shelter for those who cannot afford to pay for them.

20. Scientist: Some critics of public funding for this research project have maintained that only if it can be indicated how the public will benefit from the project is continued public funding for it justified. If the critics were right about this, then there would not be the tremendous public support for the project that even its critics acknowledge.

If the scientist's claims are true, which one of the following must also be true?

(A) The benefits derived from the research project are irrelevant to whether or not its funding is justified.

(B) Continued public funding for the research project is justified.

(C) Public support for the research project is the surest indication of whether or not it is justified.

(D) There is tremendous public support for the research project because it can be indicated how the public will benefit from the project.

(E) That a public benefit can be indicated is not a requirement for the justification of the research project's continued public funding.

GO ON TO THE NEXT PAGE.

21. The new agriculture bill will almost surely fail to pass. The leaders of all major parties have stated that they oppose it.

    Which one of the following, if true, adds the most support for the prediction that the agriculture bill will fail to pass?

    (A) Most bills that have not been supported by even one leader of a major party have not been passed into law.

    (B) Most bills that have not been passed into law were not supported by even one member of a major party.

    (C) If the leaders of all major parties endorse the new agriculture bill, it will pass into law.

    (D) Most bills that have been passed into law were not unanimously supported by the leaders of all major parties.

    (E) Most bills that have been passed into law were supported by at least one leader of a major party.

22. The folktale that claims that a rattlesnake's age can be determined from the number of sections in its rattle is false, but only because the rattles are brittle and sometimes partially or completely break off. So if they were not so brittle, one could reliably determine a rattlesnake's age simply from the number of sections in its rattle, because one new section is formed each time a rattlesnake molts.

    Which one of the following is an assumption the argument requires in order for its conclusion to be properly drawn?

    (A) Rattlesnakes molt exactly once a year.

    (B) The rattles of rattlesnakes of different species are identical in appearance.

    (C) Rattlesnakes molt more frequently when young than when old.

    (D) The brittleness of a rattlesnake's rattle is not correlated with the length of the rattlesnake's life.

    (E) Rattlesnakes molt as often when food is scarce as they do when food is plentiful.

Questions 23–24

Tony: A new kind of videocassette has just been developed. It lasts for only half as many viewings as the old kind does but costs a third as much. Therefore, video rental stores would find it significantly more economical to purchase and stock movies recorded on the new kind of videocassette than on the old kind.

Anna: But the videocassette itself only accounts for 5 percent of the price a video rental store pays to buy a copy of a movie on video; most of the price consists of royalties the store pays to the studio that produced the movie. So the price that video rental stores pay per copy would decrease by considerably less than 5 percent, and royalties would have to be paid on additional copies.

23. Anna's reply is structured to lead to which one of the following conclusions?

    (A) The royalties paid to movie studios for movies sold on videotape are excessively large.

    (B) Video rental stores should always stock the highest-quality videocassettes available, because durability is more important than price.

    (C) The largest part of the fee a customer pays to rent a movie from a video rental store goes toward the royalties the store paid in purchasing that movie.

    (D) The cost savings to video rental stores that buy movies recorded on the cheaper videocassettes rather than movies recorded on the more durable ones will be small or nonexistent.

    (E) If the price a video rental store pays to buy a movie on videocassette does not decrease, the rental fee the store charges on the movie will not decrease.

24. Which one of the following, if true, would contribute most to a defense of Tony's position against Anna's reply?

    (A) The price that video rental stores pay for movies recorded on videocassettes is considerably less than the retail price of those movies.

    (B) A significant proportion of the movies on videocassette purchased by video rental stores are bought as replacements for worn-out copies of movies the stores already have in stock.

    (C) The royalty fee included in the price that video rental stores pay for movies on the new kind of videocassette will be half that included in the price of movies on the old kind.

    (D) Given a choice, customers are more likely to buy a movie on videocassette than to rent it if the rental fee is more than half of the purchase price.

    (E) Many of the movies rented from video rental stores, particularly children's movies, average several viewings per rental fee.

GO ON TO THE NEXT PAGE.

25. Physician: Heart disease generally affects men at an earlier age than it does women, who tend to experience heart disease after menopause. Both sexes have the hormones estrogen and testosterone, but when they are relatively young, men have ten times as much testosterone as women, and women abruptly lose estrogen after menopause. We can conclude, then, that testosterone tends to promote, and estrogen tends to inhibit, heart disease.

The physician's argument is questionable because it presumes which one of the following without providing sufficient justification?

(A) Hormones are the primary factors that account for the differences in age-related heart disease risks between women and men.

(B) Estrogen and testosterone are the only hormones that promote or inhibit heart disease.

(C) Men with high testosterone levels have a greater risk for heart disease than do postmenopausal women.

(D) Because hormone levels are correlated with heart disease they influence heart disease.

(E) Hormone levels do not vary from person to person, especially among those of the same age and gender.

26. People ought to take into account a discipline's blemished origins when assessing the scientific value of that discipline. Take, for example, chemistry. It must be considered that many of its landmark results were obtained by alchemists—a group whose superstitions and appeals to magic dominated the early development of chemical theory.

The reasoning above is most susceptible to criticism because the author

(A) fails to establish that disciplines with unblemished origins are scientifically valuable

(B) fails to consider how chemistry's current theories and practices differ from those of the alchemists mentioned

(C) uses an example to contradict the principle under consideration

(D) does not prove that most disciplines that are not scientifically valuable have origins that are in some way suspect

(E) uses the word "discipline" in two different senses

S T O P

IF YOU FINISH BEFORE TIME IS CALLED, YOU MAY CHECK YOUR WORK ON THIS SECTION ONLY.
DO NOT WORK ON ANY OTHER SECTION IN THE TEST.

SECTION III

Time—35 minutes

27 Questions

Directions: Each passage in this section is followed by a group of questions to be answered on the basis of what is <u>stated</u> or <u>implied</u> in the passage. For some of the questions, more than one of the choices could conceivably answer the question. However, you are to choose the <u>best</u> answer; that is, the response that most accurately and completely answers the question, and blacken the corresponding space on your answer sheet.

The okapi, a forest mammal of central Africa, has presented zoologists with a number of difficult questions since they first learned of its existence in 1900. The first was how to classify it. Because it was
(5) horselike in dimension, and bore patches of striped hide similar to a zebra's (a relative of the horse), zoologists first classified it as a member of the horse family. But further studies showed that, despite okapis' coloration and short necks, their closest relatives were
(10) giraffes. The okapi's rightful place within the giraffe family is confirmed by its skin-covered horns (in males), two-lobed canine teeth, and long prehensile tongue.

The next question was the size of the okapi
(15) population. Because okapis were infrequently captured by hunters, some zoologists believed that they were rare; however, others theorized that their habits simply kept them out of sight. It was not until 1985, when zoologists started tracking okapis by affixing collars
(20) equipped with radio transmitters to briefly captured specimens, that reliable information about okapi numbers and habits began to be collected. It turns out that while okapis are not as rare as some zoologists suspected, their population is concentrated in an
(25) extremely limited chain of forestland in northeastern central Africa, surrounded by savanna.

One reason for their seeming scarcity is that their coloration allows okapis to camouflage themselves even at close range. Another is that okapis do not travel
(30) in groups or with other large forest mammals, and neither frequent open riverbanks nor forage at the borders of clearings, choosing instead to keep to the forest interior. This is because okapis, unlike any other animal in the central African forest, subsist entirely on
(35) leaves: more than one hundred species of plants have been identified as part of their diet, and about twenty of these are preferred. Okapis never eat one plant to the exclusion of others; even where preferred foliage is abundant, okapis will leave much of it uneaten,
(40) choosing to move on and sample other leaves. Because of this, and because of the distribution of their food, okapis engage in individual rather than congregated foraging.

But other questions about okapi behavior arise.
(45) Why, for example, do they prefer to remain within forested areas when many of their favorite plants are found in the open border between forest and savanna? One possibility is that this is a defense against predators; another is that the okapi was pushed into the
(50) forest by competition with other large, hoofed animals,

such as the bushbuck and bongo, that specialize on the forest edges and graze them more efficiently. Another question is why okapis are absent from other nearby forest regions that would seem hospitable to them.
(55) Zoologists theorize that okapis are relicts of an era when forestland was scarce and that they continue to respect those borders even though available forestland has long since expanded.

1. Which one of the following most completely and accurately expresses the main idea of the passage?

(A) Information gathered by means of radio-tracking collars has finally provided answers to the questions about okapis that zoologists have been attempting to answer since they first learned of the mammal's existence.

(B) Because of their physical characteristics and their infrequent capture by hunters, okapis presented zoologists with many difficult questions at the start of the twentieth century.

(C) Research concerning okapis has answered some of the questions that have puzzled zoologists since their discovery, but has also raised other questions regarding their geographic concentration and feeding habits.

(D) A new way of tracking okapis using radio-tracking collars reveals that their apparent scarcity is actually a result of their coloration, their feeding habits, and their geographic concentration.

(E) Despite new research involving radio tracking, the questions that have puzzled zoologists about okapis since their discovery at the start of the twentieth century remain mostly unanswered.

GO ON TO THE NEXT PAGE.

2. The function of the third paragraph is to

   (A) pose a question about okapi behavior
   (B) rebut a theory about okapi behavior
   (C) counter the assertion that okapis are rare
   (D) explain why okapis appeared to be rare
   (E) support the belief that okapis are rare

3. Based on the passage, in its eating behavior the okapi is most analogous to

   (A) a child who eats one kind of food at a time, consuming all of it before going on to the next kind
   (B) a professor who strictly follows the outline in the syllabus, never digressing to follow up on student questions
   (C) a student who delays working on homework until the last minute, then rushes to complete it
   (D) a newspaper reader who skips from story to story, just reading headlines and eye-catching paragraphs
   (E) a deer that ventures out of the woods only at dusk and dawn, remaining hidden during the rest of the day

4. Suppose that numerous okapis are discovered living in a remote forest region in northeastern central Africa that zoologists had not previously explored. Based on their current views, which one of the following would the zoologists be most likely to conclude about this discovery?

   (A) Okapis were pushed into this forest region by competition with mammals in neighboring forests.
   (B) Okapis in this forest region forage in the border between forest and savanna.
   (C) Okapis in this forest region are not threatened by the usual predators of okapis.
   (D) Okapis moved into this forest region because their preferred foliage is more abundant there than in other forests.
   (E) Okapis lived in this forest region when forestland in the area was scarce.

5. The passage provides information intended to help explain each of the following EXCEPT:

   (A) why zoologists once believed that okapis were rare
   (B) why zoologists classified the okapi as a member of the giraffe family
   (C) why okapis choose to limit themselves to the interiors of forests
   (D) why okapis engage in individual rather than congregated foraging
   (E) why okapis leave much preferred foliage uneaten

6. Based on the passage, the author would be most likely to agree with which one of the following statements?

   (A) The number of okapis is many times larger than zoologists had previously believed it to be.
   (B) Radio-tracking collars have enabled scientists to finally answer all the questions about the okapi.
   (C) Okapis are captured infrequently because their habits and coloration make it difficult for hunters to find them.
   (D) Okapis are concentrated in a limited geographic area because they prefer to eat one plant species to the exclusion of others.
   (E) The number of okapis would steadily increase if okapis began to forage in the open border between forest and savanna.

GO ON TO THE NEXT PAGE.

Tragic dramas written in Greece during the fifth century B.C. engender considerable scholarly debate over the relative influence of individual autonomy and the power of the gods on the drama's action. One early
(5) scholar, B. Snell, argues that Aeschylus, for example, develops in his tragedies a concept of the autonomy of the individual. In these dramas, the protagonists invariably confront a situation that paralyzes them, so that their prior notions about how to behave or think
(10) are dissolved. Faced with a decision on which their fate depends, they must reexamine their deepest motives, and then act with determination. They are given only two alternatives, each with grave consequences, and they make their decision only after a tortured internal
(15) debate. According to Snell, this decision is "free" and "personal" and such personal autonomy constitutes the central theme in Aeschylean drama, as if the plays were devised to isolate an abstract model of human action. Drawing psychological conclusions from this
(20) interpretation, another scholar, Z. Barbu, suggests that "[Aeschylean] drama is proof of the emergence within ancient Greek civilization of the individual as a free agent."

To A. Rivier, Snell's emphasis on the decision
(25) made by the protagonist, with its implicit notions of autonomy and responsibility, misrepresents the role of the superhuman forces at work, forces that give the dramas their truly tragic dimension. These forces are not only external to the protagonist; they are also
(30) experienced by the protagonist as an internal compulsion, subjecting him or her to constraint even in what are claimed to be his or her "choices." Hence all that the deliberation does is to make the protagonist aware of the impasse, rather than motivating one
(35) choice over another. It is finally a necessity imposed by the deities that generates the decision, so that at a particular moment in the drama necessity dictates a path. Thus, the protagonist does not so much "choose" between two possibilities as "recognize" that there is
(40) only one real option.

A. Lesky, in his discussion of Aeschylus' play *Agamemnon*, disputes both views. Agamemnon, ruler of Argos, must decide whether to brutally sacrifice his own daughter. A message from the deity Artemis has
(45) told him that only the sacrifice will bring a wind to blow his ships to an important battle. Agamemnon is indeed constrained by a divine necessity. But he also deeply desires a victorious battle: "If this sacrifice will loose the winds, it is permitted to desire it fervently,"
(50) he says. The violence of his passion suggests that Agamemnon chooses a path—chosen by the gods for their own reasons—on the basis of desires that must be condemned by us, because they are his own. In Lesky's view, tragic action is bound by the constant tension
(55) between a self and superhuman forces.

7. Based on the information presented in the passage, which one of the following statements best represents Lesky's view of Agamemnon?

(A) Agamemnon's motivations are identical to those of the gods.
(B) The nature of Agamemnon's character solely determines the course of the tragedy.
(C) Agamemnon's decision-making is influenced by his military ambitions.
(D) Agamemnon is concerned only with pleasing the deity Artemis.
(E) Agamemnon is especially tragic because of his political position.

8. Which one of the following paraphrases most accurately restates the quotation from *Agamemnon* found in lines 48–49 of the passage?

(A) If the goddess has ordained that the only way I can evade battle is by performing this sacrifice, then it is perfectly appropriate for me to deeply desire this sacrifice.
(B) If the goddess has ordained that the only way I can get a wind to move my ships to battle is by performing this sacrifice, then it is perfectly appropriate for me to deeply desire victory in battle.
(C) If the goddess has ordained that the only way I can get a wind to move my ships to battle is by performing this sacrifice, then it is perfectly appropriate for me to deeply desire this sacrifice.
(D) As I alone have determined that only this sacrifice will give me victory in battle, I will perform it, without reservations.
(E) As I have determined that only deeply desiring victory in battle will guarantee the success of the sacrifice, I will perform it, as ordained by the goddess.

9. Which one of the following statements best expresses Rivier's view, as presented in the passage, of what makes a drama tragic?

(A) The tragic protagonist is deluded by the gods into thinking he or she is free.
(B) The tragic protagonist struggles for a heroism that belongs to the gods.
(C) The tragic protagonist wrongly seeks to take responsibility for his or her actions.
(D) The tragic protagonist cannot make a decision that is free of divine compulsion.
(E) The tragic protagonist is punished for evading his or her responsibilities.

GO ON TO THE NEXT PAGE.

10. It can be inferred from the passage that the central difference between the interpretations of Lesky and Rivier is over which one of the following points?

(A) whether or not the tragic protagonist is aware of the consequences of his or her actions
(B) whether or not the tragic protagonist acknowledges the role of the deities in his or her life
(C) whether or not the tragic protagonist's own desires have relevance to the outcome of the drama
(D) whether or not the actions of the deities are relevant to the moral evaluation of the character's action
(E) whether or not the desires of the tragic protagonist are more ethical than those of the deities

11. Which one of the following summaries of the plot of a Greek tragedy best illustrates the view attributed to Rivier in the passage?

(A) Although she knows that she will be punished for violating the law of her city, a tragic figure bravely decides to bury her dead brother over the objections of local authorities.
(B) Because of her love for her dead brother, a tragic figure, although aware that she will be punished for violating the law of her city, accedes to the gods' request that she bury his body.
(C) After much careful thought, a tragic figure decides to disobey the dictates of the gods and murder her unfaithful husband.
(D) A tragic figure, defying a curse placed on his family by the gods, leads his city into a battle that he realizes will prove futile.
(E) After much careful thought, a tragic figure realizes that he has no alternative but to follow the course chosen by the gods and murder his father.

12. The quotation in lines 21–23 suggests that Barbu assumes which one of the following about Aeschylean drama?

(A) Aeschylean drama helped to initiate a new understanding of the person in ancient Greek society.
(B) Aeschylean drama introduced new ways of understanding the role of the individual in ancient Greek society.
(C) Aeschylean drama is the original source of the understanding of human motivation most familiar to the modern Western world.
(D) Aeschylean drama accurately reflects the way personal autonomy was perceived in ancient Greek society.
(E) Aeschylean drama embodies the notion of freedom most familiar to the modern Western world.

13. All of the following statements describe Snell's view of Aeschylus' tragic protagonists, as it is presented in the passage, EXCEPT:

(A) They are required to choose a course of action with grave consequences.
(B) Their final choices restore harmony with supernatural forces.
(C) They cannot rely on their customary notions of appropriate behavior.
(D) They are compelled to confront their true motives.
(E) They are aware of the available choices.

14. The primary purpose of the passage is to

(A) argue against one particular interpretation of Greek tragedy
(B) establish that there are a variety of themes in Greek tragedy
(C) present aspects of an ongoing scholarly debate about Greek tragedy
(D) point out the relative merits of different scholarly interpretations of Greek tragedy
(E) suggest the relevance of Greek tragedy to the philosophical debate over human motivation

GO ON TO THE NEXT PAGE.

Philosopher Denise Meyerson views the Critical Legal Studies (CLS) movement as seeking to debunk orthodox legal theory by exposing its contradictions. However, Meyerson argues that CLS proponents tend
(5) to see contradictions where none exist, and that CLS overrates the threat that conflict poses to orthodox legal theory.

According to Meyerson, CLS proponents hold that the existence of conflicting values in the law implies
(10) the absence of any uniquely right solution to legal cases. CLS argues that these conflicting values generate equally plausible but opposing answers to any given legal question, and, consequently, that the choice between the conflicting answers must necessarily be
(15) arbitrary or irrational. Meyerson denies that the existence of conflicting values makes a case irresolvable, and asserts that at least some such cases can be resolved by ranking the conflicting values. For example, a lawyer's obligation to preserve a client's
(20) confidences may entail harming other parties, thus violating moral principle. This conflict can be resolved if it can be shown that in certain cases the professional obligation overrides ordinary moral obligations.

In addition, says Meyerson, even when the two
(25) solutions are equally compelling, it does not follow that the choice between them must be irrational. On the contrary, a solution that is not rationally required need not be unreasonable. Meyerson concurs with another critic that instead of concentrating on the choice
(30) between two compelling alternatives, we should rather reflect on the difference between both of these answers on the one hand, and some utterly unreasonable answer on the other—such as deciding a property dispute on the basis of which claimant is louder. The
(35) acknowledgment that conflicting values can exist, then, does not have the far-reaching implications imputed by CLS; even if some answer to a problem is not the only answer, opting for it can still be reasonable.

Last, Meyerson takes issue with the CLS charge
(40) that legal formalism, the belief that there is a quasi-deductive method capable of giving solutions to problems of legal choice, requires objectivism, the belief that the legal process has moral authority. Meyerson claims that showing the law to be
(45) unambiguous does not demonstrate its legitimacy: consider a game in which participants compete to steal the item of highest value from a shop; while a person may easily identify the winner in terms of the rules, it does not follow that the person endorses the rules of
(50) the game. A CLS scholar might object that legal cases are unlike games, in that one cannot merely apply the rules without appealing to, and therefore endorsing, external considerations of purpose, policy, and value. But Meyerson replies that such considerations may be
(55) viewed as part of, not separate from, the rules of the game.

15. Which one of the following best expresses the main idea of the passage?

(A) The arguments of the Critical Legal Studies movement are under attack not only by legal theorists, but also by thinkers in related areas such as philosophy.

(B) In critiquing the Critical Legal Studies movement, Meyerson charges that the positions articulated by the movement's proponents overlook the complexity of actual legal dilemmas.

(C) Meyerson objects to the propositions of the Critical Legal Studies movement because she views them as being self-contradictory.

(D) Meyerson poses several objections to the tenets of the Critical Legal Studies movement, but her most important argument involves constructing a hierarchy of conflicting values.

(E) Meyerson seeks to counter the claims that are made by proponents of the Critical Legal Studies movement in their effort to challenge conventional legal theory.

16. The primary purpose of the reference to a game in the last paragraph is to

(A) provide an example of how a principle has previously been applied

(B) demonstrate a point by means of an analogy

(C) emphasize the relative unimportance of an activity

(D) contrast two situations by exaggerating their differences

(E) dismiss an idea by portraying it as reprehensible

GO ON TO THE NEXT PAGE.

17. The author's primary purpose in the passage is to

    (A) evaluate divergent legal doctrines
    (B) explain how a controversy arose
    (C) advocate a new interpretation of legal tradition
    (D) describe a challenge to a school of thought
    (E) refute claims made by various scholars

18. It can be inferred from the passage that Meyerson would be most likely to agree with which one of the following statements about "external considerations" (line 53)?

    (A) How one determines the extent to which these considerations are relevant depends on one's degree of belief in the legal process.
    (B) The extent to which these considerations are part of the legal process depends on the extent to which the policies and values can be endorsed.
    (C) When these considerations have more moral authority than the law, the former should outweigh the latter.
    (D) If one uses these considerations in determining a legal solution, one is assuming that the policies and values are desirable.
    (E) Whether these considerations are separate from or integral to the legal process is a matter of debate.

19. The phrase "far-reaching implications" (line 36) refers to the idea that

    (A) any choice made between conflicting solutions to a legal question will be arbitrary
    (B) every legal question will involve the consideration of a set of values
    (C) two or more alternative solutions to a legal question may carry equal moral weight
    (D) no legal question will have a single correct answer
    (E) the most relevant criterion for judging solutions is the degree of rationality they possess

20. Which one of the following most accurately describes the organization of the final paragraph in the passage?

    (A) A criticism is identified and its plausibility is investigated.
    (B) The different arguments made by two opponents of a certain viewpoint are advanced.
    (C) The arguments for and against a certain position are outlined, then a new position is offered to reconcile them.
    (D) A belief is presented and its worth is debated on the basis of its practical consequences.
    (E) Two different solutions are imagined in order to summarize a controversy.

21. It can be inferred from the passage that proponents of the Critical Legal Studies movement would be most likely to hold which one of the following views about the law?

    (A) It incorporates moral principles in order to yield definitive solutions to legal problems.
    (B) It does not necessarily imply approval of any policies or values.
    (C) It is insufficient in itself to determine the answer to a legal question.
    (D) It is comparable to the application of rules in a game.
    (E) It can be used to determine the best choice between conflicting values.

GO ON TO THE NEXT PAGE.

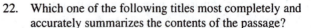

While historians once propagated the myth that Africans who were brought to the New World as slaves contributed little of value but their labor, a recent study by Amelia Wallace Vernon helps to dispel this notion
(5) by showing that Africans introduced rice and the methods of cultivating it into what is now the United States in the early eighteenth century. She uncovered, for example, an 1876 document that details that in 1718 starving French settlers instructed the captain of a
(10) slave ship bound for Africa to trade for 400 Africans including some "who know how to cultivate rice." This discovery is especially compelling because the introduction of rice into what is now the United States had previously been attributed to French Acadians,
(15) who did not arrive until the 1760s.

Vernon interviewed elderly African Americans who helped her discover the locations where until about 1920 their forebears had cultivated rice. At the heart of Vernon's research is the question of why, in an
(20) economy dedicated to maximizing cotton production, African Americans grew rice. She proposes two intriguing answers, depending on whether the time is before or after the end of slavery. During the period of slavery, plantation owners also ate rice and therefore
(25) tolerated or demanded its "after-hours" cultivation on patches of land not suited to cotton. In addition, growing the rice gave the slaves some relief from a system of regimented labor under a field supervisor, in that they were left alone to work independently.

(30) After the abolition of slavery, however, rice cultivation is more difficult to explain: African Americans had acquired a preference for eating corn, there was no market for the small amounts of rice they produced, and under the tenant system—in which
(35) farmers surrendered a portion of their crops to the owners of the land they farmed—owners wanted only cotton as payment. The labor required to transform unused land to productive ground would thus seem completely out of proportion to the reward—except
(40) that, according to Vernon, the transforming of the land itself was the point.

Vernon suggests that these African Americans did not transform the land as a means to an end, but rather as an end in itself. In other words, they did not
(45) transform the land in order to grow rice—for the resulting rice was scarcely worth the effort required to clear the land—but instead transformed the land because they viewed land as an extension of self and home and so wished to nurture it and make it their
(50) own. In addition to this cultural explanation, Vernon speculates that rice cultivation might also have been a political act, a next step after the emancipation of the slaves: the symbolic claiming of plantation land that the U.S. government had promised but failed to parcel
(55) off and deed to newly freed African Americans.

22. Which one of the following titles most completely and accurately summarizes the contents of the passage?

(A) "The Introduction of Rice Cultivation into what is now the United States by Africans and Its Continued Practice in the Years During and After Slavery"

(B) "The Origin of Rice Cultivation in what is now the United States and Its Impact on the Economy from 1760 to 1920"

(C) "Widespread Rice Cultivation by African Americans under the Tenant System in the Years After the Abolition of Slavery"

(D) "Cultural and Political Contributions of Africans who were Brought to what is now the United States in the Eighteenth Century"

(E) "African American Tenant Farmers and their Cultivation of Rice in an Economy Committed to the Mass Production of Cotton"

23. Which one of the following most completely and accurately describes the author's attitude toward Vernon's study?

(A) respectful of its author and skeptical toward its theories

(B) admiring of its accomplishments and generally receptive to its theories

(C) appreciative of the effort it required and neutral toward its theories

(D) enthusiastic about its goals but skeptical of its theories

(E) accepting of its author's motives but overtly dismissive of its theories

GO ON TO THE NEXT PAGE.

24. As described in the last paragraph of the passage, rice cultivation after slavery is most analogous to which one of the following?

    (A) A group of neighbors plants flower gardens on common land adjoining their properties in order to beautify their neighborhood and to create more of a natural boundary between properties.

    (B) A group of neighbors plants a vegetable garden for their common use and to compete with the local market's high-priced produce by selling vegetables to other citizens who live outside the neighborhood.

    (C) A group of neighbors initiates an effort to neuter all the domestic animals in their neighborhood out of a sense of civic duty and to forestall the city taking action of its own to remedy the overpopulation.

    (D) A group of neighbors regularly cleans up the litter on a vacant lot in their neighborhood out of a sense of ownership over the lot and to protest the city's neglect of their neighborhood.

    (E) A group of neighbors renovates an abandoned building so they can start a program to watch each other's children out of a sense of communal responsibility and to offset the closing of a day care center in their neighborhood.

25. Which one of the following most completely and accurately describes the organization of the passage?

    (A) A historical phenomenon is presented, several competing theories about the phenomenon are described, and one theory having the most support is settled upon.

    (B) A historical discovery is presented, the method leading to the discovery is provided, and two questions left unanswered by the discovery are identified.

    (C) A historical fact is presented, a question raised by the fact is described, and two answers to the question are given.

    (D) A historical question is raised, possible answers to the question are speculated upon, and two reasons for difficulty in answering the question are given.

    (E) A historical question is raised, a study is described that answers the question, and a number of issues surrounding the study are discussed.

26. The passage cites which one of the following as a reason that rice cultivation in the context of the tenant system was difficult to explain?

    (A) Landowners did not eat rice and thus would not tolerate its cultivation on tenant lands.

    (B) Rice was not considered acceptable payment to landowners for the use of tenant lands.

    (C) Tenant farmers did not have enough time "after hours" to cultivate the rice properly.

    (D) The labor required to cultivate rice was more strenuous than that required for cotton.

    (E) Tenant lands used primarily to grow cotton were not suited to rice.

27. The author's primary purpose in the passage is to

    (A) describe the efforts of a historian to uncover evidence for a puzzling phenomenon

    (B) illustrate the historical background of a puzzling phenomenon

    (C) present a historian's theories about a puzzling phenomenon

    (D) criticize the work of previous historians regarding a puzzling phenomenon

    (E) analyze the effects of a puzzling phenomenon on an economic system

S T O P

IF YOU FINISH BEFORE TIME IS CALLED, YOU MAY CHECK YOUR WORK ON THIS SECTION ONLY.
DO NOT WORK ON ANY OTHER SECTION IN THE TEST.

SECTION IV

Time – 35 minutes

25 Questions

Directions: The questions in this section are based on the reasoning contained in brief statements or passages. For some questions, more than one of the choices could conceivably answer the question. However, you are to choose the best answer; that is, the response that most accurately and completely answers the question. You should not make assumptions that are by commonsense standards implausible, superfluous, or incompatible with the passage. After you have chosen the best answer, blacken the corresponding space on your answer sheet.

1. A government ought to protect and encourage free speech, because free speech is an activity that is conducive to a healthy nation and thus is in the best interest of its people.

The main conclusion above follows logically if which one of the following is assumed?

(A)   An activity that is in the best interest of the people ought to be protected and encouraged by a nation's government.

(B)   Basic, inalienable rights of the people ought to be protected and encouraged by government.

(C)   An activity that helps a government to govern ought to be protected and encouraged by it.

(D)   A government ought to protect and encourage an activity that is conducive to the interests of that government.

(E)   Universal human rights that are in the best interest of the people ought to be protected and encouraged by a nation's government.

2. The current theory about earthquakes holds that they are caused by adjoining plates of rock sliding past each other; the plates are pressed together until powerful forces overcome the resistance. As plausible as this may sound, at least one thing remains mysterious on this theory. The overcoming of such resistance should create enormous amounts of heat. But so far no increases in temperature unrelated to weather have been detected following earthquakes.

Which one of the following most accurately expresses the main point of the argument?

(A)   No increases in temperature have been detected following earthquakes.

(B)   The current theory does not fully explain earthquake data.

(C)   No one will ever be sure what the true cause of earthquakes is.

(D)   Earthquakes produce enormous amounts of heat that have so far gone undetected.

(E)   Contrary to the current theory, earthquakes are not caused by adjoining plates of rock sliding past one another.

3. Legal theorist: It is unreasonable to incarcerate anyone for any other reason than that he or she is a serious threat to the property or lives of other people. The breaking of a law does not justify incarceration, for lawbreaking proceeds either from ignorance of the law or of the effects of one's actions, or from the free choice of the lawbreaker. Obviously mere ignorance cannot justify incarcerating a lawbreaker, and even free choice on the part of the lawbreaker fails to justify incarceration, for free choice proceeds from the desires of an agent, and the desires of an agent are products of genetics and environmental conditioning, neither of which is controlled by the agent.

The claim in the first sentence of the passage plays which one of the following roles in the argument?

(A)   It is offered as a premise that helps to show that no actions are under the control of the agent.

(B)   It is offered as background information necessary to understand the argument.

(C)   It is offered as the main conclusion that the argument is designed to establish.

(D)   It is offered as evidence for the stated claim that protection of life and property is more important than retribution for past illegal acts.

(E)   It is offered as evidence for the stated claim that lawbreaking proceeds from either ignorance of the law, or ignorance of the effects of one's actions, or free choice.

GO ON TO THE NEXT PAGE.

4. A certain gene can be stimulated by chemicals in cigarette smoke, causing lung cells to metabolize the chemicals in a way that makes the cells cancerous. Yet smokers in whom this gene is not stimulated have as high a risk of developing lung cancer from smoking as other smokers do.

If the statements above are true, it can be concluded on the basis of them that

(A) stimulation of the gene by chemicals in cigarette smoke is not the only factor affecting the risk for smokers of developing lung cancer
(B) nonsmokers have as high a risk of developing lung cancer as do smokers in whom the gene has not been stimulated
(C) smokers in whom the gene has been stimulated are more likely to develop lung cancer than are other smokers
(D) the gene is more likely to be stimulated by chemicals in cigarette smoke than by other chemicals
(E) smokers are less likely to develop lung cancer if they do not have the gene

5. In a poll of eligible voters conducted on the eve of a mayoral election, more of those polled stated that they favored Panitch than stated that they favored any other candidate. Despite this result, another candidate, Yeung, defeated Panitch by a comfortable margin.

Each of the following, if true, contributes to a resolution of the discrepancy described above EXCEPT:

(A) Of Yeung's supporters, a smaller percentage were eligible to vote than the percentage of Panitch's supporters who were eligible to vote.
(B) A third candidate, Mulhern, conducted a press conference on the morning of the election and withdrew from the race.
(C) The poll's questions were designed by staff members of Panitch's campaign.
(D) Of the poll respondents supporting Yeung, 70 percent described the election as "important" or "very important," while 30 percent of respondents supporting Panitch did the same.
(E) The poll, conducted on a Monday, surveyed persons in the downtown area, and the percentage of Yeung's supporters who work downtown is lower than that of Panitch's supporters.

6. Commissioner: Budget forecasters project a revenue shortfall of a billion dollars in the coming fiscal year. Since there is no feasible way to increase the available funds, our only choice is to decrease expenditures. The plan before you outlines feasible cuts that would yield savings of a billion dollars over the coming fiscal year. We will be able to solve the problem we face, therefore, only if we adopt this plan.

The reasoning in the commissioner's argument is flawed because this argument

(A) relies on information that is far from certain
(B) confuses being an adequate solution with being a required solution
(C) inappropriately relies on the opinions of experts
(D) inappropriately employs language that is vague
(E) takes for granted that there is no way to increase available funds

7. Critic: Emily Dickinson's poetry demonstrates that meaning cannot reside entirely within a poem itself, but is always the unique result of an interaction between a reader's system of beliefs and the poem; and, of course, any two readers from different cultures or eras have radically different systems of beliefs.

If the critic's statements are true, each of the following could be true EXCEPT:

(A) A reader's interpretation of a poem by Dickinson is affected by someone else's interpretation of it.
(B) A modern reader and a nineteenth-century reader interpret one of Shakespeare's sonnets in the same way.
(C) A reader's interpretation of a poem evolves over time.
(D) Two readers from the same era arrive at different interpretations of the same poem.
(E) A reader's enjoyment of a poem is enhanced by knowing the poet's interpretation of it.

GO ON TO THE NEXT PAGE.

8. Archaeologist: The fact that the ancient Egyptians and the Maya both built pyramids is often taken as evidence of a historical link between Old- and New-World civilizations that is earlier than any yet documented. But while these buildings are similar to each other, there are important differences in both design and function. The Egyptian pyramids were exclusively tombs for rulers, whereas the Mayan pyramids were used as temples. This shows conclusively that there was no such link between Old- and New-World civilizations.

Which one of the following most accurately describes a flaw in the archaeologist's argument?

(A) The argument equivocates with respect to the term "evidence."
(B) The argument appeals to emotion rather than to reason.
(C) The argument assumes the conclusion it is trying to prove.
(D) The argument incorrectly relies on words whose meanings are vague or imprecise.
(E) The argument presumes that no other evidence is relevant to the issue at hand.

9. Manuscripts written by first-time authors generally do not get serious attention by publishers except when these authors happen to be celebrities. My manuscript is unlikely to be taken seriously by publishers for I am a first-time author who is not a celebrity.

The structure of which one of the following arguments is most similar to the structure of the argument above?

(A) Challengers generally do not win elections unless the incumbent has become very unpopular. The incumbent in this election has become very unpopular. Therefore, the challenger may win.
(B) Fruit salad that contains bananas is ordinarily a boring dish unless it contains two or more exotic fruits. This fruit salad has bananas in it, and the only exotic fruit it has is guava. Thus, it will probably be boring.
(C) Thursday's city council meeting is likely to be poorly attended. Traditionally, council meetings are sparsely attended if zoning issues are the only ones on the agenda. The agenda for Thursday is exclusively devoted to zoning.
(D) The bulk of an estate generally goes to the spouse, if surviving, and otherwise goes to the surviving children. In this case there is no surviving spouse; hence the bulk of the estate is likely to go to the surviving children.
(E) Normally about 40 percent of the deer population will die over the winter unless it is extremely mild. The percentage of the deer population that died over the recent winter was the normal 40 percent. I conclude that the recent winter was not unusually mild.

10. Twelve healthy volunteers with the Apo-A-IV-1 gene and twelve healthy volunteers who instead have the Apo-A-IV-2 gene each consumed a standard diet supplemented daily by a high-cholesterol food. A high level of cholesterol in the blood is associated with an increased risk of heart disease. After three weeks, the blood cholesterol levels of the subjects in the second group were unchanged, whereas the blood cholesterol levels of those with the Apo-A-IV-1 gene rose 20 percent.

Which one of the following is most strongly supported by the information above?

(A) Approximately half the population carries a gene that lowers cholesterol levels.
(B) Most of those at risk of heart disease may be able to reduce their risk by adopting a low-cholesterol diet.
(C) The bodies of those who have the Apo-A-IV-2 gene excrete cholesterol when blood cholesterol reaches a certain level.
(D) The presence of the Apo-A-IV-1 gene seems to indicate that a person has a lower risk of heart disease.
(E) The presence of the Apo-A-IV-2 gene may inhibit the elevation of blood cholesterol.

GO ON TO THE NEXT PAGE.

11. High school students who feel that they are not succeeding in school often drop out before graduating and go to work. Last year, however, the city's high school dropout rate was significantly lower than the previous year's rate. This is encouraging evidence that the program instituted two years ago to improve the morale of high school students has begun to take effect to reduce dropouts.

Which one of the following, if true about the last year, most seriously weakens the argument?

(A) There was a recession that caused a high level of unemployment in the city.

(B) The morale of students who dropped out of high school had been low even before they reached high school.

(C) As in the preceding year, more high school students remained in school than dropped out.

(D) High schools in the city established placement offices to assist their graduates in obtaining employment.

(E) The antidropout program was primarily aimed at improving students' morale in those high schools with the highest dropout rates.

12. The television show *Henry* was not widely watched until it was scheduled for Tuesday evenings immediately after *That's Life*, the most popular show on television. During the year after the move, *Henry* was consistently one of the ten most-watched shows on television. Since *Henry*'s recent move to Wednesday evenings, however, it has been watched by far fewer people. We must conclude that *Henry* was widely watched before the move to Wednesday evenings because it followed *That's Life* and not because people especially liked it.

Which one of the following, if true, most strengthens the argument?

(A) *Henry* has been on the air for three years, but *That's Life* has been on the air for only two years.

(B) The show that replaced *Henry* on Tuesdays has persistently had a low number of viewers in the Tuesday time slot.

(C) The show that now follows *That's Life* on Tuesdays has double the number of viewers it had before being moved.

(D) After its recent move to Wednesday, *Henry* was aired at the same time as the second most popular show on television.

(E) *That's Life* was not widely watched during the first year it was aired.

Questions 13–14

Joseph: My encyclopedia says that the mathematician Pierre de Fermat died in 1665 without leaving behind any written proof for a theorem that he claimed nonetheless to have proved. Probably this alleged theorem simply cannot be proved, since—as the article points out—no one else has been able to prove it. Therefore it is likely that Fermat was either lying or else mistaken when he made his claim.

Laura: Your encyclopedia is out of date. Recently someone has in fact proved Fermat's theorem. And since the theorem is provable, your claim—that Fermat was lying or mistaken—clearly is wrong.

13. Joseph's statement that "this alleged theorem simply cannot be proved" plays which one of the following roles in his argument?

(A) an assumption for which no support is offered

(B) a subsidiary conclusion on which his argument's main conclusion is based

(C) a potential objection that his argument anticipates and attempts to answer before it is raised

(D) the principal claim that his argument is structured to refute

(E) background information that neither supports nor undermines his argument's conclusion

14. Which one of the following most accurately describes a reasoning error in Laura's argument?

(A) It purports to establish its conclusion by making a claim that, if true, would actually contradict that conclusion.

(B) It mistakenly assumes that the quality of a person's character can legitimately be taken to guarantee the accuracy of the claims that person has made.

(C) It mistakes something that is necessary for its conclusion to follow for something that ensures that the conclusion follows.

(D) It uses the term "provable" without defining it.

(E) It fails to distinguish between a true claim that has mistakenly been believed to be false and a false claim that has mistakenly been believed to be true.

GO ON TO THE NEXT PAGE.

15. It is not good for a university to have class sizes that are very large or very small, or to have professors with teaching loads that are very light or very heavy. After all, crowded classes and overworked faculty cripple the institution's ability to recruit and retain both qualified students and faculty.

Which one of the following, if added as a premise to the argument, most helps to justify its conclusion?

(A) Professors who have very light teaching loads tend to focus their remaining time on research.
(B) Classes that have very low numbers of students tend to have a lot of classroom discussion.
(C) Very small class sizes or very light teaching loads indicate incompetence in classroom instruction.
(D) Very small class sizes or very light teaching loads are common in the worst and the best universities.
(E) Professors with very light teaching loads have no more office hours for students than professors with normal teaching loads.

16. Sales manager: The highest priority should be given to the needs of the sales department, because without successful sales the company as a whole would fail.

Shipping manager: There are several departments other than sales that also must function successfully for the company to succeed. It is impossible to give the highest priority to all of them.

The shipping manager criticizes the sales manager's argument by pointing out

(A) that the sales department taken by itself is not critical to the company's success as a whole
(B) the ambiguity of the term "highest priority"
(C) that departments other than sales are more vital to the company's success
(D) an absurd consequence of its apparent assumption that a department's necessity earns it the highest priority
(E) that the sales manager makes a generalization from an atypical case

17. Researchers have found that people who drink five or more cups of coffee a day have a risk of heart disease 2.5 times the average after corrections are made for age and smoking habits. Members of the research team say that, on the basis of their findings, they now limit their own daily coffee intake to two cups.

Which one of the following, if true, indicates that the researchers' precaution might NOT have the result of decreasing their risk of heart disease?

(A) The study found that for people who drank three or more cups of coffee daily, the additional risk of heart disease increased with each extra daily cup.
(B) Per capita coffee consumption has been declining over the past 20 years because of the increasing popularity of soft drinks and also because of health worries.
(C) The study did not collect information that would show whether variations in level of coffee consumption are directly related to variations in level of stress, a major causal factor in heart disease.
(D) Subsequent studies have consistently shown that heavy smokers consume coffee at about 3 times the rate of nonsmokers.
(E) Subsequent studies have shown that heavy coffee consumption tends to cause an elevated blood-cholesterol level, an immediate indicator of increased risk of heart disease.

GO ON TO THE NEXT PAGE.

18. People who have political power tend to see new technologies as a means of extending or protecting their power, whereas they generally see new ethical arguments and ideas as a threat to it. Therefore, technical ingenuity usually brings benefits to those who have this ingenuity, whereas ethical inventiveness brings only pain to those who have this inventiveness.

Which one of the following statements, if true, most strengthens the argument?

(A) Those who offer new ways of justifying current political power often reap the benefits of their own innovations.

(B) Politically powerful people tend to reward those who they believe are useful to them and to punish those who they believe are a threat.

(C) Ethical inventiveness and technical ingenuity are never possessed by the same individuals.

(D) New technologies are often used by people who strive to defeat those who currently have political power.

(E) Many people who possess ethical inventiveness conceal their novel ethical arguments for fear of retribution by the politically powerful.

19. Birds need so much food energy to maintain their body temperatures that some of them spend most of their time eating. But a comparison of a bird of a seed-eating species to a bird of a nectar-eating species that has the same overall energy requirement would surely show that the seed-eating bird spends more time eating than does the nectar-eating bird, since a given amount of nectar provides more energy than does the same amount of seeds.

The argument relies on which one of the following questionable assumptions?

(A) Birds of different species do not generally have the same overall energy requirements as each other.

(B) The nectar-eating bird does not sometimes also eat seeds.

(C) The time it takes for the nectar-eating bird to eat a given amount of nectar is not longer than the time it takes the seed-eating bird to eat the same amount of seeds.

(D) The seed-eating bird does not have a lower body temperature than that of the nectar-eating bird.

(E) The overall energy requirements of a given bird do not depend on factors such as the size of the bird, its nest-building habits, and the climate of the region in which it lives.

20. Consumer advocate: The introduction of a new drug into the marketplace should be contingent upon our having a good understanding of its social impact. However, the social impact of the newly marketed antihistamine is far from clear. It is obvious, then, that there should be a general reduction in the pace of bringing to the marketplace new drugs that are now being tested.

Which one of the following, if true, most strengthens the argument?

(A) The social impact of the new antihistamine is much better understood than that of most new drugs being tested.

(B) The social impact of some of the new drugs being tested is poorly understood.

(C) The economic success of some drugs is inversely proportional to how well we understand their social impact.

(D) The new antihistamine is chemically similar to some of the new drugs being tested.

(E) The new antihistamine should be on the market only if most new drugs being tested should be on the market also.

GO ON TO THE NEXT PAGE.

21. Tina: For centuries oceans and human eccentricity have been linked in the literary and artistic imagination. Such linkage is probably due to the European Renaissance practice of using ships as asylums for the socially undesirable.

    Sergio: No. Oceans have always been viewed as mysterious and unpredictable—qualities that people have invariably associated with eccentricity.

    Tina's and Sergio's statements lend the most support to the claim that they disagree about which one of the following statements?

    (A) Eccentric humans were considered socially undesirable during the European Renaissance.
    (B) Oceans have always been viewed as mysterious and unpredictable.
    (C) The linkage between oceans and eccentricity explains the European Renaissance custom of using ships as asylums.
    (D) People have never attributed the same qualities to oceans and eccentrics.
    (E) The linkage between oceans and eccentricity predates the European Renaissance.

22. In a recent study, a group of subjects had their normal daily caloric intake increased by 25 percent. This increase was entirely in the form of alcohol. Another group of similar subjects had alcohol replace nonalcoholic sources of 25 percent of their normal daily caloric intake. All subjects gained body fat over the course of the study, and the amount of body fat gained was the same for both groups.

    Which one of the following is most strongly supported by the information above?

    (A) Alcohol is metabolized more quickly by the body than are other foods or drinks.
    (B) In the general population, alcohol is the primary cause of gains in body fat.
    (C) An increased amount of body fat does not necessarily imply a weight gain.
    (D) Body fat gain is not dependent solely on the number of calories one consumes.
    (E) The proportion of calories from alcohol in a diet is more significant for body fat gain than are the total calories from alcohol.

23. When investigators discovered that the director of a local charity had repeatedly overstated the number of people his charity had helped, the director accepted responsibility for the deception. However, the investigators claimed that journalists were as much to blame as the director was for inflating the charity's reputation, since they had naïvely accepted what the director told them, and simply reported as fact the numbers he gave them.

    Which one of the following principles, if valid, most helps to justify the investigators' claim?

    (A) Anyone who works for a charitable organization is obliged to be completely honest about the activities of that organization.
    (B) Anyone who knowingly aids a liar by trying to conceal the truth from others is also a liar.
    (C) Anyone who presents as factual a story that turns out to be untrue without first attempting to verify that story is no less responsible for the consequences of that story than anyone else is.
    (D) Anyone who lies in order to advance his or her own career is more deserving of blame than someone who lies in order to promote a good cause.
    (E) Anyone who accepts responsibility for a wrongful act that he or she committed is less deserving of blame than someone who tries to conceal his or her own wrongdoing.

GO ON TO THE NEXT PAGE.

24. Telephone companies are promoting "voice mail" as an alternative to the answering machine. By recording messages from callers when a subscriber does not have access to his or her telephone, voice mail provides a service similar to that of an answering machine. The companies promoting this service argue that it will soon make answering machines obsolete, since it is much more convenient, more flexible, and less expensive than an answering machine.

Which one of the following, if true, most calls into question the argument made by the companies promoting voice mail?

(A) Unlike calls made to owners of answering machines, all telephone calls made to voice-mail subscribers are completed, even if the line called is in use at the time of the call.

(B) The surge in sales of answering machines occurred shortly after they were first introduced to the electronics market.

(C) Once a telephone customer decides to subscribe to voice mail, that customer can cancel the service at any time.

(D) Answering machines enable the customer to hear who is calling before the customer decides whether to answer the telephone, a service voice mail does not provide.

(E) The number of messages a telephone answering machine can record is limited by the length of the magnetic tape on which calls are recorded.

25. The judgment that an artist is great always rests on assessments of the work the artist has produced. A series of great works is the only indicator of greatness. Therefore, to say that an artist is great is just to summarize the quality of his or her known works, and the artist's greatness can provide no basis for predicting the quality of the artist's unknown or future works.

Which one of the following contains questionable reasoning most similar to that in the argument above?

(A) The only way of knowing whether someone has a cold is to observe symptoms. Thus, when a person is said to have a cold, this means only that he or she has displayed the symptoms of a cold, and no prediction about the patient's future symptoms is justified.

(B) Although colds are very common, there are some people who never or only very rarely catch colds. Clearly these people must be in some way physiologically different from people who catch colds frequently.

(C) Someone who has a cold is infected by a cold virus. No one can be infected by the same cold virus twice, but there are indefinitely many different cold viruses. Therefore, it is not possible to predict from a person's history of infection how susceptible he or she will be in the future.

(D) The viruses that cause colds are not all the same, and they differ in their effects. Therefore, although it may be certain that a person has a cold, it is impossible to predict how the cold will progress.

(E) Unless a person displays cold symptoms, it cannot properly be said that the person has a cold. But each of the symptoms of a cold is also the symptom of some other disease. Therefore, one can never be certain that a person has a cold.

S T O P

IF YOU FINISH BEFORE TIME IS CALLED, YOU MAY CHECK YOUR WORK ON THIS SECTION ONLY.
DO NOT WORK ON ANY OTHER SECTION IN THE TEST.

Acknowledgment is made to the following sources from which material has been adapted for use in this test booklet:

Whit Gibbons, "Zoos have a role in preserving species." ©1994 by The Tuscaloosa News.

Theodore Rosengarten, "The Secret of the Marshes." ©1994 by The New York Times.

SIGNATURE _____

LSAT WRITING SAMPLE TOPIC

Houlihan must choose between two job offers. Write an argument in favor of one of the two, taking into account the following guidelines:

- Houlihan, a recent graduate of journalism school, is concerned about repaying her student loans.
- Houlihan's career goal is to have a column in a major newspaper.

The Herald, the only daily paper in a small town, has offered Houlihan a job as a reporter. According to its editor, Houlihan's initial job responsibility would be writing about local politics, including school board activities, city elections, and tax assessments. Houlihan would have sole responsibility for the focus of her assigned stories and would have the opportunity to develop other stories on her own. Because of its small staff, journalists for *The Herald* are expected to move into positions of responsibility quickly. The editor of *The Herald* can pay Houlihan only a modest salary, but the cost of living in the town is low and a modest salary will be more than enough to cover her living expenses.

The Sun Journal, one of two daily newspapers in a major city, has offered Houlihan a job on its metropolitan desk. The entry-level job involves more fact checking and research than actual reporting. Promotion to staff writer, which usually takes 12 to 18 months, is a reward for hard work and perseverance. At the staff writer level, there are many reporters and competition for the best assignments is fierce. Houlihan's first assignment would likely be to the police beat, covering local crime. It would probably be five years or so before she would be covering stories, such as profiles of prominent people in business and government, that are likely to be picked up by the national news services. The cost of living in the city is high and Houlihan will have to budget carefully if she is to cover her living expenses.

Directions:

1. Use the Answer Key on the next page to check your answers.

2. Use the Scoring Worksheet below to compute your raw score.

3. Use the Score Conversion Chart to convert your raw score into the 120-180 scale.

Scoring Worksheet

1. Enter the number of questions you answered correctly in each section.

Number Correct

SECTION I . . . . . . ——
SECTION II . . . . . ——
SECTION III . . . . . ——
SECTION IV . . . . . ——

2. Enter the sum here: ——
This is your Raw Score.

Conversion Chart

For Converting Raw Score to the 120-180 LSAT Scaled Score
LSAT Form 9LSS43

Reported Score	Raw Score Lowest	Raw Score Highest
180	98	101
179	97	97
178	96	96
177	95	95
176	94	94
175	93	93
174	91	92
173	90	90
172	89	89
171	88	88
170	87	87
169	85	86
168	84	84
167	82	83
166	81	81
165	79	80
164	78	78
163	76	77
162	75	75
161	73	74
160	72	72
159	70	71
158	68	69
157	67	67
156	65	66
155	63	64
154	62	62
153	60	61
152	58	59
151	57	57
150	55	56
149	53	54
148	52	52
147	50	51
146	49	49
145	47	48
144	46	46
143	44	45
142	42	43
141	41	41
140	39	40
139	38	38
138	37	37
137	35	36
136	34	34
135	32	33
134	31	31
133	29	30
132	28	28
131	27	27
130	26	26
129	24	25
128	23	23
127	22	22
126	20	21
125	19	19
124	18	18
123	17	17
122	15	16
121	—*	—*
120	0	14

*There is no raw score that will produce this scaled score for this form.

SECTION I

1.	D	8.	A	15.	B	22.	A
2.	A	9.	D	16.	A	23.	D
3.	C	10.	C	17.	B		
4.	D	11.	B	18.	C		
5.	B	12.	A	19.	C		
6.	D	13.	B	20.	D		
7.	A	14.	E	21.	A		

SECTION II

1.	A	8.	A	15.	A	22.	E
2.	E	9.	C	16.	B	23.	D
3.	B	10.	D	17.	B	24.	C
4.	C	11.	D	18.	A	25.	D
5.	B	12.	E	19.	C	26.	B
6.	B	13.	D	20.	E		
7.	D	14.	D	21.	A		

SECTION III

1.	C	8.	C	15.	E	22.	A
2.	D	9.	D	16.	B	23.	B
3.	D	10.	C	17.	D	24.	D
4.	E	11.	E	18.	E	25.	C
5.	E	12.	D	19.	A	26.	B
6.	C	13.	B	20.	A	27.	C
7.	C	14.	C	21.	C		

SECTION IV

1.	A	8.	E	15.	C	22.	D
2.	B	9.	B	16.	D	23.	C
3.	C	10.	E	17.	C	24.	D
4.	A	11.	A	18.	B	25.	A
5.	A	12.	C	19.	C		
6.	B	13.	B	20.	A		
7.	B	14.	C	21.	E		

The Official LSAT PrepTest

3

1

- **June 2000**
  PrepTest 31

- **Form 1LSS45**

SECTION I
Time—35 minutes

23 Questions

Directions: Each group of questions in this section is based on a set of conditions. In answering some of the questions, it may be useful to draw a rough diagram. Choose the response that most accurately and completely answers each question and blacken the corresponding space on your answer sheet.

Questions 1–6

Four boys—Fred, Juan, Marc, and Paul—and three girls—Nita, Rachel, and Trisha—will be assigned to a row of five adjacent lockers, numbered consecutively 1 through 5, arranged along a straight wall. The following conditions govern the assignment of lockers to the seven children:

Each locker must be assigned to either one or two children, and each child must be assigned to exactly one locker.

Each shared locker must be assigned to one girl and one boy.

Juan must share a locker, but Rachel cannot share a locker.

Nita's locker cannot be adjacent to Trisha's locker.

Fred must be assigned to locker 3.

1. Which one of the following is a complete and accurate list of the children who must be among those assigned to shared lockers?

   (A) Fred, Juan
   (B) Juan, Paul
   (C) Juan, Marc, Paul
   (D) Juan, Marc, Trisha
   (E) Juan, Nita, Trisha

2. If Trisha is assigned to locker 3 and Marc alone is assigned to locker 1, then which one of the following must be true?

   (A) Juan is assigned to locker 4.
   (B) Juan is assigned to locker 5.
   (C) Paul is assigned to locker 2.
   (D) Rachel is assigned to locker 2.
   (E) Rachel is assigned to locker 5.

3. If the four boys are assigned to consecutively numbered lockers and Juan is assigned to locker 5, then which one of the following is a complete and accurate list of lockers each of which CANNOT be a shared locker?

   (A) locker 2
   (B) locker 4
   (C) locker 1, locker 2
   (D) locker 1, locker 4
   (E) locker 2, locker 4

4. Once Rachel has been assigned to a locker, what is the maximum number of different lockers each of which could be the locker to which Juan is assigned?

   (A) one
   (B) two
   (C) three
   (D) four
   (E) five

5. If the first three lockers are assigned to girls, which one of the following must be true?

   (A) Juan is assigned to locker 1.
   (B) Nita is assigned to locker 3.
   (C) Trisha is assigned to locker 1.
   (D) Juan is assigned to the same locker as Trisha.
   (E) Paul is assigned to the same locker as Trisha.

6. If lockers 1 and 2 are each assigned to one boy and are not shared lockers, then locker 4 must be assigned to

   (A) Juan
   (B) Paul
   (C) Rachel
   (D) Juan and Nita
   (E) Marc and Trisha

GO ON TO THE NEXT PAGE.

Questions 7–13

A music store carries exactly ten types of CDs—both new and used of each of jazz, opera, pop, rap, and soul. The store is having a sale on some of these types of CDs. The following conditions must apply:

Used pop is on sale; new opera is not.
If both types of pop are on sale, then all soul is.
If both types of jazz are on sale, then no rap is.
If neither type of jazz is on sale, then new pop is.
If either type of rap is on sale, then no soul is.

7. Which one of the following could be a complete and accurate list of the types of CDs that are on sale?

(A) new jazz, used jazz, used opera, used pop, new rap
(B) new jazz, used pop, used rap, new soul
(C) used opera, used pop, new rap, used rap
(D) used opera, new pop, used pop, new soul
(E) used jazz, used pop, new soul, used soul

8. If new soul is not on sale, then which one of the following must be true?

(A) New rap is not on sale.
(B) New rap is on sale.
(C) Used opera is not on sale.
(D) At least one type of jazz is not on sale.
(E) At least one type of pop is not on sale.

9. If both types of jazz are on sale, then which one of the following is the minimum number of types of new CDs that could be included in the sale?

(A) one
(B) two
(C) three
(D) four
(E) five

10. Which one of the following CANNOT be true?

(A) Neither type of opera and neither type of rap is on sale.
(B) Neither type of jazz and neither type of opera is on sale.
(C) Neither type of opera and neither type of soul is on sale.
(D) Neither type of jazz and neither type of soul is on sale.
(E) Neither type of jazz and neither type of rap is on sale.

11. If neither type of jazz is on sale, then each of the following must be true EXCEPT:

(A) Used opera is on sale.
(B) New rap is not on sale.
(C) Used rap is not on sale.
(D) New soul is on sale.
(E) Used soul is on sale.

12. If new soul is the only type of new CD on sale, then which one of the following CANNOT be true?

(A) Used jazz is not on sale.
(B) Used opera is not on sale.
(C) Used rap is not on sale.
(D) Used soul is on sale.
(E) Used soul is not on sale.

13. If exactly four of the five types of used CDs are the only CDs on sale, then which one of the following could be true?

(A) Used jazz is not on sale.
(B) Used opera is not on sale.
(C) Used rap is not on sale.
(D) Neither type of jazz is on sale.
(E) Neither type of rap and neither type of soul is on sale.

GO ON TO THE NEXT PAGE.

Questions 14–18

During a single week, from Monday through Friday, tours will be conducted of a company's three divisions—Operations, Production, Sales. Exactly five tours will be conducted that week, one each day. The schedule of tours for the week must conform to the following restrictions:

Each division is toured at least once.
The Operations division is not toured on Monday.
The Production division is not toured on Wednesday.
The Sales division is toured on two consecutive days, and on no other days.
If the Operations division is toured on Thursday, then the Production division is toured on Friday.

14. Which one of the following CANNOT be true of the week's tour schedule?

(A) The division that is toured on Monday is also toured on Tuesday.
(B) The division that is toured on Monday is also toured on Friday.
(C) The division that is toured on Tuesday is also toured on Thursday.
(D) The division that is toured on Wednesday is also toured on Friday.
(E) The division that is toured on Thursday is also toured on Friday.

15. If in addition to the Sales division one other division is toured on two consecutive days, then it could be true of the week's tour schedule both that the

(A) Production division is toured on Monday and that the Operations division is toured on Thursday
(B) Production division is toured on Tuesday and that the Sales division is toured on Wednesday
(C) Operations division is toured on Tuesday and that the Production division is toured on Friday
(D) Sales division is toured on Monday and that the Operations division is toured on Friday
(E) Sales division is toured on Wednesday and that the Production division is toured on Friday

16. If in the week's tour schedule the division that is toured on Tuesday is also toured on Friday, then for which one of the following days must a tour of the Production division be scheduled?

(A) Monday
(B) Tuesday
(C) Wednesday
(D) Thursday
(E) Friday

17. If in the week's tour schedule the division that is toured on Monday is not the division that is toured on Tuesday, then which one of the following could be true of the week's schedule?

(A) A tour of the Sales division is scheduled for some day earlier in the week than is any tour of the Production division.
(B) A tour of the Operations division is scheduled for some day earlier in the week than is any tour of the Production division.
(C) The Sales division is toured on Monday.
(D) The Production division is toured on Tuesday.
(E) The Operations division is toured on Wednesday.

18. If in the week's tour schedule the division that is toured on Tuesday is also toured on Wednesday, then which one of the following must be true of the week's tour schedule?

(A) The Production division is toured on Monday.
(B) The Operations division is toured on Tuesday.
(C) The Sales division is toured on Wednesday.
(D) The Sales division is toured on Thursday.
(E) The Production division is toured on Friday.

GO ON TO THE NEXT PAGE.

Questions 19–23

A crew of up to five workers is to install a partition in at most three days. The crew completes five tasks in this order: framing, wallboarding, taping, sanding, priming. The crew is selected from the following list, which specifies exactly the tasks each person can do:

George: taping
Helena: sanding, priming
Inga: framing, priming
Kelly: framing, sanding
Leanda: wallboarding, taping
Maricita: sanding
Olaf: wallboarding, priming

The following conditions must apply:
At least one task is done each day.
Taping and priming are done on different days.
Each crew member does at least one task during the installation, but no more than one task a day.
Each task is done by exactly one worker, completed the day it is started and before the next task begins.

19. Which one of the following could be a complete and accurate list of the members of the crew?

(A) George, Helena, Inga, Kelly
(B) George, Helena, Kelly, Leanda
(C) Helena, Inga, Kelly, Olaf
(D) Helena, Inga, Maricita, Olaf
(E) George, Helena, Leanda, Maricita, Olaf

20. If the installation takes three days, and if the same two crew members work on the first and third days, then which one of the following could be the pair of crew members who work on those two days?

(A) Helena and Inga
(B) Inga and Kelly
(C) Inga and Leanda
(D) Kelly and Olaf
(E) Leanda and Olaf

21. Each of the following could be a complete and accurate list of the members of the crew EXCEPT:

(A) Helena, Inga, Kelly, Maricita
(B) Inga, Kelly, Leanda, Olaf
(C) George, Helena, Inga, Leanda
(D) Inga, Leanda, Maricita, Olaf
(E) Kelly, Leanda, Maricita, Olaf

22. If the installation takes three days, and if the sanding is done on the third day, then which one of the following could be a list of all the crew members who work on the second day?

(A) Inga
(B) Kelly
(C) Olaf
(D) George and Helena
(E) Leanda and Olaf

23. Which one of the following could be a pair of members of the crew both of whom work on the same days as each other and each of whom perform two tasks?

(A) George and Maricita
(B) Helena and Kelly
(C) Inga and Leanda
(D) Kelly and Leanda
(E) Leanda and Olaf

S T O P

IF YOU FINISH BEFORE TIME IS CALLED, YOU MAY CHECK YOUR WORK ON THIS SECTION ONLY.
DO NOT WORK ON ANY OTHER SECTION IN THE TEST.

SECTION II

Time—35 minutes

24 Questions

<u>Directions:</u> The questions in this section are based on the reasoning contained in brief statements or passages. For some questions, more than one of the choices could conceivably answer the question. However, you are to choose the <u>best</u> answer; that is, the response that most accurately and completely answers the question. You should not make assumptions that are by commonsense standards implausible, superfluous, or incompatible with the passage. After you have chosen the best answer, blacken the corresponding space on your answer sheet.

1. Moralist: TV talk shows are contributing to the moral decline in our country. By constantly being shown the least moral people in our society, viewers begin to think that such people are the norm, and that there is something wrong with being morally upright.

   TV talk show host: Well, if there is such a decline, it's not because of TV talk shows: we simply show people what they want to see. What can be wrong with letting the viewers decide? Furthermore, if restrictions were put on my show, that would amount to censorship, which is wrong.

   The moralist's and the TV talk show host's statements provide the most support for holding that they disagree about whether

   (A)   TV talk shows should be censored
   (B)   people's moral standards have changed
   (C)   TV talk shows influence people's conception of what is the norm
   (D)   TV talk shows, by presenting immoral guests, are causing a moral decline
   (E)   it is wrong not to let the viewers decide what they want to see

2. For the last three years, entomologists have been searching for a parasite to help control a whitefly that has recently become a serious crop pest. Believing this new pest to be a variety of sweet-potato whitefly, the entomologists confined their search to parasites of the sweet-potato whitefly. Genetic research now shows the new pest to be a distinct species, the silverleaf whitefly. Therefore, the search for a parasite has so far been wasted effort.

   Which one of the following is an assumption on which the argument relies?

   (A)   All varieties of the sweet-potato whitefly are serious crop pests.
   (B)   If a crop pest has a parasite, that parasite can always be used to control that pest.
   (C)   The chances of successfully identifying a useful parasite of the new pest have increased since the proper identification of the pest.
   (D)   No parasite of the sweet-potato whitefly is also a parasite of the silverleaf whitefly.
   (E)   In the last three years, the entomologists found no parasites of the sweet-potato whitefly.

3. Announcement for a television program: Are female physicians more sensitive than male physicians to the needs of women patients? To get the answer, we'll ask physicians of both sexes this question. Tune in tomorrow.

   Which one of the following, if true, identifies a flaw in the plan for the program?

   (A)   Physicians are in general unwilling to describe the treatment style of other physicians.
   (B)   There still are fewer women than men who are physicians, so a patient might not have the opportunity to choose a woman as a physician.
   (C)   Those who are best able to provide answers to the question are patients, rather than physicians.
   (D)   Since medical research is often performed on men, not all results are fully applicable to women as patients.
   (E)   Women as patients are now beginning to take a more active role in managing their care and making sure that they understand the medical alternatives.

GO ON TO THE NEXT PAGE.

4. Doctor: The practice of using this therapy to treat the illness cannot be adequately supported by the claim that any therapy for treating the illness is more effective than no therapy at all. What must also be taken into account is that this therapy is expensive and complicated.

Which one of the following most accurately expresses the main point of the doctor's argument?

(A) The therapy is more effective than no treatment at all for the illness.

(B) The therapy is more effective than other forms of treatment for the illness.

(C) The therapy is more expensive and complicated than other forms of treatment for the illness.

(D) The therapy should not be used to treat the illness unless it is either effective or inexpensive.

(E) The therapy's possible effectiveness in treating the illness is not sufficient justification for using it.

5. Television executives recently announced that advertising time on television will cost 10 to 15 percent more next fall than it cost last fall. The executives argued that in spite of this increase, advertisers will continue to profit from television advertising, and so advertising time will be no harder to sell next fall than it was last fall.

Which one of the following, if true, would most support the television executives' argument?

(A) Most costs of production and distribution of products typically advertised on television are expected to rise 3 to 7 percent in the next year.

(B) The system for rating the size of the audience watching any given television advertisement will change next fall.

(C) Next fall advertising time on television will no longer be available in blocks smaller than 30 seconds.

(D) The amount of television advertising time purchased by providers of services is increasing, while the amount of such time purchased by providers of products is decreasing.

(E) A recent survey has shown that the average number of hours people spend watching television is increasing at the rate of 2 percent every two months.

6. It is proposed to allow the sale, without prescription, of a medication that physicians currently prescribe to treat the common ear inflammation called "swimmer's ear." The principal objection is that most people lack the expertise for proper self-diagnosis and might not seek medical help for more serious conditions in the mistaken belief that they have swimmer's ear. Yet in a recent study, of 1,000 people who suspected that they had swimmer's ear, 84 percent had made a correct diagnosis—a slightly better accuracy rate than physicians have in diagnosing swimmer's ear. Thus, clearly, most people can diagnose swimmer's ear in themselves without ever having to consult a physician.

Which one of the following, if true, most undermines the conclusion?

(A) Cases in which swimmer's ear progresses to more serious infections are very rare.

(B) Most of those who suspected incorrectly that they had swimmer's ear also believed that they had other ailments that in fact they did not have.

(C) Most of the people who diagnosed themselves correctly had been treated by a physician for a prior occurrence of swimmer's ear.

(D) Physicians who specialize in ear diseases are generally able to provide more accurate diagnoses than those provided by general practitioners.

(E) For many people who develop swimmer's ear, the condition disappears without medical or pharmaceutical intervention.

GO ON TO THE NEXT PAGE.

7. Social critic: The whole debate over the legal right of
    rock singers to utter violent lyrics misses the point.
    Legally, there is very little that may not be said.
    But not everything that may legally be said, ought
    to be said. Granted, violence predates the rise in
    popularity of such music. Yet words also have the
    power to change the way we see and the way we
    act.

    Which one of the following is most strongly supported
    by the passage?

    (A)   If rock music that contains violent lyrics is
          morally wrong, then it should be illegal.
    (B)   The law should be changed so that the
          government is mandated to censor rock music
          that contains violent lyrics.
    (C)   Violent rock song lyrics do not incite violence,
          they merely reflect the violence in society.
    (D)   If rock musicians voluntarily censor their violent
          lyrics, this may help to reduce violence in
          society.
    (E)   Stopping the production of rock music that
          contains violent lyrics would eliminate much of
          the violence within society.

8. For all species of higher animals, reproduction requires
    the production of eggs but not necessarily the production
    of sperm. There are some species whose members are all
    female; the eggs produced by a rare female-only species
    of salamander hatch without fertilization. This has the
    drawback that all offspring have genetic codes nearly
    identical to that of the single parent, making the species
    less adaptive than species containing both male and
    female members.

    If the statements above are true, each of the following
    could be true EXCEPT:

    (A)   There are some species of salamanders that have
          both male and female members.
    (B)   There are some species of higher animals none of
          whose members produce eggs.
    (C)   There is a significant number of female-only
          species of higher animals.
    (D)   Some species of higher animals containing both
          female and male members are not very adaptive.
    (E)   Some offspring of species of higher animals
          containing both female and male members have
          genetic codes more similar to one parent than to
          the other parent.

9. As part of a survey, approximately 10,000 randomly
    selected individuals were telephoned and asked a
    number of questions about their income and savings.
    Those conducting the survey observed that the older the
    person being queried, the more likely it was that he or
    she would refuse to answer any of the questions. This
    finding clearly demonstrates that, in general, people are
    more willing when they are younger than when they are
    older to reveal personal financial information to
    strangers over the telephone.

    The argument above is vulnerable to criticism on the
    grounds that the argument

    (A)   offers no evidence that the individuals queried
          would have responded differently had they been
          asked the same questions in years prior to the
          survey
    (B)   fails to specify the exact number of people who
          were telephoned as part of the survey
    (C)   assumes without warrant that age is the main
          determinant of personal income and savings
          levels
    (D)   assumes from the outset what it purports to
          establish on the basis of a body of statistical
          evidence
    (E)   provides no reason to believe that what is true of
          a given age group in general is also true of all
          individuals within that age group

                    GO ON TO THE NEXT PAGE.

10. If something would have been justifiably regretted if it had occurred, then it is something that one should not have desired in the first place. It follows that many forgone pleasures should not have been desired in the first place.

The conclusion above follows logically if which one of the following is assumed?

(A) One should never regret one's pleasures.
(B) Forgone pleasures that were not desired would not have been justifiably regretted.
(C) Everything that one desires and then regrets not having is a forgone pleasure.
(D) Many forgone pleasures would have been justifiably regretted.
(E) Nothing that one should not have desired in the first place fails to be a pleasure.

11. Several thousand years ago, people in what is now North America began to grow corn, which grows faster and produces more food per unit of land than do the grains these people had grown previously. Corn is less nutritious than those other grains, however, and soon after these people established corn as their staple grain crop, they began having nutrition-related health problems. Yet the people continued to grow corn as their staple grain, although they could have returned to growing the more nutritious grains.

Which one of the following, if true, most helps to explain why the people mentioned continued to grow corn as their staple grain crop?

(A) The variety of corn that the people relied on as their staple grain produced more food than did the ancestors of that variety.
(B) Modern varieties of corn are more nutritious than were the varieties grown by people in North America several thousand years ago.
(C) The people did not domesticate large animals for meat or milk, either of which could supply nutrients not provided by corn.
(D) Some of the grain crops that could have been planted instead of corn required less fertile soil in order to flourish than corn required.
(E) The people discovered some years after adopting corn as their staple grain that a diet that supplemented corn with certain readily available nongrain foods significantly improved their health.

12. Some biologists believe that the capacity for flight first developed in marine reptiles, claiming that feathers are clearly developed from scales. Other biologists rightly reject this suggestion, pointing out that bats have no scales and that nonmarine reptiles also have scales. Those who believe that flight first developed in tree-dwelling reptiles reject the claim that the limbs of land-dwelling reptiles might have developed into wings. They insist that it is more likely that tree-dwelling reptiles developed wings to assist their leaps from branch to branch.

Which one of the following most accurately describes the role played in the passage by the claim that nonmarine reptiles have scales?

(A) It is cited as evidence against the claim that the capacity for flight first developed in marine reptiles.
(B) It is cited as evidence against the claim that the capacity for flight first developed in land-dwelling animals.
(C) It is cited as evidence against the claim that the capacity for flight first developed in tree-dwelling reptiles.
(D) It weakens the claim that tree-dwelling reptiles were the first kind of reptile to develop the capacity for flight.
(E) It corroborates the observation that some mammals without scales, such as bats, developed the capacity to fly.

GO ON TO THE NEXT PAGE.

13. Studies have shown that, contrary to popular belief, middle-aged people have more fear of dying than do elderly people.

    Each of the following, if true, contributes to an explanation of the phenomenon shown by the studies EXCEPT:

    (A) The longer one lives, the more likely it is that one has come to terms with dying.
    (B) Middle-aged people have more people dependent upon them than people of any other age group.
    (C) Many people who suffer from depression first become depressed in middle age.
    (D) The longer one lives, the more imperturbable one becomes.
    (E) Middle-aged people have a more acute sense of their own mortality than do people of any other age group.

14. Historian: Leibniz, the seventeenth-century philosopher, published his version of calculus before Newton did. But then Newton revealed his private notebooks, which showed he had been using these ideas for at least a decade before Leibniz's publication. Newton also claimed that he had disclosed these ideas to Leibniz in a letter shortly before Leibniz's publication. Yet close examination of the letter shows that Newton's few cryptic remarks did not reveal anything important about calculus. Thus, Leibniz and Newton each independently discovered calculus.

    Which one of the following is an assumption required by the historian's argument?

    (A) Leibniz did not tell anyone about calculus prior to publishing his version of it.
    (B) No third person independently discovered calculus prior to Newton and Leibniz.
    (C) Newton believed that Leibniz was able to learn something important about calculus from his letter to him.
    (D) Neither Newton nor Leibniz knew that the other had developed a version of calculus prior to Leibniz's publication.
    (E) Neither Newton nor Leibniz learned crucial details about calculus from some third source.

15. For a ten-month period, the total monthly sales of new cars within the country of Calistan remained constant. During this period the monthly sales of new cars manufactured by Marvel Automobile Company doubled, and its share of the new car market within Calistan increased correspondingly. At the end of this period, emission standards were imposed on new cars sold within Calistan. During the three months following this imposition, Marvel Automobile Company's share of the Calistan market declined substantially even though its monthly sales within Calistan remained constant at the level reached in the last month of the ten-month period.

    If the statements above are true, which one of the following CANNOT be true?

    (A) The total monthly sales within Calistan of new cars by companies other than Marvel Automobile Company decreased over the three months following the imposition of the emission standards.
    (B) Over the three months before the imposition of the emission standards, the combined market share of companies other than Marvel Automobile Company selling new cars in Calistan decreased.
    (C) If the emission standards had not been imposed, Marvel Automobile Company would have lost an even larger share of the number of new cars sold in Calistan than, in fact, it did.
    (D) A decrease in the total monthly sales of new cars within Calistan will occur if the emission standards remain in effect.
    (E) Since the imposition of the emission standards, Marvel Automobile Company's average profit on each new car sold within Calistan has increased.

GO ON TO THE NEXT PAGE.

Questions 16–17

Because addictive drugs are physically harmful, their use by athletes is never justified. Purists, however, claim that taking massive doses of even such nonaddictive drugs as aspirin and vitamins before competing should also be prohibited because they are unnatural. This is ridiculous; almost everything in sports is unnatural, from high-tech running shoes to padded boxing gloves to highly-specialized bodybuilding machines. Yet, none of these is prohibited on the basis of its being unnatural. Furthermore, we should be attending to far more serious problems that plague modern sports and result in unnecessary deaths and injuries. Therefore, the use of nonaddictive drugs by athletes should not be prohibited.

16. Which one of the following statements, if true, would be the strongest challenge to the author's conclusion?

   (A) Massive doses of aspirin and vitamins enhance athletic performance.
   (B) Addictive drugs are just as unnatural as nonaddictive drugs like aspirin and vitamins.
   (C) Unnecessary deaths and injuries occur in other walks of life besides modern sports.
   (D) There would be more unnecessary deaths and injuries if it were not for running shoes, boxing gloves, and bodybuilding machines.
   (E) Taking massive doses of aspirin or vitamins can be physically harmful.

17. Which one of the following can be inferred from the passage above?

   (A) The fact that something is unnatural is not a sufficient reason for banning it.
   (B) There is nothing unnatural about the use of nonaddictive drugs by athletes.
   (C) The use of addictive drugs by athletes should be prohibited because addictive drugs are unnatural.
   (D) Some of the unnecessary deaths and injuries in modern sports are caused by the use of addictive drugs by athletes.
   (E) The use of addictive drugs by athletes is a less serious problem than are unnecessary injuries.

18. Not all works of art represent something, but some do, and their doing so is relevant to our aesthetic experience of them; representation is therefore an aesthetically relevant property. Whether a work of art possesses this property is dependent upon context. Yet there are no clear criteria for determining whether context-dependent properties are present in an object, so there cannot be any clear criteria for determining whether an object qualifies as art.

The reasoning above is questionable because it fails to exclude the possibility that

   (A) because some works of art are nonrepresentational, there is no way of judging our aesthetic experience of them
   (B) an object may have some aesthetic properties and not be a work of art
   (C) aesthetically relevant properties other than representation can determine whether an object is a work of art
   (D) some works of art may have properties that are not relevant to our aesthetic experience of them
   (E) some objects that represent things other than themselves are not works of art

19. If the flowers Drew received today had been sent by someone who knows Drew well, that person would have known that Drew prefers violets to roses. Yet Drew received roses. On the other hand, if the flowers had been sent by someone who does not know Drew well, then that person would have sent a signed card with the flowers. Yet Drew received no card. Therefore, the florist must have made some sort of mistake: either Drew was supposed to receive violets, or a card, or these flowers were intended for someone else.

Which one of the following statements, if true, most weakens the argument?

   (A) Most people send roses when they send flowers.
   (B) Some people send flowers for a reason other than the desire to please.
   (C) Someone who does not know Drew well would be unlikely to send Drew flowers.
   (D) The florist has never delivered the wrong flowers to Drew before.
   (E) Some people who know Drew well have sent Drew cards along with flowers.

GO ON TO THE NEXT PAGE.

20. One of the most vexing problems in historiography is dating an event when the usual sources offer conflicting chronologies of the event. Historians should attempt to minimize the number of competing sources, perhaps by eliminating the less credible ones. Once this is achieved and several sources are left, as often happens, historians may try, though on occasion unsuccessfully, to determine independently of the usual sources which date is more likely to be right.

Which one of the following inferences is most strongly supported by the information above?

(A) We have no plausible chronology of most of the events for which attempts have been made by historians to determine the right date.

(B) Some of the events for which there are conflicting chronologies and for which attempts have been made by historians to determine the right date cannot be dated reliably by historians.

(C) Attaching a reliable date to any event requires determining which of several conflicting chronologies is most likely to be true.

(D) Determining independently of the usual sources which of several conflicting chronologies is more likely to be right is an ineffective way of dating events.

(E) The soundest approach to dating an event for which the usual sources give conflicting chronologies is to undermine the credibility of as many of these sources as possible.

21. Bank deposits are credited on the date of the transaction only when they are made before 3 P.M. Alicia knows that the bank deposit was made before 3 P.M. So, Alicia knows that the bank deposit was credited on the date of the transaction.

Which one of the following exhibits both of the logical flaws exhibited by the argument above?

(A) Journalists are the only ones who will be permitted to ask questions at the press conference. Since Marjorie is a journalist, she will be permitted to ask questions.

(B) We know that Patrice works only on Thursday. Today is Thursday, so it follows that Patrice is working today.

(C) It is clear that George knows he will be promoted to shift supervisor, because George will be promoted to shift supervisor only if Helen resigns, and George knows Helen will resign.

(D) John believes that 4 is a prime number and that 4 is divisible by 2. Hence John believes that there is a prime number divisible by 2.

(E) Pat wants to become a social worker. It is well known that social workers are poorly paid. Pat apparently wants to be poorly paid.

22. On the surface, Melville's *Billy Budd* is a simple story with a simple theme. However, if one views the novel as a religious allegory, then it assumes a richness and profundity that place it among the great novels of the nineteenth century. However, the central question remains: Did Melville intend an allegorical reading? Since there is no textual or historical evidence that he did, we should be content with reading *Billy Budd* as a simple tragedy.

Which one of the following most accurately expresses the principle underlying the argument?

(A) Given a choice between an allegorical and a nonallegorical reading of a novel, one should choose the latter.

(B) The only relevant evidence in deciding in which genre to place a novel is the author's stated intention.

(C) In deciding between rival readings of a novel, one should choose the one that is most favorable to the work.

(D) Without relevant evidence as to a novel's intended reading, one should avoid viewing the work allegorically.

(E) The only relevant evidence in deciding the appropriate interpretation of a text is the text itself.

GO ON TO THE NEXT PAGE.

Questions 23–24

Town councillor: The only reason for the town to have ordinances restricting where skateboarding can be done would be to protect children from danger. Skateboarding in the town's River Park is undoubtedly dangerous, but we should not pass an ordinance prohibiting it. If children cannot skateboard in the park, they will most certainly skateboard in the streets. And skateboarding in the streets is more dangerous than skateboarding in the park.

23. The pattern of reasoning in which one of the following is most similar to that in the town councillor's argument?

(A) The reason for requiring environmental reviews is to ensure that projected developments do not harm the natural environment. Currently, environmental concerns are less compelling than economic concerns, but in the long run, the environment must be protected. Therefore, the requirement for environmental reviews should not be waived.

(B) Insecticides are designed to protect crops against insect damage. Aphids damage tomato crops, but using insecticides against aphids kills wasps that prey on insecticide-resistant pests. Since aphids damage tomato crops less than the insecticide-resistant pests do, insecticides should not be used against aphids on tomato crops.

(C) The purpose of compulsory vaccination for schoolchildren was to protect both the children themselves and others in the community against smallpox. Smallpox was indeed a dreadful disease, but it has now been eliminated from the world's population. So children should not be vaccinated against it.

(D) The function of a sealer on wood siding is to retard deterioration caused by weather. However, cedar is a wood that is naturally resistant to weather-related damage and thus does not need additional protection. Sealers, therefore, should not be applied to cedar siding.

(E) Traffic patterns that involve one-way streets are meant to accelerate the flow of traffic in otherwise congested areas. However, it would be detrimental to the South Main Street area to have traffic move faster. So traffic patterns involving one-way streets should not be implemented there.

24. Which one of the following principles, if established, would provide the strongest support for the town councillor's argument?

(A) Ordinances that restrict the recreational activities of a town's inhabitants should not be passed unless those activities pose a danger to participants.

(B) Since the town could be legally liable for accidents that occur on public property, town ordinances should restrict any unnecessarily dangerous activities in publicly owned areas.

(C) Since safety in a recreational activity depends on the level of skill of the participant in that activity, the regulation of children's recreational activities should be left to the discretion of the children's parents.

(D) If recreational activities constitute a danger to the participants in those activities, then the town council should enact ordinances prohibiting those activities.

(E) Ordinances that seek to eliminate dangers should not be enacted if their enactment would lead to dangers that are greater than those they seek to eliminate.

S T O P

IF YOU FINISH BEFORE TIME IS CALLED, YOU MAY CHECK YOUR WORK ON THIS SECTION ONLY.
DO NOT WORK ON ANY OTHER SECTION IN THE TEST.

SECTION III

Time—35 minutes

26 Questions

<u>Directions:</u> The questions in this section are based on the reasoning contained in brief statements or passages. For some questions, more than one of the choices could conceivably answer the question. However, you are to choose the <u>best</u> answer; that is, the response that most accurately and completely answers the question. You should not make assumptions that   e by commonsense standards implausible, superfluous, or incompatible with the passage. After you have chosen the best ai.   er, blacken the corresponding space on your answer sheet.

1. Journalist: One reason many people believe in extrasensory perception (ESP) is that they have heard of controlled experiments in which ESP is purportedly demonstrated. However, ESP is a myth and the public is deluded by these experiments, for a prominent researcher has admitted to falsifying data on psychic phenomena in order to obtain additional grants.

   The reasoning in the journalist's argument is flawed because this argument

   (A) uses an irrelevant personal attack on the integrity of someone
   (B) infers that something must be a myth from the fact that the general public believes it
   (C) presupposes that, in general, only evidence from experiments can support beliefs
   (D) implies that all scientists who depend on grants to support their research are unreliable
   (E) overgeneralizes from the example of one deceptive researcher

2. One way kidney stones can form is when urine produced in the kidneys is overly concentrated with calcium or oxalate. Reducing dietary calcium has been thought, therefore, to decrease the likelihood that calcium will concentrate and form additional stones. Oddly enough, for many people the chances of recurrence are decreased by increasing calcium intake.

   Which one of the following, if true, most helps to resolve the apparent discrepancy described above?

   (A) Laboratory studies on animals with kidney stones reveal that they rarely get additional stones once calcium supplements are added to the diet.
   (B) Increasing dietary oxalate while reducing dietary calcium does not reduce the chances of kidney stone recurrence.
   (C) Kidney stone development is sometimes the result of an inherited disorder that can result in excessive production of calcium and oxalate.
   (D) Increasing calcium intake increases the amount of calcium eliminated through the intestines, which decreases the amount to be filtered by the kidneys.
   (E) Some kidney stones are composed of uric acid rather than a combination of calcium and oxalate.

3. David: Forbidding companies from hiring permanent replacements for striking employees would be profoundly unfair. Such companies would have little leverage in their negotiations with strikers.

   Lin: No, the companies would still have sufficient leverage in negotiations if they hired temporary replacements.

   Which one of the following statements is most strongly supported by the exchange between David and Lin?

   (A) David does not believe that the freedom to hire temporary replacements gives companies any leverage in their negotiations with strikers.
   (B) David and Lin believe that companies should be allowed as much leverage in negotiations as the striking employees.
   (C) David and Lin disagree over the amount of leverage companies lose in their negotiations with strikers by not being able to hire permanent replacements.
   (D) David and Lin disagree over how much leverage should be accorded companies in their negotiations with strikers.
   (E) Lin believes it is unfair to forbid companies from hiring permanent replacements for their striking employees.

GO ON TO THE NEXT PAGE.

4. A favorable biography of a politician omits certain incriminating facts about the politician that were available to anyone when the book was written. The book's author claims that, because he was unaware of these facts when he wrote the book, he is not accountable for the fact that readers were misled by this omission. In a biographer, however, ignorance of this kind cannot be used to evade blame for misleading readers.

Which one of the following principles, if established, does most to justify the position advanced by the passage?

(A) An author of a biography should not be blamed for whether the book is perceived to be favorable or unfavorable by readers of the biography.

(B) An author of a biography should be blamed for readers' misperceptions only when facts are omitted deliberately in order to mislead the readers.

(C) An author of a biography should not be blamed for omitting facts if those facts would have supported the author's view.

(D) An author of a biography should be blamed for misleading readers only if facts are omitted to which the author alone had access when the biography was written.

(E) An author of a biography should be blamed for readers' misperceptions caused by omitting facts that were widely available when the biography was written.

5. Logician: I have studied and thoroughly mastered the laws of logic. So to argue that I sometimes violate the laws of logic in ordinary conversation would be like arguing that some physicist circumvents the laws of physics in everyday life.

The reasoning in the logician's argument is questionable because this argument

(A) ignores the fact that our conception of physical laws undergoes constant change

(B) presents no evidence that physics is as difficult to master as logic

(C) fails to rule out the possibility that some physicist could circumvent the laws of physics in everyday life

(D) treats two kinds of things that differ in important respects as if they do not differ

(E) has a conclusion that contradicts what is asserted in its premise

6. One thousand people in Denmark were questioned about their views on banning cigarette advertising. The sample comprised adults who are representative of the general population, and who, ten years previously, had been questioned on the same issue. Interestingly, their opinions changed little. Results show that 31 percent are in favor of such a ban, 24 percent are against it, 38 percent are in favor, but only for certain media, and 7 percent have no opinion.

The survey results in the passage best support which one of the following conclusions?

(A) People's opinions never change very much.

(B) A minority of Denmark's population feels that banning cigarette advertising would set a bad precedent.

(C) Most of Denmark's population is not seriously concerned about cigarette advertising.

(D) Most of Denmark's population favors some sort of ban on cigarette advertising.

(E) Most of Denmark's population does not smoke cigarettes.

7. Passenger volume in the airline industry has declined dramatically over the past two years, and thus fewer travelers and fewer planes are using airports. Since airport expansion can be warranted only by increases in air traffic volume, and since it will probably be at least five years before passenger volume returns to and then exceeds its previous level, it seems surprising that now is the time that airports are going ahead with plans to expand their passenger terminal facilities.

Which one of the following, if true, provides the best reason in favor of the airports' timing of their planned expansions?

(A) It is generally more difficult to finance major construction projects when the economy is in a period of decline.

(B) Low volume in passenger air travel permits airport expansion with relatively little inconvenience to the public.

(C) A rise in fuel costs that is expected in the near future will drive up the cost of all forms of transportation, including airline travel.

(D) When passenger volume begins to grow again after a period of decline, most airlines can, initially, absorb the increase without adding new routes or new planes.

(E) A sustained decline in passenger travel could lead to the failure of many airlines and the absorption of their routes by those airlines that survive.

GO ON TO THE NEXT PAGE.

8. Books updating the classification systems used by many libraries are not free—in fact they are very expensive. The only way to sell copies of them is to make the potential buyers believe they need to adopt the most recent system. Thus, these frequent changes in the classification systems are just a ploy by the publishers to make libraries buy their products.

The reasoning above is most vulnerable to criticism because it

(A) claims without providing warrant that the books are unreasonably expensive
(B) concludes that a possible ulterior motive must be the only motive
(C) fails to consider that there may be potential buyers of these books other than libraries
(D) concludes that there is no need ever to change classification systems
(E) fails to consider that the libraries cannot afford to buy every book they want

9. During the three months before and the three months after a major earthquake in California, students at a college there happened to be keeping a record of their dreams. After experiencing the earthquake, half of the students reported dreaming about earthquakes. During the same six months, a group of college students in Ontario who had never experienced an earthquake also recorded their dreams. Almost none of the students in Ontario reported dreaming about earthquakes. So it is clear that experiencing an earthquake can cause people to dream about earthquakes.

Which one of the following, if true, most strengthens the argument?

(A) Before the California earthquake, no more of the students in California than of those in Ontario recorded dreams about earthquakes.
(B) The students in California were members of a class studying dreams and dream recollection, but the students in Ontario were not.
(C) Before they started keeping records of their dreams, many of the students in California had experienced at least one earthquake.
(D) The students in Ontario reported having more dreams overall, per student, than the students in California did.
(E) The students in Ontario who reported having dreams about earthquakes recorded the dreams as having occurred after the California earthquake.

10. It is wrong to waste our natural resources, and it is an incredible waste of resources to burn huge amounts of trash in incinerators. When trash is recycled, fewer resources are wasted. Because less trash will be recycled if an incinerator is built, the city should not build an incinerator.

Which one of the following can be properly inferred from the statements above?

(A) All of the city's trash that is not recycled goes into incinerators.
(B) By recycling more trash, the city can stop wasting resources entirely.
(C) The most effective way to conserve resources is to recycle trash.
(D) If the city is to avoid wasting resources, huge amounts of trash cannot be burned in any city incinerator.
(E) If the city does not burn trash, it will not waste resources.

11. Human intelligence is not possible without human emotions. A computer is something that can never have emotions, so for that reason alone a computer will never be able to display intelligence.

Which one of the following is an assumption on which the argument depends?

(A) A computer could have emotions only if it could display intelligence.
(B) Computer technology will not greatly advance beyond its current state.
(C) Someone or something is intelligent only if it can identify its emotions.
(D) The greater the capacity to feel emotions, the more intelligence there is.
(E) Being intelligent requires the capacity to have emotions.

GO ON TO THE NEXT PAGE.

12. Several recent studies establish that most people would want to be informed if they had any serious medical condition. In each study, over 80 percent of the people surveyed indicated that they would want to be told.

Each of the following, if true, weakens the argument EXCEPT:

(A) In another recent study, most of the people surveyed indicated that they would not want to be told if they had a serious medical condition.
(B) People often do not indicate their true feelings when responding to surveys.
(C) Some of the researchers conducting the studies had no background in medicine.
(D) Some questions asked in the studies suggested that reasonable people would want to be told if they had a serious medical condition.
(E) The people surveyed in the studies were all young students in introductory psychology courses.

13. Historian: Political regimes that routinely censor various forms of expression on the grounds that they undermine public morality inevitably attempt to expand the categories of proscribed expression to include criticisms that these regimes perceive to threaten their power. Accordingly, many totalitarian regimes classify as blasphemous or pornographic those writings that would, if widely influential, reduce public passivity.

Which one of the following is an assumption on which the historian's reasoning depends?

(A) Unless a piece of writing expresses something that is widely believed, it is unlikely to be very popular.
(B) Not all political regimes that routinely censor forms of expression on the grounds that they erode public morality are totalitarian regimes.
(C) A totalitarian regime can perceive loss of public passivity as a threat to its power.
(D) Widespread public passivity is usually needed for a regime to retain political power.
(E) Most writings that totalitarian regimes label blasphemous or pornographic would, if widely influential, reduce public passivity.

14. Ethicist: Both ASA and TPA are clot-dissolving agents. Recent studies show that the more expensive agent, TPA, would save at most two more lives than would ASA out of every 50 cardiac patients to whom they are postoperatively administered. However, since the relatives of the patients who die simply because they were given the less expensive medicine would be particularly grieved, the financial saving involved in using ASA over TPA must also be weighed against such considerations.

Which one of the following most accurately expresses the conclusion of the ethicist's argument?

(A) ASA should never be given to postoperative cardiac patients in place of TPA.
(B) TPA is a slightly more effective clot-dissolving agent than ASA.
(C) The extra expense of TPA cannot be weighed simply against the few additional lives saved.
(D) ASA is a less expensive clot-dissolving agent than TPA.
(E) Relatives of a patient who has died grieve more if the patient received ASA rather than TPA.

15. Ashley: Words like "of" and "upon," unlike "pencil" and "shirt," do not refer to anything.

Joshua: I agree; and since such words are meaningless, they should be abandoned.

Joshua's remarks indicate that he interpreted Ashley's statement to imply that

(A) only words that refer to something have meaning
(B) words that are not useful are meaningless
(C) words that refer to something are meaningful
(D) if a word is not useful, it should be abandoned
(E) all words that refer to something are useful

GO ON TO THE NEXT PAGE.

16. Ethicist: Some would ban cloning on the grounds that clones would be subpeople, existing to indulge the vanity of their "originals." It is not illegal, however, to use one person as a vehicle for the ambitions of another. Some people push their children to achieve in academics or athletics. You do not have to have been born in a test tube to be an extension of someone else's ego.

The assertion that it is not illegal to use one person as a vehicle for another's ambitions is used in the ethicist's argument in which one of the following ways?

(A)   It supports the ethicist's view that society does not value individuality as much as many opponents of cloning think it does.

(B)   It supports the conclusion that forcing children to pursue academic success is not objectionable.

(C)   It is implied by the ethicist's conviction that clones are not subpeople.

(D)   It supports the ethicist's view that vanity's being the motivation for cloning is not enough of a reason to ban cloning.

(E)   It describes a legal position that the ethicist argues should be changed.

17. Selena: Asteroid impact on the Earth caused the extinction of the dinosaurs by raising vast clouds of dust, thus blocking the Sun's rays and cooling the planet beyond the capacity of the dinosaurs, or perhaps the vegetation that supported them, to adapt. A worldwide dust layer provides evidence of asteroid impact at approximately the correct time, and a huge crater exists on the edge of the Yucatán peninsula in Mexico.

Trent: That asteroid crater is not large enough for the requisite amount of dust to have been produced. Besides, the extinction of dinosaur species took many years, not just one or two. So the extinctions must have been due not to asteroid impact on the Earth but to some other kind of cause.

Trent's argument assumes that

(A)   any collision of an asteroid with the Earth would have occurred on a land area rather than an ocean

(B)   dinosaurs in the neighborhood of an asteroid impact but not within the zone of direct impact would have survived such an impact

(C)   any event that takes place over a long period of time has many different kinds of causes

(D)   dust from the impact of an asteroid on the Earth would not have had any cooling effect on the climate

(E)   no more than one large asteroid struck the Earth during the period when the dinosaurs were becoming extinct

18. It is impossible to do science without measuring. It is impossible to measure without having first selected units of measurement. Hence, science is arbitrary, since the selection of a unit of measurement—kilometer, mile, fathom, etc.—is always arbitrary.

The pattern of reasoning in which one of the following is most similar to that in the argument above?

(A)   Long hours of practice are necessary for developing musical skill. One must develop one's musical skill in order to perform difficult music. But long hours of practice are tedious. So performing difficult music is tedious.

(B)   You have to advertise to run an expanding business, but advertising is expensive. Hence, it is expensive to run a business.

(C)   It is permissible to sit on the park benches. To sit on the park benches one must walk to them. One way to walk to them is by walking on the grass. So it is permissible to walk on the grass.

(D)   It is impossible to be a manager without evaluating people. The process of evaluation is necessarily subjective. Thus, people resent managers because they resent being evaluated subjectively.

(E)   Some farming on the plains requires irrigation. This irrigation now uses water pumped from aquifers. But aquifers have limited capacity and continued pumping will eventually exhaust them. Thus, a new source of water will have to be found in order for such farming to continue indefinitely.

GO ON TO THE NEXT PAGE.

Questions 19–20

Professor Beckstein: American Sign Language is the native language of many North Americans. Therefore, it is not a foreign language, and for that reason alone, no student should be permitted to satisfy the university's foreign language requirement by learning it.

Professor Sedley: According to your argument, students should not be allowed to satisfy the university's foreign language requirement by learning French or Spanish either, since they too are the native languages of many North Americans. Yet many students currently satisfy the requirement by studying French or Spanish, and it would be ridiculous to begin prohibiting them from doing so.

19. Their statements commit Professors Beckstein and Sedley to disagreeing about which one of the following?

   (A) whether American Sign Language is the native language of a significant number of North Americans

   (B) whether any North American whose native language is not English should be allowed to fulfill the university's foreign language requirement by studying his or her own native language

   (C) whether the university ought to retain a foreign language requirement

   (D) whether any other universities in North America permit their students to fulfill a foreign language requirement by learning American Sign Language

   (E) whether the fact that a language is the native language of many North Americans justifies prohibiting its use to fulfill the university's foreign language requirement

20. Professor Sedley uses which one of the following strategies of argumentation in responding to Professor Beckstein's argument?

   (A) attempting to demonstrate that the reasoning used to reach a certain conclusion leads to another conclusion that is undesirable

   (B) trying to show that a certain conclusion contradicts some of the evidence used to support it

   (C) questioning an opponent's authority to address the issue under discussion

   (D) offering an alternative explanation of the facts used to arrive at a specific conclusion

   (E) agreeing with the conclusion of a particular argument while rejecting the evidence used to support the conclusion

21. So-called "engineered foods," usually in powder or liquid form, consist of protein that is distilled from natural sources and supplemented with vitamins and minerals. Although the amino acids contained in such products stimulate the production of growth hormones, these hormones produce growth in connective tissue rather than in muscle mass; this does not improve muscle strength. Hence, athletes, who need to improve their muscular strength, should not consume engineered foods.

The argument depends on assuming which one of the following?

   (A) An increase in muscle mass produces an increase in strength.

   (B) People who are not athletes require neither stronger connective tissue nor muscle strength.

   (C) If an engineered food does not improve muscle strength, there is no other substantial advantage to athletes from consuming it.

   (D) Consuming engineered foods that provide nutrients that can be obtained more easily elsewhere is unhealthy.

   (E) Growth of muscle mass enhances muscle strength only when accompanied by growth of connective tissue.

22. Some types of organisms originated through endosymbiosis, the engulfing of one organism by another so that a part of the former becomes a functioning part of the latter. An unusual nucleomorph, a structure that contains DNA and resembles a cell nucleus, has been discovered within a plant known as a chlorarachniophyte. Two versions of a particular gene have been found in the DNA of this nucleomorph, and one would expect to find only a single version of this gene if the nucleomorph were not the remains of an engulfed organism's nucleus.

Which one of the following is most strongly supported by the information above?

   (A) Only organisms of types that originated through endosymbiosis contain nucleomorphs.

   (B) A nucleomorph within the chlorarachniophyte holds all of the genetic material of some other organism.

   (C) Nucleomorphs originated when an organism endosymbiotically engulfed a chlorarachniophyte.

   (D) Two organisms will not undergo endosymbiosis unless at least one of them contains a nucleomorph.

   (E) Chlorarachniophytes emerged as the result of two organisms having undergone endosymbiosis.

GO ON TO THE NEXT PAGE.

23. Reviewer: Although finalism—the view that there are purposes in nature—has been universally rejected, this book launches another attack on that view. Its arguments are based on a complete misunderstanding of the operation of pure chance in nature and so it fails as a critique of finalism. Finalism, therefore, is clearly more plausible than people have thought.

Which one of the following is most closely parallel in its flawed reasoning to the flawed reasoning in the reviewer's argument?

(A) No literary historian still believes the claim that a single author wrote every word of this collection of works. Evidence on which that claim is based can be shown to be false by manuscript dating techniques, but these dating results have not been cited before. Therefore, it is quite likely that a single author did write every word of this collection of works.

(B) Few botanists deny that a recently discovered fern is the same species represented in ancient fossils. The botanists who first discovered this specimen deny that it is the same species as the ancient one, but they have spent little time studying the specimen. Therefore, the specimen is likely to be the same species represented in the ancient fossils.

(C) Bicycle engineers no longer believe that aluminum is as good a frame material as titanium. An engineer at Ace Bicycles has argued that aluminum is not as good as titanium because it breaks under pressure. But he is confused about the kind of pressure exerted on bicycles. Therefore, the claim that aluminum is as good a frame material as titanium makes more sense than bicycle engineers believe.

(D) Experts agree that red wines from France's Bordeaux region are the best in the world, and five are on this year's list of the world's top ten red wines. However, the best currently available Bordeaux wines are more than one year old, whereas other countries' best are not. Therefore, it is false that Bordeaux red wines are the best in the world this year.

(E) Sociologists agree that the psychological development of children may be impaired by watching too much television, though researchers argued recently that the quality of the parent-child relationship is more developmentally significant than television viewing. These researchers did not consider the long-term impact of television on children, so it is quite likely that the psychological development of children is impaired by watching too much television.

24. Appliance dealer: Appliance manufacturers commonly modify existing models without giving the modified versions new model names. Some people have complained that this practice makes it impossible for consumers to be certain that the appliance they are about to purchase is identical to the one they may have seen at a neighbor's or read about in a consumer magazine. Yet manufacturers' modifications to existing models are invariably improvements that benefit the buyer. Therefore, consumers have little reason to object to this practice.

Which one of the following, if true, most seriously weakens the dealer's argument?

(A) Appliances are generally purchased with the expectation that they will continue to be used for several years.

(B) Appliances usually carry a model number that provides substantially more detailed information about the product than does the model name.

(C) Appliance manufacturers frequently sell identical products under several different model names.

(D) Improved versions of appliances typically become available before vendors have stopped selling the older versions of the appliance with the same model name.

(E) The high cost of product advertising makes appliance manufacturers generally reluctant to change model names to reflect modifications to their products.

GO ON TO THE NEXT PAGE.

25. In our solar system only one of the nine planets—Earth—qualifies as fit to sustain life. Nonetheless, using this ratio, and considering the astonishingly large number of planetary systems in the universe, we must conclude that the number of planets fit to sustain some form of life is extremely large.

The argument is questionable because it presumes which one of the following without providing justification?

(A) If a planet is Earthlike, then life will arise on it.
(B) Our solar system is similar to many other planetary systems in the universe.
(C) The conditions necessary for life to begin are well understood.
(D) Life similar to Earth's could evolve under conditions very different from those on Earth.
(E) Most other planetary systems in the universe have nine planets.

26. Sociologist: Suggestions for improved efficiency that derive from employers are unlikely to elicit positive responses from employees, who tend to resent suggestions they did not generate. An employer should therefore engage the employee in a nonthreatening dialogue that emphasizes the positive contributions of the employee to the development of such ideas. Then the ideas employers want to try will be implemented more quickly and effectively.

Which one of the following principles, if valid, most helps to justify the sociologist's reasoning?

(A) Employees are more likely to accept suggestions for improved efficiency when these suggestions are not obviously directed at them.
(B) Employees are more likely to carry out ideas for improved efficiency that they believe they have participated in generating.
(C) Employees are more likely to implement ideas for improved efficiency that derive from a dialogue in which they have participated than from a dialogue in which they have not participated.
(D) Employees are more likely to generate good ideas for improved efficiency when they do not feel resentment about the process that attempts to formulate such ideas.
(E) Employees are more likely to resent employers who attempt to implement the employers' rather than the employees' ideas for improved efficiency.

S T O P

IF YOU FINISH BEFORE TIME IS CALLED, YOU MAY CHECK YOUR WORK ON THIS SECTION ONLY.
DO NOT WORK ON ANY OTHER SECTION IN THE TEST.

SECTION IV

Time—35 minutes

28 Questions

Directions: Each passage in this section is followed by a group of questions to be answered on the basis of what is stated or implied in the passage. For some of the questions, more than one of the choices could conceivably answer the question. However, you are to choose the best answer; that is, the response that most accurately and completely answers the question, and blacken the corresponding space on your answer sheet.

By the year 2030, the Earth's population is expected to increase to 10 billion; ideally, all would enjoy standards of living equivalent to those of present-day industrial democracies. However, if 10 billion
(5) people consume critical natural resources such as copper, nickel, and petroleum at the current per capita rates of industrialized countries, and if new resources are not discovered or substitutes developed, such an ideal would last a decade or less. Moreover, projections
(10) based on the current rate of waste production in many industrialized countries suggest that 10 billion people would generate enough solid waste every year to bury a large city and its surrounding suburbs 100 meters deep.

These estimates are not meant to predict a grim
(15) future. Instead they emphasize the incentives for recycling, conservation, and a switch to alternative materials. They also suggest that the traditional model of industrial activity, in which individual manufacturing processes take in raw materials and
(20) generate products to be sold plus waste to be disposed of, should be transformed into a more integrated model: an industrial ecosystem. In such a system the consumption of energy and materials is optimized, wastes and pollution are minimized, and the effluents
(25) of one process—whether they are spent catalysts from petroleum refining or discarded plastic containers from consumer products—serve as the raw material for another process.

Materials in an ideal industrial ecosystem would
(30) not be depleted any more than are materials in a biological ecosystem, in which plants synthesize nutrients that feed herbivores, some of which in turn feed a chain of carnivores whose waste products and remains eventually feed further generations of plants.
(35) A chunk of steel could potentially show up one year in a tin can, the next year in an automobile, and 10 years later in the skeleton of a building. Some manufacturers are already making use of "designed offal" in the manufacture of metals and some plastics: tailoring the
(40) production of waste from a manufacturing process so that the waste can be fed directly back into that process or a related one. Such recycling still requires the expenditure of energy and the unavoidable generation of some wastes and harmful by-products, but at much
(45) lower levels than are typical today.

The ideal industrial ecosystem, in which there is an economically viable role for every product of a manufacturing process, will not be attained soon; current technology is often inadequate to the task.
(50) However, if industrialized nations embrace major and minor changes in their current industrial practices and developing nations bypass older, less ecologically sound technologies, it should be possible to develop a more closed industrial ecosystem that would be more
(55) sustainable than current industrial practices, especially in the face of decreasing supplies of raw materials and increasing problems of waste and pollution.

1. According to the passage, which one of the following is currently an obstacle to the implementation of an ideal industrial ecosystem?

(A) the unwillingness of manufacturers to change their industrial practices

(B) the unwillingness of industrialized countries to reduce their standards of living to a level that is sustainable for the entire world

(C) the unwillingness of developing nations to adopt new technologies that are more ecologically sound than those used by industrialized countries

(D) the inability of technology to provide a profitable use for every by-product of the manufacturing process

(E) the failure of the industrial ecosystem approach to provide sufficient quantities of manufactured goods

GO ON TO THE NEXT PAGE.

2. The author of the passage would most probably agree with which one of the following statements about standards of living?

   (A) An increase in the standard of living in developing countries will be accompanied by a decrease in the standard of living in industrialized countries.

   (B) It is likely that the standard of living of both industrialized and developing countries will decrease substantially by the year 2030.

   (C) The current standard of living of industrialized countries cannot be sustained if the population of the world increases.

   (D) All countries could enjoy a high standard of living without depleting natural resources if industrialized and developing countries implemented an ideal industrial ecosystem.

   (E) Supplies of critical natural resources will be in serious danger of depletion by the year 2030 unless the current standard of living of both industrialized and developing countries is reduced.

3. The author of the passage would most probably agree with which one of the following statements about the use of "designed offal" (line 38)?

   (A) It is a harmful step that requires the consumption of critical natural resources and results in the generation of waste and harmful by-products.

   (B) It is not an entirely helpful step because it draws attention away from the central problems that still need to be solved.

   (C) It is a temporary solution that will not contribute to the establishment of an industrial ecosystem.

   (D) It is a promising step in the right direction, but it does not solve all of the problems that need to be addressed.

   (E) It is the most practical solution to the environmental problems facing the world.

4. The author mentions all of the following as advantages of replacing current industrial practices with an industrial ecosystem approach EXCEPT:

   (A) The amount of waste produced by industrial processes would be reduced.

   (B) The amount of harmful by-products produced by industrial processes would be reduced.

   (C) The use of alternative sources of energy to provide power for industrial processes would be increased.

   (D) The consumption of raw materials used in industrial processes would be optimized.

   (E) Better use would be made of the waste produced by industrial processes.

5. Of the following, which one is the best example of the use of "designed offal" (line 38) as it is defined in the passage?

   (A) A paper container manufacturer purchases recycled newspaper that is turned into pulp and used as the raw material for producing paper containers.

   (B) A demolition company strips brass fixtures from condemned buildings, reconditions the fixtures, and sells them to home renovation companies.

   (C) A steel company buys metal taken from discarded automobiles, melts it down, and uses it in the production of steel beams.

   (D) An automobile manufacturer turns the plastic left over from its production of automobile body panels into insulation for its automobile doors.

   (E) A plastics company receives recycled beverage containers, reprocesses the containers, and uses the reprocessed material to produce polyester fiber.

GO ON TO THE NEXT PAGE.

Thurgood Marshall's litigation of *Brown v. Board of Education* in 1952—the landmark case, decided in 1954, that made segregation illegal in United States public schools—was not his first case before the U.S.
(5) Supreme Court. Some legal scholars claim that the cases he presented to the court in the sixteen years before his successful argument for desegregation of public schools were necessary forerunners of that case: preliminary tests of legal strategies and early erosions
(10) of the foundations of discrimination against African Americans that paved the way for success in *Brown*.

When Marshall joined the legal staff of the National Association for the Advancement of Colored People (NAACP) in 1936, the organization was
(15) divided on how to proceed against the legal doctrine that for forty years had promoted "separate but equal" facilities for African Americans in educational institutions, in public transportation, and various other civic amenities. One approach was to emphasize that
(20) facilities were not in fact equal and to pursue litigation whose practical goal was the improvement both of opportunity for African Americans and of the facilities themselves. A second, more theoretical, approach was to argue that the concept of separate but equal facilities
(25) for the races was by its very nature impossible to fulfill, rendering the doctrine self-contradictory and hence legally unsound. Marshall correctly believed that the latter approach would eventually be the one to bring repeal of the doctrine, but felt it necessary in the
(30) short term to argue several cases using the former approach, in order to demonstrate the numerous ways in which segregation prevented real equality and thus to prepare the courts to recognize the validity of the theoretical argument.
(35) While Marshall enjoyed several successes arguing for the equalization of facilities and opportunities in such areas as voting practices and accommodations for graduate students at public universities, it would be twelve years before he evolved a strategy for arguing
(40) against pervasive discriminatory practices that enabled him to make the leap from individual instances of inequality to the broader social argument needed to later invalidate "separate but equal." In 1948, Marshall litigated *Shelley v. Kraemer*, in which he convinced the
(45) court to outlaw housing discrimination practiced by private parties. Although the court had previously supported such practices implicitly under a doctrine that excused private dealings from the legal requirement for equal protection of citizens under law,
(50) Marshall presented sociological data demonstrating that, in sum and over time, these individual transactions constituted a pattern of insupportable discrimination. Marshall later used this strategy when arguing against individual schools' enrollment
(55) restrictions in *Brown*; scholars argue that his successful use of the strategy in *Shelley* prepared the court to accept such data as convincing evidence for finding "separate but equal" insupportable on its face.

6. Which one of the following titles most accurately describes the contents of the passage?

(A) "Broader Social Patterns: Theoretical Arguments Heard in the Supreme Court, 1936–1952"

(B) "Thurgood Marshall: The Growth of His Career, 1936–1952"

(C) "Toward Change: The Development of Thurgood Marshall's Argument against 'Separate but Equal,' 1936–1952"

(D) "Separate but Not Equal: The Impact of *Brown v. Board of Education* on School Segregation"

(E) "Conflict and Compromise: Early Divisions in the NAACP's Attack on School Segregation"

7. It can most reasonably be inferred from the passage that Marshall's legal strategy for attacking the "separate but equal" doctrine

(A) sought to answer critics within the NAACP

(B) suggested Marshall thought the court would never accept the validity of a theoretical argument

(C) satisfied the requirement that cases first be argued in lower court

(D) presumed that the court could only gradually be convinced to overturn the "separate but equal" doctrine

(E) reflected Marshall's preference to seek practical goals

8. According to the passage, sociological data presented by Marshall in *Shelley v. Kraemer* showed that

(A) numerous examples of individual discriminatory enrollment policies in public schools amounted to a general pattern of discrimination

(B) numerous examples of individual discriminatory transactions by private parties amounted to a general pattern of housing discrimination

(C) the legal requirement for equal treatment of citizens was not applicable to private transactions

(D) the pattern of discrimination in housing transactions was due to inequities in financial resources

(E) the pattern of discrimination in the enrollment policies of public schools was similar to the pattern of insupportable discrimination in housing transactions

GO ON TO THE NEXT PAGE.

9. The passage suggests that the scholars referred to in the passage would be most likely to believe which one of the following statements?

(A) Without Marshall's argument in *Shelley v. Kraemer*, the court would probably have overturned "separate but equal" for political reasons.

(B) Without Marshall's argument in *Shelley v. Kraemer*, the court would probably not have ruled in his favor on *Brown v. Board of Education*.

(C) Without Marshall's argument in *Shelley v. Kraemer*, the court would probably not have excused private dealings from the legal requirement for equal protection of citizens under law.

(D) Without Marshall's argument in *Shelley v. Kraemer*, the court would probably never have relied on sociological data in any future cases.

(E) Without Marshall's argument in *Shelley v. Kraemer*, the court would probably have overturned discriminatory housing transactions on other grounds.

10. According to the passage, the more theoretical approach to proceeding against the "separate but equal" doctrine was to

(A) show that the doctrine often resulted in unequal opportunities for African Americans

(B) argue that the doctrine was legally unsound because it contradicted itself

(C) adopt a short-term strategy to prepare for the use of a long-term strategy

(D) erode its foundations by successfully arguing individual cases

(E) demonstrate that the separate facilities provided for African Americans were not in fact equitable

11. The function of the third paragraph is to

(A) provide support for the view presented in the first paragraph

(B) sharpen the distinction made in the second paragraph

(C) question the claim made in the first paragraph

(D) summarize the argument made in the first two paragraphs

(E) counter the criticism of "separate but equal" made in the second paragraph

12. The primary purpose of the passage is to

(A) reveal the details of Marshall's career before he litigated *Brown v. Board of Education*

(B) examine the effects of a particular legal doctrine on the lives of African Americans

(C) describe the strategy contributing to a successful legal argument

(D) provide guidance to other litigators who attempt to overturn legal doctrines

(E) call attention to an unsound legal doctrine by focusing on the strategy of its successful challenger

GO ON TO THE NEXT PAGE.

Donna Haraway's *Primate Visions* is the most ambitious book on the history of science yet written from a feminist perspective, embracing not only the scientific construction of gender but also the interplay
(5) of race, class, and colonial and postcolonial culture with the "Western" construction of the very concept of nature itself. Primatology is a particularly apt vehicle for such themes because primates seem so much like ourselves that they provide ready material for
(10) scientists' conscious and unconscious projections of their beliefs about nature and culture.

Haraway's most radical departure is to challenge the traditional disjunction between the active knower (scientist/historian) and the passive object
(15) (nature/history). In Haraway's view, the desire to understand nature, whether in order to tame it or to preserve it as a place of wild innocence, is based on a troublingly masculinist and colonialist view of nature as an entity distinct from us and subject to our control.
(20) She argues that it is a view that is no longer politically, ecologically, or even scientifically viable. She proposes an approach that not only recognizes diverse human actors (scientists, government officials, laborers, science fiction writers) as contributing to our
(25) knowledge of nature, but that also recognizes the creatures usually subsumed under nature (such as primates) as active participants in creating that knowledge as well. Finally, she insists that the perspectives afforded by these different agents cannot
(30) be reduced to a single, coherent reality—there are necessarily only multiple, interlinked, partial realities.

This iconoclastic view is reflected in Haraway's unorthodox writing style. Haraway does not weave the many different elements of her work into one unified,
(35) overarching Story of Primatology; they remain distinct voices that will not succumb to a master narrative. This fragmented approach to historiography is familiar enough in historiographical theorizing but has rarely been put into practice by historians of science. It
(40) presents a complex alternative to traditional history, whether strictly narrative or narrative with emphasis on a causal argument.

Haraway is equally innovative in the way she incorporates broad cultural issues into her analysis.
(45) Despite decades of rhetoric from historians of science about the need to unite issues deemed "internal" to science (scientific theory and practice) and those considered "external" to it (social issues, structures, and beliefs), that dichotomy has proven difficult to set
(50) aside. Haraway simply ignores it. The many readers in whom this separation is deeply ingrained may find her discussions of such popular sources as science fiction, movies, and television distracting, and her statements concerning such issues as nuclear war bewildering and
(55) digressive. To accept her approach one must shed a great many assumptions about what properly belongs to the study of science.

13. The passage is primarily concerned with discussing which one of the following?

(A) the roles played by gender and class in Western science in general, and in the field of primatology in particular

(B) two different methods of writing the history of science

(C) the content and style of a proposal to reform the scientific approach to nature

(D) the theoretical bases and the cultural assumptions underlying a recent book on the history of women in science

(E) the effect of theoretical positions on writing styles in books on the history of science

14. Which one of the following best describes the attitude of the author of the passage toward *Primate Visions*?

(A) The book is highly original and exciting, but will be difficult for many readers to accept.

(B) The book is admirable primarily because of the extensive research it reflects.

(C) Although far from ground breaking, the book is elegantly and coherently written.

(D) While commendably imaginative, the book is, in the end, less than convincing.

(E) The book's thesis is promising and provocative but half-heartedly argued.

15. The passage suggests which one of the following about the traditional scientific approach to nature?

(A) Scientists have traditionally preferred to tame nature rather than to preserve it.

(B) Scientists have traditionally sought to counter the masculinist and colonialist aspects of Western culture.

(C) Scientists have traditionally assumed that primates were more active participants in the creation of knowledge than were other forms of natural life.

(D) Scientists have traditionally endeavored to conceal the role of government officials and laborers in the construction of scientific knowledge.

(E) Scientists have traditionally regarded nature as something separate from themselves.

GO ON TO THE NEXT PAGE.

16. The passage suggests that Haraway would most probably agree with which one of the following statements about scientists observing animal behavior in the field?

   (A) Those scientists who have been properly trained in field techniques will all record similar observations about the animals they are studying.

   (B) Primatologists are more likely to record accurate and sensitive observations about the animals they are studying than are other animal behaviorists.

   (C) Scientists studying primate behavior will probably record more accurate and sensitive observations than will scientists studying animals that are less like ourselves.

   (D) Scientists who study primates will probably be more likely than will scientists studying other animals to interpret an animal's behavior in terms of the scientists' own beliefs.

   (E) Scientists who take a passive role in interactions with the animals they study will probably record observations similar to those recorded by scientists taking a more active role.

17. The "iconoclastic view" mentioned in line 32 refers to which one of the following?

   (A) the assertion that there is no way to construct a unified and comprehensive reality out of the different fragments that contribute to the construction of scientific knowledge

   (B) the advocacy of the incorporation of many different sources, both literary and scholarly, into the construction of a unified and overarching Story of Primatology

   (C) the argument that the traditional scientific disjunction between active knower and passive object has had troubling political and ecological repercussions

   (D) the thesis that the projection of scientists' beliefs about nature and culture onto the study of primates has burdened primatology with masculinist and colonialist preconceptions

   (E) the contention that scientists have not succeeded in breaking out of the confines of either traditional narrative history or history organized around a causal argument

18. Which one of the following best exemplifies the type of "traditional history" mentioned in line 40 of the passage?

   (A) a chronological recounting of the life and work of Marie Curie, with special attention paid to the circumstances that led to her discovery of radium

   (B) a television series that dramatizes one scientist's prediction about human life in the twenty-second century

   (C) the transcript of a series of conversations among several scientists of radically opposing philosophies, in which no resolution or conclusion is reached

   (D) a newspaper editorial written by a scientist trying to arouse public support for a certain project by detailing the practical benefits to be gained from it

   (E) detailed mathematical notes recording the precise data gathered from a laboratory experiment

19. According to the author of the passage, which one of the following statements is true of the historiographical method employed by Haraway in *Primate Visions*?

   (A) It is a particularly effective approach in discussions of social issues.

   (B) It is an approach commonly applied in historiography in many disciplines.

   (C) It is generally less effective than traditional approaches.

   (D) It has rarely been used by historians emphasizing causal arguments.

   (E) It has rarely been practiced by historians of science.

20. The author uses the term "rhetoric" in line 45 most probably in order to do which one of the following?

   (A) underscore the importance of clear and effective writing in historiographical works

   (B) highlight the need for historians of science to study modes of language

   (C) emphasize the fact that historians of science have been unable to put innovative ideas into practice

   (D) criticize the excessive concern for form over content in the writings of historians of science

   (E) characterize the writing style and analytical approach employed by Haraway

GO ON TO THE NEXT PAGE.

Some philosophers find the traditional, subjective approach to studying the mind outdated and ineffectual. For them, the attempt to describe the sensation of pain or anger, for example, or the
(5) awareness that one is aware, has been surpassed by advances in fields such as psychology, neuroscience, and cognitive science. Scientists, they claim, do not concern themselves with how a phenomenon feels from the inside; instead of investigating private evidence
(10) perceivable only to a particular individual, scientists pursue hard data—such as the study of how nerves transmit impulses to the brain—which is externally observable and can be described without reference to any particular point of view. With respect to features of
(15) the universe such as those investigated by chemistry, biology, and physics, this objective approach has been remarkably successful in yielding knowledge. Why, these philosophers ask, should we suppose the mind to be any different?
(20) But philosophers loyal to subjectivity are not persuaded by appeals to science when such appeals conflict with the data gathered by introspection. Knowledge, they argue, relies on the data of experience, which includes subjective experience. Why
(25) should philosophy ally itself with scientists who would reduce the sources of knowledge to only those data that can be discerned objectively?

On the face of it, it seems unlikely that these two approaches to studying the mind could be reconciled.
(30) Because philosophy, unlike science, does not progress inexorably toward a single truth, disputes concerning the nature of the mind are bound to continue. But what is particularly distressing about the present debate is that genuine communication between the two sides is
(35) virtually impossible. For reasoned discourse to occur, there must be shared assumptions or beliefs. Starting from radically divergent perspectives, subjectivists and objectivists lack a common context in which to consider evidence presented from each other's
(40) perspectives.

The situation may be likened to a debate between adherents of different religions about the creation of the universe. While each religion may be confident that its cosmology is firmly grounded in its respective
(45) sacred text, there is little hope that conflicts between their competing cosmologies could be resolved by recourse to the texts alone. Only further investigation into the authority of the texts themselves would be sufficient.
(50) What would be required to resolve the debate between the philosophers of mind, then, is an investigation into the authority of their differing perspectives. How rational is it to take scientific description as the ideal way to understand the nature of
(55) consciousness? Conversely, how useful is it to rely solely on introspection for one's knowledge about the workings of the mind? Are there alternative ways of gaining such knowledge? In this debate, epistemology—the study of knowledge—may itself
(60) lead to the discovery of new forms of knowledge about how the mind works.

21. Which one of the following most accurately summarizes the main point of the passage?

(A) In order to gain new knowledge of the workings of the mind, subjectivists must take into consideration not only the private evidence of introspection but also the more objective evidence obtainable from disciplines such as psychology, neuroscience, and cognitive science.

(B) In rejecting the traditional, subjective approach to studying the mind, objectivists have made further progress virtually impossible because their approach rests on a conception of evidence that is fundamentally incompatible with that employed by subjectivists.

(C) Because the subjectivist and objectivist approaches rest on diametrically opposed assumptions about the kinds of evidence to be used when studying the mind, the only way to resolve the dispute is to compare the two approaches' success in obtaining knowledge.

(D) Although subjectivists and objectivists appear to employ fundamentally irreconcilable approaches to the study of the mind, a common ground for debate may be found if both sides are willing to examine the authority of the evidence on which their competing theories depend.

(E) While the success of disciplines such as chemistry, biology, and physics appears to support the objectivist approach to studying the mind, the objectivist approach has failed to show that the data of introspection should not qualify as evidence.

22. Which one of the following most likely reflects the author's belief about the current impasse between subjectivists and objectivists?

(A) It cannot be overcome because of the radically different conceptions of evidence favored by each of the two sides.

(B) It is resolvable only if the two sides can find common ground from which to assess their competing conceptions of evidence.

(C) It is unavoidable unless both sides recognize that an accurate understanding of the mind requires both types of evidence.

(D) It is based on an easily correctable misunderstanding between the two sides about the nature of evidence.

(E) It will prevent further progress until alternate ways of gaining knowledge about the mind are discovered.

GO ON TO THE NEXT PAGE.

23. The author's primary purpose in writing the passage is to

(A) suggest that there might be valid aspects to both the subjective and the objective approaches to studying the mind
(B) advocate a possible solution to the impasse undermining debate between subjectivists and objectivists
(C) criticize subjectivist philosophers for failing to adopt a more scientific methodology
(D) defend the subjective approach to studying the mind against the charges leveled against it by objectivists
(E) evaluate the legitimacy of differing conceptions of evidence advocated by subjectivists and objectivists

24. According to the passage, subjectivists advance which one of the following claims to support their charge that objectivism is faulty?

(A) Objectivism rests on evidence that conflicts with the data of introspection.
(B) Objectivism restricts the kinds of experience from which philosophers may draw knowledge.
(C) Objectivism relies on data that can be described and interpreted only by scientific specialists.
(D) Objectivism provides no context in which to view scientific data as relevant to philosophical questions.
(E) Objectivism concerns itself with questions that have not traditionally been part of philosophical inquiry.

25. The author discusses the work of scientists in lines 7–14 primarily to

(A) contrast the traditional approach to studying the mind with the approach advocated by objectivists
(B) argue that the attempt to describe the sensation of pain should be done without reference to any particular point of view
(C) explain why scientists should not concern themselves with describing how a phenomenon feels from the inside
(D) criticize subjectivists for thinking there is little to be gained from studying the mind scientifically
(E) clarify why the objectivists' approach has been successful in disciplines such as chemistry, biology, and physics

26. The author characterizes certain philosophers as "loyal to subjectivity" (line 20) for each of the following reasons EXCEPT:

(A) These philosophers believe scientists should adopt the subjective approach when studying phenomena such as how nerves transmit impulses to the brain.
(B) These philosophers favor subjective evidence about the mind over objective evidence about the mind when the two conflict.
(C) These philosophers maintain that subjective experience is essential to the study of the mind.
(D) These philosophers hold that objective evidence is only a part of the full range of experience.
(E) These philosophers employ evidence that is available only to a particular individual.

27. Based on the passage, which one of the following is most clearly an instance of the objectivist approach to studying the mind?

(A) collecting accounts of dreams given by subjects upon waking in order to better understand the nature of the subconscious
(B) interviewing subjects during extremes of hot and cold weather in order to investigate a connection between weather and mood
(C) recording subjects' evaluation of the stress they experienced while lecturing in order to determine how stress affects facility at public speaking
(D) analyzing the amount of a certain chemical in subjects' bloodstreams in order to investigate a proposed link between the chemical and aggressive behavior
(E) asking subjects to speak their thoughts aloud as they attempt to learn a new skill in order to test the relationship between mental understanding and physical performance

28. Which one of the following is most closely analogous to the debate described in the hypothetical example given by the author in the fourth paragraph?

(A) a debate among investigators attempting to determine a criminal's identity when conflicting physical evidence is found at the crime scene
(B) a debate among jurors attempting to determine which of two conflicting eyewitness accounts of an event is to be believed
(C) a debate between two archaeologists about the meaning of certain written symbols when no evidence exists to verify either's claim
(D) a debate between two museum curators about the value of a painting that shows clear signs of both genuineness and forgery
(E) a debate between two historians who draw conflicting conclusions about the same event based on different types of historical data

S T O P
IF YOU FINISH BEFORE TIME IS CALLED, YOU MAY CHECK YOUR WORK ON THIS SECTION ONLY.
DO NOT WORK ON ANY OTHER SECTION IN THE TEST.

Acknowledgment is made to the following sources from which material has been adapted for use in this test booklet:

Barbara Ehrenreich, "The Economics of Cloning." ©1993 by Time Inc.

Paul Reidinger, "The Long March to Brown." ©1994 by ABA Journal.

SIGNATURE _____   / /
                                                    DATE

LSAT WRITING SAMPLE TOPIC

The Norton Community Travel Club is considering two travel packages for its annual summer vacation trip. Write an argument for selecting one trip over the other, keeping two guidelines in mind:

- The club is committed to serving the needs and interests of its membership, drawn from a retirement community and a subdivision of moderately priced homes.
- Club members are eager to keep costs down as much as possible.

Worldwide Travel Agency has offered a two-week guided tour of three South American countries. The group will travel together in an air-conditioned bus and stop at major attractions. All members will be expected to be packed and ready to leave each morning at a designated time. Round-trip airfare, meals, and accommodations are included in the price of the trip. While serviceable, the accommodations are not first-class; first-class accommodations are available to those who pay an additional fee. Worldwide is an experienced travel agency that has been running this particular tour for fifteen years. The agency has a reputation for knowledgeable, personable tour guides.

For the same price, Leisure Tours has offered a three-week trip to three major South American cities. Included in the fee will be round-trip airfare, airfare to each of the three cities, and a shared room in highly rated hotels; the cost of meals is not included in the price. On the first day of each stop, Leisure Tours schedules a guided tour of the city, provides brochures and maps, and offers suggestions for those wishing to take side trips. Otherwise, there are no planned activities. Leisure Tours, a relatively new company, recently received an award for superior service from the Association of Business Executives. Leisure Tour's president is a well-known travel writer.

Directions:

1. Use the Answer Key on the next page to check your answers.

2. Use the Scoring Worksheet below to compute your raw score.

3. Use the Score Conversion Chart to convert your raw score into the 120-180 scale.

Scoring Worksheet

1. Enter the number of questions you answered correctly in each section.

	Number Correct
SECTION I	_____
SECTION II	_____
SECTION III	_____
SECTION IV	_____

2. Enter the sum here: _____

   This is your Raw Score.

Conversion Chart

For Converting Raw Score to the 120-180 LSAT Scaled Score
LSAT Form 1LSS45

Reported Score	Raw Score Lowest	Raw Score Highest
180	98	101
179	97	97
178	96	96
177	95	95
176	94	94
175	93	93
174	92	92
173	91	91
172	90	90
171	88	89
170	87	87
169	86	86
168	85	85
167	83	84
166	82	82
165	81	81
164	79	80
163	78	78
162	76	77
161	75	75
160	73	74
159	71	72
158	70	70
157	68	69
156	66	67
155	65	65
154	63	64
153	61	62
152	60	60
151	58	59
150	56	57
149	54	55
148	53	53
147	51	52
146	49	50
145	47	48
144	46	46
143	44	45
142	42	43
141	41	41
140	39	40
139	37	38
138	36	36
137	34	35
136	32	33
135	31	31
134	29	30
133	28	28
132	26	27
131	25	25
130	24	24
129	22	23
128	21	21
127	20	20
126	19	19
125	18	18
124	16	17
123	15	15
122	14	14
121	13	13
120	0	12

SECTION I

1.	E	8.	E	15.	B	22.	E
2.	B	9.	A	16.	A	23.	D
3.	D	10.	D	17.	E		
4.	C	11.	A	18.	A		
5.	A	12.	A	19.	B		
6.	C	13.	C	20.	D		
7.	E	14.	C	21.	A		

SECTION II

1.	D	8.	B	15.	A	22.	D
2.	D	9.	A	16.	E	23.	B
3.	C	10.	D	17.	A	24.	E
4.	E	11.	E	18.	C		
5.	E	12.	A	19.	B		
6.	C	13.	C	20.	B		
7.	D	14.	E	21.	C		

SECTION III

1.	E	8.	B	15.	A	22.	E
2.	D	9.	A	16.	D	23.	C
3.	C	10.	D	17.	E	24.	D
4.	E	11.	E	18.	A	25.	B
5.	D	12.	C	19.	E	26.	B
6.	D	13.	C	20.	A		
7.	B	14.	C	21.	C		

SECTION IV

1.	D	8.	B	15.	E	22.	B
2.	D	9.	B	16.	D	23.	B
3.	D	10.	B	17.	A	24.	B
4.	C	11.	A	18.	A	25.	A
5.	D	12.	C	19.	E	26.	A
6.	C	13.	C	20.	C	27.	D
7.	D	14.	A	21.	D	28.	E

The Official LSAT PrepTest

32

- October 2000
  PrepTest 32

- Form OLSS47

SECTION I

Time—35 minutes

25 Questions

<u>Directions:</u> The questions in this section are based on the reasoning contained in brief statements or passages. For some questions, more than one of the choices could conceivably answer the question. However, you are to choose the <u>best</u> answer; that is, the response that most accurately and completely answers the question. You should not make assumptions that are by commonsense standards implausible, superfluous, or incompatible with the passage. After you have chosen the best answer, blacken the corresponding space on your answer sheet.

1. Editorial: The structure of the present school calendar was established to satisfy the requirements of early-twentieth-century agricultural life. In those days, farmers needed their children to have long breaks during which they could remain at home and help with the harvest. The contemporary school year is thus made up of periods of study interspersed with long breaks. But agricultural life no longer occupies most of our citizens, so we can now make changes that serve the interests of children. Therefore, long breaks should be removed from the school calendar.

Which one of the following is an assumption on which the editorial's argument depends?

(A)   During long breaks children have a tendency to forget what they have learned.

(B)   Children of farmers need to continue observing a school calendar made up of periods of study interspersed with long breaks.

(C)   Long breaks in the school calendar should be replaced with breaks that are no longer than workers' average vacations.

(D)   A change in the present school calendar that shortened breaks would serve the interests of agricultural life.

(E)   A school calendar made up of periods of study without long breaks would serve the interests of children more than a school calendar with long breaks.

2. Leatherbacks, the largest of the sea turtles, when subjected to the conditions of captivity, are susceptible to a wide variety of fatal diseases with which they would never come in contact if they lived in the wild. It is surprising, therefore, that the likelihood that a leatherback will reach its theoretical maximum life expectancy is about the same whether that animal is living in captivity or in the wild.

Which one of the following, if true, most helps to resolve the apparent discrepancy?

(A)   Fewer diseases attack leatherbacks than attack other large aquatic reptiles.

(B)   The average life expectancy of sea turtles in general is longer than that of almost all other marine animals.

(C)   Most leatherbacks that perish in the wild are killed by predators.

(D)   Few zoologists have sufficient knowledge to establish an artificial environment that is conducive to the well-being of captive leatherbacks.

(E)   The size of a leatherback is an untrustworthy indicator of its age.

GO ON TO THE NEXT PAGE.

3. Chairperson: The board of directors of our corporation should not allow the incentives being offered by two foreign governments to entice us to expand our operations into their countries without further consideration of the issue. Although there is an opportunity to increase our profits by expanding our operations there, neither of these countries is politically stable.

The chairperson's reasoning most closely conforms to which one of the following principles?

(A) A corporation should never expand operations into countries that are politically unstable.
(B) Corporations should expand operations into countries when there is a chance of increasing profits.
(C) Political stability is the most important consideration in deciding whether to expand operations into a country.
(D) Corporations should always be cautious about expanding operations into politically unstable countries.
(E) Boards of directors should always disregard governmental incentives when considering where to expand corporate operations.

4. Maria: Thomas Edison was one of the most productive inventors of his time, perhaps of all time. His contributions significantly shaped the development of modern lighting and communication systems. Yet he had only a few months of formal schooling. Therefore, you do not need a formal education to make crucial contributions to technological advancement.

Frank: That is definitely not true anymore. Since Edison's day there have been many new developments in technology; to make crucial contributions today you need much more extensive technical knowledge than was needed then.

Frank's reasoning in his response to Maria is most vulnerable to criticism on the grounds that it

(A) fails to address the possibility that technical knowledge may be acquired without formal education
(B) does not consider whether there have been improvements in formal education since Edison's day
(C) relies on using the term "crucial" differently from the way Maria used it
(D) presumes that no other inventor of Edison's time could have been as productive as Edison
(E) fails to criticize or question any of Maria's statements about Edison

5. In some countries, there is a free flow of information about infrastructure, agriculture, and industry, whereas in other countries, this information is controlled by a small elite. In the latter countries, the vast majority of the population is denied vital information about factors that determine their welfare. Thus, these countries are likely to experience more frequent economic crises than other countries do.

The conclusion follows logically if which one of the following is assumed?

(A) It is more likely that people without political power will suffer from economic crises than it is that people in power will.
(B) Economic crises become more frequent as the amount of information available to the population about factors determining its welfare decreases.
(C) In nations in which the government controls access to information about infrastructure, agriculture, and industry, economic crises are common.
(D) The higher the percentage of the population that participates in economic decisions, the better those decisions are.
(E) A small elite that controls information about infrastructure, agriculture, and industry is likely to manipulate that information for its own benefit.

GO ON TO THE NEXT PAGE.

6. Hana said she was not going to invite her brothers to her birthday party. However, among the gifts Hana received at her party was a recording in which she had expressed an interest. Since her brothers had planned to give her that recording, at least some of Hana's brothers must have been among the guests at Hana's birthday party after all.

A reasoning error in the argument is that the argument

(A) disregards the possibility that a change of mind might be justified by a change in circumstances

(B) treats the fact of someone's presence at a given event as a guarantee that that person had a legitimate reason to be at that event

(C) uses a term that is intrinsically evaluative as though that term was purely descriptive

(D) fails to establish that something true of some people is true of only those people

(E) overlooks the possibility that a person's interest in one kind of thing is compatible with that person's interest in a different kind of thing

7. If you have no keyboarding skills at all, you will not be able to use a computer. And if you are not able to use a computer, you will not be able to write your essays using a word processing program.

If the statements above are true, which one of the following must be true?

(A) If you have some keyboarding skills, you will be able to write your essays using a word processing program.

(B) If you are not able to write your essays using a word processing program, you have no keyboarding skills.

(C) If you are able to write your essays using a word processing program, you have at least some keyboarding skills.

(D) If you are able to use a computer, you will probably be able to write your essays using a word processing program.

(E) If you are not able to write your essays using a word processing program, you are not able to use a computer.

Questions 8–9

Rossi: It is undemocratic for people to live under a government in which their interests are not represented. So children should have the right to vote, since sometimes the interests of children are different from those of their parents.

Smith: Granted, children's interests are not always the same as their parents'; governmental deficits incurred by their parents' generation will later affect their own generation's standard of living. But even if children are told about the issues affecting them, which is not generally the case, their conceptions of what can or should be done are too simple, and their time horizons are radically different from those of adults, so we cannot give them the responsibility of voting.

8. Which one of the following most accurately describes Rossi's argument?

(A) It makes an appeal to a general principle.

(B) It denies the good faith of an opponent.

(C) It relies on evaluating the predictable consequences of a proposal.

(D) It substitutes description for giving a rationale for a policy.

(E) It employs a term on two different occasions in different senses.

9. Smith's statements can most directly be used as part of an argument for which one of the following views?

(A) A democratic government does not infringe on the rights of any of its citizens.

(B) Children have rights that must be respected by any political authority that rules over them.

(C) News programs for children would give them enough information to enable them to vote in an informed way.

(D) If there are any limitations on full democracy that result from denying the vote to children, such limitations must be accepted.

(E) If parents do not adequately represent their children's interests in the political sphere, those interests will be adequately represented by someone else.

GO ON TO THE NEXT PAGE.

10. To accommodate the personal automobile, houses are built on widely scattered lots far from places of work and shopping malls are equipped with immense parking lots that leave little room for wooded areas. Hence, had people generally not used personal automobiles, the result would have to have been a geography of modern cities quite different from the one we have now.

The argument's reasoning is questionable because the argument

(A) infers from the idea that the current geography of modern cities resulted from a particular cause that it could only have resulted from that cause

(B) infers from the idea that the current geography of modern cities resulted from a particular cause that other facets of modern life resulted from that cause

(C) overlooks the fact that many technological innovations other than the personal automobile have had some effect on the way people live

(D) takes for granted that shopping malls do not need large parking lots even given the use of the personal automobile

(E) takes for granted that people ultimately want to live without personal automobiles

11. Many of the presidents and prime ministers who have had the most successful foreign policies had no prior experience in foreign affairs when they assumed office. Although scholars and diplomats in the sacrosanct inner circle of international affairs would have us think otherwise, anyone with an acute political sense, a disciplined temperament, and a highly developed ability to absorb and retain information can quickly learn to conduct a successful foreign policy. In fact, prior experience alone will be of little value to a foreign policymaker who lacks all three of these traits.

If all of the statements above are true, which one of the following must be true?

(A) Scholars and diplomats have more experience in foreign affairs than most presidents and prime ministers bring to office.

(B) Prior experience in foreign affairs is neither a sufficient nor a necessary condition for a president or prime minister to have a successful foreign policy.

(C) Prior experience in foreign affairs is a necessary but not sufficient condition for a president or prime minister to have a successful foreign policy.

(D) An acute political sense, a disciplined temperament, and a highly developed ability to absorb and retain information are each necessary conditions for a president or prime minister to have a successful foreign policy.

(E) A president or prime minister with years of experience in foreign affairs will have a more successful foreign policy than one who does not have experience in foreign affairs.

12. Navigation in animals is defined as the animal's ability to find its way from unfamiliar territory to points familiar to the animal but beyond the immediate range of the animal's senses. Some naturalists claim that polar bears can navigate over considerable distances. As evidence, they cite an instance of a polar bear that returned to its home territory after being released over 500 kilometers (300 miles) away.

Which one of the following, if true, casts the most doubt on the validity of the evidence offered in support of the naturalists' claim?

(A) The polar bear stopped and changed course several times as it moved toward its home territory.

(B) The site at which the polar bear was released was on the bear's annual migration route.

(C) The route along which the polar bear traveled consisted primarily of snow and drifting ice.

(D) Polar bears are only one of many species of mammal whose members have been known to find their way home from considerable distances.

(E) Polar bears often rely on their extreme sensitivity to smell in order to scent out familiar territory.

GO ON TO THE NEXT PAGE.

Questions 13–14

City council member: Despite the city's desperate need to exploit any available source of revenue, the mayor has repeatedly blocked council members' attempts to pass legislation imposing real estate development fees. It is clear that in doing so the mayor is sacrificing the city's interests to personal interests. The mayor cites figures to show that, in the current market, fees of the size proposed would significantly reduce the number of building starts and thus, on balance, result in a revenue loss to the city. But the important point is that the mayor's family is heavily involved in real estate development and thus has a strong financial interest in the matter.

13. Which one of the following most accurately and completely expresses the main conclusion of the city council member's argument?

(A) Imposing real estate development fees is the best way for the city to exploit the available sources of revenue.

(B) The city would benefit financially from the passage of legislation imposing real estate development fees.

(C) In blocking council members' attempts to impose real estate development fees, the mayor is sacrificing the city's interests to personal interests.

(D) Significantly reducing the number of building starts would not, on balance, result in revenue loss to the city.

(E) The mayor's family has a strong financial interest in preventing the passage of legislation that would impose real estate development fees.

14. The reasoning in the city council member's argument is flawed because

(A) the issue of the mayor's personal interest in the proposed legislation is irrelevant to any assessment of the mayor's action with respect to that legislation

(B) the mayor's course of action being personally advantageous is not inconsistent with the mayor's action being advantageous for the city

(C) the council member's own absence of personal interest in the proposed legislation has not been established

(D) that a person or a municipality has a need for something does not, in itself, establish that that person or that municipality has a right to that thing

(E) the possibility remains open that the mayor's need to avoid loss of family revenue is as desperate as the city's need to increase municipal revenue

15. Seemingly inconsequential changes in sea temperature due to global warming eventually result in declines in fish and seabird populations. A rise of just two degrees prevents the vertical mixing of seawater from different strata. This restricts the availability of upwelling nutrients to phytoplankton. Since zooplankton, which feed upon phytoplankton, feed the rest of the food chain, the declines are inevitable.

Which one of the following most accurately describes the role played in the argument by the statement that zooplankton feed upon phytoplankton?

(A) It is a hypothesis supported by the fact that phytoplankton feed on upwelling nutrients.

(B) It is intended to provide an example of the ways in which the vertical mixing of seawater affects feeding habits.

(C) It helps show how global temperature changes affect larger sea animals indirectly.

(D) It is offered as one reason that global warming must be curtailed.

(E) It is offered in support of the idea that global warming poses a threat to all organisms.

GO ON TO THE NEXT PAGE.

16. Retailers that excel in neither convenience nor variety of merchandise tend not to be very successful. Yet many successful retailers excel in just one of the areas and meet competitors' standards for the other. Hence, a retailer's success need not depend on excellence in both areas.

The structure of the reasoning in the argument above is most parallel to that in which one of the following?

(A) Runners who have only average speed and endurance are unlikely to win long-distance races. Some long-distance champions, however, win by being above average in speed or endurance only; therefore, being above average in both speed and endurance is not necessary.

(B) Bicyclists who have only average speed are unlikely to win short races, but in a long-distance race such bicyclists can win if they have better-built bicycles than average and better endurance than average. Therefore, most bicycle races are not won by bicyclists with above-average speed.

(C) Excellence in a particular swimming stroke is not always necessary in order for a swimmer to win a race that requires each swimmer to use several different strokes in sequence, and many swimmers win these races without being the best at any of the strokes. Therefore, anyone who does excel at all the strokes is almost certain to win.

(D) Apples that are neither especially firm nor especially flavorful are unsuitable for baking; yet while flavor is essential for both baking and eating, many flavorful apples that are soft are suitable for eating. Hence, the apples that are best for eating need not be both firm and flavorful.

(E) Most plants that are neither ornamental nor edible are useless and are thus classified as weeds; yet many such plants are useful for purposes other than food or ornamentation, and are thus not classified as weeds. Hence, not all inedible and non-ornamental plants are weeds.

17. Detective: Because the embezzler must have had specialized knowledge and access to internal financial records, we can presume that the embezzler worked for XYZ Corporation as either an accountant or an actuary. But an accountant would probably not make the kind of mistakes in ledger entries that led to the discovery of the embezzlement. Thus it is likely that the embezzler is one of the actuaries.

Each of the following weakens the detective's argument EXCEPT:

(A) The actuaries' activities while working for XYZ Corporation were more closely scrutinized by supervisors than were the activities of the accountants.

(B) There is evidence of breaches in computer security at the time of the embezzlement that could have given persons outside of XYZ Corporation access to internal financial records.

(C) XYZ Corporation employs eight accountants, whereas it has only two actuaries on its staff.

(D) An independent report released before the crime took place concluded that XYZ Corporation was vulnerable to embezzlement.

(E) Certain security measures at XYZ Corporation made it more difficult for the actuaries to have access to internal financial records than for the accountants.

GO ON TO THE NEXT PAGE.

18. Until 1985 all commercial airlines completely replenished the cabin air in planes in flight once every 30 minutes. Since then the rate has been once every hour. The less frequently cabin air is replenished in a plane in flight, the higher the level of carbon dioxide in that plane and the easier it is for airborne illnesses to be spread.

Which one of the following is most strongly supported by the information above?

(A) In 1985 there was a loosening of regulations concerning cabin air in commercial airline flights.

(B) People who fly today are more likely to contract airborne illnesses than were people who flew prior to 1985.

(C) Low levels of carbon dioxide in cabin air make it impossible for airborne illnesses to spread.

(D) In 1980 the rate at which the cabin air was replenished in commercial airliners was sufficient to protect passengers from the effects of carbon dioxide buildup.

(E) In 1980 the level of carbon dioxide in the cabin air on a two-hour commercial airline flight was lower than it is today on a similar flight.

19. There is no genuinely altruistic behavior. Everyone needs to have a sufficient amount of self-esteem, which crucially depends on believing oneself to be useful and needed. Behavior that appears to be altruistic can be understood as being motivated by the desire to reinforce that belief, a clearly self-interested motivation.

A flaw in the argument is that it

(A) presupposes that anyone who is acting out of self-interest is being altruistic

(B) illicitly infers that behavior is altruistic merely because it seems altruistic

(C) fails to consider that self-esteem also depends on maintaining an awareness of one's own value

(D) presumes, without providing justification, that if one does not hold oneself in sufficient self-esteem one cannot be useful or needed

(E) takes for granted that any behavior that can be interpreted as self-interested is in fact self-interested

20. Current maps showing the North American regions where different types of garden plants will flourish are based on weather data gathered 60 years ago from a few hundred primitive weather stations. New maps are now being compiled using computerized data from several thousand modern weather stations and input from home gardeners across North America. These maps will be far more useful.

Each of the following, if true, helps to support the claim that the new maps will be more useful EXCEPT:

(A) Home gardeners can provide information on plant flourishing not available from weather stations.

(B) Some of the weather stations currently in use are more than 60 years old.

(C) Weather patterns can be described more accurately when more information is available.

(D) Weather conditions are the most important factor in determining where plants will grow.

(E) Weather patterns have changed in the past 60 years.

21. A smoker trying to quit is more likely to succeed if his or her doctor greatly exaggerates the dangers of smoking. Similar strategies can be used to break other habits. But since such strategies involve deception, individuals cannot easily adopt them unless a doctor or some other third party provides the warning.

Which one of the following is an assumption on which the argument depends?

(A) People tend to believe whatever doctors tell them.

(B) Most of the techniques that help people quit smoking can also help people break other habits.

(C) The more the relevant danger is exaggerated, the more likely one is to break one's habit.

(D) People generally do not find it easy to deceive themselves.

(E) A doctor is justified in deceiving a patient whenever doing so is likely to make the patient healthier.

GO ON TO THE NEXT PAGE.

22. Most people who shop for groceries no more than three times a month buy prepared frozen dinners regularly. In Hallstown most people shop for groceries no more than three times a month. Therefore, in Hallstown most people buy prepared frozen dinners regularly.

Which one of the following arguments has a flawed pattern of reasoning most like the flawed reasoning in the argument above?

(A) It is clear that most drivers in West Ansland are safe drivers since there are very few driving accidents in West Ansland and most accidents there are not serious.

(B) It is clear that John cannot drive, since he does not own a car and no one in his family who does not own a car can drive.

(C) It is clear that Fernando's friends usually drive to school, since all of his friends can drive and all of his friends go to school.

(D) It is clear that most people in Highland County drive sedans, since most people who commute to work drive sedans and most people in Highland County commute to work.

(E) It is clear that most of Janine's friends are good drivers, since she accepts rides only from good drivers and she accepts rides from most of her friends.

23. Editorial: This political party has repeatedly expressed the view that increasing spending on education is a worthy goal. On other occasions, however, the same party has claimed that the government should not increase spending on education. So this party's policy is clearly inconsistent.

The argument in the editorial depends on assuming which one of the following?

(A) It is inconsistent for a legislator both to claim that increasing spending on education is a worthy goal and to vote against increasing spending on education.

(B) A consistent course of action in educational policy is usually the course of action that will reduce spending on education in the long run.

(C) Even if a goal is a morally good one, one should not necessarily try to achieve it.

(D) A consistent political policy does not hold that an action that comprises a worthy goal should not be performed.

(E) Members of one political party never have inconsistent views on how to best approach a political issue.

24. Science journalist: Brown dwarfs are celestial objects with more mass than planets but less mass than stars. They are identified by their mass and whether or not lithium is present in their atmospheres. Stars at least as massive as the Sun have lithium remaining in their atmospheres because the mixing of elements in their internal nuclear furnaces is incomplete. Stars with less mass than the Sun have no lithium because the element has been fully mixed into their nuclear furnaces and consumed. A brown dwarf does not have a fully functional nuclear furnace and so its lithium cannot be consumed.

Which one of the following is most strongly supported by the science journalist's statements?

(A) Any celestial object without lithium in its atmosphere is a star with less mass than the Sun.

(B) Any celestial object with lithium in its atmosphere has a nuclear furnace that has incompletely mixed the object's elements.

(C) No celestial object that has no lithium in its atmosphere is a brown dwarf.

(D) No celestial object with lithium in its atmosphere has less mass than the Sun.

(E) No celestial object less massive than a brown dwarf has lithium in its atmosphere.

25. Native speakers perceive sentences of their own language as sequences of separate words. But this perception is an illusion. This is shown by the fact that travelers who do not know a local language hear an unintelligible, uninterrupted stream of sound, not sentences with distinct words.

Which one of the following is an assumption on which the argument depends?

(A) It is impossible to understand sentences if they are in fact uninterrupted streams of sound.

(B) Those who do not know a language cannot hear the way speech in that language actually sounds.

(C) People pay less close attention to the way their own language sounds than they do to the way an unfamiliar language sounds.

(D) Accomplished non-native speakers of a language do not perceive sentences as streams of sound.

(E) Native speakers' perceptions of their own language are not more accurate than are the perceptions of persons who do not know that language.

S T O P

IF YOU FINISH BEFORE TIME IS CALLED, YOU MAY CHECK YOUR WORK ON THIS SECTION ONLY.
DO NOT WORK ON ANY OTHER SECTION IN THE TEST.

SECTION II

Time—35 minutes

27 Questions

Directions: Each passage in this section is followed by a group of questions to be answered on the basis of what is stated or implied in the passage. For some of the questions, more than one of the choices could conceivably answer the question. However, you are to choose the best answer; that is, the response that most accurately and completely answers the question, and blacken the corresponding space on your answer sheet.

Is it necessary for defense lawyers to believe that the clients they defend are innocent of the charges against them? Some legal scholars hold that lawyers' sole obligation is to provide the best defense they are
(5) capable of, claiming that in democratic societies all people accused of crimes are entitled to the best possible legal representation. They argue that lawyers have no right to judge defendants because it is the job of the courts to determine guilt or innocence and the
(10) job of the lawyer to represent the defendant before the court. They believe that the lawyer's responsibility is to state those facts that will assist each client's case, construct sound arguments based on these facts, and identify flaws in the arguments of opposing counsel.
(15) According to these scholars, the lawyer's role is not to express or act on personal opinions but to act as an advocate, saying only what defendants would say if they possessed the proper training or resources with which to represent themselves.

(20) But such a position overlooks the fact that the defense lawyer's obligation is twofold: to the defendant, certainly, but no less so to the court and, by extension, to society. For this reason, lawyers, great as their obligation to defendants is, should not, as officers
(25) of the court, present to the court assertions that they know to be false. But by the same principle, lawyers who are convinced that their clients are guilty should not undertake to demonstrate their innocence. Guilty defendants should not be entitled to false or insincere
(30) representation. When lawyers know with certainty that a defendant is guilty, it is their duty not to deny this. Rather, they should appraise the case as much as possible in their client's favor, after giving due consideration to the facts on the other side, and then
(35) present any extenuating circumstances and argue for whatever degree of leniency in sentencing they sincerely believe is warranted. In cases where it is uncertain whether the client is guilty but the lawyer sincerely believes the client may well be innocent, the
(40) lawyer should of course try to prove that the client is innocent.

The lawyer's obligation to the court and to society also ultimately benefits the defendant, because the "best defense" can only truly be provided by an
(45) advocate who, after a careful analysis of the facts, is convinced of the merits of the case. The fact that every client is entitled to a defense does not mean that defense lawyers should take every case they are offered. Lawyers should not be mere mouthpieces for a
(50) defendant but instead advocates for the rights of the defendant given the facts of the case.

1. Which one of the following most accurately expresses the main idea of the passage?

(A) Some legal scholars defend a morally questionable view that defense lawyers' sole obligation to their clients is to provide the best defense, while it is the court's job to determine guilt or innocence.

(B) Defense lawyers should put aside personal judgments about their clients' guilt when determining how best to proceed when representing a client.

(C) In a democracy, all persons accused of crimes have a right to an attorney who will state the facts, construct sound arguments, and identify flaws in the arguments of opposing counsel.

(D) Lawyers should be mindful of their duty to society as well as to their clients and base the decision as to whether, and how, to defend a client on the facts of the case.

(E) Defense attorneys are obligated to defend clients who request their professional services, especially when the attorney is absolutely convinced of the client's innocence.

2. Which one of the following most accurately describes the author's attitude toward the twofold obligation introduced in lines 20–23?

(A) confident that it enables defense lawyers to balance their competing responsibilities to the court and to society

(B) certain that it prevents defense lawyers from representing clients whom they know to be guilty

(C) satisfied that it helps defense lawyers to uncover the relevant facts of a case

(D) pleased that it does not interfere with common defense strategies used by defense lawyers

(E) convinced that it does not represent a conflict of interest for defense lawyers

GO ON TO THE NEXT PAGE.

3. Which one of the following sentences would most logically begin a paragraph immediately following the end of the passage?

    (A) In keeping with this role, defense lawyers should base their cases upon the foundations of honesty, substantive accuracy, and selectivity.

    (B) Therefore, the practice of law remains morally dubious, in that misrepresentation may achieve acquittal for an attorney's client.

    (C) Consequently, the defendant's right to legal representation varies from case to case, depending on the severity of the alleged crime and the defense lawyer's personal interpretation of the case.

    (D) Thus, the lawyers' obligations are threefold—to be faithful to the dictates of the court, society, and themselves by proving their professional worth in securing acquittal for the clients whom they represent.

    (E) Therefore, judges or other officials of the court should interrogate defense attorneys regarding any prior knowledge they may have of their clients' innocence or guilt.

4. According to the passage, the legal scholars mentioned in lines 15–19 believe that it is a defense lawyer's role to be

    (A) a source of legal information that can help a jury to reach decisions that are fair and equitable

    (B) a thorough investigator of all relevant evidence

    (C) a diligent representative of the client's position

    (D) a facilitator and expediter of the cause of justice

    (E) an energetic advocate of the client's right to legal representation

5. The relationship of the information contained in the two sentences at lines 28–31 to that in the sentence at lines 7–11 can most accurately be described as

    (A) no significant relationship because they represent two unrelated factual statements

    (B) the author's opinion opposing another opinion reported by the author in the earlier lines

    (C) a hypothetical situation supporting a statement reported by the author in the earlier lines

    (D) agreement in general with the earlier position but disagreement over the particulars

    (E) essentially equivalent assertions arising from different perspectives

6. It can be inferred from the passage that the author holds that a defense attorney who argues in court that a client is innocent

    (A) should sincerely believe that the client may be innocent

    (B) would be right to do so even if the attorney knows that the client is actually guilty

    (C) is assuming the role of mouthpiece for the client

    (D) has favored the obligation to the client over that to society

    (E) has typically not researched the facts of the case thoroughly

7. The primary purpose of the passage is to

    (A) show that ethical dilemmas in the legal profession can complicate the defense lawyer's role

    (B) argue that the defense lawyer's duty to the court and society complements effective legal representation for the client

    (C) explain why the actual guilt or innocence of a defendant is not an important issue to many defense attorneys

    (D) discuss some of the issues that a defense lawyer must resolve prior to accepting a case

    (E) reveal how the practice of law strengthens the values and principles of democratic societies

GO ON TO THE NEXT PAGE.

Many educators in Canada and the United States advocate multicultural education as a means of achieving multicultural understanding. There are, however, a variety of proposals as to what multicultural
(5) education should consist of. The most modest of these proposals holds that schools and colleges should promote multicultural understanding by teaching about other cultures, teaching which proceeds from within the context of the majority culture. Students should
(10) learn about other cultures, proponents claim, but examination of these cultures should operate with the methods, perspectives, and values of the majority culture. These values are typically those of liberalism: democracy, tolerance, and equality of persons.

(15) Critics of this first proposal have argued that genuine understanding of other cultures is impossible if the study of other cultures is refracted through the distorting lens of the majority culture's perspective. Not all cultures share liberal values. Their value
(20) systems have arisen in often radically different social and historical circumstances, and thus, these critics argue, cannot be understood and adequately appreciated if one insists on approaching them solely from within the majority culture's perspective.

(25) In response to this objection, a second version of multicultural education has developed that differs from the first in holding that multicultural education ought to adopt a neutral stance with respect to the value differences among cultures. The values of one culture
(30) should not be standards by which others are judged; each culture should be taken on its own terms. However, the methods of examination, study, and explanation of cultures in this second version of multicultural education are still identifiably Western.
(35) They are the methods of anthropology, social psychology, political science, and sociology. They are, that is, methods which derive from the Western scientific perspective and heritage.

Critics of this second form of multicultural
(40) education argue as follows: The Western scientific heritage is founded upon an epistemological system that prizes the objective over the subjective, the logical over the intuitive, and the empirically verifiable over the mystical. The methods of social-scientific
(45) examination of cultures are thus already value laden; the choice to examine and understand other cultures by these methods involves a commitment to certain values such as objectivity. Thus, the second version of multicultural education is not essentially different from
(50) the first. Scientific discourse has a privileged place in Western cultures, but the discourses of myth, tradition, religion, and mystical insight are often the dominant forms of thought and language of non-Western cultures. To insist on trying to understand nonscientific
(55) cultures by the methods of Western science is not only distorting, but is also an expression of an attempt to maintain a Eurocentric cultural chauvinism: the chauvinism of science. According to this objection, it is only by adopting the (often nonscientific) perspectives
(60) and methods of the cultures studied that real understanding can be achieved.

8. Which one of the following most accurately states the main point of the passage?

(A) Proponents of two proposals for promoting multicultural understanding disagree about both the goal of multicultural education and the means for achieving this goal.

(B) Proponents of two proposals for promoting multicultural understanding claim that education should be founded upon an epistemological system that recognizes the importance of the subjective, the intuitive, and the mystical.

(C) Proponents of two proposals for promoting multicultural understanding claim that it is not enough to refrain from judging non-Western cultures if the methods used to study these cultures are themselves Western.

(D) Critics of two proposals for promoting multicultural understanding disagree about the extent to which a culture's values are a product of its social and historical circumstances.

(E) Critics of two proposals for promoting multicultural understanding claim these proposals are not value neutral and are therefore unable to yield a genuine understanding of cultures with a different value system.

9. Critics who raise the objection discussed in the second paragraph would be most likely to agree with which one of the following?

(A) The social and historical circumstances that give rise to a culture's values cannot be understood by members of a culture with different values.

(B) The historical and social circumstances of a culture can play an important role in the development of that culture's values.

(C) It is impossible for one culture to successfully study another culture unless it does so from more than one cultural perspective.

(D) Genuine understanding of another culture is impossible unless that culture shares the same cultural values.

(E) The values of liberalism cannot be adequately understood if we approach them solely through the methods of Western science.

GO ON TO THE NEXT PAGE.

10. Which one of the following most accurately describes the organization of the passage as a whole?

(A) Difficulties in achieving a goal are contrasted with the benefits of obtaining that goal.

(B) A goal is argued to be unrealizable by raising objections to the means proposed to achieve it.

(C) Two means for achieving a goal are presented along with an objection to each.

(D) Difficulties in achieving a goal are used to defend several radical revisions to that goal.

(E) The desirability of a goal is used to defend against a number of objections to its feasibility.

11. The version of multicultural education discussed in the first paragraph is described as "modest" (line 5) most likely because it

(A) relies on the least amount of speculation about non-Western cultures

(B) calls for the least amount of change in the educational system

(C) involves the least amount of Eurocentric cultural chauvinism

(D) is the least distorting since it employs several cultural perspectives

(E) deviates least from a neutral stance with respect to differences in values

12. Given the information in the passage, which one of the following would most likely be considered objectionable by proponents of the version of multicultural education discussed in the third paragraph?

(A) a study of the differences between the moral codes of several Western and non-Western societies

(B) a study of a given culture's literature to determine the kinds of personal characteristics the culture admires

(C) a study that employs the methods of Western science to investigate a nonscientific culture

(D) a study that uses the literary theories of one society to criticize the literature of a society that has different values

(E) a study that uses the methods of anthropology and sociology to criticize the values of Western culture

13. Which one of the following, if true, would provide the strongest objection to the criticism in the passage of the second version of multicultural education?

(A) It is impossible to adopt the perspectives and methods of a culture unless one is a member of that culture.

(B) Many non-Western societies have value systems that are very similar to one another.

(C) Some non-Western societies use their own value system when studying cultures that have different values.

(D) Students in Western societies cannot understand their culture's achievements unless such achievements are treated as the subject of Western scientific investigations.

(E) Genuine understanding of another culture is necessary for adequately appreciating that culture.

GO ON TO THE NEXT PAGE.

In studying the autobiographies of Native Americans, most scholars have focused on as-told-to life histories that were solicited, translated, recorded, and edited by non-Native American collaborators—that
(5) emerged from "bicultural composite authorship." Limiting their studies to such written documents, these scholars have overlooked traditional, preliterate modes of communicating personal history. In addition, they have failed to address the cultural constructs of the
(10) highly diverse Native American peoples, who prior to contact with nonindigenous cultures did not share with Europeans the same assumptions about self, life, and writing that underlie the concept of an autobiography— that indeed constitute the English word's root meaning.

(15) The idea of self was, in a number of pre-contact Native American cultures, markedly inclusive: identity was not merely individual, but also relational to a society, a specific landscape, and the cosmos. Within these cultures, the expression of life experiences tended
(20) to be oriented toward current events: with the participation of fellow tribal members, an individual person would articulate, reenact, or record important experiences as the person lived them, a mode of autobiography seemingly more fragmented than the
(25) European custom of writing down the recollections of a lifetime. Moreover, expression itself was not a matter of writing but of language, which can include speech and signs. Oral autobiography comprised songs, chants, stories, and even the process whereby one repeatedly
(30) took on new names to reflect important events and deeds in one's life. Dance and drama could convey personal history; for example, the advent of a vision to one person might require the enactment of that vision in the form of a tribal pageant.

(35) One can view as autobiographical the elaborate tattoos that symbolized a warrior's valorous deeds, and such artifacts as a decorated shield that communicated the accomplishments and aspirations of its maker, or a robe that was emblazoned with the pictographic history
(40) of the wearer's battles and was sometimes used in reenactments. Also autobiographical, and indicative of high status within the tribe, would have been a tepee painted with symbolic designs to record the achievements and display the dreams or visions of its
(45) owner, who was often assisted in the painting by other tribal members.

A tribe would, then, have contributed to the individual's narrative not merely passively, by its social codes and expectations, but actively by joining
(50) in the expression of that narrative. Such intracultural collaboration may seem alien to the European style of autobiography, yet any autobiography is shaped by its creator's ideas about the audience for which it is intended; in this sense, autobiography is justly called a
(55) simultaneous individual story and cultural narrative. Autobiographical expressions by early Native Americans may additionally have been shaped by the cultural perspectives of the people who transmitted them.

14. Which one of the following most accurately expresses the main conclusion of the passage?

(A) Scholars have tended to overlook the nuances of concepts about identity that existed in some of the early Native American cultures.

(B) As demonstrated by early Native Americans, autobiography can exist in a variety of media other than written documents.

(C) The Native American life histories collected and recorded by non-Native American writers differ from European-style autobiographies in their depictions of an individual's relation to society.

(D) Early Native Americans created autobiographies with forms and underlying assumptions that frequently differ from those of European-style autobiographies.

(E) The autobiographical forms traditionally used by Native Americans are more fragmented than European forms and thus less easily recognizable as personal history.

15. Which one of the following phrases best conveys the author's attitude toward the earlier scholarship on Native American autobiographies that is mentioned in the passage?

(A) "failed to address" (line 9)
(B) "highly diverse" (line 10)
(C) "markedly inclusive" (line 16)
(D) "seemingly more fragmented" (line 24)
(E) "alien to the European style" (line 51)

GO ON TO THE NEXT PAGE.

16. Which one of the following most accurately conveys the meaning of the phrase "bicultural composite authorship" as it is used in line 5 of the passage?

    (A) written by a member of one culture but based on the artifacts and oral traditions of another culture

    (B) written by two people, each of whom belongs to a different culture but contributes in the same way to the finished product

    (C) compiled from the writings of people who come from different cultures and whose identities cannot be determined

    (D) written originally by a member of one culture but edited and revised by a member of another culture

    (E) written by a member of one culture but based on oral communication by a member of another culture

17. Which one of the following most accurately describes the function of the third paragraph within the passage as a whole?

    (A) to refute traditional interpretations of certain artifacts

    (B) to present evidence that undermines a theory

    (C) to provide examples that support an argument

    (D) to contrast several different modes of expression

    (E) to enumerate specific instances in which a phenomenon recurred

18. The author of the passage refers to "self, life, and writing" (lines 12–13) most probably in order to

    (A) identify concepts about which Europeans and Native Americans had contrasting ideas

    (B) define a word that had a different meaning for early Native Americans than it has for contemporary Native Americans

    (C) illustrate how words can undergo a change in meaning after their introduction into the language

    (D) posit a fundamental similarity in the origins of a concept in both European and Native American cultures

    (E) explain how the assumptions that underlie European-style autobiography arose

19. Which one of the following would be most consistent with the ideas about identity that the author attributes to pre-contact Native American cultures?

    (A) A person who is born into one tribe but is brought up by members of another tribe retains a name given at birth.

    (B) A pictograph that represents a specific person incorporates the symbol for a constellation.

    (C) A similar ritual for assuming a new name is used in diverse communities.

    (D) A name given to one member of a community cannot be given to another member of the same community.

    (E) A decorated shield that belonged to an individual cannot be traced to a particular tribe.

GO ON TO THE NEXT PAGE.

Most scientists who study the physiological effects of alcoholic beverages have assumed that wine, like beer or distilled spirits, is a drink whose only active ingredient is alcohol. Because of this assumption, these
(5) scientists have rarely investigated the effects of wine as distinct from other forms of alcoholic beverages. Nevertheless, unlike other alcoholic beverages, wine has for centuries been thought to have healthful effects that these scientists—who not only make no distinction
(10) among wine, beer, and distilled spirits but also study only the excessive or abusive intake of these beverages—have obscured.

Recently, a small group of researchers has questioned this assumption and investigated the effects
(15) of moderate wine consumption. While alcohol has been shown conclusively to have negative physiological effects—for example, alcohol strongly affects the body's processing of lipids (fats and other substances including cholesterol), causing dangerous increases in
(20) the levels of these substances in the blood, increases that are a large contributing factor in the development of premature heart disease—the researchers found that absorption of alcohol into the bloodstream occurs much more slowly when subjects drink wine than when they
(25) drink distilled spirits. More remarkably, it was discovered that deaths due to premature heart disease in the populations of several European countries decreased dramatically as the incidence of moderate wine consumption increased. One preliminary study
(30) linked this effect to red wine, but subsequent research has shown identical results whether the wine was white or red. What could explain such apparently healthful effects?

For one thing, the studies show increased activity
(35) of a natural clot-breaking compound used by doctors to restore blood flow through blocked vessels in victims of heart disease. In addition, the studies of wine drinkers indicate increased levels of certain compounds that may help to prevent damage from high lipid levels.
(40) And although the link between lipid processing and premature heart disease is one of the most important discoveries in modern medicine, in the past 20 years researchers have found several additional important contributing factors. We now know that endothelial
(45) cell reactivity (which affects the thickness of the innermost walls of blood vessels) and platelet adhesiveness (which influences the degree to which platelets cause blood to clot) are each linked to the development of premature heart disease. Studies show
(50) that wine appears to have ameliorating effects on both of these factors: it decreases the thickness of the innermost walls of blood vessels, and it reduces platelet adhesiveness. One study demonstrated a decrease in platelet adhesiveness among individuals who drank
(55) large amounts of grape juice. This finding may be the first step in confirming speculation that the potentially healthful effects of moderate wine intake may derive from the concentration of certain natural compounds found in grapes and not present in other alcoholic
(60) beverages.

20. Which one of the following most accurately states the author's main point in the passage?

(A) Because of their assumption that alcohol is the only active ingredient in wine, beer, and distilled spirits, scientists have previously studied these beverages in ways that obscure their healthful effects.

(B) A new study of moderate wine consumption calls into question the belief that premature heart disease is caused solely by the presence of high lipid levels in the bloodstream.

(C) Researchers have found that alcohol from moderate wine consumption is absorbed into the bloodstream more slowly than is alcohol from other alcoholic beverages.

(D) Although it has long been held that moderate wine consumption has healthful effects, scientific studies have yet to prove such effects definitively.

(E) Wine, unlike other alcoholic beverages, appears to have a number of significant healthful effects that may be tied to certain natural compounds found in grapes.

21. In the first paragraph, the author most likely refers to the centuries-old belief that wine has healthful effects in order to

(A) demonstrate that discoveries in the realm of science often bear out popular beliefs

(B) provide evidence for the theory that moderate wine consumption ameliorates factors that contribute to premature heart disease

(C) argue that traditional beliefs are no less important than scientific evidence when investigating health matters

(D) suggest that a prevailing scientific assumption might be mistaken

(E) refute the argument that science should take cues from popular beliefs

GO ON TO THE NEXT PAGE.

22. According to the passage, each of the following might help to prevent premature heart disease EXCEPT:

   (A)   an increase in the degree to which platelets cause blood to clot

   (B)   an increase in the body's ability to remove lipids from the bloodstream

   (C)   an increase in the amount of time it takes alcohol to be absorbed into the bloodstream

   (D)   increased activity of a natural compound that reduces blood clotting

   (E)   increased levels of compounds that prevent damage from high lipid levels

23. Which one of the following, if true, would most strengthen the passage's position concerning the apparently healthful effects of moderate wine consumption?

   (A)   Subjects who consumed large amounts of grape juice exhibited decreased thickness of the innermost walls of their blood vessels.

   (B)   Subjects who were habitual drinkers of wine and subjects who were habitual drinkers of beer exhibited similar lipid levels in their bloodstreams.

   (C)   Subjects who drank grape juice exhibited greater platelet adhesiveness than did subjects who drank no grape juice.

   (D)   Subjects who drank excessive amounts of wine suffered from premature heart disease at roughly the same rate as moderate wine drinkers.

   (E)   Subjects who possess a natural clot-breaking compound were discovered to have a certain gene that is absent from subjects who do not possess the compound.

24. It can be inferred from the passage that the author would most likely agree with which one of the following statements?

   (A)   Scientists should not attempt to study the possible healthful effects of moderate consumption of beer and distilled spirits.

   (B)   The conclusion that alcohol affects lipid processing should be questioned in light of studies of moderate wine consumption.

   (C)   Moderate consumption of wine made from plums or apples rather than grapes would be unlikely to reduce the risk of premature heart disease.

   (D)   Red wine consumption has a greater effect on reducing death rates from premature heart disease than does white wine consumption.

   (E)   Beer and distilled spirits contain active ingredients other than alcohol whose effects tend to be beneficial.

25. Based on the passage, the author's attitude toward the scientists discussed in the first paragraph can most accurately be described as

   (A)   highly enthusiastic

   (B)   tacitly approving

   (C)   grudgingly accepting

   (D)   overtly critical

   (E)   clearly outraged

26. In the passage, the author is primarily concerned with doing which one of the following?

   (A)   advocating a particular method of treatment

   (B)   criticizing popular opinion

   (C)   correcting a scientific misconception

   (D)   questioning the relevance of newly discovered evidence

   (E)   countering a revolutionary hypothesis

27. The author suggests each of the following in the passage EXCEPT:

   (A)   Greater platelet adhesiveness increases the risk of premature heart disease.

   (B)   The body's ability to process lipids is compromised by the presence of alcohol in the bloodstream.

   (C)   Doctors have access to a natural compound that breaks down blood clots.

   (D)   High lipid levels are dangerous because they lead to increased endothelial cell reactivity and platelet adhesiveness.

   (E)   Moderate wine consumption appears to decrease the thickness of the interior walls of blood vessels.

S T O P

IF YOU FINISH BEFORE TIME IS CALLED, YOU MAY CHECK YOUR WORK ON THIS SECTION ONLY.
DO NOT WORK ON ANY OTHER SECTION IN THE TEST.

SECTION III

Time—35 minutes

24 Questions

Directions: Each group of questions in this section is based on a set of conditions. In answering some of the questions, it may be useful to draw a rough diagram. Choose the response that most accurately and completely answers each question and blacken the corresponding space on your answer sheet.

Questions 1–6

Of the eight students—George, Helen, Irving, Kyle, Lenore, Nina, Olivia, and Robert—in a seminar, exactly six will give individual oral reports during three consecutive days—Monday, Tuesday, and Wednesday. Exactly two reports will be given each day—one in the morning and one in the afternoon—according to the following conditions:

Tuesday is the only day on which George can give a report.

Neither Olivia nor Robert can give an afternoon report.

If Nina gives a report, then on the next day Helen and Irving must both give reports, unless Nina's report is given on Wednesday.

1. Which one of the following could be the schedule of students' reports?

   (A) Mon. morning: Helen; Mon. afternoon: Robert
       Tues. morning: Olivia; Tues. afternoon: Irving
       Wed. morning: Lenore; Wed. afternoon: Kyle
   (B) Mon. morning: Irving; Mon. afternoon: Olivia
       Tues. morning: Helen; Tues. afternoon: Kyle
       Wed. morning: Nina; Wed. afternoon: Lenore
   (C) Mon. morning: Lenore; Mon. afternoon: Helen
       Tues. morning: George; Tues. afternoon: Kyle
       Wed. morning: Robert; Wed. afternoon: Irving
   (D) Mon. morning: Nina; Mon. afternoon: Helen
       Tues. morning: Robert; Tues. afternoon: Irving
       Wed. morning: Olivia; Wed. afternoon: Lenore
   (E) Mon. morning: Olivia; Mon. afternoon: Nina
       Tues. morning: Irving; Tues. afternoon: Helen
       Wed. morning: Kyle; Wed. afternoon: George

2. If Kyle and Lenore do not give reports, then the morning reports on Monday, Tuesday, and Wednesday, respectively, could be given by

   (A) Helen, George, and Nina
   (B) Irving, Robert, and Helen
   (C) Nina, Helen, and Olivia
   (D) Olivia, Robert, and Irving
   (E) Robert, George, and Helen

3. Which one of the following is a pair of students who, if they give reports on the same day as each other, must give reports on Wednesday?

   (A) George and Lenore
   (B) Helen and Nina
   (C) Irving and Robert
   (D) Kyle and Nina
   (E) Olivia and Kyle

4. If George, Nina, and Robert give reports and they do so on different days from one another, which one of the following could be true?

   (A) Helen gives a report on Wednesday.
   (B) Nina gives a report on Monday.
   (C) Nina gives a report on Tuesday.
   (D) Olivia gives a report on Monday.
   (E) Robert gives a report on Wednesday.

5. If Kyle gives the afternoon report on Tuesday, and Helen gives the afternoon report on Wednesday, which one of the following could be the list of the students who give the morning reports on Monday, Tuesday, and Wednesday, respectively?

   (A) Irving, Lenore, and Nina
   (B) Lenore, George, and Irving
   (C) Nina, Irving, and Lenore
   (D) Robert, George, and Irving
   (E) Robert, Irving, and Lenore

6. If Helen, Kyle, and Lenore, not necessarily in that order, give the three morning reports, which one of the following must be true?

   (A) Helen gives a report on Monday.
   (B) Irving gives a report on Monday.
   (C) Irving gives a report on Wednesday.
   (D) Kyle gives a report on Tuesday.
   (E) Kyle gives a report on Wednesday.

GO ON TO THE NEXT PAGE.

Questions 7–11

The organizer of a reading club will select at least five and at most six works from a group of nine works. The group consists of three French novels, three Russian novels, two French plays, and one Russian play. The organizer's selection of works must conform to the following requirements:

No more than four French works are selected.

At least three but no more than four novels are selected.

At least as many French novels as Russian novels are selected.

If both French plays are selected, then the Russian play is not selected.

7. Which one of the following could be the organizer's selection of works?

(A) one French novel, two Russian novels, one French play, one Russian play
(B) two French novels, one Russian novel, two French plays, one Russian play
(C) two French novels, two Russian novels, two French plays
(D) three French novels, one Russian novel, two French plays
(E) three French novels, two Russian novels, one Russian play

8. Which one of the following could be true about the organizer's selection of works?

(A) No Russian novels are selected.
(B) Exactly one French novel is selected.
(C) All three plays are selected.
(D) All three Russian novels are selected.
(E) All five French works are selected.

9. If the works selected include three French novels, which one of the following could be a complete and accurate list of the remaining works selected?

(A) one Russian novel
(B) two French plays
(C) one Russian novel, one Russian play
(D) one Russian novel, two French plays
(E) two Russian novels, one French play

10. The organizer must at least select

(A) one French novel and one French play
(B) one French novel and one Russian play
(C) one Russian novel and one French play
(D) two French novels
(E) two Russian novels

11. Any one of the following could be true about the organizer's selection of works EXCEPT:

(A) No Russian novels and exactly one play are selected.
(B) Exactly one Russian novel and both French plays are selected.
(C) Exactly two French novels and the Russian play are selected.
(D) Exactly two French novels and exactly two plays are selected.
(E) Exactly two Russian novels and exactly one play are selected.

GO ON TO THE NEXT PAGE.

3

Questions 12–18

At a concert, exactly eight compositions—F, H, L, O, P, R, S, and T—are to be performed exactly once each, consecutively and one composition at a time. The order of their performance must satisfy the following conditions:

T is performed either immediately before F or immediately after R.

At least two compositions are performed either after F and before R, or after R and before F.

O is performed either first or fifth.

The eighth composition performed is either L or H.

P is performed at some time before S.

At least one composition is performed either after O and before S, or after S and before O.

12. Which one of the following lists the compositions in an order in which they could be performed during the concert, from first through eighth?

 (A) L, P, S, R, O, T, F, H
 (B) O, T, P, F, S, H, R, L
 (C) P, T, F, S, L, R, O, H
 (D) P, T, F, S, O, R, L, H
 (E) T, F, P, R, O, L, S, H

13. P CANNOT be performed

 (A) second
 (B) third
 (C) fourth
 (D) sixth
 (E) seventh

14. If T is performed fifth and F is performed sixth, then S must be performed either

 (A) fourth or seventh
 (B) third or sixth
 (C) third or fourth
 (D) second or seventh
 (E) first or fourth

15. If O is performed immediately after T, then F must be performed either

 (A) first or second
 (B) second or third
 (C) fourth or sixth
 (D) fourth or seventh
 (E) sixth or seventh

16. If S is performed fourth, which one of the following could be an accurate list of the compositions performed first, second, and third, respectively?

 (A) F, H, P
 (B) H, P, L
 (C) O, P, R
 (D) O, P, T
 (E) P, R, T

17. If P is performed third and S is performed sixth, the composition performed fifth must be either

 (A) F or H
 (B) F or O
 (C) F or T
 (D) H or L
 (E) O or R

18. If exactly two compositions are performed after F but before O, then R must be performed

 (A) first
 (B) third
 (C) fourth
 (D) sixth
 (E) seventh

GO ON TO THE NEXT PAGE.

Questions 19–24

On each of exactly seven consecutive days (day 1 through day 7), a pet shop features exactly one of three breeds of kitten—Himalayan, Manx, Siamese—and exactly one of three breeds of puppy—Greyhound, Newfoundland, Rottweiler. The following conditions must apply:

Greyhounds are featured on day 1.
No breed is featured on any two consecutive days.
Any breed featured on day 1 is not featured on day 7.
Himalayans are featured on exactly three days, but not on day 1.
Rottweilers are not featured on day 7, nor on any day that features Himalayans.

19. Which one of the following could be the order in which the breeds of kitten are featured in the pet shop, from day 1 through day 7 ?

   (A)   Himalayan, Manx, Siamese, Himalayan, Manx, Himalayan, Siamese
   (B)   Manx, Himalayan, Siamese, Himalayan, Manx, Himalayan, Manx
   (C)   Manx, Himalayan, Manx, Himalayan, Siamese, Manx, Siamese
   (D)   Siamese, Himalayan, Manx, Himalayan, Siamese, Siamese, Himalayan
   (E)   Siamese, Himalayan, Siamese, Himalayan, Manx, Siamese, Himalayan

20. If Himalayans are not featured on day 2, which one of the following could be true?

   (A)   Manx are featured on day 3.
   (B)   Siamese are featured on day 4.
   (C)   Rottweilers are featured on day 5.
   (D)   Himalayans are featured on day 6.
   (E)   Greyhounds are featured on day 7.

21. Which one of the following could be true?

   (A)   Greyhounds and Siamese are both featured on day 2.
   (B)   Greyhounds and Himalayans are both featured on day 7.
   (C)   Rottweilers and Himalayans are both featured on day 4.
   (D)   Rottweilers and Manx are both featured on day 5.
   (E)   Newfoundlands and Manx are both featured on day 6.

22. If Himalayans are not featured on day 7, then which one of the following pairs of days CANNOT feature both the same breed of kitten and the same breed of puppy?

   (A)   day 1 and day 3
   (B)   day 2 and day 6
   (C)   day 3 and day 5
   (D)   day 4 and day 6
   (E)   day 5 and day 7

23. Which one of the following could be true?

   (A)   There are exactly four breeds that are each featured on three days.
   (B)   Greyhounds are featured on every day that Himalayans are.
   (C)   Himalayans are featured on every day that Greyhounds are.
   (D)   Himalayans are featured on every day that Rottweilers are not.
   (E)   Rottweilers are featured on every day that Himalayans are not.

24. If Himalayans are not featured on day 7, which one of the following could be true?

   (A)   Greyhounds are featured on days 3 and 5.
   (B)   Newfoundlands are featured on day 3.
   (C)   Rottweilers are featured on day 6.
   (D)   Rottweilers are featured only on day 3.
   (E)   Rottweilers are featured on exactly three days.

S T O P

IF YOU FINISH BEFORE TIME IS CALLED, YOU MAY CHECK YOUR WORK ON THIS SECTION ONLY.
DO NOT WORK ON ANY OTHER SECTION IN THE TEST.

SECTION IV

Time—35 minutes

25 Questions

<u>Directions:</u> The questions in this section are based on the reasoning contained in brief statements or passages. For some questions, more than one of the choices could conceivably answer the question. However, you are to choose the <u>best</u> answer; that is, the response that most accurately and completely answers the question. You should not make assumptions that are by commonsense standards implausible, superfluous, or incompatible with the passage. After you have chosen the best answer, blacken the corresponding space on your answer sheet.

1. Yuriko: Our city's campaign to persuade parents to have their children vaccinated ought to be imitated by your city. In the 16 months since the enactment of legislation authorizing the campaign, vaccinations in our city have increased by 30 percent.

    Susan: But the major part of that increase occurred in the first 6 months after that legislation was enacted, right after your city's free neighborhood health clinics opened, and before the vaccination campaign really got going.

    In responding to Yuriko, Susan does which one of the following?

    (A)   She denies Yuriko's assumption that Susan's city wants to increase the vaccination rate for children.

    (B)   She cites facts that tend to weaken the force of the evidence with which Yuriko supports her recommendation.

    (C)   She introduces evidence to show that the campaign Yuriko advocates is only effective for a short period of time.

    (D)   She advances the claim that a campaign such as Yuriko recommends is not necessary because most parents already choose to have their children vaccinated.

    (E)   She presents evidence to suggest that vaccination campaigns are usually ineffective.

2. The process by which nylon is manufactured releases large amounts of the gas nitrous oxide, which is harmful to the environment. Since the processing of cotton fiber does not release environmentally harmful gases, there would be less environmental damage done if cotton fiber rather than nylon were used to make products such as thread and rope.

    Which one of the following, if true, would weaken the argument?

    (A)   Even if the quantity of nitrous oxide released into the environment decreased, many environmental problems would remain unsolved.

    (B)   Even if only some of the thread and rope that is currently being made from nylon were instead made from cotton fiber, some environmental damage would be avoided.

    (C)   If cotton fiber replaced nylon in the production of thread and rope, there would be a resulting increase in the amount of nylon used in other manufactured products.

    (D)   If the quantity of nylon manufactured annually decreased substantially, the volume of several pollutants that are released into the environment during its manufacture would be reduced.

    (E)   If thread and rope continue to be made from nylon, the production of cotton fiber will not increase as rapidly as it would if all thread and rope were to be made from cotton fiber.

GO ON TO THE NEXT PAGE.

3. John: It was wrong of you to blame me for that traffic accident. You know full well that the accident was due to my poor vision, and I certainly cannot be held responsible for the fact that my vision has deteriorated.

   Michiko: But I can hold you responsible for your hazardous driving, because you know how poor your vision is. People are responsible for the consequences of actions that they voluntarily undertake, if they know that those actions risk such consequences.

   The principle that Michiko invokes, if established, would justify which one of the following judgments?

   (A)   Colleen was responsible for missing her flight home from Paris, because she decided to take one more trip to the Eiffel Tower even though she knew she might not have sufficient time to get to the airport if she did so.
   (B)   Colleen was responsible for having offended her brother when she reported to him an offensive comment made about his colleague, although she did not know her brother would mistakenly understand the comment to be about himself.
   (C)   Colleen was responsible for her automobile's having been stolen two weeks ago, because she did not take any of the precautions that the town police recommended in the antitheft manual they published last week.
   (D)   Colleen was responsible for her cat's being frightened, because, even though it was her brother who allowed the door to slam shut, she knew that cats are often frightened by loud noises.
   (E)   Colleen was not responsible for losing her job, because, knowing that her position was in danger of being eliminated, she did everything possible to preserve it.

4. Psychiatrist: Take any visceral emotion you care to consider. There are always situations in which it is healthy to try to express that emotion. So, there are always situations in which it is healthy to try to express one's anger.

   The conclusion of the argument follows logically if which one of the following is assumed?

   (A)   Anger is always expressible.
   (B)   Anger is a visceral emotion.
   (C)   Some kinds of emotions are unhealthy to express.
   (D)   All emotions that are healthy to express are visceral.
   (E)   An emotion is visceral only if it is healthy to express.

5. Cigarette companies claim that manufacturing both low- and high-nicotine cigarettes allows smokers to choose how much nicotine they want. However, a recent study has shown that the levels of nicotine found in the blood of smokers who smoke one pack of cigarettes per day are identical at the end of a day's worth of smoking, whatever the level of nicotine in the cigarettes they smoke.

   Which one of the following, if true, most helps to explain the finding of the nicotine study?

   (A)   Blood cannot absorb more nicotine per day than that found in the smoke from a package of the lowest-nicotine cigarettes available.
   (B)   Smokers of the lowest-nicotine cigarettes available generally smoke more cigarettes per day than smokers of high-nicotine cigarettes.
   (C)   Most nicotine is absorbed into the blood of a smoker even if it is delivered in smaller quantities.
   (D)   The level of tar in cigarettes is higher in low-nicotine cigarettes than it is in some high-nicotine cigarettes.
   (E)   When taking in nicotine by smoking cigarettes is discontinued, the level of nicotine in the blood decreases steadily.

6. Editorial: The premier's economic advisor assures her that with the elimination of wasteful spending the goal of reducing taxes while not significantly decreasing government services can be met. But the premier should not listen to this advisor, who in his youth was convicted of embezzlement. Surely his economic advice is as untrustworthy as he is himself, and so the premier should discard any hope of reducing taxes without a significant decrease in government services.

   Which one of the following is a questionable argumentative strategy employed in the editorial's argument?

   (A)   rejecting a proposal on the grounds that a particular implementation of the proposal is likely to fail
   (B)   trying to win support for a proposal by playing on people's fears of what could happen otherwise
   (C)   criticizing the source of a claim rather than examining the claim itself
   (D)   taking lack of evidence for a claim as evidence undermining that claim
   (E)   presupposing what it sets out to establish

GO ON TO THE NEXT PAGE.

Questions 7–8

Figorian Wildlife Commission: The development of wetlands in industrialized nations for residential and commercial uses has endangered many species. To protect wildlife we must regulate such development in Figoria: future wetland development must be offset by the construction of replacement wetland habitats. Thus, development would cause no net reduction of wetlands and pose no threat to the species that inhabit them.

Figorian Development Commission: Other nations have flagrantly developed wetlands at the expense of wildlife. We have conserved. Since Figorian wetland development might not affect wildlife and is necessary for growth, we should allow development. We have as much right to govern our own resources as countries that have already put their natural resources to commercial use.

7. Which one of the following is an assumption on which the argument advanced by the Figorian Wildlife Commission depends?

    (A) More species have been endangered by the development of wetlands than have been endangered by any other type of development.
    (B) The species indigenous to natural wetland habitats will survive in specially constructed replacement wetlands.
    (C) In nations that are primarily agricultural, wetland development does not need to be regulated.
    (D) Figorian regulation of development has in the past protected and preserved wildlife.
    (E) The species that inhabit Figorian wetlands are among the most severely threatened of the designated endangered species.

8. Which one of the following principles, if accepted, would most strongly support the Figorian Development Commission's position against the Figorian Wildlife Commission's position?

    (A) National resources should be regulated by international agreement when wildlife is endangered.
    (B) The right of future generations to have wildlife preserved supersedes the economic needs of individual nations.
    (C) Only when a reduction of populations of endangered species by commercial development has been found should regulation be implemented to prevent further damage.
    (D) Environmental regulation must aim at preventing any further environmental damage and cannot allow for the different degrees to which different nations have already harmed the environment.
    (E) It is imprudent to allow further depletion of natural resources.

9. High blood cholesterol levels are bad for the heart. Like meat, eggs, and poultry, shellfish contains cholesterol. But shellfish is not necessarily bad for the heart; it is very low in saturated fat, which affects blood cholesterol levels much more than dietary cholesterol does.

    Which one of the following, if true, most strengthens the argument?

    (A) Meat and eggs are high in saturated fat.
    (B) Small quantities of foods high in saturated fat are not bad for the heart.
    (C) Shellfish has less cholesterol per gram than meat, eggs, and poultry do.
    (D) Foods low in saturated fat promote low blood cholesterol.
    (E) A serving of meat or poultry is typically larger than a serving of shellfish.

10. Every moral theory developed in the Western tradition purports to tell us what a good life is. However, most people would judge someone who perfectly embodied the ideals of any one of these theories not to be living a good life—the kind of life they would want for themselves and their children.

    The statements above, if true, most strongly support which one of the following?

    (A) Most people desire a life for themselves and their children that is better than a merely good life.
    (B) A person who fits the ideals of one moral theory in the Western tradition would not necessarily fit the ideals of another.
    (C) Most people have a conception of a good life that does not match that of any moral theory in the Western tradition.
    (D) A good life as described by moral theories in the Western tradition cannot be realized.
    (E) It is impossible to develop a theory that accurately describes what a good life is.

GO ON TO THE NEXT PAGE.

11. Biologist: Humans have five fingers because we descended from a fish with five phalanges in its fins. Despite our prejudices to the contrary, our configuration of fingers is no more or less useful than several other possible configurations, e.g., six per hand. So, if humans had descended from a fish with six phalanges in its fins and had six fingers on each hand, then we would be just as content with that configuration.

Which one of the following, if true, most strengthens the biologist's argument?

(A) Everyone is equally content with our present configuration of fingers.
(B) Humans are never equally content with two things of unequal usefulness.
(C) Humans are always equally content with two things of equal usefulness.
(D) The perceived usefulness of our configuration of fingers is an illusory result of our prejudices.
(E) At least one species of fish had six phalanges in its fins.

12. Surrealist: Many artists mistakenly think that models need be taken only from outside the psyche. Although human sensibility can confer beauty upon even the most vulgar external objects, using the power of artistic representation solely to preserve and reinforce objects that would exist even without artists is an ironic waste.

Which one of the following most accurately expresses the conclusion of the surrealist's argument?

(A) An artist's work should not merely represent objects from outside the psyche.
(B) Artistic representation is used solely to preserve and reinforce objects.
(C) Artists should not base all their work on mere representation.
(D) Great art can confer beauty even upon very vulgar external objects.
(E) True works of art rarely represent objects from outside the psyche.

13. Harrold Foods is attempting to dominate the soft-drink market by promoting "Hero," its most popular carbonated drink product, with a costly new advertising campaign. But survey results show that, in the opinion of 72 percent of all consumers, "Hero" already dominates the market. Since any product with more than 50 percent of the sales in a market is, by definition, dominant in that market, Harrold Foods dominates the market now and need only maintain its current market share in order to continue to do so.

The argument commits which one of the following errors in reasoning?

(A) failing to exclude the possibility that what appears to be the result of a given market condition may in fact be the cause of that condition
(B) mistaking a condition required if a certain result is to obtain for a condition that by itself is sufficient to guarantee that result
(C) treating the failure to establish that a certain claim is false as equivalent to a demonstration that that claim is true
(D) taking evidence that a claim is believed to be true to constitute evidence that the claim is in fact true
(E) describing survey results that were obtained in the past as if they are bound to obtain in the future as well

GO ON TO THE NEXT PAGE.

14. Theoretically, analog systems are superior to digital systems. A signal in a pure analog system can be infinitely detailed, while digital systems cannot produce signals that are more precise than their digital units. With this theoretical advantage there is a practical disadvantage, however. Since there is no limit on the potential detail of the signal, the duplication of an analog representation allows tiny variations from the original, which are errors. These errors tend to accumulate as signals are duplicated, until this "noise" obliterates the information embodied in the original signal.

The statements above, if true, most strongly support which one of the following?

(A) Many ideas that work well in theory do not work well in practice.
(B) Analog representation of information is impractical because we do not need infinitely detailed information.
(C) Digital systems are the best information systems because error cannot occur in the emission of digital signals.
(D) Analog systems are inferior to digital systems for most practical purposes.
(E) Digital systems are preferable to analog systems when the signal must be reproduced many times.

15. Psychologist: Doctors should never prescribe sedatives for people with insomnia. Most cases of insomnia that psychologists treat are known to be caused by psychological stress. This suggests that insomniacs do not need drugs that alter their biochemistry, but rather need psychotherapy to help them alleviate the stress causing their insomnia.

Each of the following describes a flaw in the psychologist's reasoning EXCEPT:

(A) It presumes, without providing warrant, that insomnia contributes to an inability to cope with stress.
(B) It fails to consider the possibility that sedatives are the only treatment known to be effective for cases of insomnia not caused by stress.
(C) It neglects the possibility that for some people psychotherapy is a completely ineffective treatment for stress.
(D) It overlooks the possibility that sedatives could help insomniacs cope with stress.
(E) It presumes, without providing justification, that the cases of insomnia psychologists treat are representative of all cases of insomnia.

16. Numerous paintings and engravings representing warfare can be found in remains of all civilizations going back to and including the Neolithic period, when agriculture was first developed. However, no paintings or engravings of warfare are found dating from before the Neolithic period. Therefore, warfare must have first developed as a result of the transition to an agricultural society.

Which one of the following is an assumption required by the argument?

(A) Paintings and engravings were the dominant forms of artistic expression during the Neolithic period.
(B) Warfare in the Neolithic period was always motivated by territorial disputes over agricultural land.
(C) There was no warfare prior to the period in which paintings and engravings of warfare were first created.
(D) Warfare is the inevitable result of the development of a civilization.
(E) Paintings and engravings of agricultural life began to be made at the same time as paintings and engravings of warfare.

17. An antidote for chicken pox has been developed, but researchers warn that its widespread use could be dangerous, despite the fact that this drug has no serious side effects and is currently very effective at limiting the duration and severity of chicken pox.

Which one of the following, if true, helps most to reconcile the apparent discrepancy indicated above?

(A) The drug is extremely expensive and would be difficult to make widely available.
(B) The drug has to be administered several times a day, so patient compliance is likely to be low.
(C) The drug does not prevent the spread of chicken pox from one person to another, even when the drug eventually cures the disease in the first person.
(D) When misused by taking larger-than-prescribed doses, the drug can be fatal.
(E) Use of the drug contributes to the development of deadlier forms of chicken pox that are resistant to the drug.

GO ON TO THE NEXT PAGE.

18. The tendency toward overspecialization in the study of artifacts is unfortunate. Scholars can enhance their understanding of a certain artistic period by studying art from earlier periods that had a significant influence on it. For instance, because of its influence on Spanish artisans, a proper understanding of Arabic porcelain is indispensable for a proper understanding of Spanish porcelain.

Of the following, which one most closely conforms to the principle that the passage as a whole illustrates?

(A) To understand completely the major trends in research on aging, one must understand the influences these trends exert on society's view of aging.

(B) To understand fully the historical events of this century, a historian must have an understanding of similar events in earlier centuries.

(C) To appreciate fully the French language, one must understand the other languages that share its linguistic ancestry.

(D) To understand properly any academic discipline, one must have at least a superficial acquaintance with the practices of the wider academic community.

(E) To understand completely Aristotle's philosophy, one must be well acquainted with the philosophy of his intellectual mentor, Plato.

19. Editorial: Medical schools spend one hour teaching preventive medicine for every ten hours spent teaching curative medicine, even though doctors' use of the techniques of preventive medicine cuts down medical costs greatly. Therefore, if their goal is to make medicine more cost-effective, medical schools spend insufficient time teaching preventive medicine.

Which one of the following is an assumption on which the editorial's argument depends?

(A) Preventive medicine makes use of technologies that are lower in initial cost than the technologies used within the practice of curative medicine.

(B) Every hour devoted to the teaching of preventive medicine reduces medical costs by 10 percent or more.

(C) Medical schools could increase their total number of teaching hours.

(D) Improvements in doctors' use of the techniques of curative medicine would only increase overall medical costs.

(E) The time required to teach preventive medicine thoroughly is greater than one hour for every ten that are now spent teaching curative medicine.

20. Dana: It is wrong to think that the same educational methods should be used with all children. Many children have been raised in more communal environments than others and would therefore learn better through group, rather than individual, activities. A child's accustomed style of learning should always dictate what method is used.

Pat: No, not always. The flexibility of being able to work either on one's own or in a group is invaluable in a world where both skills are in demand.

The conversation lends the most support to the claim that Dana and Pat disagree on which one of the following?

(A) All children can learn valuable skills from individual activities.

(B) All children should learn to adapt to various educational methods.

(C) Many children would learn better through group, rather than individual, activities.

(D) The main purpose of education is to prepare children to meet the demands of the job market as adults.

(E) It is sometimes desirable to tailor educational methods to the way a child learns best.

GO ON TO THE NEXT PAGE.

21. Experimental psychology requires the application of statistics to interpret empirical data and assess their significance. A person will not be able to understand such applications without training in statistics. Therefore, the more training one has in statistics, the better one will be at research in experimental psychology.

Which one of the following arguments exhibits a flawed pattern of reasoning most similar to that exhibited by the argument above?

(A) Most people need the love and support of others; without it, they become depressed and unhappy. Therefore, in most instances, the more love and support a person receives, the happier that person will be.

(B) Since in most jobs there are annual wage or salary increases, the longer one has worked, the more raises one will have received. Therefore, in a typical job, the longer one has worked, the greater one's income will be.

(C) The main cause of heart attacks is arteriosclerosis, the buildup of plaque on the interior wall of the coronary arteries. It develops over an extended period of time. Therefore, if one is at risk for arteriosclerosis, one becomes more likely to suffer a heart attack as one gets older.

(D) Since many disease processes are biochemical in nature, unless one understands chemistry one will not be able to understand the explanations for many diseases. Therefore, if one has no training in chemistry, one will not be able to master medicine.

(E) Since most disease processes are biochemical in nature, an understanding of chemistry will enable one to understand most diseases. Therefore, one needs little more than training in chemistry to be able to master medicine.

22.

Item Removed From Scoring

GO ON TO THE NEXT PAGE.

23. Some vegetarians have argued that there are two individually sufficient reasons for not eating meat—one based on health considerations, and the other based on the aversion to living at the expense of other conscious creatures. But suppose that eating meat were essential to good health for humans. Then it would be less clear that an aversion to living at the expense of other conscious creatures is enough of a reason to stop eating meat.

   Which one of the following most accurately describes the role played in the argument by the supposition that eating meat is essential to good health?

   (A) It is used to disprove the vegetarian position that we should not eat meat.
   (B) It is used to show that the two types of reasons cited in favor of vegetarianism are independent.
   (C) It is used to disprove the claim that a vegetarian diet is healthy.
   (D) It is used to weaken the claim that the consciousness of animals is a sufficient reason for not eating meat.
   (E) It is used to show that there is no sufficient reason for not eating meat.

24. The increasing complexity of scientific inquiry has led to a proliferation of multiauthored technical articles. Reports of clinical trials involving patients from several hospitals are usually coauthored by physicians from each participating hospital. Likewise, physics papers reporting results from experiments using subsystems developed at various laboratories generally have authors from each laboratory.

   If all of the statements above are true, which one of the following must be true?

   (A) Clinical trials involving patients from several hospitals are never conducted solely by physicians from just one hospital.
   (B) Most reports of clinical trials involving patients from several hospitals have multiple authors.
   (C) When a technical article has multiple authors, they are usually from several different institutions.
   (D) Physics papers authored by researchers from multiple laboratories usually report results from experiments using subsystems developed at each laboratory.
   (E) Most technical articles are authored solely by the researchers who conducted the experiments these articles report.

25. Helena: Extroversion, or sociability, is not biologically determined. Children whose biological parents are introverted, when adopted by extroverts, tend to be more sociable than children of introverted parents who are not adopted.

   Jay: Your conclusion does not follow. Some of these children adopted by extroverts remain introverted no matter how young they are when adopted.

   Jay's response suggests that he interpreted Helena's remarks to mean that

   (A) biological factors play only a partial role in a child being extroverted
   (B) most but not all children whose biological parents are introverted become extroverted when adopted by extroverts
   (C) children whose biological parents are introverted, when adopted by extroverts, tend not to be more sociable than children of introverted parents who are not adopted
   (D) biological factors do not play any role in a child being extroverted
   (E) environmental factors can sometimes be more influential than biological factors in determining extroversion

S T O P

**IF YOU FINISH BEFORE TIME IS CALLED, YOU MAY CHECK YOUR WORK ON THIS SECTION ONLY.
DO NOT WORK ON ANY OTHER SECTION IN THE TEST.**

Acknowledgment is made to the following sources from which material has been adapted for use in this test booklet:

A.S. Cutler, "Lawyers Should Not Accept Unlawful Cases." ©1983 by Greenhaven Press, Inc.

Carl Sagan, "*Cosmos*." ©1980 by Carl Sagan Productions, Inc.

LSAT WRITING SAMPLE TOPIC

Helene has recently purchased an established art gallery and is trying to decide which of two artists to feature in her first show as owner. Write an argument supporting one artist over the other based on the following criteria:

- Helene is aware that the gallery has gained a reputation for featuring traditional artwork but wants to begin promoting art that is more exciting and contemporary in style.
- Helene needs to at least break even on the show, so it is important that the show draw a good crowd and generate several sales of the works of the featured artist.

Celia has only recently been showing her artwork. She has never had her own show and has never sold a piece of her art. Yet, a highly respected art magazine focusing on contemporary art has recently published a favorable review of Celia's work, describing her as "an exciting young artist poised to take the art world by storm." Celia has enthusiastically responded to Helene's queries about the possibility of coordinating a show. Further, Celia has connections with a group of young artists who have begun to receive favorable reviews for their highly creative work. Featuring Celia's work in the show would likely lead to later exhibitions of the work of these other artists.

Andre is a well-established artist who has had many shows and has sold several works in the past year. Recent reviews of Andre's work have been favorable, but less glowing than in the past. Still, Andre's shows tend to be well attended, and he has a loyal following; many of those attending would likely be influential dealers and wealthy collectors of traditional art. In addition, Andre has a longstanding contract with a major publisher of expensive, high-quality art books and Helene would be entitled to royalties if this publisher were to produce a catalog to accompany Andre's show at her gallery. Andre would have to be convinced to participate in the show but would probably be willing to do so because the gallery that Helene purchased is well-known for being supportive of his style of art.

Directions:

1. Use the Answer Key on the next page to check your answers.

2. Use the Scoring Worksheet below to compute your raw score.

3. Use the Score Conversion Chart to convert your raw score into the 120-180 scale.

Scoring Worksheet

1. Enter the number of questions you answered correctly in each section.

	Number Correct
SECTION I.	_____
SECTION II	_____
SECTION III.	_____
SECTION IV.	_____

2. Enter the sum here: _____
   This is your Raw Score.

Conversion Chart

For Converting Raw Score to the 120-180 LSAT Scaled Score
LSAT Form 0LSS47

Reported Score	Raw Score Lowest	Raw Score Highest
180	98	101
179	97	97
178	96	96
177	95	95
176	94	94
175	93	93
174	92	92
173	91	91
172	90	90
171	88	89
170	87	87
169	86	86
168	85	85
167	83	84
166	82	82
165	80	81
164	79	79
163	77	78
162	75	76
161	74	74
160	72	73
159	70	71
158	69	69
157	67	68
156	65	66
155	64	64
154	62	63
153	60	61
152	58	59
151	57	57
150	55	56
149	53	54
148	52	52
147	50	51
146	48	49
145	47	47
144	45	46
143	44	44
142	42	43
141	40	41
140	39	39
139	37	38
138	36	36
137	35	35
136	33	34
135	32	32
134	30	31
133	29	29
132	28	28
131	27	27
130	26	26
129	24	25
128	23	23
127	22	22
126	21	21
125	20	20
124	19	19
123	18	18
122	17	17
121	—*	—*
120	0	16

*There is no raw score that will produce this scaled score for this form.

SECTION I

1.	E	8.	A	15.	C	22.	D
2.	C	9.	D	16.	A	23.	D
3.	D	10.	A	17.	D	24.	C
4.	A	11.	B	18.	E	25.	E
5.	B	12.	B	19.	E		
6.	D	13.	C	20.	B		
7.	C	14.	B	21.	D		

SECTION II

1.	D	8.	E	15.	A	22.	A
2.	E	9.	B	16.	E	23.	A
3.	A	10.	C	17.	C	24.	C
4.	C	11.	B	18.	A	25.	D
5.	B	12.	D	19.	B	26.	C
6.	A	13.	A	20.	E	27.	D
7.	B	14.	D	21.	D		

SECTION III

1.	C	8.	A	15.	E	22.	B
2.	D	9.	C	16.	C	23.	A
3.	B	10.	D	17.	C	24.	D
4.	A	11.	A	18.	D		
5.	D	12.	A	19.	E		
6.	B	13.	E	20.	B		
7.	C	14.	A	21.	D		

SECTION IV

1.	B	8.	C	15.	A	22.	*
2.	C	9.	D	16.	C	23.	D
3.	A	10.	C	17.	E	24.	B
4.	B	11.	C	18.	E	25.	D
5.	A	12.	A	19.	E		
6.	C	13.	D	20.	B		
7.	B	14.	E	21.	A		

*Item removed from scoring.

The Official LSAT PrepTest®

- December 2000
  PrepTest 33

- Form 0LSS46

SECTION I
Time—35 minutes
25 Questions

Directions: The questions in this section are based on the reasoning contained in brief statements or passages. For some questions, more than one of the choices could conceivably answer the question. However, you are to choose the best answer; that is, the response that most accurately and completely answers the question. You should not make assumptions that are by commonsense standards implausible, superfluous, or incompatible with the passage. After you have chosen the best answer, blacken the corresponding space on your answer sheet.

1. Marmosets are the only primates other than humans known to display a preference for using one hand rather than the other. Significantly more marmosets are left-handed than are right-handed. Since infant marmosets engage in much imitative behavior, researchers hypothesize that it is by imitation that infant marmosets learn which hand to use, so that offspring reared by left-handed parents generally share their parents' handedness.

Which one of the following, if true, most supports the researchers' hypothesis?

(A) A study conducted on adult marmosets revealed that many were right-handed.

(B) Right-handed marmosets virtually all have at least one sibling who is left-handed.

(C) According to the study, 33 percent of marmosets are ambidextrous, showing equal facility using either their left hand or their right hand.

(D) Ninety percent of humans are right-handed, but those who are left-handed are likely to have at least one left-handed parent.

(E) Marmosets raised in captivity with right-handed adult marmosets to whom they are not related are more likely to be right-handed than left-handed.

2. Sheila: It has been argued that using computer technology to add color to a movie originally filmed in black and white damages the integrity of the original film. But no one argues that we should not base a movie on a novel or a short story because doing so would erode the value of the book or story. The film adaptation of the written work is a new work that stands on its own. Judgments of it do not reflect on the original. Similarly, the colorized film is a new work distinct from the original and should be judged on its own merit. It does not damage the integrity of the original black-and-white film.

Sheila's argument uses which one of the following techniques of argumentation?

(A) It appeals to an analogy between similar cases.

(B) It offers a counterexample to a general principle.

(C) It appeals to popular opinion on the matter at issue.

(D) It distinguishes facts from value judgments.

(E) It draws an inference from a general principle and a set of facts.

GO ON TO THE NEXT PAGE.

Questions 3–4

Juan: Unlike the ancient Olympic games on which they are based, the modern Olympics include professional as well as amateur athletes. But since amateurs rarely have the financial or material resources available to professionals, it is unlikely that the amateurs will ever offer a serious challenge to professionals in those Olympic events in which amateurs compete against professionals. Hence, the presence of professional athletes violates the spirit of fairness essential to the games.

Michiko: But the idea of the modern Olympics is to showcase the world's finest athletes, regardless of their backgrounds or resources. Hence, professionals should be allowed to compete.

3. Which one of the following most accurately expresses the point at issue between Juan and Michiko?

(A)   whether the participation of both amateur and professional athletes is in accord with the ideals of the modern Olympics

(B)   whether both amateur and professional athletes competed in the ancient Olympic games upon which the modern Olympics are based

(C)   whether the athletes who compete in the modern Olympics are the world's finest

(D)   whether any amateur athletes have the financial or material resources that are available to professional athletes

(E)   whether governments sponsor professional as well as amateur athletes in the modern Olympics

4. Which one of the following, if true, most seriously undermines Juan's argument?

(A)   In general, amateur athletes tend to outnumber professional athletes in the modern Olympics.

(B)   In certain events in the modern Olympics the best few competitors are amateurs; in certain other events the best few competitors are professionals.

(C)   The concept of "amateur" and "professional" athletics would have been unfamiliar to the ancient Greeks on whose games the modern Olympics are based.

(D)   In the modern Olympics there has been no noticeable correlation between the financial or material resources expended on the training of individual athletes and the eventual performance of those athletes.

(E)   Many amateur athletes who take part in international competitions receive no financial or material support from the governments of the countries that the amateurs represent.

Questions 5–6

A recent national study of the trash discarded in several representative areas confirmed that plastics constitute a smaller proportion of all trash than paper products do, whether the trash is measured by weight or by volume. The damage that a given weight or volume of trash does to the environment is roughly the same whether the trash consists of plastics or paper products. Contrary to popular opinion, therefore, the current use of plastics actually does less harm to the environment nationwide than that of paper products.

5. The main conclusion of the argument is that

(A)   plastics constitute a smaller proportion of the nation's total trash than do paper products

(B)   the ratio of weight to volume is the same for plastic trash as it is for paper trash

(C)   popular opinion regards the use of paper products as less harmful to the environment than the use of products made from plastic

(D)   contrary to popular opinion, a shift away from the use of paper products to the use of plastics would benefit the environment nationwide

(E)   at this time more harm is being done to the environment nationwide by the use of paper than by the use of plastics

6. Which one of the following, if true, most strengthens the argument?

(A)   A given weight of paper product may increase in volume after manufacture and before being discarded as trash.

(B)   According to popular opinion, volume is a more important consideration than weight in predicting the impact of a given quantity of trash on the environment.

(C)   The sum of damage caused to the environment by paper trash and by plastic trash is greater than that caused by any other sort of trash that was studied.

(D)   The production of any paper product is more harmful to the environment than is the production of an equal weight or volume of any plastic.

(E)   The proportion of plastic trash to paper trash varies from one part of the country to another.

GO ON TO THE NEXT PAGE.

7. Consultant: Most workers do not have every item they produce judged for quality, but each piece a freelance writer authors is evaluated. That is why freelance writers produce such high-quality work.

The consultant's statements, if true, most strongly support which one of the following?

(A) A piece authored by a freelance writer is generally evaluated more strictly than the majority of items most workers produce.
(B) By having every piece of their work evaluated, some workers are caused to produce high-quality work.
(C) No other workers produce higher quality work than do freelance writers.
(D) Only freelance writers have every item they produce evaluated for quality.
(E) Some workers produce high-quality work in spite of the fact that not every item they produce is judged for quality.

8. Few animals brave the midday heat of the Sahara desert. An exception is the silver ant, which chooses this time of day to leave its nest and scout for food, typically the corpses of heat-stricken animals. Even the silver ant, however, must be careful: at such times they can become victims of the heat themselves.

Which one of the following, if true, LEAST helps to explain the silver ant's choice of scavenging times?

(A) The chief predators of the silver ant must take cover from the sun during midday.
(B) The cues that silver ants use to navigate become less reliable as the afternoon progresses.
(C) Other scavengers remove any remaining corpses as soon as the temperature begins to drop in the afternoon.
(D) The temperature inside the silver ants' nests often exceeds the surface temperature during the hottest times of the day.
(E) Silver ants cool themselves by climbing onto small pieces of dried vegetation to take advantage of random light breezes.

9. The same task triggers different levels of awareness of one's surroundings, called environmental awareness, in different individuals. Mathematical puzzles, for example, cause most people to increase such an awareness. Some people—those who formulate the answer visually, imagining the numbers in their mind's eye—will, in an attempt to freeze the picture, experience a decrease in environmental awareness while solving the puzzle. Other people's environmental awareness may rise during the exercise, because their brains are signaling a rest at the end of every stage of problem solving.

Which one of the following is most strongly supported by the information above?

(A) There are some people for whom mathematical puzzles do not cause an increase in their level of environmental awareness.
(B) People who visually formulate answers differ from other problem solvers in that the former are aware of their surroundings.
(C) People tend to be more aware of their surroundings when solving mathematical problems than when solving nonmathematical problems.
(D) Mathematical problem solvers who rely on visual techniques become aware of their surroundings only during periods of rest.
(E) Mathematical problem solving requires frequent periods of rest in the form of increased awareness of the problem solver's surroundings.

10. Art historian: Great works of art have often elicited outrage when first presented; in Europe, Stravinsky's *Rite of Spring* prompted a riot, and Manet's *Déjeuner sur l'herbe* elicited outrage and derision. So, since it is clear that art is often shocking, we should not hesitate to use public funds to support works of art that many people find shocking.

Which one of the following is an assumption that the art historian's argument requires in order for its conclusion to be properly drawn?

(A) Most art is shocking.
(B) Stravinsky and Manet received public funding for their art.
(C) Art used to be more shocking than it currently is.
(D) Public funds should support art.
(E) Anything that shocks is art.

GO ON TO THE NEXT PAGE.

11. Researchers have discovered that caffeine can be as physically addictive as other psychoactive substances. Some people find that they become unusually depressed, drowsy, or even irritable if they do not have their customary dose of caffeine. This is significant because as many people consume caffeine as consume any one of the other addictive psychoactive substances.

Which one of the following can be logically concluded from the information above?

(A) There is no psychoactive substance to which more people are physically addicted than are addicted to caffeine.

(B) A physical addiction to a particular psychoactive substance will typically give rise to diverse psychological symptoms.

(C) Not all substances to which people can become physically addicted are psychoactive.

(D) If one is physically addicted to a psychoactive substance, one will become unusually depressed when one is no longer ingesting that substance.

(E) If alcohol is a physically addictive psychoactive substance, there are not more people who consume alcohol than consume caffeine.

12. A nationwide poll of students, parents, and teachers showed that over 90 percent believe that an appropriate percentage of their school's budget is being spent on student counseling programs. It seems, then, that any significant increase in a school's budget should be spent on something other than student counseling programs.

Which one of the following describes a flaw in the reasoning of the argument above?

(A) The argument confuses a mere coincidence with a causal relationship.

(B) The argument confuses the percentage of the budget spent on a program with the overall amount spent on that program.

(C) The argument fails to justify its presumption that what is true of a part of the budget is also true of the total budget.

(D) The argument fails to consider the possibility that money could be saved by training students as peer counselors.

(E) The argument fails to consider that if more money is spent on a program, then more money cannot also be used for other purposes.

13. Ethicist: Studies have documented the capacity of placebos to reduce pain in patients who believe that they are receiving beneficial drugs. Some doctors say that they administer placebos because medically effective treatment reinforced by the placebo effect sometimes helps patients recover faster than good treatment alone. But administering placebos is nonetheless ethically questionable, for even if a placebo benefits a patient, a doctor might, for example, have prescribed it just to give the patient satisfaction that something was being done.

The ethicist's argument depends on which one of the following assumptions?

(A) A patient's psychological satisfaction is not a consideration in administering medical treatment.

(B) The motivation for administering a placebo can be relevant to the ethical justification for doing so.

(C) Medical treatment that relies on the placebo effect alone is ethically indefensible.

(D) The pain relief produced by the placebo effect justifies the deception involved in administering a placebo.

(E) Administering a placebo is not ethically justified if that treatment is not prescribed by a doctor.

GO ON TO THE NEXT PAGE.

14. After the United Nations Security Council authorized military intervention by a coalition of armed forces intended to halt civil strife in a certain country, the parliament of one UN member nation passed a resolution condemning its own prime minister for promising to commit military personnel to the action. A parliamentary leader insisted that the overwhelming vote for the resolution did not imply the parliament's opposition to the anticipated intervention; on the contrary, most members of parliament supported the UN plan.

Which one of the following, if true, most helps to resolve the apparent discrepancy presented above?

(A) The UN Security Council cannot legally commit the military of a member nation to armed intervention in other countries.

(B) In the parliamentary leader's nation, it is the constitutional prerogative of the parliament, not of the prime minister, to initiate foreign military action.

(C) The parliament would be responsible for providing the funding necessary in order to contribute military personnel to the UN intervention.

(D) The public would not support the military action unless it was known that the parliament supported the action.

(E) Members of the parliament traditionally are more closely attuned to public sentiment, especially with regard to military action, than are prime ministers.

15. People who are good at playing the game Drackedary are invariably skilled with their hands. Mary is a very competent watchmaker. Therefore, Mary would make a good Drackedary player.

The flawed pattern of reasoning in the argument above is most similar to that in which one of the following?

(A) People with long legs make good runners. Everyone in Daryl's family has long legs. Therefore, Daryl would make a good runner.

(B) People who write for a living invariably enjoy reading. Julie has been a published novelist for many years. Therefore, Julie enjoys reading.

(C) All race car drivers have good reflexes. Chris is a champion table tennis player. Therefore, Chris would make a good race car driver.

(D) The role of Santa Claus in a shopping mall is often played by an experienced actor. Erwin has played Santa Claus in shopping malls for years. Therefore, Erwin must be an experienced actor.

(E) Any good skier can learn to ice-skate eventually. Erica is a world-class skier. Therefore, Erica could learn to ice-skate in a day or two.

16. Notice to subscribers: In order for us to provide you with efficient and reliable newspaper service, please note the following policies. You will be billed for home delivery every four weeks, in advance. If you do not receive delivery, call us promptly to receive a replacement copy. Credit can be given only if the missed copy is reported to us within twenty-four hours and only if a replacement copy is unavailable. Request for temporary nondelivery must be made at least three days prior to the first day on which delivery is to stop. No subscription will be canceled unless the subscriber explicitly requests the cancellation beforehand and in writing.

The Daily Gazette

If *The Daily Gazette* denies each of the following subscriber's requests, each of the denials could be justified solely on the basis of the policy stated above EXCEPT:

(A) Mr. Rathanan did not send in his advance payment two weeks ago; he states that his inaction was intended as cancellation and requests that he not be charged for the past two weeks of delivery of *The Daily Gazette*.

(B) Dr. Broder called *The Daily Gazette* Monday morning to report that her Sunday edition had not been delivered; she requests credit instead of the offered replacement copy.

(C) *The Daily Gazette* was delivered to Ms. Herrera during her one-week vacation even though she called on a Wednesday to stop delivery the following Monday for the entire week; she requests credit for the full week's delivery.

(D) Although Ms. Jackson telephoned *The Daily Gazette* at the beginning of June requesting that her subscription be canceled on June 30, delivery was continued until July 3 when she called to complain; she requests that she not be charged for the papers delivered in July.

(E) Ms. Silverman was out of town on Sunday and Monday and when she returned on Tuesday she found that her Sunday edition had not been delivered; she called *The Daily Gazette* on Tuesday afternoon requesting credit for the undelivered copy.

GO ON TO THE NEXT PAGE.

17. Expert witness: Ten times, and in controlled circumstances, a single drop of the defendant's blood was allowed to fall onto the fabric. And in all ten cases, the stained area was much less than the expected 9.5 cm^2. In fact, the stained area was always between 4.5 and 4.8 cm^2. I conclude that a single drop of the defendant's blood stains much less than 9.5 cm^2 of the fabric.

Which one of the following, if true, most undermines the value of the evidence for the expert witness's conclusion?

(A) If similar results had been found after 100 test drops of the defendant's blood, the evidence would be even stronger.

(B) Expert witnesses have sometimes been known to fudge their data to accord with the prosecution's case.

(C) In an eleventh test drop of the defendant's blood, the area stained was also less than 9.5 cm^2—this time staining 9.3 cm^2.

(D) Another person's blood was substituted, and in otherwise identical circumstances, stained between 9.8 and 10.6 cm^2 of the fabric.

(E) Not all expert witnesses are the authorities in their fields that they claim to be.

18. The use of space-based satellites to study environmental conditions on Earth is an important development in the conservation movement's history. Environmental problems may now be observed long before they otherwise would be noticed, allowing for intervention before they reach the crisis stage. It is no wonder that environmentalists fail to consider both that spacecraft may damage the ozone layer and that this damage could be serious enough to warrant discontinuing spaceflight.

The reasoning above most closely conforms to which one of the following principles?

(A) People tend to ignore possible objectionable consequences of actions that support their activities.

(B) A negative consequence of an activity may be outweighed by its great positive consequences.

(C) Technology usually has at least some negative impact on the environment, even if it is largely beneficial.

(D) Even well-intentioned attempts to solve problems sometimes make them worse.

(E) Attempts to employ technology often have unforeseen consequences that may be negative.

19. Historian: The spread of literacy informs more people of injustices and, in the right circumstances, leads to increased capacity to distinguish true reformers from mere opportunists. However, widespread literacy invariably emerges before any comprehensive system of general education; thus, in the interim, the populace is vulnerable to clever demagogues calling for change. Consequently, some relatively benign regimes may ironically be toppled by their own "enlightened" move to increase literacy.

Which one of the following is an assumption on which the historian's argument depends?

(A) A demagogue can never enlist the public support necessary to topple an existing regime unless a comprehensive system of general education is in place.

(B) Without literacy there can be no general awareness of the injustice in a society.

(C) Any comprehensive system of general education will tend to preserve the authority of benign regimes.

(D) A lack of general education affects the ability to differentiate between legitimate and illegitimate calls for reform.

(E) Any benign regime that fails to provide comprehensive general education will be toppled by a clever demagogue.

20. Recently discovered prehistoric rock paintings on small islands off the northern coast of Norway have archaeologists puzzled. The predominant theory about northern cave paintings was that they were largely a description of the current diets of the painters. This theory cannot be right, because the painters must have needed to eat the sea animals populating the waters north of Norway if they were to make the long journey to and from the islands, and there are no paintings that unambiguously depict such creatures.

Each of the following, if true, weakens the argument against the predominant theory about northern cave paintings EXCEPT:

(A) Once on these islands, the cave painters hunted and ate land animals.

(B) Parts of the cave paintings on the islands did not survive the centuries.

(C) The cave paintings that were discovered on the islands depicted many land animals.

(D) Those who did the cave paintings that were discovered on the islands had unusually advanced techniques of preserving meats.

(E) The cave paintings on the islands were done by the original inhabitants of the islands who ate the meat of land animals.

21. Attacks on an opponent's character should be avoided in political debates. Such attacks do not confront the opponent's argument; instead they attempt to cast doubt on the opponent's moral right to be in the debate at all.

Which one of the following principles, if valid, most helps to justify the reasoning above?

(A) Attacks on an opponent's character result from an inability to confront the opponent's argument properly.

(B) Attacks on an opponent's character should not impress those watching a political debate.

(C) Debating techniques that do not confront every argument should be avoided.

(D) Attacking the character of one's opponent does nothing to preserve one's moral right to enter into further political debates.

(E) Questions of character should be raised in political debate if they are relevant to the opponent's argument.

22. Lawyer: Did Congleton assign the best available graphic artist to the project?
Witness: Yes.
Lawyer: And the best writer?
Witness: Yes.
Lawyer: In fact everyone she assigned to work on the project was top notch?
Witness: That's true.
Lawyer: So, you lied to the court when you said, earlier, that Congleton wanted the project to fail?

Each of the following accurately describes a flaw in the lawyer's reasoning displayed above EXCEPT:

(A) It takes for granted that Congleton was not forced to assign the people she did to the project.

(B) It takes for granted that the project could fail only if Congleton wanted it to fail.

(C) It ignores the possibility that Congleton knew that the people assigned to the project would not work well together.

(D) It ignores the possibility that the witness failed to infer from known facts what should have been inferred and therefore was not lying.

(E) It ignores the possibility that Congleton failed to allot enough time or resources to the project team.

23. An air traveler in Beijing cannot fly to Lhasa without first flying to Chengdu. Unfortunately, an air traveler in Beijing must fly to Xian before flying to Chengdu. Any air traveler who flies from Beijing to Lhasa, therefore, cannot avoid flying to Xian.

The pattern of reasoning exhibited by the argument above is most similar to that exhibited by which one of the following?

(A) A doctor cannot prescribe porozine for a patient without first prescribing anthroxine for that patient. Unfortunately, anthroxine makes most patients who take it feel either extremely drowsy or else extremely nervous. It is likely, therefore, that a patient who has taken porozine has felt extremely nervous.

(B) An ice-sculpture artist cannot reach the yellow level of achievement without first achieving the green level. The green level is impossible to achieve unless the white level has already been achieved. Therefore, an ice-sculpture artist who has reached the yellow level must have previously achieved the white level.

(C) One cannot properly identify a mushroom without first examining its spores. A powerful microscope can be used to examine the spores of a mushroom. A powerful microscope, therefore, is necessary for anyone wishing to identify mushrooms properly.

(D) It is impossible to be fluent in a language without knowing its grammatical rules. A person who knows the grammatical rules of a language has learned them by means of exhaustive and difficult study or else by growing up in an environment in which the language is spoken. There are two major ways, therefore, for a person to become fluent in a language.

(E) In the City Ballet Company any dancer who has danced in *Giselle* has also danced in *Sleeping Beauty*, and some dancers who have danced in *Sleeping Beauty* have also danced in *Swan Lake*. Therefore, some dancers in the City Ballet Company who have danced in *Giselle* have also danced in *Swan Lake*.

GO ON TO THE NEXT PAGE.

24. Supervisor: Our next budget proposal will probably be approved, because normally about half of all budget proposals that the vice president considers are approved, and our last five budget proposals have all been turned down.

The supervisor's reasoning is flawed because it presumes, without giving warrant, that

(A)   the last five budget proposals' having been turned down guarantees that the next five budget proposals will be approved

(B)   the vice president is required to approve at least half of all budget proposals submitted

(C)   having the last five budget proposals turned down affects the likelihood that the next budget proposal will be turned down

(D)   the majority of the last five budget proposals deserved to be turned down

(E)   the likelihood that a budget proposal will be approved is influenced by the amount of money that budget proposal requests

25. The number of airplanes equipped with a new anticollision device has increased steadily during the past two years. During the same period, it has become increasingly common for key information about an airplane's altitude and speed to disappear suddenly from air traffic controllers' screens. The new anticollision device, which operates at the same frequency as air traffic radar, is therefore responsible for the sudden disappearance of key information.

Which one of the following, if true, most seriously weakens the argument?

(A)   The new anticollision device has already prevented a considerable number of mid-air collisions.

(B)   It was not until the new anticollision device was introduced that key information first began disappearing suddenly from controllers' screens.

(C)   The new anticollision device is scheduled to be moved to a different frequency within the next two to three months.

(D)   Key information began disappearing from controllers' screens three months before the new anticollision device was first tested.

(E)   The sudden disappearance of key information from controllers' screens has occurred only at relatively large airports.

S T O P

IF YOU FINISH BEFORE TIME IS CALLED, YOU MAY CHECK YOUR WORK ON THIS SECTION ONLY.
DO NOT WORK ON ANY OTHER SECTION IN THE TEST.

SECTION II
Time—35 minutes
28 Questions

Directions: Each passage in this section is followed by a group of questions to be answered on the basis of what is stated or implied in the passage. For some of the questions, more than one of the choices could conceivably answer the question. However, you are to choose the best answer; that is, the response that most accurately and completely answers the question, and blacken the corresponding space on your answer sheet.

Many political economists believe that the soundest indicator of the economic health of a nation is the nation's gross national product (GNP) per capita—a figure reached by dividing the total value of the goods
(5) produced yearly in a nation by its population and taken to be a measure of the welfare of the nation's residents. But there are many factors affecting residents' welfare that are not captured by per capita GNP; human indicators, while sometimes more difficult to calculate
(10) or document, provide sounder measures of a nation's progress than does the indicator championed by these economists. These human indicators include nutrition and life expectancy; birth weight and level of infant mortality; ratio of population level to availability of
(15) resources; employment opportunities; and the ability of governments to provide services such as education, clean water, medicine, public transportation, and mass communication for their residents.

The economists defend their use of per capita GNP
(20) as the sole measure of a nation's economic health by claiming that improvements in per capita GNP eventually stimulate improvements in human indicators. But, in actuality, this often fails to occur. Even in nations where economic stimulation has
(25) brought about substantial improvements in per capita GNP, economic health as measured by human indicators does not always reach a level commensurate with the per capita GNP. Nations that have achieved a relatively high per capita GNP, for example, sometimes
(30) experience levels of infant survival, literacy, nutrition, and life expectancy no greater than levels in nations where per capita GNP is relatively low. In addition, because per capita GNP is an averaged figure, it often presents a distorted picture of the wealth of a nation;
(35) for example, in a relatively sparsely populated nation where a small percentage of residents receives most of the economic benefits of production while the majority receives very little benefit, per capita GNP may nevertheless be high. The welfare of a nation's
(40) residents is a matter not merely of total economic benefit, but also of the distribution of economic benefits across the entire society. Measuring a nation's economic health only by total wealth frequently obscures a lack of distribution of wealth across the
(45) society as a whole.

In light of the potential for such imbalances in distribution of economic benefits, some nations have begun to realize that their domestic economic efforts are better directed away from attempting to raise per
(50) capita GNP and instead toward ensuring that the

conditions measured by human indicators are salutary. They recognize that unless a shift in focus away from using material wealth as the sole indicator of economic success is effected, the well-being of the nation may be
(55) endangered, and that nations that do well according to human indicators may thrive even if their per capita GNP remains stable or lags behind that of other nations.

1. Which one of the following titles most accurately expresses the main point of the passage?

(A) "The Shifting Meaning of Per Capita GNP: A Historical Perspective"
(B) "A Defense of Per Capita GNP: An Economist's Rejoinder"
(C) "The Preferability of Human Indicators as Measures of National Economic Health"
(D) "Total Wealth vs. Distribution of Wealth as a Measure of Economic Health"
(E) "A New Method of Calculating Per Capita GNP to Measure National Economic Health"

2. The term "welfare" is used in the first paragraph to refer most specifically to which one of the following?

(A) the overall quality of life for individuals in a nation
(B) the services provided to individuals by a government
(C) the material wealth owned by individuals in a nation
(D) the extent to which the distribution of wealth among individuals in a nation is balanced
(E) government efforts to redistribute wealth across society as a whole

GO ON TO THE NEXT PAGE.

3. The passage provides specific information about each of the following EXCEPT:

(A) how per capita GNP is calculated

(B) what many political economists believe to be an accurate measure of a nation's economic health

(C) how nations with a relatively low per capita GNP can sometimes be economically healthier than nations whose per capita GNP is higher

(D) why human indicators may not provide the same picture of a nation's economic health that per capita GNP does

(E) how nations can adjust their domestic economic efforts to bring about substantial improvements in per capita GNP

4. Which one of the following scenarios, if true, would most clearly be a counterexample to the views expressed in the last paragraph of the passage?

(A) The decision by a nation with a low level of economic health as measured by human indicators to focus on increasing the levels of human indicators results in slower growth in its per capita GNP.

(B) The decision by a nation with a low level of economic health as measured by human indicators to focus on increasing domestic production of goods results in significant improvements in the levels of human indicators.

(C) The decision by a nation with a low level of economic health as measured by human indicators to focus on increasing the levels of human indicators results in increased growth in per capita GNP.

(D) The decision by a nation with a low per capita GNP to focus on improving its level of economic health as measured by human indicators fails to bring about an increase in per capita GNP.

(E) The decision by a nation with a low per capita GNP to focus on increasing domestic production of goods fails to improve its economic health as measured by human indicators.

5. The primary function of the last paragraph of the passage is to

(A) offer a synthesis of the opposing positions outlined in the first two paragraphs

(B) expose the inadequacies of both positions outlined in the first two paragraphs

(C) summarize the argument made in the first two paragraphs

(D) correct a weakness in the political economists' position as outlined in the second paragraph

(E) suggest policy implications of the argument made in the first two paragraphs

6. Based on the passage, the political economists discussed in the passage would be most likely to agree with which one of the following statements?

(A) A change in a nation's per capita GNP predicts a similar future change in the state of human indicators in that nation.

(B) The level of human indicators in a nation is irrelevant to the welfare of the individuals in that nation.

(C) A high per capita GNP in a nation usually indicates that the wealth in the nation is not distributed across the society as a whole.

(D) The welfare of a nation's residents is irrelevant to the economic health of the nation.

(E) The use of indicators other than material wealth to measure economic well-being would benefit a nation.

7. In the passage, the author's primary concern is to

(A) delineate a new method of directing domestic economic efforts

(B) point out the weaknesses in one standard for measuring a nation's welfare

(C) explain the fact that some nations have both a high per capita GNP and a low quality of life for its citizens

(D) demonstrate that unequal distribution of wealth is an inevitable result of a high per capita GNP

(E) argue that political economists alone should be responsible for economic policy decisions

GO ON TO THE NEXT PAGE.

The autobiographical narrative *Incidents in the Life of a Slave Girl, Written by Herself* (1861), by Harriet A. Jacobs, a slave of African descent, not only recounts an individual life but also provides, implicitly and

(5) explicitly, a perspective on the larger United States culture from the viewpoint of one denied access to it. Jacobs, as a woman and a slave, faced the stigmas to which those statuses were subject. Jacobs crafted her narrative, in accordance with the mainstream literary

(10) genre of the sentimental domestic novel, as an embodiment of cherished cultural values such as the desirability of marriage and the sanctity of personal identity, home, and family. She did so because she was writing to the free women of her day—the principal

(15) readers of domestic novels—in the hopes that they would sympathize with and come to understand her unique predicament as a female slave. By applying these conventions of the genre to her situation, Jacobs demonstrates to her readers that family and domesticity

(20) are no less prized by those forced into slavery, thus leading her free readers to perceive those values within a broader social context.

Some critics have argued that, by conforming to convention, Jacobs shortchanged her own experiences;

(25) one critic, for example, claims that in Jacobs's work the purposes of the domestic novel overshadow those of the typical slave narrative. But the relationship between the two genres is more complex: Jacobs's attempt to frame her story as a domestic novel creates a

(30) tension between the usual portrayal of women in this genre and her actual experience, often calling into question the applicability of the hierarchy of values espoused by the domestic novel to those who are in her situation. Unlike the traditional romantic episodes in

(35) domestic novels in which a man and woman meet, fall in love, encounter various obstacles but eventually marry, Jacobs's protagonist must send her lover, a slave, away in order to protect him from the wrath of her jealous master. In addition, by the end of the

(40) narrative, Jacobs's protagonist achieves her freedom by escaping to the north, but she does not achieve the domestic novel's ideal of a stable home complete with family, as the price she has had to pay for her freedom is separation from most of her family, including one of

(45) her own children. Jacobs points out that slave women view certain events and actions from a perspective different from that of free women, and that they must make difficult choices that free women need not. Her narrative thus becomes an antidomestic novel, for

(50) Jacobs accepts readily the goals of the genre, but demonstrates that its hierarchy of values does not apply when examined from the perspective of a female slave, suggesting thereby that her experience, and that of any female slave, cannot be fully understood without

(55) shedding conventional perspectives.

8. The author of the passage displays which one of the following attitudes toward the position of the critics mentioned in line 23?

(A) complete rejection
(B) reluctant rejection
(C) complete neutrality
(D) reluctant agreement
(E) complete agreement

9. According to the passage, Jacobs's narrative departs from the conventions of a typical domestic novel in which one of the following ways?

(A) Jacobs's protagonist does not ultimately achieve her freedom.
(B) Jacobs's protagonist does not wish for the same ideals as the protagonists of domestic novels.
(C) Jacobs's protagonist does not encounter various obstacles in her quest for love.
(D) Jacobs's protagonist does not ultimately achieve the ideals of home and family.
(E) Jacobs's protagonist does not experience the stigmas to which women and slaves were subject.

10. It can most reasonably be inferred from the passage that the critics mentioned in line 23 hold which one of the following views?

(A) The mixture of literary genres in a single narrative often creates a useful tension that adds value to the narrative.
(B) The mixture of literary genres in a single narrative tends to cause the goals of both genres to be compromised.
(C) The mixture of literary genres in a single narrative tends to favor the genre having the greater degree of realism.
(D) The mixture of literary genres in a single narrative tends to favor the genre having the lesser degree of sentimentality.
(E) The mixture of literary genres in a single narrative can sometimes cause the goals of one of the genres to be compromised.

GO ON TO THE NEXT PAGE.

11. Which one of the following, if true, would most support the position of the critics mentioned in line 23?

(A) Most readers of Jacobs's narrative when it was first published concluded that it was simply a domestic novel and were thus disinclined to see it as an attempt to provoke thought.

(B) Many reviewers of Jacobs's narrative included passionate statements in their reviews calling for the immediate abolition of slavery.

(C) Most scholars believe that Jacobs's narrative would not have been able to communicate its message effectively if it had not adopted the conventions of the domestic novel.

(D) Jacobs's narrative was modeled not only after domestic novels of the period but after realistic novels whose goal was to point out social injustices.

(E) Jacobs's goal in crafting her narrative was not only to preach against the injustices of slavery but also to tell a powerful story that would make those injustices vivid to readers.

12. The author describes Jacobs's narrative as an "antidomestic novel" (line 49) for which one of the following reasons?

(A) Jacobs's protagonist does not lament her separation from her family.

(B) Jacobs's protagonist is disinclined toward stereotypical domestic aspirations.

(C) Jacobs's narrative reveals the limitations of the hierarchy of values espoused by the domestic novel genre.

(D) Jacobs's narrative implicitly suggests that the desire for domestic ideals contributes to the protagonist's plight.

(E) Jacobs's narrative condemns domestic values as a hindrance to its protagonist's development of personal identity.

13. With which one of the following statements would the author of the passage be most likely to agree?

(A) Some authors of slave narratives allowed the purposes of the genre to overshadow their own experiences.

(B) The slave narrative, no less than the domestic novel, constitutes a literary genre.

(C) Authors who write in a particular genre must obey the conventions of that genre.

(D) An autobiography, no less than a novel, should tell a powerful story.

(E) Autobiographies should be evaluated not on their literary merit but on their historical accuracy.

14. Which one of the following principles most likely governs the author's evaluation of Jacobs's narrative?

(A) Those autobiographical narratives that capture the mood of a particular period are thereby more valuable.

(B) Those autobiographical narratives that focus on accurately depicting the events in the individual's life are thereby more valuable.

(C) Those autobiographical narratives that force readers to view certain familiar cultural values in a wider context are thereby more valuable.

(D) Those autobiographical narratives that are written from a perspective familiar to the majority of their readers are thereby more valuable.

(E) Those autobiographical narratives that employ the conventions of another literary genre are thereby more valuable.

GO ON TO THE NEXT PAGE.

Experts anticipate that global atmospheric concentrations of carbon dioxide (CO_2) will have doubled by the end of the twenty-first century. It is known that CO_2 can contribute to global warming by
(5) trapping solar energy that is being reradiated as heat from the Earth's surface. However, some research has suggested that elevated CO_2 levels could enhance the photosynthetic rates of plants, resulting in a lush world of agricultural abundance, and that this CO_2
(10) fertilization effect might eventually decrease the rate of global warming. The increased vegetation in such an environment could be counted on to draw more CO_2 from the atmosphere. The level of CO_2 would thus increase at a lower rate than many experts have
(15) predicted.

However, while a number of recent studies confirm that plant growth would be generally enhanced in an atmosphere rich in CO_2, they also suggest that increased CO_2 would differentially increase the growth
(20) rate of different species of plants, which could eventually result in decreased agricultural yields. Certain important crops such as corn and sugarcane that currently have higher photosynthetic efficiencies than other plants may lose that edge in an atmosphere
(25) rich in CO_2. Patterson and Flint have shown that these important crops may experience yield reductions because of the increased performance of certain weeds. Such differences in growth rates between plant species could also alter ecosystem stability. Studies have
(30) shown that within rangeland regions, for example, a weedy grass grows much better with plentiful CO_2 than do three other grasses. Because this weedy grass predisposes land to burning, its potential increase may lead to greater numbers of and more severe wildfires in
(35) future rangeland communities.

It is clear that the CO_2 fertilization effect does not guarantee the lush world of agricultural abundance that once seemed likely, but what about the potential for the increased uptake of CO_2 to decrease the rate of global
(40) warming? Some studies suggest that the changes accompanying global warming will not improve the ability of terrestrial ecosystems to absorb CO_2. Billings' simulation of global warming conditions in wet tundra grasslands showed that the level of CO_2
(45) actually increased. Plant growth did increase under these conditions because of warmer temperatures and increased CO_2 levels. But as the permafrost melted, more peat (accumulated dead plant material) began to decompose. This process in turn liberated more CO_2 to
(50) the atmosphere. Billings estimated that if summer temperatures rose four degrees Celsius, the tundra would liberate 50 percent more CO_2 than it does currently. In a warmer world, increased plant growth, which could absorb CO_2 from the atmosphere, would
(55) not compensate for this rapid increase in decomposition rates. This observation is particularly important because high-latitude habitats such as the tundra are expected to experience the greatest temperature increase.

15. Which one of the following best states the main point of the passage?

(A) Elevated levels of CO_2 would enhance photosynthetic rates, thus increasing plant growth and agricultural yields.

(B) Recent studies have yielded contradictory findings about the benefits of increased levels of CO_2 on agricultural productivity.

(C) The possible beneficial effects of increased levels of CO_2 on plant growth and global warming have been overstated.

(D) Increased levels of CO_2 would enhance the growth rates of certain plants, but would inhibit the growth rates of other plants.

(E) Increased levels of CO_2 would increase plant growth, but the rate of global warming would ultimately increase.

16. The passage suggests that the hypothesis mentioned in the first paragraph is not entirely accurate because it fails to take into account which one of the following in predicting the effects of increased vegetation on the rate of global warming?

(A) Increased levels of CO_2 will increase the photosynthetic rates of many species of plants.

(B) Increased plant growth cannot compensate for increased rates of decomposition caused by warmer temperatures.

(C) Low-latitude habitats will experience the greatest increases in temperature in an atmosphere high in CO_2.

(D) Increased levels of CO_2 will change patterns of plant growth and thus will alter the distribution of peat.

(E) Increases in vegetation can be counted on to draw more CO_2 from the atmosphere.

17. Which one of the following best describes the function of the last paragraph of the passage?

(A) It presents research that may undermine a hypothesis presented in the first paragraph.

(B) It presents solutions for a problem discussed in the first and second paragraphs.

(C) It provides an additional explanation for a phenomenon described in the first paragraph.

(D) It provides experimental data in support of a theory described in the preceding paragraph.

(E) It raises a question that may cast doubt on information presented in the preceding paragraph.

GO ON TO THE NEXT PAGE.

18. The passage suggests that Patterson and Flint would be most likely to agree with which one of the following statements about increased levels of CO_2 in the Earth's atmosphere?

    (A) They will not increase the growth rates of most species of plants.

    (B) They will inhibit the growth of most crops, thus causing substantial decreases in agricultural yields.

    (C) They are unlikely to increase the growth rates of plants with lower photosynthetic efficiencies.

    (D) They will increase the growth rates of certain species of plants more than the growth rates of other species of plants.

    (E) They will not affect the photosynthetic rates of plants that currently have the highest photosynthetic efficiencies.

19. The author would be most likely to agree with which one of the following statements about the conclusions drawn on the basis of the research on plant growth mentioned in the first paragraph of the passage?

    (A) The conclusions are correct in suggesting that increased levels of CO_2 will increase the photosynthetic rates of certain plants.

    (B) The conclusions are correct in suggesting that increased levels of CO_2 will guarantee abundances of certain important crops.

    (C) The conclusions are correct in suggesting that increased plant growth will reverse the process of global warming.

    (D) The conclusions are incorrect in suggesting that enhanced plant growth could lead to abundances of certain species of plants.

    (E) The conclusions are incorrect in suggesting that vegetation can draw CO_2 from the atmosphere.

20. The passage supports which one of the following statements about peat in wet tundra grasslands?

    (A) More of it would decompose if temperatures rose four degrees Celsius.

    (B) It could help absorb CO_2 from the atmosphere if temperatures rose four degrees Celsius.

    (C) It will not decompose unless temperatures rise four degrees Celsius.

    (D) It decomposes more quickly than peat found in regions at lower latitudes.

    (E) More of it accumulates in regions at lower latitudes.

21. Which one of the following, if true, is LEAST consistent with the hypothesis mentioned in lines 22–25 of the passage?

    (A) The roots of a certain tree species grow more rapidly when the amount of CO_2 in the atmosphere increases, thus permitting the trees to expand into habitats formerly dominated by grasses with high photosynthetic efficiencies.

    (B) When grown in an atmosphere high in CO_2, certain weeds with low photosynthetic efficiencies begin to thrive in cultivated farmlands formerly dominated by agricultural crops.

    (C) When trees of a species with a high photosynthetic efficiency and grasses of a species with a low photosynthetic efficiency were placed in an atmosphere high in CO_2, the trees grew more quickly than the grasses.

    (D) When two different species of grass with equivalent photosynthetic efficiency were placed in an atmosphere high in CO_2, one species grew much more rapidly and crowded the slower-growing species out of the growing area.

    (E) The number of leguminous plants decreased in an atmosphere rich in CO_2, thus diminishing soil fertility and limiting the types of plant species that could thrive in certain habitats.

22. According to the passage, Billings' research addresses which one of the following questions?

    (A) Which kind of habitat will experience the greatest temperature increase in an atmosphere high in CO_2?

    (B) How much will summer temperatures rise if levels of CO_2 double by the end of the twenty-first century?

    (C) Will enhanced plant growth necessarily decrease the rate of global warming that has been predicted by experts?

    (D) Would plant growth be differentially enhanced if atmospheric concentrations of CO_2 were to double by the end of the twenty-first century?

    (E) Does peat decompose more rapidly in wet tundra grasslands than it does in other types of habitats when atmospheric concentrations of CO_2 increase?

GO ON TO THE NEXT PAGE.

By the time Bentham turned his interest to the subject, late in the eighteenth century, most components of modern evidence law had been assembled. Among common-law doctrines regarding
(5) evidence there were, however, principles that today are regarded as bizarre; thus, a well-established (but now abandoned) rule forbade the parties to a case from testifying. Well into the nineteenth century, even defendants in criminal cases were denied the right to
(10) testify to facts that would prove their innocence.

Although extreme in its irrationality, this proscription was in other respects quite typical of the law of evidence. Much of that law consisted of rules excluding relevant evidence, usually on some rational
(15) grounds. Hearsay evidence was generally excluded because absent persons could not be cross-examined. Yet such evidence was mechanically excluded even where out-of-court statements were both relevant and reliable, but the absent persons could not appear in
(20) court (for example, because they were dead).

The morass of evidentiary technicalities often made it unlikely that the truth would emerge in a judicial contest, no matter how expensive and protracted. Reform was frustrated both by the vested interests of
(25) lawyers and by the profession's reverence for tradition and precedent. Bentham's prescription was revolutionary: virtually all evidence tending to prove or disprove the issue in dispute should be admissible. Narrow exceptions were envisioned: instances in
(30) which the trouble or expense of presenting or considering proof outweighed its value, confessions to a Catholic priest, and a few other instances.

One difficulty with Bentham's nonexclusion principle is that some kinds of evidence are inherently
(35) unreliable or misleading. Such was the argument underlying the exclusions of interested-party testimony and hearsay evidence. Bentham argued that the character of evidence should be weighed by the jury: the alternative was to prefer ignorance to knowledge.
(40) Yet some evidence, although relevant, is actually more likely to produce a false jury verdict than a true one. To use a modern example, evidence of a defendant's past bank robberies is excluded, since the prejudicial character of the evidence substantially outweighs its
(45) value in helping the jury decide correctly. Further, in granting exclusions such as sacramental confessions, Bentham conceded that competing social interests or values might override the desire for relevant evidence. But then, why not protect conversations between social
(50) workers and their clients, or parents and children?

Despite concerns such as these, the approach underlying modern evidence law began to prevail soon after Bentham's death: relevant evidence should be admitted unless there are clear grounds of policy for
(55) excluding it. This clear-grounds proviso allows more exclusions than Bentham would have liked, but the main thrust of the current outlook is Bentham's own nonexclusion principle, demoted from a rule to a presumption.

23. Which one of the following is the main idea of the passage?

(A) Bentham questioned the expediency of modern rules of legal evidence.
(B) Bentham's proposed reform of rules of evidence was imperfect but beneficial.
(C) Bentham's nonexclusion principle should be reexamined in the light of subsequent developments.
(D) Rules of legal evidence inevitably entail imperfect mediations of conflicting values and constraints.
(E) Despite their impairment of judicial efficiency, rules of legal evidence are resistant to change.

24. The author's attitude toward eighteenth-century lawyers can best be described as

(A) sympathetic
(B) critical
(C) respectful
(D) scornful
(E) ambivalent

25. The author mentions "conversations between social workers and their clients" (lines 49–50) most probably in order to

(A) suggest a situation in which application of the nonexclusion principle may be questionable
(B) cite an example of objections that were raised to Bentham's proposed reform
(C) illustrate the conflict between competing social interests
(D) demonstrate the difference between social interests and social values
(E) emphasize that Bentham's exceptions to the nonexclusion principle covered a wide range of situations

GO ON TO THE NEXT PAGE.

26. Which one of the following statements concerning the history of the law of evidence is supported by information in the passage?

    (A)   Common-law rules of evidence have been replaced by modern principles.

    (B)   Modern evidence law is less rigid than was eighteenth-century evidence law.

    (C)   Some current laws regarding evidence do not derive from common-law doctrines.

    (D)   The late eighteenth century marked the beginning of evidence law.

    (E)   Prior to the eighteenth century, rules of evidence were not based on common law.

27. The passage is primarily concerned with which one of the following?

    (A)   suggesting the advantages and limitations of a legal reform

    (B)   summarizing certain deficiencies of an outmoded legal system

    (C)   justifying the apparent inadequacies of current evidence law

    (D)   detailing objections to the nonexclusion principle

    (E)   advocating reexamination of a proposal that has been dismissed by the legal profession

28. According to the fourth paragraph of the passage, what specifically does Bentham characterize as preference of ignorance to knowledge?

    (A)   uncritical acceptance of legal conventions

    (B)   failure to weigh the advantages of legal reform

    (C)   exclusion of sacramental confessions

    (D)   refusal to allow the jury to hear and assess relevant testimony

    (E)   rejection of exceptions to Bentham's nonexclusion principle

S T O P

IF YOU FINISH BEFORE TIME IS CALLED, YOU MAY CHECK YOUR WORK ON THIS SECTION ONLY.
DO NOT WORK ON ANY OTHER SECTION IN THE TEST.

SECTION III

Time—35 minutes

25 Questions

<u>Directions:</u> The questions in this section are based on the reasoning contained in brief statements or passages. For some questions, more than one of the choices could conceivably answer the question. However, you are to choose the <u>best</u> answer; that is, the response that most accurately and completely answers the question. You should not make assumptions that are by commonsense standards implausible, superfluous, or incompatible with the passage. After you have chosen the best answer, blacken the corresponding space on your answer sheet.

1. North American eastern white cedars grow both on cliff faces and in forests. Cedars growing on exposed cliff faces receive very few nutrients, and rarely grow bigger than one-tenth the height of cedars growing in forests, where they benefit from moisture and good soil. Yet few eastern white cedars found in forests are as old as four hundred years, while many on cliff faces are more than five hundred years old.

   Which one of the following, if true, most helps to explain the difference in the ages of the cedars on cliff faces and those in forests?

   (A) The conditions on cliff faces are similar to those in most other places where there are few tall trees.

   (B) In areas where eastern white cedars grow, forest fires are relatively frequent, but fires cannot reach cliff faces.

   (C) Trees that are older than a few hundred years start to lose the protective outer layer of their bark.

   (D) The roots of cedars on cliff faces lodge in cracks in the cliff, and once the roots are so large that they fill a crack, the tree is unable to grow any taller.

   (E) Eastern white cedar wood is too soft to be used for firewood or modern buildings, but it is occasionally used to make furniture.

2. Brewer: All children should be given the opportunity to participate in competitive sports; these activities provide an unsurpassed opportunity to engage children's emotions and so stimulate them to put maximum effort into attaining high athletic standards.

   Polanski: I disagree. Competitive athletics does, over time, produce a handful of highly motivated children with a desire to excel at an activity, but many children have no taste for competition, and to make them participate would only cause them to develop an antipathy toward athletics.

   Polanski's response most strongly supports the contention that Polanski misunderstood Brewer to be asserting that

   (A) characteristics acquired by playing competitive sports carry over into the rest of one's life

   (B) winning at competitive sports is essential to motivation to excel at athletics

   (C) children should put more effort into athletic activities than any other form of activity

   (D) children should be required to participate in competitive sports regardless of their interests

   (E) children cannot be motivated without their emotions being engaged

GO ON TO THE NEXT PAGE.

3. The most common bird in Stillwater Marsh is a species of marsh hen, yet this species is rarely seen, even by experienced bird-watchers who seek it. In fact, this bird is seen far less frequently than any other bird inhabiting the marsh, including those that are much smaller and much less abundant.

Each of the following, if true, helps to reconcile the statements above EXCEPT:

(A) The coloration of the marsh hen blends in particularly well with the marsh grass where the marsh hen nests.

(B) The marsh hen's call is harsh and repetitive, whereas the calls of many other marsh birds are pleasant and melodious.

(C) Unlike many small marsh birds, which dash along the banks of the marsh, the marsh hen remains completely still for long periods of time.

(D) Many marsh birds are most active during daylight hours, but the marsh hen is usually most active at night.

(E) Although many small marsh birds fly in groups to several feeding areas each day, the marsh hen tends to be solitary and flies only when it is in danger.

4. Limited research indicates that therapeutic intervention before the onset of mental disorders can mitigate factors identified as major contributors to them. But a much more comprehensive research program is needed to verify these results and allow for the design of specific health care measures. Thus, in order to explore a potential means of cost-effectively helping people prone to mental disorders, we should increase funding for intervention research.

Which one of the following, if true, most strengthens the argument?

(A) Most minor mental disorders are more expensive to treat than other minor health problems.

(B) Prevention research can be coordinated by drawing together geneticists, neurologists, and behavioral scientists.

(C) Reducing known risk factors for mental disorders is relatively inexpensive compared to the long-term treatment required.

(D) Current funding for intervention research is now higher than it has ever been before.

(E) Once a mental disorder disappears, there is a fair chance that it will recur, given that complete cures are rare.

5. The radiation absorbed by someone during an ordinary commercial airline flight is no more dangerous than that received during an ordinary dental X-ray. Since a dental X-ray does negligible harm to a person, we can conclude that the radiation absorbed by members of commercial airline flight crews will also do them negligible harm.

A flaw in the argument is its failure to consider that

(A) there may be many forms of dangerous radiation other than X-rays and the kinds of radiation absorbed by members of commercial airline flight crews

(B) receiving a dental X-ray may mitigate other health risks, whereas flying does not

(C) exposure to X-rays of higher intensity than dental X-rays may be harmful

(D) the longer and the more often one is exposed to radiation, the more radiation one absorbs and the more seriously one is harmed

(E) flying at high altitude involves risks in addition to exposure to minor radiation

6. The recent cleaning of frescoes in the Sistine Chapel has raised important aesthetic issues. Art historians are now acutely aware that the colors of the works they study may differ from the works' original colors. Art historians have concluded from this that interpretations of the frescoes that seemed appropriate before the frescoes' restoration may no longer be appropriate.

Which one of the following principles, if valid, most helps to justify the art historians' reasoning?

(A) The appropriateness of an interpretation of an artwork is relative to the general history of the period in which the interpretation is made.

(B) The restoration of an artwork may alter it such that it will have colors that the artist did not intend for it to have.

(C) The colors of an artwork are relevant to an appropriate interpretation of that work.

(D) Art historians are the best judges of the value of an artwork.

(E) Interpretations of an artwork are appropriate if they originated during the period when the work was created.

GO ON TO THE NEXT PAGE.

7. Unlike newspapers in the old days, today's newspapers and televised news programs are full of stories about murders and assaults in our city. One can only conclude from this change that violent crime is now out of control, and, to be safe from personal attack, one should not leave one's home except for absolute necessities.

    Which one of the following, if true, would cast the most serious doubt on the conclusion?

    (A) Newspapers and televised news programs have more comprehensive coverage of violent crime than newspapers did in the old days.
    (B) National data show that violent crime is out of control everywhere, not just in the author's city.
    (C) Police records show that people experience more violent crimes in their own neighborhoods than they do outside their neighborhoods.
    (D) Murder comprised a larger proportion of violent crimes in the old days than it does today.
    (E) News magazines play a more important role today in informing the public about crime than they did in the old days.

8. Most people invest in the stock market without doing any research of their own. Some of these people rely solely on their broker's advice, whereas some others make decisions based merely on hunches. Other people do some research of their own, but just as often rely only on their broker or on hunches. Only a few always do their own research before investing. Nonetheless, a majority of investors in the stock market make a profit.

    If the statements in the passage are true, which one of the following must also be true?

    (A) Some people who make a profit on their investments in the stock market do so without doing any research of their own.
    (B) Most people who invest in the stock market either rely solely on their broker or make decisions based merely on hunches.
    (C) Some people who do investment research on their own, while just as often relying on their broker or on hunches, make a profit in the stock market.
    (D) Most people who invest in the stock market without doing any research of their own make a profit.
    (E) Most people who rely solely on their broker rather than on hunches make a profit in the stock market.

9. At some point in any discussion of societal justice, the only possible doctrinal defense seems to be "That is the way we do things here." Different communities that each recognize the dignity and equality of all citizens will, for example, nevertheless settle on somewhat different provisions for the elderly. So we can see that general principles of justice are never sufficient to determine the details of social policies fixed within a particular state.

    Which one of the following statements, if true, most strengthens the argument concerning the general principles of justice?

    (A) Although two socialist states each adhered to the same electoral principles, one had a different type of machine for counting ballots in public elections than the other did.
    (B) Two democratic industrial states, both subscribing to capitalistic economic principles, differed markedly in the respective proportions of land they devoted to forestry.
    (C) Although each adhered to its own principles, a democracy and a monarchy each had the same distribution of wealth in its population.
    (D) Two states founded on and adhering to similar principles of justice had different requirements that had to be met in order to be eligible for government-subsidized day care.
    (E) Two societies based on different principles of justice, each adhering to its own principles, had the same unemployment benefits.

10. The importance of the ozone layer to terrestrial animals is that it entirely filters out some wavelengths of light but lets others through. Holes in the ozone layer and the dangers associated with these holes are well documented. However, one danger that has not been given sufficient attention is that these holes could lead to severe eye damage for animals of many species.

    Which one of the following is most strongly supported by the statements above, if they are true?

    (A) All wavelengths of sunlight that can cause eye damage are filtered out by the ozone layer, where it is intact.
    (B) Few species of animals live on a part of the earth's surface that is not threatened by holes in the ozone layer.
    (C) Some species of animals have eyes that will not suffer any damage when exposed to unfiltered sunlight.
    (D) A single wavelength of sunlight can cause severe damage to the eyes of most species of animals.
    (E) Some wavelengths of sunlight that cause eye damage are more likely to reach the earth's surface where there are holes in the ozone layer than where there are not.

GO ON TO THE NEXT PAGE.

Questions 11–12

Some people claim that the reason herbs are not prescribed as drugs by licensed physicians is that the medical effectiveness of herbs is seriously in doubt. No drug can be offered for sale, however, unless it has regulatory-agency approval for medicinal use in specific illnesses or conditions. It costs about $200 million to get regulatory-agency approval for a drug, and only the holder of a patent can expect to recover such large expenses. Although methods of extracting particular substances from herbs can be patented, herbs themselves and their medicinal uses cannot be. Therefore, under the current system licensed physicians cannot recommend the medicinal use of herbs.

11. The argument depends on the assumption that

(A) the medical ineffectiveness of many herbs as treatments for specific illnesses or conditions is well established

(B) the only time a substance is properly used as a drug is when it is prescribed as a drug by a licensed physician

(C) a licensed physician cannot recommend the medicinal use of an herb unless that herb is offered for sale as a drug

(D) some other substances, besides herbs, are not available as drugs because the illnesses they could effectively treat are too uncommon to allow those substances to be marketed profitably as drugs

(E) the cost of medical care would be substantially reduced if faster ways of obtaining regulatory-agency approval for new drugs could be found

12. Which one of the following most accurately describes the argumentative technique used in the argument?

(A) questioning a claim about why something is the case by supplying an alternative explanation

(B) attacking the validity of the data on which a competing claim is based

(C) revealing an inconsistency in the reasoning used to develop an opposing position

(D) identifying all plausible explanations for why something is the case and arguing that all but one of them can be eliminated

(E) testing a theory by determining the degree to which a specific situation conforms to the predictions of that theory

13. Editorialist: Some people argue that ramps and other accommodations for people using wheelchairs are unnecessary in certain business areas because those areas are not frequented by wheelchair users. What happens, however, is that once ramps and other accommodations are installed in these business areas, people who use wheelchairs come there to shop and work.

Which one of the following is most strongly supported by the editorialist's statements?

(A) Owners of business areas not frequented by wheelchair users generally are reluctant to make modifications.

(B) Businesses that install proper accommodations for wheelchair users have greater profits than those that do not.

(C) Many businesses fail to make a profit because they do not accommodate wheelchair users.

(D) Most businesses are not modified to accommodate wheelchair users.

(E) Some business areas are not frequented by wheelchair users because the areas lack proper accommodations.

14. Many people think that the only way to remedy the problem of crime is by increasing the number of police officers, but recent statistics show that many major cities had similar ratios of police officers to citizens, yet diverged widely in their crime rates.

The statistics cited function in the argument to

(A) establish that the number of police officers does not need to be increased

(B) illustrate the need for increasing the number of police officers in major cities

(C) prove that there are factors other than the number of police officers that are more important in reducing the crime rate

(D) demonstrate that there is no relation between the number of police officers and the crime rate

(E) suggest that the number of police officers is not the only influence on the crime rate

GO ON TO THE NEXT PAGE.

15. Scientists hoping to understand and eventually reverse damage to the fragile ozone layer in the Earth's upper atmosphere used a spacecraft to conduct crucial experiments. These experiments drew criticism from a group of environmentalists who observed that a single trip by the spacecraft did as much harm to the ozone layer as a year's pollution by the average factory, and that since the latter was unjustifiable so must be the former.

The reasoning in the environmentalists' criticism is questionable because it

(A) treats as similar two cases that are different in a critical respect

(B) justifies a generalization on the basis of a single instance

(C) fails to distinguish the goal of reversing harmful effects from the goal of preventing those harmful effects

(D) attempts to compare two quantities that are not comparable in any way

(E) presupposes that experiments always do harm to their subjects

16. Curator: Since ancient times, the fine arts were developed and sustained with the aid of large subsidies from the aristocracies and religious institutions that were the public sectors of their day; it is doubtful that the arts would have survived without these subsidies. Clearly, contemporary societies should fulfill their obligation as stewards of cultural heritage without the assistance of aristocracies or religious institutions, so governments must help finance the maintenance, advancement, and enrichment of the fine arts today.

The curator's argument depends on assuming which one of the following?

(A) The fine arts would be more highly developed now if they had been given greater governmental subsidies in the past.

(B) If contemporary governments help to maintain and enrich the fine arts, private support for the arts will become unnecessary.

(C) In contemporary societies, aristocracies and religious institutions are not willing to help finance the fine arts.

(D) Serving as stewards of cultural heritage requires that contemporary societies help to maintain the fine arts.

(E) Maintenance, advancement, and enrichment of the fine arts in any era require governmental subsidies.

17. In a business whose owners and employees all belong to one family, the employees can be paid exceptionally low wages. Hence, general operating expenses are much lower than they would be for other business ventures, making profits higher. So a family business is a family's surest road to financial prosperity.

The reasoning in the argument is flawed because the argument

(A) ignores the fact that businesses that achieve high levels of customer satisfaction are often profitable even if they pay high wages

(B) presumes, without providing justification, that businesses that pay the lowest wages have the lowest general operating expenses and thus the highest profits

(C) ignores the fact that in a family business, paying family members low wages may itself reduce the family's prosperity

(D) presumes, without providing justification, that family members are willing to work for low wages in a family business because they believe that doing so promotes the family's prosperity

(E) presumes, without providing justification, that only businesses with low general operating expenses can succeed

GO ON TO THE NEXT PAGE.

18. Studies have shown that photosynthesis, the process by which plants manufacture life-sustaining proteins from sunlight and carbon, is actually intensified if the level of carbon dioxide in the atmosphere is increased. Since carbon dioxide levels are increased by the burning of fossil fuels and by other human industrial activities, it is obvious that these industrial activities are purely beneficial to agriculture and those of us who depend upon it.

The flawed reasoning in the argument above is most similar to that in which one of the following?

(A) Because a high fiber diet has been shown to be more healthful than a low fiber diet, a diet in which foods with a low fiber content have been entirely replaced by foods with a high fiber content is bound to be even more healthful.

(B) Because exercise has been shown to prevent a number of diseases, injuries, and other human ills, clearly no harm, and a lot of good, can come from exercise.

(C) Consistently consuming more calories than one expends inevitably leads to excessive weight gain, so if one wishes to avoid the health problems associated with this condition, one ought to fast periodically.

(D) It has been shown that one can obtain more vitamins and minerals from fresh fruits and vegetables than from processed fruits and vegetables. One ought, therefore, to completely abandon consumption of the latter in favor of the former.

(E) Excessive use of penicillin tends to increase one's susceptibility to penicillin-resistant infections. The best policy, therefore, is to avoid using penicillin, thereby strengthening the body's innate ability to resist disease.

19. Raphaela: Forcing people to help others is morally wrong. Therefore, no government has the right to redistribute resources via taxation. Anyone who wants can help others voluntarily.

Edward: Governments do have that right, insofar as they give people the freedom to leave and hence not to live under their authority.

Raphaela and Edward disagree about the truth of which one of the following?

(A) Any government that does not permit emigration would be morally wrong to redistribute resources via taxation.

(B) Any government that permits emigration has the right to redistribute resources via taxation.

(C) Every government should allow people to help others voluntarily.

(D) Any government that redistributes resources via taxation forces people to help others.

(E) Any government that forces people to help others should permit emigration.

20. Galanin is a protein found in the brain. In an experiment, rats that consistently chose to eat fatty foods when offered a choice between lean and fatty foods were found to have significantly higher concentrations of galanin in their brains than did rats that consistently chose lean over fatty foods. These facts strongly support the conclusion that galanin causes rats to crave fatty foods.

Which one of the following, if true, most supports the argument?

(A) The craving for fatty foods does not invariably result in a rat's choosing those foods over lean foods.

(B) The brains of the rats that consistently chose to eat fatty foods did not contain significantly more fat than did the brains of rats that consistently chose lean foods.

(C) The chemical components of galanin are present in both fatty foods and lean foods.

(D) The rats that preferred fatty foods had the higher concentrations of galanin in their brains before they were offered fatty foods.

(E) Rats that metabolize fat less efficiently than do other rats develop high concentrations of galanin in their brains.

21. Some government economists view their home countries as immune to outside influence. But economies are always open systems; international trade significantly affects prices and wages. Just as physicists learned the shortcomings of a mechanics based on idealizations such as the postulation of perfectly frictionless bodies, government economists must look beyond national borders if their nations' economies are to prosper.

The argument's conclusion follows logically if which one of the following is assumed?

(A) A national economy cannot prosper unless every significant influence on it has been examined by that nation's government economists.

(B) Economics is weakly analogous to the physical sciences.

(C) Economic theories relying on idealizations are generally less accurate than economic theories that do not rely on idealizations.

(D) International trade is the primary significant variable influencing prices and wages.

(E) Some government economists have been ignoring the effects of international trade on prices and wages.

GO ON TO THE NEXT PAGE.

22. If relativity theory is correct, no object can travel forward in time at a speed greater than the speed of light. Yet quantum mechanics predicts that the tachyon, a hypothetical subatomic particle, travels faster than light. Thus, if relativity theory is correct, either quantum mechanics' prediction about tachyons is erroneous or tachyons travel backward in time.

The pattern of reasoning in which one of the following arguments is most similar to that in the argument above?

(A) According to a magazine article, the view that present-day English is a descendant of the ancient Proto-Indo-European language is incorrect. Rather, English more likely descended from a Finno-Ugric language, judging from the similarities between English and other languages of Finno-Ugric descent.

(B) If the defendant committed the crime, then either the defendant had a motive or the defendant is irrational, for only irrational persons act with no motive. If the psychologist is correct, then the defendant is not rational; on the other hand, according to the evidence, the defendant had a strong motive. Thus, since there is no reason to disbelieve the evidence, the defendant is guilty.

(C) The human brain can survive without oxygen only for a few minutes, according to modern medicine. Surprisingly, a reliable witness reported that a shaman has survived for an entire week buried five feet underground. Thus, if modern medicine is not wrong, either the witness is mistaken or the shaman's brain did not suffer any lack of oxygen.

(D) Alexander the Great was buried either in Alexandria or in Siwa, Egypt. However, the burial place is more likely to be Siwa. A limestone table engraved by Ptolemy, Alexander's lieutenant, was found in Siwa, attesting to Alexander's burial place.

(E) If the big bang theory is correct, the universe is currently expanding: the galaxies are moving away from each other and from the center of an original explosion. The same theory also predicts that, eventually, the gravitational forces among galaxies will counterbalance the galaxies' kinetic energy. It follows that, at some point, the universe will stop expanding.

23. Maria won this year's local sailboat race by beating Sue, the winner in each of the four previous years. We can conclude from this that Maria trained hard.

The conclusion follows logically if which one of the following is assumed?

(A) Sue did not train as hard as Maria trained.
(B) If Maria trained hard, she would win the sailboat race.
(C) Maria could beat a four-time winner only if she trained hard.
(D) If Sue trained hard, she would win the sailboat race.
(E) Sue is usually a faster sailboat racer than Maria.

GO ON TO THE NEXT PAGE.

24. Dietician: "The French Paradox" refers to the unusual concurrence in the population of France of a low incidence of heart disease and a diet high in fat. The most likely explanation is that the French consume a high quantity of red wine, which mitigates the ill effects of the fat they eat. So North Americans, with nearly the highest rate of heart disease in the world, should take a cue from the French: if you want to be healthier without cutting fat intake, drink more red wine.

Which one of the following statements, if true, most seriously undermines the conclusion of the dietician's argument?

(A) French men consume as much red wine as French women do, yet French men have a higher rate of heart disease than do French women.

(B) A greater intake of red wine among North Americans would likely lead to a higher incidence of liver problems and other illnesses.

(C) Not all French people have a diet that includes large amounts of fat and a high quantity of red wine.

(D) All evidence suggests that the healthiest way to decrease the chance of heart disease is to exercise and keep a diet low in fat.

(E) Many other regions have much lower rates of heart disease than France, though their populations consume even less red wine than do North Americans.

25. We are in a new industrial revolution that requires management trainees to develop "action learning" from real experience within business and industry, rather than getting tied up with theory and academia. Business schools seem unable, on their own, to tear themselves away from their largely academic roots and move closer to the realities of today's business and industry; too often, trainees in business schools find themselves studying hypothetical cases instead of real ones. Furthermore, business schools have been slow to respond to the needs of business. Therefore, business schools should allow business executives to set curricula for management trainees that could then be taught by academics.

The argument relies on which one of the following assumptions?

(A) Academics in business schools have no practical business experience that is valuable.

(B) Academics in business schools deal only with hypothetical situations in their business case studies.

(C) Academics are not capable of teaching curricula suitable for relevant management training.

(D) Academic training outside of business schools is more responsive to the needs of business than is training within business schools.

(E) Today's business executives have valuable insight into business that academics in business schools do not have.

S T O P

IF YOU FINISH BEFORE TIME IS CALLED, YOU MAY CHECK YOUR WORK ON THIS SECTION ONLY.
DO NOT WORK ON ANY OTHER SECTION IN THE TEST.

SECTION IV

Time—35 minutes

23 Questions

Directions: Each group of questions in this section is based on a set of conditions. In answering some of the questions, it may be useful to draw a rough diagram. Choose the response that most accurately and completely answers each question and blacken the corresponding space on your answer sheet.

Questions 1–5

Each of seven television programs—H, J, L, P, Q, S, V—is assigned a different rank: from first through seventh (from most popular to least popular). The ranking is consistent with the following conditions:
    J and L are each less popular than H.
    J is more popular than Q.
    S and V are each less popular than L.
    P and S are each less popular than Q.
    S is not seventh.

1. Which one of the following could be the order of the programs, from most popular to least popular?

    (A) J, H, L, Q, V, S, P
    (B) H, L, Q, J, S, P, V
    (C) H, J, Q, L, S, V, P
    (D) H, J, V, L, Q, S, P
    (E) H, L, V, J, Q, P, S

2. If J is more popular than L, and S is more popular than P, then which one of the following must be true of the ranking?

    (A) J is second.
    (B) J is third.
    (C) L is third.
    (D) Q is third.
    (E) P is seventh.

3. Which one of the following programs CANNOT be ranked third?

    (A) L
    (B) J
    (C) Q
    (D) V
    (E) P

4. If V is more popular than Q and J is less popular than L, then which one of the following could be true of the ranking?

    (A) P is more popular than S.
    (B) S is more popular than V.
    (C) P is more popular than L.
    (D) J is more popular than V.
    (E) Q is more popular than V.

5. If Q is more popular than L, then each of the following must be true of the ranking EXCEPT:

    (A) H is first.
    (B) L is fourth.
    (C) V is not fourth.
    (D) J is not third.
    (E) Q is third.

GO ON TO THE NEXT PAGE.

Questions 6–12

Bird-watchers explore a forest to see which of the following six kinds of birds—grosbeak, harrier, jay, martin, shrike, wren—it contains. The findings are consistent with the following conditions:

If harriers are in the forest, then grosbeaks are not.
If jays, martins, or both are in the forest, then so are harriers.
If wrens are in the forest, then so are grosbeaks.
If jays are not in the forest, then shrikes are.

6. Which one of the following could be a complete and accurate list of the birds NOT in the forest?

(A) jays, shrikes
(B) harriers, grosbeaks
(C) grosbeaks, jays, martins
(D) grosbeaks, martins, shrikes, wrens
(E) martins, shrikes

7. If both martins and harriers are in the forest, then which one of the following must be true?

(A) Shrikes are the only other birds in the forest.
(B) Jays are the only other birds in the forest.
(C) The forest contains neither jays nor shrikes.
(D) There are at least two other kinds of birds in the forest.
(E) There are at most two other kinds of birds in the forest.

8. If jays are not in the forest, then which one of the following must be false?

(A) Martins are in the forest.
(B) Harriers are in the forest.
(C) Neither martins nor harriers are in the forest.
(D) Neither martins nor shrikes are in the forest.
(E) Harriers and shrikes are the only birds in the forest.

9. Which one of the following is the maximum number of the six kinds of birds the forest could contain?

(A) two
(B) three
(C) four
(D) five
(E) six

10. Which one of the following pairs of birds CANNOT be among those birds contained in the forest?

(A) jays, wrens
(B) jays, shrikes
(C) shrikes, wrens
(D) jays, martins
(E) shrikes, martins

11. If grosbeaks are in the forest, then which one of the following must be true?

(A) Shrikes are in the forest.
(B) Wrens are in the forest.
(C) The forest contains both wrens and shrikes.
(D) At most two kinds of birds are in the forest.
(E) At least three kinds of birds are in the forest.

12. Suppose the condition is added that if shrikes are in the forest, then harriers are not. If all other conditions remain in effect, then which one of the following could be true?

(A) The forest contains both jays and shrikes.
(B) The forest contains both wrens and shrikes.
(C) The forest contains both martins and shrikes.
(D) Jays are not in the forest, whereas martins are.
(E) Only two of the six kinds of birds are not in the forest.

GO ON TO THE NEXT PAGE.

4

Questions 13–18

From among ten stones, a jeweler will select six, one for each of six rings. Of the stones, three—F, G, and H—are rubies; three—J, K, and M—are sapphires; and four—W, X, Y, and Z—are topazes. The selection of stones must meet the following restrictions:

At least two of the topazes are selected.
If exactly two of the sapphires are selected, exactly one of the rubies is selected.
If W is selected, neither H nor Z is selected.
If M is selected, W is also selected.

13. Which one of the following could be the selection of stones?

   (A)   F, G, H, M, X, Y
   (B)   F, G, J, K, M, W
   (C)   F, G, J, K, W, X
   (D)   G, H, J, X, Y, Z
   (E)   G, H, K, W, X, Z

14. Which one of the following must be true?

   (A)   G is selected.
   (B)   J is selected.
   (C)   X is selected.
   (D)   Of at least one of the three types of stones, exactly one stone is selected.
   (E)   Of at least one of the three types of stones, exactly three stones are selected.

15. If Z is selected, which one of the following could be true?

   (A)   All three of the sapphires are selected.
   (B)   Both J and M are selected.
   (C)   Both K and M are selected.
   (D)   None of the rubies is selected.
   (E)   None of the sapphires is selected.

16. If exactly two rubies are selected, which one of the following must be true?

   (A)   H is selected.
   (B)   J is selected.
   (C)   Z is selected.
   (D)   Exactly one sapphire is selected.
   (E)   Exactly two topazes are selected.

17. Which one of the following must be true?

   (A)   The selection of stones includes at least one ruby.
   (B)   The selection of stones includes at most two rubies.
   (C)   The selection of stones includes either F or Z, or both.
   (D)   The selection of stones includes either X or Y, or both.
   (E)   The selection of stones includes either X or Z, or both.

18. If J and M are the only sapphires selected, which one of the following could be true?

   (A)   F and G are both selected.
   (B)   F and X are both selected.
   (C)   G and H are both selected.
   (D)   G and K are both selected.
   (E)   Y and Z are both selected.

GO ON TO THE NEXT PAGE.

Questions 19–23

There are exactly ten stores and no other buildings on Oak Street. On the north side of the street, from west to east, are stores 1, 3, 5, 7, and 9; on the south side of the street, also from west to east, are stores 2, 4, 6, 8, and 10. The stores on the north side are located directly across the street from those on the south side, facing each other in pairs, as follows: 1 and 2; 3 and 4; 5 and 6; 7 and 8; 9 and 10. Each store is decorated with lights in exactly one of the following colors: green, red, and yellow. The stores have been decorated with lights according to the following conditions:

   No store is decorated with lights of the same color as those of any store adjacent to it.
   No store is decorated with lights of the same color as those of the store directly across the street from it.
   Yellow lights decorate exactly one store on each side of the street.
   Red lights decorate store 4.
   Yellow lights decorate store 5.

19. Which one of the following could be an accurate list of the colors of the lights that decorate stores 2, 4, 6, 8, and 10, respectively?

   (A)   green, red, green, red, green
   (B)   green, red, green, yellow, red
   (C)   green, red, yellow, red, green
   (D)   yellow, green, red, green, red
   (E)   yellow, red, green, red, yellow

20. If green lights decorate store 7, then each of the following statements could be false EXCEPT:

   (A)   Green lights decorate store 2.
   (B)   Green lights decorate store 10.
   (C)   Red lights decorate store 8.
   (D)   Red lights decorate store 9.
   (E)   Yellow lights decorate store 2.

21. Which one of the following statements must be true?

   (A)   Green lights decorate store 10.
   (B)   Red lights decorate store 1.
   (C)   Red lights decorate store 8.
   (D)   Yellow lights decorate store 8.
   (E)   Yellow lights decorate store 10.

22. If green lights decorate five stores on the street, then which one of the following statements must be true?

   (A)   Green lights decorate store 9.
   (B)   Red lights decorate store 2.
   (C)   Red lights decorate store 7.
   (D)   Red lights decorate store 10.
   (E)   Yellow lights decorate store 8.

23. Suppose that yellow lights decorate exactly two stores, not just one, on the south side of the street and decorate exactly one store on the north side. If all of the other conditions remain the same, then which one of the following statements must be true?

   (A)   Green lights decorate store 1.
   (B)   Red lights decorate store 7.
   (C)   Red lights decorate store 10.
   (D)   Yellow lights decorate store 2.
   (E)   Yellow lights decorate store 8.

S T O P

IF YOU FINISH BEFORE TIME IS CALLED, YOU MAY CHECK YOUR WORK ON THIS SECTION ONLY.
DO NOT WORK ON ANY OTHER SECTION IN THE TEST.

Acknowledgment is made to the following sources from which material has been adapted for use in this test booklet:

Robert J. Haggerty, "Mental Illness: First, Prevent." ©1994 by the Tuscaloosa News.

Rushworth Kidder, "The North-South Affluence Gap." ©1988 by the Christian Science Publishing Society.

Donald N. McCloskey, "The Gulliver Effect." ©1995 by Scientific American, Inc.

SIGNATURE _____   / /
DATE

LSAT WRITING SAMPLE TOPIC

The mayor of Highport, a small town on the North American east coast, must decide between two development proposals, each of which precludes the successful completion of the other. The proposed projects are roughly equivalent in cost. Write an argument in support of adopting one of the proposals, with the following criteria in mind:

- New projects undertaken by the town should enhance the flow of money to the area.
- The mayor wants to maintain Highport's desirability as a tourist destination.

The first proposal is to build a light rail system connecting Highport to several nearby urban centers. Although Highport is near several major metropolitan areas, it has no public transportation system linking it to these cities, even though Highport has a large population of residents who work in the nearby cities. Highport's present infrastructure consists of old, narrow roads and while traffic congestion is usually noticeable, it is particularly bad at rush hour. In addition to providing an additional incentive for tourists to travel to Highport, having a light rail system in place would help Highport increase its tax base by attracting new residents to the town who might otherwise choose to live in urban locations more convenient to their workplaces.

The second proposal is to restore and preserve a historic military fortress that lies directly in the path of the planned light rail system. Restoration experts agree that buildings on the historic site cannot be moved and that in order to preserve the fortress the light rail project must be abandoned. Highport has a rich history of both local and national importance, and over the past decade has been successfully cultivating its attractiveness as a tourist destination, to such an extent that tourism is now Highport's largest industry. Because the military fortress is a unique piece of national history, completion of this project will ensure that Highport receives new government grants for the maintenance and preservation of national historic sites.

Directions:

1. Use the Answer Key on the next page to check your answers.

2. Use the Scoring Worksheet below to compute your raw score.

3. Use the Score Conversion Chart to convert your raw score into the 120-180 scale.

Scoring Worksheet

1. Enter the number of questions you answered correctly in each section.

	Number Correct
SECTION I.	———
SECTION II	———
SECTION III.	———
SECTION IV.	———

2. Enter the sum here: ———
   This is your Raw Score.

Conversion Chart

For Converting Raw Score to the 120-180 LSAT Scaled Score
LSAT Form 0LSS46

Reported Score	Raw Score	
	Lowest	Highest
180	98	101
179	97	97
178	96	96
177	95	95
176	94	94
175	93	93
174	92	92
173	91	91
172	90	90
171	89	89
170	87	88
169	86	86
168	85	85
167	83	84
166	81	82
165	80	80
164	78	79
163	77	77
162	75	76
161	73	74
160	72	72
159	70	71
158	68	69
157	66	67
156	65	65
155	63	64
154	61	62
153	59	60
152	58	58
151	56	57
150	54	55
149	53	53
148	51	52
147	49	50
146	48	48
145	46	47
144	45	45
143	43	44
142	42	42
141	40	41
140	39	39
139	37	38
138	36	36
137	34	35
136	33	33
135	32	32
134	31	31
133	29	30
132	28	28
131	27	27
130	26	26
129	25	25
128	24	24
127	23	23
126	22	22
125	21	21
124	20	20
123	19	19
122	18	18
121	17	17
120	0	16

SECTION I

1.	E	8.	E	15.	C	22.	B
2.	A	9.	A	16.	C	23.	B
3.	A	10.	D	17.	C	24.	C
4.	D	11.	E	18.	A	25.	D
5.	E	12.	B	19.	D		
6.	D	13.	B	20.	C		
7.	B	14.	B	21.	C		

SECTION II

1.	C	8.	A	15.	C	22.	C
2.	A	9.	D	16.	B	23.	B
3.	E	10.	E	17.	A	24.	B
4.	B	11.	A	18.	D	25.	A
5.	E	12.	C	19.	A	26.	B
6.	A	13.	B	20.	A	27.	A
7.	B	14.	C	21.	C	28.	D

SECTION III

1.	B	8.	A	15.	A	22.	C
2.	D	9.	D	16.	D	23.	C
3.	B	10.	E	17.	C	24.	B
4.	C	11.	C	18.	B	25.	E
5.	D	12.	A	19.	B		
6.	C	13.	E	20.	D		
7.	A	14.	E	21.	A		

SECTION IV

1.	C	8.	D	15.	E	22.	E
2.	A	9.	C	16.	D	23.	D
3.	E	10.	A	17.	D		
4.	D	11.	A	18.	B		
5.	B	12.	B	19.	B		
6.	D	13.	D	20.	D		
7.	E	14.	E	21.	B		

The Official LSAT PrepTest

34

- June 2001
  PrepTest 34

- Form 2LSS52

SECTION I

Time—35 minutes

26 Questions

<u>Directions:</u> Each passage in this section is followed by a group of questions to be answered on the basis of what is <u>stated</u> or <u>implied</u> in the passage. For some of the questions, more than one of the choices could conceivably answer the question. However, you are to choose the <u>best</u> answer; that is, the response that most accurately and completely answers the question, and blacken the corresponding space on your answer sheet.

Most authoritarian rulers who undertake democratic reforms do so not out of any intrinsic commitment or conversion to democratic ideals, but rather because they foresee or recognize that certain
(5) changes and mobilizations in civil society make it impossible for them to hold on indefinitely to absolute power.

Three major types of changes can contribute to a society's no longer condoning the continuation of
(10) authoritarian rule. First, the values and norms in the society alter over time, reducing citizens' tolerance for repression and concentration of power and thus stimulating their demands for freedom. In some Latin American countries during the 1970s and 1980s, for
(15) example, this change in values came about partly as a result of the experience of repression, which brought in its wake a resurgence of democratic values. As people come to place more value on political freedom and civil liberties they also become more inclined to speak
(20) out, protest, and organize for democracy, frequently beginning with the denunciation of human rights abuses.

In addition to changing norms and values, the alignment of economic interests in a society can shift.
(25) As one scholar notes, an important turning point in the transition to democracy comes when privileged people in society—landowners, industrialists, merchants, bankers—who had been part of a regime's support base come to the conclusion that the authoritarian regime is
(30) dispensable and that its continuation might damage their long-term interests. Such a large-scale shift in the economic interests of these elites was crucial in bringing about the transition to democracy in the Philippines and has also begun occurring incrementally
(35) in other authoritarian nations.

A third change derives from the expanding resources, autonomy, and self-confidence of various segments of society and of newly formed organizations both formal and informal. Students march in the streets
(40) demanding change; workers paralyze key industries; lawyers refuse to cooperate any longer in legal charades; alternative sources of information pierce and then shatter the veil of secrecy and disinformation; informal networks of production and exchange emerge
(45) that circumvent the state's resources and control. This profound development can radically alter the balance of power in a country, as an authoritarian regime that could once easily dominate and control its citizens is placed on the defensive.

(50) Authoritarian rule tends in the long run to generate all three types of changes. Ironically, all three types can be accelerated by the authoritarian regime's initial success at producing economic growth and maintaining social order—success that, by creating a period of
(55) stability, gives citizens the opportunity to reflect on the circumstances in which they live. The more astute or calculating of authoritarian rulers will recognize this and realize that their only hope of retaining some power in the future is to match these democratic social
(60) changes with democratic political changes.

1. Which one of the following most accurately expresses the main point of the passage?

(A) Authoritarian rulers tend to undertake democratic reforms only after it becomes clear that the nation's economic and social power bases will slow economic growth and disrupt social order until such reforms are instituted.

(B) Authoritarian regimes tend to ensure their own destruction by allowing opposition groups to build support among the wealthy whose economic interests are easily led away from support for the regime.

(C) Authoritarian policies tend in the long run to alienate the economic power base in a nation once it becomes clear that the regime's initial success at generating economic growth and stability will be short lived.

(D) Authoritarian principles tend in the long run to be untenable because they demand from the nation a degree of economic and social stability that is impossible to maintain in the absence of democratic institutions.

(E) Authoritarian rulers who institute democratic reforms are compelled to do so because authoritarian rule tends to bring about various changes in society that eventually necessitate corresponding political changes.

GO ON TO THE NEXT PAGE.

2. The author's attitude toward authoritarian regimes is most accurately described as which one of the following?

(A) uncertainty whether the changes in authoritarian regimes represent genuine progress or merely superficial changes

(B) puzzlement about the motives of authoritarian rulers given their tendency to bring about their own demise

(C) confidence that most authoritarian regimes will eventually be replaced by a more democratic form of government

(D) insistence that authoritarian rule constitutes an intrinsically unjust form of government

(E) concern that authoritarian rulers will discover ways to retain power without instituting democratic reforms

3. Which one of the following titles most completely summarizes the content of the passage?

(A) "Avenues for Change: The Case for Dissent in Authoritarian Regimes"

(B) "Human Rights Abuses under Authoritarian Regimes: A Case Study"

(C) "Democratic Coalitions under Authoritarian Regimes: Strategies and Solutions"

(D) "Why Authoritarian Regimes Compromise: An Examination of Societal Forces"

(E) "Growing Pains: Economic Instability in Countries on the Brink of Democracy"

4. Which one of the following most accurately describes the organization of the passage?

(A) A political phenomenon is linked to a general set of causes; this set is divided into categories and the relative importance of each category is assessed; the possibility of alternate causes is considered and rejected.

(B) A political phenomenon is linked to a general set of causes; this set is divided into categories and an explication of each category is presented; the causal relationship is elaborated upon and reaffirmed.

(C) A political phenomenon is identified; the possible causes of the phenomenon are described and placed into categories; one possible cause is preferred over the others and reasons are given for the preference.

(D) A political phenomenon is identified; similarities between this phenomenon and three similar phenomena are presented; the similarities among the phenomena are restated in general terms and argued for.

(E) A political phenomenon is identified; differences between this phenomenon and three similar phenomena are presented; the differences among the phenomena are restated in general terms and argued for.

5. It can most reasonably be inferred from the passage that

(A) many authoritarian rulers would eventually institute democratic reform even if not pressured to do so

(B) citizen dissatisfaction in authoritarian regimes is highest when authoritarian rule is first imposed

(C) popular support for authoritarian regimes is lowest when economic conditions are weak

(D) absolute power in an authoritarian society cannot be maintained indefinitely if the society does not condone the regime

(E) citizens view human rights abuses as the only objectionable aspect of authoritarian regimes

6. Given the information in the passage, authoritarian rulers who institute democratic reforms decide to do so on the basis of which one of the following principles?

(A) Rulers should act in ways that allow occasional curbs on their power if the health of the nation requires it.

(B) Rulers should act in ways that offer the greatest amount of personal freedoms to citizens.

(C) Rulers should act in ways that speed the transition from authoritarian rule to democracy.

(D) Rulers should act in ways that ensure the long-term health of the nation's economy.

(E) Rulers should act in ways that maximize their long-term political power.

GO ON TO THE NEXT PAGE.

The term "blues" is conventionally used to refer to a state of sadness or melancholy, but to conclude from this that the musical genre of the same name is merely an expression of unrelieved sorrow is to miss its deeper
(5) meaning. Despite its frequent focus on such themes as suffering and self-pity, and despite the censure that it has sometimes received from church communities, the blues, understood more fully, actually has much in common with the traditional religious music known as
(10) spirituals. Each genre, in its own way, aims to bring about what could be called a spiritual transformation: spirituals produce a religious experience and the blues elicits an analogous response. In fact the blues has even been characterized as a form of "secular spiritual." The
(15) implication of this apparently contradictory terminology is clear: the blues shares an essential aspect of spirituals. Indeed, the blues and spirituals may well arise from a common reservoir of experience, tapping into an aesthetic that underlies many aspects of
(20) African American culture.

Critics have noted that African American folk tradition, in its earliest manifestations, does not sharply differentiate reality into sacred and secular strains or into irreconcilable dichotomies between good and evil,
(25) misery and joy. This is consistent with the apparently dual aspect of the blues and spirituals. Spirituals, like the blues, often express longing or sorrow, but these plaintive tones are indicative of neither genre's full scope: both aim at transforming their participants'
(30) spirits to elation and exaltation. In this regard, both musical forms may be linked to traditional African American culture in North America and to its ancestral cultures in West Africa, in whose traditional religions worshippers play an active role in invoking the
(35) divine—in creating the psychological conditions that are conducive to religious experience. These conditions are often referred to as "ecstasy," which is to be understood here with its etymological connotation of standing out from oneself, or rather from one's
(40) background psychological state and from one's centered concept of self.

Working in this tradition, blues songs serve to transcend negative experiences by invoking the negative so that it can be transformed through the
(45) virtuosity and ecstatic mastery of the performer. This process produces a double-edged irony that is often evident in blues lyrics themselves; consider, for example the lines "If the blues was money, I'd be a millionaire," in which the singer reconfigures the
(50) experience of sorrow into a paradoxical asset through a kind of boasting bravado. One critic has observed that the impulse behind the blues is the desire to keep painful experiences alive in the performer and audience not just for their own sake, but also in order to coax
(55) from these experiences a lyricism that is both tragic and comic.

7. Based on the passage, with which one of the following statements would the author be most likely to agree?

(A) The emphasis on spiritual transcendence takes the blues out of the realm of folk art and into the realm of organized religion.
(B) Little of the transcendent aspect of the blues is retained in its more modern, electronically amplified, urban forms.
(C) Other forms of African American folk art rely heavily on uses of irony similar to those observed in the blues.
(D) The distinctive musical structure of blues songs is the primary means of producing tensions between sadness and transcendence.
(E) The blues may be of psychological benefit to its listeners.

8. Each of the following is indicated by the passage as a shared aspect of the blues and spirituals EXCEPT:

(A) expressions of sorrow or longing
(B) a striving to bring about a kind of spiritual transformation
(C) a possible link to ancestral West African cultures
(D) the goal of producing exalted emotions
(E) the use of traditional religious terminology in their lyrics

GO ON TO THE NEXT PAGE.

9. Which one of the following most accurately expresses what the author intends "a common reservoir of experience" (line 18) to refer to?

(A) a set of experiences that members of differing cultures frequently undergo and that similarly affects the music of those cultures

(B) a set of ordinary experiences that underlies the development of all musical forms

(C) a set of experiences that contributed to the development of both the blues and spirituals

(D) a set of musically relevant experiences that serves to differentiate reality into irreconcilable dichotomies

(E) a set of experiences arising from the folk music of a community and belonging to the community at large

10. The primary purpose of the second paragraph is to

(A) uncover the shared origin of both the blues and spirituals

(B) examine the process by which ecstasy is produced

(C) identify the musical precursors of the blues

(D) explore the sacred and secular strains of the blues

(E) trace the early development of African American folk tradition

11. The reference to "standing out from oneself" in line 39 primarily serves to

(A) distinguish the standard from the nonstandard, and thus incorrect, use of a word

(B) specify a particular sense of a word that the author intends the word to convey

(C) point out a word that incorrectly characterizes experiences arising from blues performance

(D) identify a way in which religious participation differs from blues performance

(E) indicate the intensity that a good blues artist brings to a performance

12. Which one of the following is most closely analogous to the author's account of the connections among the blues, spirituals, and certain West African religious practices?

(A) Two species of cacti, which are largely dissimilar, have very similar flowers; this has been proven to be due to the one's evolution from a third species, whose flowers are nonetheless quite different from theirs.

(B) Two species of ferns, which are closely similar in most respects, have a subtly different arrangement of stem structures; nevertheless, they may well be related to a third, older species, which has yet a different arrangement of stem structures.

(C) Two types of trees, which botanists have long believed to be unrelated, should be reclassified in light of the essential similarities of their flower structures and their recently discovered relationship to another species, from which they both evolved.

(D) Two species of grass, which may have some subtle similarities, are both very similar to a third species, and thus it can be inferred that the third species evolved from one of the two species.

(E) Two species of shrubs, which seem superficially unalike, have a significantly similar leaf structure; this may be due to their relation to a third, older species, which is similar to both of them.

GO ON TO THE NEXT PAGE.

In the eighteenth century the French naturalist Jean Baptiste de Lamarck believed that an animal's use or disuse of an organ affected that organ's development in the animal's offspring. Lamarck claimed that the
(5) giraffe's long neck, for example, resulted from its ancestors stretching to reach distant leaves. But because biologists could find no genetic mechanism to make the transmission of environmentally induced adaptations seem plausible, they have long held that
(10) inheritance of acquired characteristics never occurs. Yet new research has uncovered numerous examples of the phenomenon.

In bacteria, for instance, enzymes synthesize and break down rigid cell walls as necessary to
(15) accommodate the bacteria's growth. But if an experimenter completely removes the cell wall from a bacterium, the process of wall synthesis and breakdown is disrupted, and the bacterium continues to grow—and multiply indefinitely—without walls. This
(20) inherited absence of cell walls in bacteria results from changes in the interactions among genes, without any attendant changes in the genes themselves.

A fundamentally different kind of environmentally induced heritable characteristic occurs when specific
(25) genes are added to or eliminated from an organism. For example, a certain virus introduces a gene into fruit flies that causes the flies to be vulnerable to carbon dioxide poisoning, and fruit flies infected with the virus will pass the gene to their offspring. But if infected
(30) flies are kept warm while they are producing eggs, the virus is eliminated from the eggs and the offspring are resistant to carbon dioxide. Similarly, if an *Escherichia coli* bacterium carrying a certain plasmid—a small ring of genetic material—comes into contact with an *E. coli*
(35) bacterium lacking the plasmid, the plasmid will enter the second bacterium and become part of its genetic makeup, which it then passes to its offspring. The case of the *E. coli* is especially noteworthy for its suggestion that inheritance of acquired characteristics may have
(40) helped to speed up evolution: for example, many complex cells may have first acquired the ability to carry out photosynthesis by coming into contact with a bacterium possessing the gene for that trait, an ability that normally would have taken eons to develop
(45) through random mutation and natural selection.

The new evidence suggests that genes can be divided into two groups. Most are inherited "vertically," from ancestors. Some, however, seem to have been acquired "horizontally," from viruses,
(50) plasmids, bacteria, or other environmental agents. The evidence even appears to show that genes can be transmitted horizontally between organisms that are considered to be unrelated: from bacteria to plants, for example, or from bacteria to yeast. Such horizontal
(55) transmission may well be the mechanism for inheritance of acquired characteristics that has long eluded biologists, and that may eventually prove Lamarck's hypothesis to be correct.

13. The passage suggests that many biologists no longer believe which one of the following?

(A) An organ's use or disuse can affect that organ's development.
(B) Some but not all genes are inherited horizontally.
(C) All genes are inherited horizontally.
(D) Some but not all genes are inherited vertically.
(E) All genes are inherited vertically.

14. According to the passage, which one of the following is an acquired characteristic transmitted by altering the interaction among genes rather than by adding or eliminating a gene?

(A) invulnerability to carbon dioxide poisoning
(B) susceptibility to carbon dioxide poisoning
(C) lack of cell walls
(D) presence of cell walls
(E) possession of certain plasmids

15. The primary purpose of the last paragraph is to

(A) suggest a modification to Lamarck's hypothesis
(B) demonstrate the correctness of Lamarck's hypothesis
(C) illustrate the significance of Lamarck's hypothesis
(D) criticize scientists' rejection of Lamarck's hypothesis
(E) explain how recent discoveries may support Lamarck's hypothesis

GO ON TO THE NEXT PAGE.

16. Which one of the following, if true, offers the most support for Lamarck's hypothesis?

(A)   Deer have antlers because antlers make deer more likely to survive and reproduce.

(B)   Anteaters developed long snouts because the anteater stretches its snout in order to reach ants hidden well below ground.

(C)   Potatoes produced from synthetic genes tend to be more resistant to disease than are potatoes produced from natural genes.

(D)   Lions raised in captivity tend to have a weaker sense of direction than do lions raised in the wild.

(E)   Pups born to wild dogs tend to be more aggressive than are pups born to dogs bred for hunting.

17. According to the passage, the inheritance of acquired characteristics is particularly significant because this phenomenon

(A)   may affect the speed at which photosynthesis occurs

(B)   may help to explain the process of natural selection

(C)   may occur without affecting the composition of genes

(D)   may influence the rate at which evolution progresses

(E)   may be changed or stopped under experimental conditions

18. Which one of the following can be inferred from the passage about the absence of cell walls in some bacteria?

(A)   It can be reversed by introducing the appropriate gene.

(B)   It can be brought about by a virally introduced gene.

(C)   It can be caused by the loss of a cell wall in a single bacterium.

(D)   It can be halted, but not reversed, by restoring cell walls to a group of bacteria.

(E)   It can be transmitted horizontally to other bacteria.

GO ON TO THE NEXT PAGE.

When women are persecuted on account of their gender, they are likely to be eligible for asylum. Persecution is the linchpin of the definition of a refugee set out in the *United Nations Convention Relating to*
(5)   *the Status of Refugees*. In this document, a refugee is defined as any person facing persecution "for reasons of race, religion, nationality, membership of a particular social group, or political opinion." While persecution on the basis of gender is not explicitly
(10)   listed, this omission does not preclude victims of gender-based persecution from qualifying as refugees, nor does it reflect an intention that such persons be excluded from international protection. Rather, women persecuted on account of gender are eligible for asylum
(15)   under the category of "social group." The history of the inclusion of the social-group category in the definition of a refugee indicates that this category was intended to cover groups, such as women facing gender-based persecution, who are otherwise not covered by the
(20)   definition's specific categories.

The original definition of refugee, which came from the constitution of the International Refugee Organization, did not include social group. However, the above-mentioned *United Nations Convention* added
(25)   the category in order to provide a "safety net" for asylum-seekers who should qualify for refugee status but who fail to fall neatly into one of the enumerated categories. The drafters of the *Convention* intentionally left the precise boundaries of the social-group category
(30)   undefined to ensure that the category would retain the flexibility necessary to address unanticipated situations.

A broad interpretation of social group is supported by the *Handbook on Procedures and Criteria for*
(35)   *Determining Refugee Status* (1979) published by the office of the United Nations High Commissioner for Refugees (UNHCR). The *Handbook* describes a social group as persons of similar background, habits, or social status. This expansive interpretation of the
(40)   category is resonant with the intentions of the *Convention* drafters—a malleable category created for future asylum determinations. Since many women fleeing gender-based persecution share a common background and social status, they should fall within
(45)   the *Handbook's* definition of a social group. Furthermore, a 1985 UNHCR Executive Committee report counseled member states to use the social-group category to classify women asylum-seekers "who face harsh or inhuman treatment due to their having
(50)   transgressed the social mores of the society in which they live."

Such a pronouncement is particularly significant. A position taken by an organization such as the UNHCR is likely to exert a strong influence on the international
(55)   community. In particular, the UNHCR's position is likely to have an impact on the interpretation of national asylum laws, since the terms and definitions used in many national laws have been developed under the international consensus that UNHCR represents.

19. According to the passage, which one of the following is true about both the *United Nations Convention* and the UNHCR *Handbook*?

(A)   Both documents are likely to exert a strong influence on improving the status of women in countries that are members of the United Nations.

(B)   Both documents explicitly support granting refugee status to women fleeing gender-based persecution.

(C)   Both documents recommend using the social-group category to classify women refugees seeking asylum from persecution.

(D)   Both documents suggest that the social-group category can be applied to a wide variety of asylum-seekers.

(E)   Both documents describe a social group as persons who share a similar background and hold a similar status in society.

20. The passage suggests that which one of the following is true about the drafters of the *United Nations Convention*?

(A)   They wanted to ensure that the United Nations would be consulted as new reasons for seeking refugee status arose.

(B)   They followed the precedent set by the International Refugee Organization concerning the status of refugees seeking asylum from gender-based persecution.

(C)   They recognized that it would be difficult to list every possible reason why a person might seek refuge from persecution in the *Convention's* definition of a refugee.

(D)   They did not consider persecution on the basis of gender to be as valid a reason for seeking asylum as persecution on the basis of race, nationality, or religion.

(E)   They did not list gender as a category in the *Convention's* definition of a refugee because gender-based persecution was not a significant problem at the time the *Convention* was drafted.

GO ON TO THE NEXT PAGE.

21. Which one of the following asylum-seekers would be most likely to qualify for refugee status under the social-group category as it is described in the passage?

(A) a woman who is unable to earn enough money to support her family because she comes from a poor country

(B) a woman who has limited opportunities to improve her socioeconomic status because of racial discrimination in her country

(C) a woman who is unable to obtain an education because she is a member of a particular religious group

(D) a woman who faces persecution because she rejects the accepted norm in her country concerning arranged marriages

(E) a woman who faces persecution because she opposes her government's harsh treatment of political prisoners

22. The author describes the definition of social group in the UNHCR *Handbook* as

(A) specific but flexible
(B) obscure but substantive
(C) exhaustive and impartial
(D) general and adaptable
(E) comprehensive and exemplary

23. The author of the passage would most likely agree with which one of the following statements about the definition of a refugee in the constitution of the International Refugee Organization?

(A) It failed to include some asylum-seekers who should have been considered eligible for refugee status.

(B) It provided a strong basis to support the claim that women seeking asylum from gender-based persecution should be eligible for asylum.

(C) It reflected an awareness that some groups of refugees seeking asylum do not easily fall into specific categories.

(D) It established that a person's social-group membership may be as significant a cause of persecution as a person's race, religion, or nationality.

(E) It prevented individual nations from refusing asylum to persons who were clearly eligible for such status on the basis of the definition.

24. The author describes persecution as the "linchpin of the definition of a refugee" (line 3) in order to indicate that

(A) international acceptance of the definition was dependent on reaching consensus about what constituted persecution

(B) international concern about the number of people fleeing persecution was the primary force behind the creation of the definition

(C) persecution is a controversial term and it was difficult to reach international agreement about its exact meaning

(D) persecution is the primary reason why people are forced to leave their home countries and seek asylum elsewhere

(E) persecution is the central factor in determining whether a person is eligible for refugee status

25. The passage suggests that which one of the following is most likely to be true of the relationship between UNHCR documents concerning refugees and many nations' asylum laws?

(A) The terms and definitions in the United Nations documents are frequently interpreted more narrowly than are similar terms and definitions in many national asylum laws.

(B) Many of the specific terms and definitions in the United Nations documents represent a compilation of terms and definitions that were first used in national asylum laws.

(C) A new interpretation of a term or definition in one of the United Nations documents is likely to influence the interpretation of a similar term or definition in a national asylum law.

(D) A change in the wording of a specific definition in one of the United Nations documents must also be reflected in any similar terms or definitions contained in national asylum laws.

(E) The terms and definitions used in many national asylum laws are in direct opposition to the terms and definitions used in the United Nations documents.

26. The primary purpose of the passage is to

(A) trace the development of the definition of an important term
(B) interpret the historical circumstances leading to the development of two documents
(C) resolve two apparently contradictory interpretations of a legal document
(D) suggest an alternative solution to a much-disputed problem
(E) argue against the current definition of a specific term

S T O P

IF YOU FINISH BEFORE TIME IS CALLED, YOU MAY CHECK YOUR WORK ON THIS SECTION ONLY.
DO NOT WORK ON ANY OTHER SECTION IN THE TEST.

SECTION II

Time—35 minutes

25 Questions

Directions: The questions in this section are based on the reasoning contained in brief statements or passages. For some questions, more than one of the choices could conceivably answer the question. However, you are to choose the best answer; that is, the response that most accurately and completely answers the question. You should not make assumptions that are by commonsense standards implausible, superfluous, or incompatible with the passage. After you have chosen the best answer, blacken the corresponding space on your answer sheet.

1. In his new book on his complex scientific research, R frequently imputes bad faith to researchers disagreeing with him. A troubling aspect of R's book is his stated conviction that other investigators' funding sources often determine what "findings" those investigators report. Add to this that R has often shown himself to be arrogant, overly ambitious, and sometimes plain nasty, and it becomes clear that R's book does not merit attention from serious professionals.

    The author of the book review commits which one of the following reasoning errors?

    (A) using an attack on the character of the writer of the book as evidence that this person is not competent on matters of scientific substance
    (B) taking it for granted that an investigator is unlikely to report findings that are contrary to the interests of those funding the investigation
    (C) dismissing a scientific theory by giving a biased account of it
    (D) presenting as facts several assertions about the book under review that are based only on strong conviction and would be impossible for others to verify
    (E) failing to distinguish between the criteria of being true and of being sufficiently interesting to merit attention

2. Having an efficient, attractive subway system makes good economic sense. So, the city needs to purchase new subway cars, since the city should always do what makes good economic sense.

    The conclusion drawn above follows logically if which one of the following is assumed?

    (A) The city should invest in an efficient, attractive subway system.
    (B) Cost-effective subway cars are an integral part of an efficient subway system.
    (C) Investment in new subway cars makes better economic sense than many of the other investment options open to the city.
    (D) New subway cars are financially affordable.
    (E) New subway cars are required in order for the city to have a subway system that is efficient and attractive.

3. Restaurant manager: In response to requests from our patrons for vegetarian main dishes, we recently introduced three: an eggplant and zucchini casserole with tomatoes, brown rice with mushrooms, and potatoes baked with cheese. The first two are frequently ordered, but no one orders the potato dish, although it costs less than the other two. Clearly, then, our patrons prefer not to eat potatoes.

    Which one of the following is an error of reasoning in the restaurant manager's argument?

    (A) concluding that two things that occur at the same time have a common cause
    (B) drawing a conclusion that is inconsistent with one premise of the argument
    (C) ignoring possible differences between what people say they want and what they actually choose
    (D) attempting to prove a claim on the basis of evidence that a number of people hold that claim to be true
    (E) treating one of several plausible explanations of a phenomenon as the only possible explanation

GO ON TO THE NEXT PAGE.

4. For newborns of age four to six weeks whose mothers have been the primary caregivers, the following is true: When the newborns are crying due to hunger or other similar discomfort, merely hearing the mother's voice will lead to a temporary halt in crying, while the voices of others do not have this effect.

Which one of the following is most reasonably supported by the information above?

(A) Babies more easily learn to recognize the voices of their mothers than the voices of other people.
(B) A mother's voice is the first thing a baby learns to recognize.
(C) Babies associate the voice of the primary caregiver with release from discomfort.
(D) Often only a primary caregiver can provide comfort to a newborn.
(E) Discomfort in newborns is best relieved by hearing the mother's voice.

5. Many elementary schools have recently offered computer-assisted educational programs. Students' reactions after several years have been decidedly mixed. Whereas students have found computers very useful in studying arithmetic, they have found them of little help in studying science, and of no help at all with their reading and writing skills.

Which one of the following, if true, most helps to explain the students' mixed reactions?

(A) Students in these schools began reading and doing arithmetic before learning to use computers.
(B) Of the disciplines and skills mentioned, the exactness of arithmetic makes it most suitable to computer-assisted education.
(C) Many elementary school teachers are reluctant to use computer technology in their classrooms.
(D) Young students are more likely to maintain interest in training programs that use the newest computers and video graphics than in those that do not.
(E) The elementary schools have offered more computer-assisted programs in reading and writing than in arithmetic and science.

6. The notion that one might be justified in behaving irrationally in the service of a sufficiently worthy end is incoherent. For if such an action is justified, then one would be behaving rationally, not irrationally.

Which one of the following arguments is most similar in its reasoning to the argument above?

(A) A representative of the law, such as a judge or a police officer, ought not to commit crimes. For if representatives of the law commit crimes, they will be ineffective in preventing crime.
(B) One cannot intend to spill a glass of water accidentally. Spilling it accidentally means that the act will not have been done intentionally.
(C) One cannot live the good life and be unhappy. If one's own neighbors see that one is unhappy, then they will see that one is not living the good life.
(D) Doctors cannot perform self-diagnosis, for they cannot objectively evaluate their own symptoms, and thus will be practicing poor medicine.
(E) One ought not to have both a cat and a goldfish. The goldfish is the natural prey of the cat, so it is unethical to place it at the cat's disposal.

GO ON TO THE NEXT PAGE.

7. A certain moral system holds that performing good actions is praiseworthy only when one overcomes a powerful temptation in order to perform them. Yet this same moral system also holds that performing good actions out of habit is sometimes praiseworthy.

Which one of the following, if true, does the most to reconcile the apparent conflict in the moral system described above?

(A) People who perform good actions out of habit have often acquired this habit after years of having resisted temptation.

(B) Most people face strong moral temptation from time to time but few people have to endure it regularly.

(C) People virtually always perform actions they think are good, regardless of what other people may think.

(D) Since it is difficult to tell what is going on in another person's mind, it is often hard to know exactly how strongly a person is tempted.

(E) It is far more common for people to perform good actions out of habit than for them to do so against strong temptation.

8. Conservationist: The risk to airplane passengers from collisions between airplanes using the airport and birds from the wildlife refuge is negligible. In the 10 years since the refuge was established, only 20 planes have been damaged in collisions with birds, and no passenger has been injured as a result of such a collision. The wildlife refuge therefore poses no safety risk.

Pilot: You neglect to mention that 17 of those 20 collisions occurred within the past 2 years, and that the number of birds in the refuge is rapidly increasing. As the number of collisions between birds and airplanes increases, so does the likelihood that at least one such collision will result in passenger injuries.

The pilot counters the conservationist by

(A) attempting to show that the conservationist's description of the facts is misleading

(B) questioning the conservationist's motives for reaching a certain conclusion

(C) asserting that dangerous situations inevitably become more dangerous with the passage of time

(D) discrediting the moral principle on which the conservationist's argument is based

(E) disputing the accuracy of the figures cited by the conservationist

9. A university study reported that between 1975 and 1983 the length of the average workweek in a certain country increased significantly. A governmental study, on the other hand, shows a significant decline in the length of the average workweek for the same period. Examination of the studies shows, however, that they used different methods of investigation; thus there is no need to look further for an explanation of the difference in the studies' results.

The argument's reasoning is flawed because the argument fails to

(A) distinguish between a study produced for the purposes of the operation of government and a study produced as part of university research

(B) distinguish between a method of investigation and the purpose of an investigation

(C) recognize that only one of the studies has been properly conducted

(D) recognize that two different methods of investigation can yield identical results

(E) recognize that varying economic conditions result in the average workweek changing in length

10. Although the charter of Westside School states that the student body must include some students with special educational needs, no students with learning disabilities have yet enrolled in the school. Therefore, the school is currently in violation of its charter.

The conclusion of the argument follows logically if which one of the following is assumed?

(A) All students with learning disabilities have special educational needs.

(B) The school currently has no students with learning disabilities.

(C) The school should enroll students with special educational needs.

(D) The only students with special educational needs are students with learning disabilities.

(E) The school's charter cannot be modified in order to avoid its being violated.

GO ON TO THE NEXT PAGE.

11. Some psychologists claim that, in theory, the best way to understand another person would be through deep empathy, whereby one would gain a direct and complete grasp of that person's motivations. But suppose they are right; then there would be no way at all to achieve understanding, since it is psychologically impossible to gain a direct and complete grasp of another person's motivations. But obviously one can understand other people; thus these psychologists are wrong.

The argument is most vulnerable to the criticism that it

(A) fails to adequately define the key phrase "deep empathy"

(B) assumes something that it later denies, resulting in a contradiction

(C) confuses a theoretically best way of accomplishing something with the only way of accomplishing it

(D) accepts a claim on mere authority, without requiring sufficient justification

(E) fails to consider that other psychologists may disagree with the psychologists cited

12. The five senses have traditionally been viewed as distinct yet complementary. Each sense is thought to have its own range of stimuli that are incapable of stimulating the other senses. However, recent research has discovered that some people taste a banana and claim that they are tasting blue, or see a color and say that it has a specific smell. This shows that such people, called synesthesiacs, have senses that do not respect the usual boundaries between the five recognized senses.

Which one of the following statements, if true, most seriously weakens the argument?

(A) Synesthesiacs demonstrate a general, systematic impairment in their ability to use and understand words.

(B) Recent evidence strongly suggests that there are other senses besides sight, touch, smell, hearing, and taste.

(C) The particular ways in which sensory experiences overlap in synesthesiacs follow a definite pattern.

(D) The synesthetic phenomenon has been described in the legends of various cultures.

(E) Synesthesiacs can be temporarily rid of their synesthetic experiences by the use of drugs.

13. Essayist: One of the claims of laissez-faire economics is that increasing the minimum wage reduces the total number of minimum-wage jobs available. In a recent study, however, it was found that after an increase in the minimum wage, fast-food restaurants kept on roughly the same number of minimum-wage employees as before the increase. Therefore, laissez-faire economics is not entirely accurate.

The essayist's argument depends on assuming which one of the following?

(A) If laissez-faire economics makes an incorrect prediction about the minimum wage, then all the doctrines of laissez-faire economics are inaccurate.

(B) Minimum-wage job availability at fast-food restaurants included in the study was representative of minimum-wage job availability in general.

(C) No study has ever found that a business has decreased the number of its minimum-wage employees after an increase in the minimum wage.

(D) The fast-food restaurants included in the study did not increase the average wage paid to employees.

(E) The national unemployment rate did not increase following the increase in the minimum wage.

14. Some people claim that every human discovery or invention is an instance of self-expression. But what they seem to ignore is that, trivially, anything we do is self-expressive. So, until they can give us a more interesting interpretation of their claim, we are not obliged to take their claim seriously.

Which one of the following, if true, provides the most support for the reasoning above?

(A) All claims that are trivial are uninteresting.

(B) Most people do not take trivial claims seriously.

(C) No claims that are trivial are worthy of serious consideration.

(D) Every claim is open to both interesting and uninteresting interpretations.

(E) Every interpretation is either trivial or uninteresting.

GO ON TO THE NEXT PAGE.

Questions 15–16

Camera manufacturers typically advertise their products by citing the resolution of their cameras' lenses, the resolution of a lens being the degree of detail the lens is capable of reproducing in the image it projects onto the film. Differences between cameras in this respect are irrelevant for practical photography, however, since all modern lenses are so excellent that they project far more detail onto the film than any photographic film is capable of reproducing in a developed image.

15. Which one of the following most accurately states the main point of the argument?

(A) Camera manufacturers ought to concentrate on building other desirable qualities into their cameras' lenses, rather than concentrating only on the lenses' resolution.

(B) Apart from differences in resolution, there is no practical difference among modern cameras in the quality of the images that they produce.

(C) Advertised differences among cameras in the resolution of their lenses have no practical bearing on the cameras' relative quality as photographic tools.

(D) In concentrating their advertising on the issue of image quality, manufacturers are making a mistake about the interests of potential purchasers of cameras.

(E) Differences among photographic films in the amount of detail they reproduce have a more significant effect on the quality of the developed image than do differences in the resolution of camera lenses.

16. The argument depends on assuming which one of the following?

(A) The definition of the term "resolution" does not capture an important determinant of the quality of photographic instruments and materials.

(B) In determining the amount of detail reproduced in the developed photographic image, differences in the resolutions of available lenses do not compound the deficiencies of available film.

(C) Variations in the method used to process the film do not have any significant effect on the film's resolution.

(D) Flawless photographic technique is needed to achieve the maximum image resolution possible with the materials and equipment being used.

(E) The only factors important in determining the degree of detail reproduced in the final photographic print are the resolution of the camera's lens and the resolution of the film.

17. Dietary researcher: A recent study reports that laboratory animals that were fed reduced-calorie diets lived longer than laboratory animals whose caloric intake was not reduced. In response, some doctors are advocating reduced-calorie diets, in the belief that North Americans' life spans can thereby be extended. However, this conclusion is not supported. Laboratory animals tend to eat much more than animals in their natural habitats, which leads to their having a shorter life expectancy. Restricting their diets merely brings their caloric intake back to natural, optimal levels and reinstates their normal life spans.

Which one of the following, if true, would most weaken the dietary researcher's argument?

(A) North Americans, on average, consume a higher number of calories than the optimal number of calories for a human diet.

(B) North Americans with high-fat, low-calorie diets generally have a shorter life expectancy than North Americans with low-fat, low-calorie diets.

(C) Not all scientific results that have important implications for human health are based on studies of laboratory animals.

(D) Some North Americans who follow reduced-calorie diets are long-lived.

(E) There is a strong correlation between diet and longevity in some species of animals.

GO ON TO THE NEXT PAGE.

18. Editorialist: The positions advanced by radical environmentalists often contain hypotheses that are false and proposals that are economically infeasible. But there is a positive role to be played even by these extremists, for the social and political inertia that attends environmental issues is so stubborn that even small areas of progress can be made only if the populace fears environmental disaster, however untenable the reasons for those fears may be.

Which one of the following most accurately expresses the main conclusion of the editorialist's argument?

(A)   The little progress that has been made in improving the environment is mainly due to the fear created by radical environmentalists.

(B)   Radical environmentalists, by promoting their views, stimulate progress on environmental issues.

(C)   Social and political inertia is most effectively overcome by an extremely fearful populace, regardless of whether its fears are well-founded.

(D)   Radical environmentalists often put forth untenable positions in order to produce the fear that is required to bring about moderate reforms.

(E)   Radical environmentalists advocate positions without regard for factual support or economic feasibility.

19. People should avoid taking the antacid calcium carbonate in doses larger than half a gram, for despite its capacity to neutralize stomach acids, calcium carbonate can increase the calcium level in the blood and thus impair kidney function. Moreover, just half a gram of it can stimulate the production of gastrin, a stomach hormone that triggers acid secretion.

Which one of the following is most strongly supported by the information above?

(A)   Cessation of gastrin production is a more effective method of controlling excess stomach acid than is direct neutralization of stomach acid.

(B)   People who avoid taking more than half a gram of calcium carbonate are less likely than average to suffer from impaired kidney function.

(C)   Doses of calcium carbonate smaller than half a gram can reduce stomach acid more effectively than much larger doses do.

(D)   Half a gram of calcium carbonate can causally contribute to both the secretion and the neutralization of stomach acids.

(E)   Impaired kidney function may increase the level of calcium in the blood.

Questions 20–21

Professor Chan: The literature department's undergraduate courses should cover only true literary works, and not such frivolous material as advertisements.

Professor Wigmore: Advertisements might or might not be true literary works but they do have a powerfully detrimental effect on society—largely because people cannot discern their real messages. The literature department's courses give students the critical skills to analyze and understand texts. Therefore, it is the literature department's responsibility to include the study of advertisements in its undergraduate courses.

20. Which one of the following principles most strongly supports Professor Wigmore's argument?

(A)   Advertisements ought to be framed in such a way that their real messages are immediately clear.

(B)   Any text that is subtly constructed and capable of affecting people's thought and action ought to be considered a form of literature.

(C)   All undergraduate students ought to take at least one course that focuses on the development of critical skills.

(D)   The literature department's courses ought to enable students to analyze and understand any text that could have a harmful effect on society.

(E)   Any professor teaching an undergraduate course in the literature department ought to be free to choose the material to be covered in that course.

21. Which one of the following is an assumption on which Professor Wigmore's argument depends?

(A)   Texts that are true literary works never have a detrimental effect on society.

(B)   Courses offered by the literature department cannot include both true literary works and material such as advertisements.

(C)   Students who take courses in the literature department do not get from those courses other skills besides those needed to analyze and understand texts.

(D)   Forms of advertising that convey their message entirely through visual images do not have a detrimental effect on society.

(E)   The literature department's responsibility is not limited to teaching students how to analyze true literary works.

GO ON TO THE NEXT PAGE.

22. Sociologist: Some people argue that capital punishment for theft was an essential part of the labor discipline of British capitalism. Critics of such a view argue that more people were executed for theft in preindustrial England than were executed in England after industrialization. But such a criticism overlooks the fact that industrialization and capitalism are two very different social phenomena, and that the latter predated the former by several centuries.

Which one of the following most accurately describes the role played in the passage by the point that capitalism and industrialization are distinct?

(A) It is cited as some evidence against the claim that capital punishment for theft was an essential part of the labor discipline of British capitalism.

(B) It is cited as a direct contradiction of the claim that capital punishment for theft was an essential part of the labor discipline of British capitalism.

(C) It is an attempt to conclusively prove the claim that capital punishment for theft was an essential part of the labor discipline of British capitalism.

(D) It is cited as a fact supporting the critics of the view that capital punishment for theft was an essential part of the labor discipline of British capitalism.

(E) It is an attempt to undermine the criticism cited against the claim that capital punishment for theft was an essential part of the labor discipline of British capitalism.

23. To be horrific, a monster must be threatening. Whether or not it presents psychological, moral, or social dangers, or triggers enduring infantile fears, if a monster is physically dangerous then it is threatening. In fact, even a physically benign monster is horrific if it inspires revulsion.

Which one of the following logically follows from the statements above?

(A) Any horror-story monster that is threatening is also horrific.

(B) A monster that is psychologically dangerous, but that does not inspire revulsion, is not horrific.

(C) If a monster triggers infantile fears but is not physically dangerous, then it is not horrific.

(D) If a monster is both horrific and psychologically threatening, then it does not inspire revulsion.

(E) All monsters that are not physically dangerous, but that are psychologically dangerous and inspire revulsion, are threatening.

GO ON TO THE NEXT PAGE.

24. Lawyer: The defendant wanted to clear the snow off his car and in doing so knocked snow on the sidewalk. This same snow melted and refroze, forming ice on which the plaintiff fell, breaking her hip. We argue that the defendant maliciously harmed the plaintiff, because malice is intention to cause harm and the defendant intentionally removed the snow from his car and put it on the sidewalk, which, unbeknownst to the defendant at the time, would subsequently cause the injury suffered by the plaintiff.

The flawed reasoning in which one of the following is most similar to that in the lawyer's argument?

(A)   Alice asked her sister to lie in court. Unbeknownst to Alice's sister, lying in court is against the law. So what Alice asked her sister to do was illegal.

(B)   Bruce wanted to eat the mincemeat pie. Unbeknownst to Bruce, the mincemeat pie was poisonous. So Bruce wanted to eat poison.

(C)   Cheryl denigrated the wine. Cheryl's sister had picked out the wine. So though she may not have realized it, Cheryl indirectly denigrated her sister.

(D)   Deon had lunch with Ms. Osgood. Unbeknownst to Deon, Ms. Osgood is generally thought to be an industrial spy. So Deon had lunch with an industrial spy.

(E)   Edwina bought a car from Mr. Yancy, then resold it. Unbeknownst to Edwina, Mr. Yancy had stolen the car. So Edwina sold a stolen car.

25. Although wood-burning stoves are more efficient than open fireplaces, they are also more dangerous. The smoke that wood-burning stoves release up the chimney is cooler than the smoke from an open flame. Thus it travels more slowly and deposits more creosote, a flammable substance that can clog a chimney—or worse, ignite inside it.

Which one of the following, if true, most seriously weakens the argument?

(A)   The most efficient wood-burning stoves produce less creosote than do many open fireplaces.

(B)   The amount of creosote produced depends not only on the type of flame but on how often the stove or fireplace is used.

(C)   Open fireplaces pose more risk of severe accidents inside the home than do wood-burning stoves.

(D)   Open fireplaces also produce a large amount of creosote residue.

(E)   Homeowners in warm climates rarely use fireplaces or wood-burning stoves.

S T O P

IF YOU FINISH BEFORE TIME IS CALLED, YOU MAY CHECK YOUR WORK ON THIS SECTION ONLY.
DO NOT WORK ON ANY OTHER SECTION IN THE TEST.

SECTION III
Time—35 minutes
26 Questions

Directions: The questions in this section are based on the reasoning contained in brief statements or passages. For some questions, more than one of the choices could conceivably answer the question. However, you are to choose the best answer; that is, the response that most accurately and completely answers the question. You should not make assumptions that are by commonsense standards implausible, superfluous, or incompatible with the passage. After you have chosen the best answer, blacken the corresponding space on your answer sheet.

1. If a doctor gives a patient only a few options for lifestyle modification, the patient is more likely to adhere to the doctor's advice than if the doctor gives the patient many options.

   Which one of the following most accurately expresses the principle illustrated above?

   (A) People are especially likely to ignore the advice they get from doctors if they are confused about that advice.
   (B) People dislike calculating the best of a variety of choices unless they can see a clear difference among the benefits that would result from each choice.
   (C) The tendency people have to alter their behavior varies inversely with the number of alternatives available to them for behavior modification.
   (D) Most people are unlikely to follow their doctor's advice unless they can vividly imagine the consequences of not following the advice.
   (E) In getting good results, the clarity with which a doctor instructs a patient is of equal importance to the accuracy of the doctor's diagnosis on which that instruction is based.

2. To acquire a better understanding of the structure and development of the human personality, some psychologists study the personalities of animals.

   Each of the following, if true, contributes to an explanation of the practice mentioned above EXCEPT:

   (A) The actions of humans and animals are believed to be motivated by similar instincts, but these instincts are easier to discern in animals.
   (B) The law forbids certain experiments on humans but permits them on animals.
   (C) It is generally less expensive to perform experiments on animals than it is to perform them on humans.
   (D) Proper understanding of human personality is thought to provide a model for better understanding the personality of animals.
   (E) Field observations of the behavior of young animals often inspire insightful hypotheses about human personality development.

3. Sigatoka disease drastically reduces the yield of banana trees and is epidemic throughout the areas of the world where bananas are grown. The fungus that causes the disease can be controlled with fungicides, but the fungicides can pose a health hazard to people living nearby. The fungicides are thus unsuitable for small banana groves in populated areas. Fortunately, most large banana plantations are in locations so isolated that fungicides can be used safely there. Therefore, most of the world's banana crop is not seriously threatened by Sigatoka disease.

   Which one of the following is an assumption on which the argument depends?

   (A) It will eventually be possible to breed strains of bananas that are resistant to Sigatoka disease.
   (B) Large plantations produce most or all of the world's bananas.
   (C) Sigatoka disease spreads more slowly on large plantations than in small banana groves.
   (D) Sigatoka disease is the only disease that threatens bananas on a worldwide scale.
   (E) Most of the banana trees that have not been exposed to the Sigatoka fungus grow in small banana groves.

GO ON TO THE NEXT PAGE.

4. A group of 1,000 students was randomly selected from three high schools in a medium-sized city and asked the question, "Do you plan to finish your high school education?" More than 89 percent answered "Yes." This shows that the overwhelming majority of students want to finish high school, and that if the national dropout rate among high school students is high, it cannot be due to a lack of desire on the part of the students.

The reasoning of the argument above is questionable because the argument

(A) fails to justify its presumption that 89 percent is an overwhelming majority
(B) attempts to draw two conflicting conclusions from the results of one survey
(C) overlooks the possibility that there may in fact not be a high dropout rate among high school students
(D) contradicts itself by admitting that there may be a high dropout rate among students while claiming that most students want to finish high school
(E) treats high school students from a particular medium-sized city as if they are representative of high school students nationwide

5. Columnist: A democratic society cannot exist unless its citizens have established strong bonds of mutual trust. Such bonds are formed and strengthened only by participation in civic organizations, political parties, and other groups outside the family. It is obvious then that widespread reliance on movies and electronic media for entertainment has an inherently corrosive effect on democracy.

Which one of the following is an assumption on which the columnist's argument depends?

(A) Anyone who relies on movies and electronic media for entertainment is unable to form a strong bond of mutual trust with a citizen.
(B) Civic organizations cannot usefully advance their goals by using electronic media.
(C) Newspapers and other forms of print media strengthen, rather than weaken, democratic institutions.
(D) Relying on movies and electronic media for entertainment generally makes people less likely to participate in groups outside their families.
(E) People who rely on movies and electronic media for entertainment are generally closer to their families than are those who do not.

6. Standard archaeological techniques make it possible to determine the age of anything containing vegetable matter, but only if the object is free of minerals containing carbon. Prehistoric artists painted on limestone with pigments composed of vegetable matter, but it is impossible to collect samples of this prehistoric paint without removing limestone, a mineral containing carbon, with the paint. Therefore, it is not possible to determine the age of prehistoric paintings on limestone using standard archaeological techniques.

Which one of the following, if true, most seriously weakens the argument?

(A) There exist several different techniques for collecting samples of prehistoric pigments on limestone.
(B) Laboratory procedures exist that can remove all the limestone from a sample of prehistoric paint on limestone.
(C) The age of the limestone itself can be determined from samples that contain no vegetable-based paint.
(D) Prehistoric artists did not use anything other than vegetable matter to make their paints.
(E) The proportion of carbon to other elements in limestone is the same in all samples of limestone.

GO ON TO THE NEXT PAGE.

Questions 7–8

Dr. Jones: The new technology dubbed "telemedicine" will provide sustained improvement in at least rural patient care since it allows rural physicians to televise medical examinations to specialists who live at great distances—specialists who will thus be able to provide advice the rural patient would otherwise not receive.

Dr. Carabella: Not so. Telemedicine might help rural patient care initially. However, small hospitals will soon realize that they can minimize expenses by replacing physicians with technicians who can use telemedicine to transmit examinations to large medical centers, resulting in fewer patients being able to receive traditional, direct medical examinations. Eventually, it will be the rare individual who ever gets truly personal attention. Hence, rural as well as urban patient care will suffer.

7. Which one of the following is a point at issue between Dr. Jones and Dr. Carabella?

(A) whether medical specialists in general offer better advice than rural physicians

(B) whether telemedicine technology will be installed only in rural hospitals and rural medical centers

(C) whether telemedicine is likely to be widely adopted in rural areas in future years

(D) whether the patients who most need the advice of medical specialists are likely to receive it through telemedicine

(E) whether the technology of telemedicine will benefit rural patients in the long run

8. Dr. Carabella uses which one of the following strategies in responding to Dr. Jones?

(A) listing a set of considerations to show that a prescribed treatment that seems to be benefiting a patient in fact harms that patient

(B) describing the application of the technology discussed by Dr. Jones as one step that initiates a process that leads to an undesirable end

(C) citing evidence that Dr. Jones lacks the professional training to judge the case at issue

(D) invoking medical statistics that cast doubt on the premises used in Dr. Jones's argument

(E) providing grounds for dismissing Dr. Jones's interpretation of a key term in medical technology

9. Lines can be parallel in a Euclidean system of geometry. But the non-Euclidean system of geometry that has the most empirical verification is regarded by several prominent physicists as correctly describing the universe we inhabit. If these physicists are right, in our universe there are no parallel lines.

Which one of the following is an assumption that is required by the argument?

(A) There are no parallel lines in the non-Euclidean system of geometry that has the most empirical verification.

(B) Most physicists have not doubted the view that the universe is correctly described by the non-Euclidean system of geometry that has the most empirical verification.

(C) There are no parallel lines in every non-Euclidean system of geometry that has any empirical verification.

(D) The universe is correctly described by the non-Euclidean system of geometry that has the most empirical verification if prominent physicists maintain that it is.

(E) Only physicists who are not prominent doubt the view that the universe is correctly described by the non-Euclidean system of geometry that has the most empirical verification.

10. Philosopher: People are not intellectually well suited to live in large, bureaucratic societies. Therefore, people can find happiness, if at all, only in smaller political units such as villages.

The reasoning in the philosopher's argument is flawed because the argument takes for granted that

(A) no one can ever be happy living in a society in which she or he is not intellectually well suited to live

(B) the primary purpose of small political units such as villages is to make people happy

(C) all societies that are plagued by excessive bureaucracy are large

(D) anyone who lives in a village or other small political unit that is not excessively bureaucratic can find happiness

(E) everyone is willing to live in villages or other small political units

GO ON TO THE NEXT PAGE.

11. The present goal of the field of medicine seems to be to extend life indefinitely. Increasingly, the ability to transplant such organs as hearts, lungs, livers, and kidneys will allow us to live longer. But we can never achieve brain transplants. There are, for a start, ten million nerves running from the brain down the neck, not to mention the millions joining the brain to the sensing organs. Clearly, then, as the transplantation of organs allows more and more people to live longer, those with degenerative brain disorders will form an ever-increasing proportion of the population.

The argument above is based on which one of the following assumptions?

(A) Degenerative brain disorders will increasingly strike younger and younger patients.
(B) It is still quite rare for people to live long enough to need more than one transplant of any given organ.
(C) There are degenerative brain disorders that will not be curable without brain transplants.
(D) Degenerative brain disorders account for a very small proportion of deaths in the population at large.
(E) More is being spent on research into degenerative brain disorders than on research into transplantation.

12. Politician: My opponents argue that the future of our city depends on compromise—that unless the city's leaders put aside their differences and work together toward common goals, the city will suffer. However, the founders of this city based the city's charter on definite principles, and anyone who compromises those principles betrays the city founders' goals. What my opponents are advocating, therefore, is nothing less than betraying the goals of the city's founders.

Critic: I'm afraid your argument is flawed. Unless you're assuming that the differences among the city's leaders are differences of principle, your argument depends on a misleading use of the term ———.

Which one of the following provides the most logical completion of the critic's statement?

(A) betray
(B) common
(C) compromise
(D) principles
(E) opponents

13. Though many insects die soon after reproducing for the first time, some may live for years after the survival of the next generation has been secured. Among the latter are some insects that work for the benefit of the ecosystem—for example, bees.

Which one of the following can be properly inferred from the information above?

(A) Survival of the species, rather than of the individual, is the goal of most insect populations.
(B) Insects that do not play a vital role in the ecosystem are more likely to die after reproducing for the first time.
(C) Most bees live well beyond the onset of the generation that follows them.
(D) Those bees that reproduce do not always die soon after reproducing for the first time.
(E) Most insects are hatched self-sufficient and do not need to be cared for by adult insects.

14. People's political behavior frequently does not match their rhetoric. Although many complain about government intervention in their lives, they tend not to reelect inactive politicians. But a politician's activity consists largely in the passage of laws whose enforcement affects voters' lives. Thus, voters often reelect politicians whose behavior they resent.

Which one of the following most accurately describes the role played in the argument by the claim that people tend not to reelect inactive politicians?

(A) It describes a phenomenon for which the argument's conclusion is offered as an explanation.
(B) It is a premise offered in support of the conclusion that voters often reelect politicians whose behavior they resent.
(C) It is offered as an example of how a politician's activity consists largely in the passage of laws whose enforcement interferes with voters' lives.
(D) It is a generalization based on the claim that people complain about government intervention in their lives.
(E) It is cited as evidence that people's behavior never matches their political beliefs.

GO ON TO THE NEXT PAGE.

15. Lea: Contemporary art has become big business. Nowadays art has less to do with self-expression than with making money. The work of contemporary artists is utterly bereft of spontaneity and creativity, as a visit to any art gallery demonstrates.

Susan: I disagree. One can still find spontaneous, innovative new artwork in most of the smaller, independent galleries.

Lea's and Susan's remarks provide the most support for holding that they disagree about whether

(A) large galleries contain creative artwork
(B) most galleries contain some artwork that lacks spontaneity and creativity
(C) contemporary art has become big business
(D) some smaller art galleries still exhibit creative new artwork
(E) contemporary art, in general, is much less concerned with self-expression than older art is

16. Ethicist: In a recent judicial decision, a contractor was ordered to make restitution to a company because of a bungled construction job, even though the company had signed a written agreement prior to entering into the contract that the contractor would not be financially liable should the task not be adequately performed. Thus, it was morally wrong for the company to change its mind and seek restitution.

Which one of the following principles, if valid, most helps to justify the ethicist's reasoning?

(A) It is morally wrong for one party not to abide by its part of an agreement only if the other party abides by its part of the agreement.
(B) It is morally wrong to seek a penalty for an action for which the agent is unable to make restitution.
(C) It is morally wrong for one person to seek to penalize another person for an action that the first person induced the other person to perform.
(D) It is morally wrong to ignore the terms of an agreement that was freely undertaken only if there is clear evidence that the agreement was legally permissible.
(E) It is morally wrong to seek compensation for an action performed in the context of a promise to forgo such compensation.

17. Zoologist: Animals can certainly signal each other with sounds and gestures. However, this does not confirm the thesis that animals possess language, for it does not prove that animals possess the ability to use sounds or gestures to refer to concrete objects or abstract ideas.

Which one of the following is an assumption on which the zoologist's argument depends?

(A) Animals do not have the cognitive capabilities to entertain abstract ideas.
(B) If an animal's system of sounds or gestures is not a language, then that animal is unable to entertain abstract ideas.
(C) When signaling each other with sounds or gestures, animals refer neither to concrete objects nor abstract ideas.
(D) If a system of sounds or gestures contains no expressions referring to concrete objects or abstract ideas, then that system is not a language.
(E) Some animals that possess a language can refer to both concrete objects and abstract ideas.

18. A person is more likely to become disabled as that person ages. Among adults in the country of East Wendell, however, the proportion receiving disability benefit payments shrinks from 4 percent among 55 to 64 year olds to 2 percent for those aged 65 to 74 and 1 percent for those aged 75 and older. The explanation of this discrepancy is that the proportion of jobs offering such a disability benefit has greatly increased in recent years.

Which one of the following, if true about East Wendell, shows that the explanation above is at best incomplete?

(A) The treatment of newly incurred disabilities is more successful now than in the past in restoring partial function in the affected area within six months.
(B) Some people receive disability benefit payments under employers' insurance plans, and some receive them from the government.
(C) Medical advances have prolonged the average lifespan beyond what it was 20 years ago.
(D) For persons receiving disability benefit payments, those payments on average represent a smaller share of their predisability income now than was the case 20 years ago.
(E) Under most employers' plans, disability benefit payments stop when an employee with a disability reaches the usual retirement age of 65.

GO ON TO THE NEXT PAGE.

19. Light is registered in the retina when photons hit molecules of the pigment rhodopsin and change the molecules' shape. Even when they have not been struck by photons of light, rhodopsin molecules sometimes change shape because of normal molecular motion, thereby introducing error into the visual system. The amount of this molecular motion is directly proportional to the temperature of the retina.

Which one of the following conclusions is most strongly supported by the information above?

(A) The temperature of an animal's retina depends on the amount of light the retina is absorbing.

(B) The visual systems of animals whose body temperature matches that of their surroundings are more error-prone in hot surroundings than in cold ones.

(C) As the temperature of the retina rises, rhodopsin molecules react more slowly to being struck by photons.

(D) Rhodopsin molecules are more sensitive to photons in animals whose retinas have large surface areas than in animals whose retinas have small surface areas.

(E) Molecules of rhodopsin are the only pigment molecules that occur naturally in the retina.

20. Critic: Political utility determines the popularity of a metaphor. In authoritarian societies, the metaphor of society as a human body governed by a head is pervasive. Therefore, the society-as-body metaphor, with its connection between society's proper functioning and governance by a head, promotes greater acceptance of authoritarian repression than do other metaphors, such as likening society to a family.

Which one of the following statements, if true, most weakens the critic's argument?

(A) In authoritarian societies, the metaphor of society as a family is just as pervasive as the society-as-body metaphor.

(B) Every society tries to justify the legitimacy of its government through the use of metaphor.

(C) The metaphor of society as a human body is sometimes used in nonauthoritarian societies.

(D) Authoritarian leaders are always searching for new metaphors for society in their effort to maintain their power.

(E) The metaphor of society as a human body governed by a head is rarely used in liberal democracies.

21. Thirty years ago, the percentage of their income that single persons spent on food was twice what it is today. Given that incomes have risen over the past thirty years, we can conclude that incomes have risen at a greater rate than the price of food in that period.

Which one of the following, if assumed, helps most to justify the conclusion drawn above?

(A) The amount of food eaten per capita today is identical to the amount of food eaten per capita thirty years ago.

(B) In general, single persons today eat healthier foods and eat less than their counterparts of thirty years ago.

(C) Single persons today, on average, purchase the same kinds of food items in the same quantities as they did thirty years ago.

(D) The prices of nonfood items single persons purchase have risen faster than the price of food over the past thirty years.

(E) Unlike single persons, families today spend about the same percentage of their income on food as they did thirty years ago.

22. Viruses can have beneficial effects. For example, some kill more-complex microorganisms, some of which are deadly to humans. But viruses have such simple structures that replacing just a few of a beneficial virus's several million atoms can make it deadly to humans. Clearly, since alterations of greater complexity than this are commonly produced by random mutations, any virus could easily become dangerous to humans.

If the statements above are true, then each of the following statements could also be true EXCEPT:

(A) Random mutation makes some deadly viruses beneficial to humans.

(B) Some organisms of greater complexity than viruses are no more likely than viruses to undergo significant alterations through random mutation.

(C) Some microorganisms that are more complex than viruses are beneficial to humans.

(D) Some viruses that fail to kill other viruses that are deadly to humans are nevertheless beneficial to humans.

(E) No virus that is deadly to organisms of greater complexity than itself is beneficial to humans.

GO ON TO THE NEXT PAGE.

23. Societies in which value is measured primarily in financial terms invariably fragment into isolated social units. But since money is not the main measure of value in nonindustrial societies, they must tend in contrast to be socially unified.

The flawed reasoning in which one of the following is most similar to that in the argument above?

(A) Animals of different genera cannot interbreed. But that does not prove that jackals and wolves cannot interbreed, for they belong to the same genus.

(B) Ecosystems close to the equator usually have more species than those closer to the poles. Thus, the Sahara Desert must contain more species than Siberia does, since the latter is farther from the equator.

(C) Insects pass through several stages of maturation: egg, larva, pupa, and adult. Since insects are arthropods, all arthropods probably undergo similar maturation processes.

(D) Poets frequently convey their thoughts via nonliteral uses of language such as metaphors and analogies. But journalists are not poets, so surely journalists always use language literally.

(E) Technologically sophisticated machines often cause us more trouble than simpler devices serving the same function. Since computers are more technologically sophisticated than pencils, they must tend to be more troublesome.

24. Ringtail opossums are an Australian wildlife species that is potentially endangered. A number of ringtail opossums that had been orphaned and subsequently raised in captivity were monitored after being returned to the wild. Seventy-five percent of these opossums were killed by foxes, a species not native to Australia. Conservationists concluded that the native ringtail opossum population was endangered not by a scarcity of food, as had been previously thought, but by non-native predator species against which the opossum had not developed natural defenses.

Which one of the following, if true, most strongly supports the conservationists' argument?

(A) There are fewer non-native predator species that prey on the ringtail opossum than there are native species that prey on the ringtail opossum.

(B) Foxes, which were introduced into Australia over 200 years ago, adapted to the Australian climate less successfully than did some other foreign species.

(C) The ringtail opossums that were raised in captivity were fed a diet similar to that which ringtail opossums typically eat in the wild.

(D) Few of the species that compete with the ringtail opossum for food sources are native to Australia.

(E) Ringtail opossums that grow to adulthood in the wild defend themselves against foxes no more successfully than do ringtail opossums raised in captivity.

GO ON TO THE NEXT PAGE.

25. Jordan: If a business invests the money necessary to implement ecologically sound practices, its market share will decrease. But if it doesn't implement these practices, it pollutes the environment and wastes resources.

Terry: But if consumers demand environmental responsibility of all businesses, no particular business will be especially hurt.

In which one of the following exchanges is the logical relationship between Jordan's and Terry's statements most similar to the logical relationship between their statements above?

(A) Jordan: Either it will rain and our plans for a picnic will be thwarted or it won't rain and the garden will go yet another day without much-needed watering.
Terry: But if it doesn't rain, we can buy a hose and water the garden with the hose.

(B) Jordan: Each person can have either an enjoyable life or a long life, for one must eat vegetables and exercise continuously to stay healthy.
Terry: That's not true: there are many happy health-conscious people.

(C) Jordan: If taxes are raised, many social problems could be solved, but if they're lowered, the economy will grow again. So we can't have both social reform and a growing economy.
Terry: But if taxes remain at their current level, neither social problems nor the economy will get worse.

(D) Jordan: If we remodel the kitchen, the house will be more valuable, but even if we do, there's no guarantee that we'll actually get more for the house when we sell it.
Terry: But if we don't remodel the kitchen, we might get even less for the house than we paid for it.

(E) Jordan: If the dam's spillway is opened, the river might flood the eastern part of town, but if the spillway is not opened, the dam might burst.
Terry: There's no real danger of the dam's bursting, but if we get more heavy rain, opening the spillway is the most prudent policy.

26. The media now devote more coverage to crime than they did ten years ago. Yet this is not because the crime rate has increased, but rather because the public is now more interested in reading and hearing about crime. After all, a crucial factor in the media's decisions about what issues to cover and to what extent to cover them is the interests of their audiences.

The proposition that the public is now more interested in reading and hearing about crime plays which one of the following roles in the argument?

(A) It supports the conclusion that the media now devote more coverage to crime than the crime rate alone justifies.

(B) It is presented as evidence that the media decide what to cover and to what extent to cover it depending on the interests of the public.

(C) It is a counterexample to the claim that the media devote more coverage to crime now than they did ten years ago.

(D) It is a generalization based on the claim that the crime rate has increased over the past ten years.

(E) It is offered as an alternative explanation of why the media devote more coverage to crime now than they did ten years ago.

S T O P

IF YOU FINISH BEFORE TIME IS CALLED, YOU MAY CHECK YOUR WORK ON THIS SECTION ONLY.
DO NOT WORK ON ANY OTHER SECTION IN THE TEST.

SECTION IV

Time—35 minutes

24 Questions

Directions: Each group of questions in this section is based on a set of conditions. In answering some of the questions, it may be useful to draw a rough diagram. Choose the response that most accurately and completely answers each question and blacken the corresponding space on your answer sheet.

Questions 1–7

Jill, Kurt, Larisa, Manny, and Olga are the clerks in a supermarket. The supermarket has exactly nine parallel aisles, numbered consecutively 1 through 9 from one end of the store to the other. Each aisle is stocked by exactly one clerk and no clerk stocks more than two aisles. Stocking assignments must meet the following conditions:

Olga stocks exactly one aisle.
Kurt stocks aisle 2.
Manny does not stock aisle 1.
Jill does not stock consecutive aisles.
Kurt stocks the only aisle between the two aisles Manny stocks.
Exactly one of Larisa's aisles is an end aisle.
Olga's aisle is numbered higher than either of Kurt's aisles, and lower than at least one of Larisa's.

1. Which one of the following clerks could stock two consecutive aisles?

   (A) Jill
   (B) Kurt
   (C) Larisa
   (D) Manny
   (E) Olga

2. Which one of the following is a pair of clerks, neither of whom could stock aisle 5?

   (A) Jill and Manny
   (B) Kurt and Olga
   (C) Larisa and Manny
   (D) Kurt and Manny
   (E) Larisa and Olga

3. Which one of the following is a complete and accurate list of clerks, any one of whom could stock aisle 3?

   (A) Jill, Kurt, Larisa
   (B) Jill, Larisa, Manny
   (C) Jill, Larisa, Olga
   (D) Jill, Kurt, Larisa, Manny
   (E) Jill, Kurt, Larisa, Olga

4. Which one of the following is a complete and accurate list of aisles, any one of which could be one of the aisles Manny stocks?

   (A) 1, 3, 4, 5
   (B) 3, 5, 7, 9
   (C) 3, 4, 5, 6
   (D) 3, 4, 5, 6, 7
   (E) 3, 5, 7

5. If Larisa's aisles are separated by the maximum number of aisles that could separate her aisles, which one of the following could be true?

   (A) Jill stocks aisle 6.
   (B) Manny stocks aisle 7.
   (C) Both of Jill's aisles are numbered lower than Olga's.
   (D) Jill stocks only even-numbered aisles.
   (E) Only one clerk stocks a higher numbered aisle than Olga does.

6. If Jill stocks aisle 3, then which one of the following CANNOT be true?

   (A) Jill stocks aisle 9.
   (B) Kurt stocks aisle 6.
   (C) Larisa stocks aisle 4.
   (D) Manny stocks aisle 4.
   (E) Olga stocks aisle 6.

7. Suppose that, rather than just one, Larisa stocks both end aisles; all other conditions remaining in effect, which one of the following CANNOT be true?

   (A) Jill stocks aisle 3.
   (B) Olga stocks aisle 6.
   (C) Olga stocks the only aisle between the two aisles that Jill stocks.
   (D) Kurt stocks only even-numbered aisles.
   (E) One of Larisa's aisles is immediately next to Olga's.

GO ON TO THE NEXT PAGE.

Questions 8–12

A five-week adult education course consists of exactly five lectures with a different lecture given each week. No lecture is given more than once. Each lecture is delivered by a different speaker. The following conditions are true about the speakers and their lectures:

Each speaker lectures on a philosopher in whom he or she specializes.

No two speakers lecture on the same philosopher.

The first week's speaker specializes in Kant, Locke, and Mill, and no other philosophers.

The second week's speaker specializes in Kant, Locke, Mill, and Nietzsche, and no other philosophers.

The third week's and fourth week's speakers each specialize in Mill and Nietzsche, and no other philosophers.

The fifth week's speaker specializes in Nietzsche, Ockham, and Plato, and no other philosophers.

8. Which one of the following statements could be true?

    (A) The first speaker lectures on Mill.
    (B) The second speaker lectures on Mill.
    (C) The second speaker lectures on Nietzsche.
    (D) The fifth speaker lectures on Nietzsche.
    (E) The fifth speaker lectures on Ockham.

9. What is the maximum possible number of different schedules for the five lectures in which those philosophers who are discussed are discussed in alphabetical order?

    (A) 2
    (B) 3
    (C) 4
    (D) 5
    (E) 6

10. Which one of the following, if known, would allow one to determine the entire lecture schedule and identify for each week the philosopher who is lectured on that week?

    (A) the weeks that Kant, Locke, and Mill are lectured on
    (B) the weeks that Kant, Mill, and Nietzsche are lectured on
    (C) the weeks that Kant, Mill, and Ockham are lectured on
    (D) the weeks that Mill, Nietzsche, and Ockham are lectured on
    (E) the weeks that Mill, Nietzsche, and Plato are lectured on

11. Assume that, of the six philosophers, Kant and Nietzsche are the only German philosophers, and Locke, Mill, and Ockham are the only British philosophers. Each of the following statements could be true EXCEPT:

    (A) The first and fourth speakers lecture on British philosophers.
    (B) The first and fourth speakers lecture on German philosophers.
    (C) The second and third speakers lecture on British philosophers.
    (D) The third and fourth speakers lecture on German philosophers.
    (E) The fourth and fifth speakers lecture on British philosophers.

12. Suppose the third speaker were a specialist not only in Mill and Nietzsche, but also in Sartre. If all of the other conditions remained the same, then each of the following could be true EXCEPT:

    (A) Mill is lectured on in the first lecture and Nietzsche in the fourth.
    (B) Mill is lectured on in the second lecture and Nietzsche in the third.
    (C) Mill is lectured on in the second lecture and Nietzsche in the fourth.
    (D) Mill is lectured on in the fourth lecture and Nietzsche in the fifth.
    (E) Nietzsche is lectured on in the second lecture and Mill in the fourth.

GO ON TO THE NEXT PAGE.

4

Exactly seven different trains—Quigley, Rockville, Sunnydale, Tilbury, Victoria, Wooster, and York—arrive at Middlebrook Station on Saturday. The following conditions govern their arrivals:

The trains arrive one at a time.
Either the York or the Wooster arrives fourth.
The Sunnydale arrives at some time after the Wooster but at some time before the York.
Both the Tilbury and the Victoria arrive at some time after the Rockville.
The Tilbury does not arrive next after the Victoria; nor does the Victoria arrive next after the Tilbury.

13. Which one of the following could be the order in which the trains arrive, from first to last?

    (A) Rockville, Tilbury, Victoria, Wooster, Sunnydale, York, Quigley
    (B) Rockville, Wooster, Quigley, York, Tilbury, Sunnydale, Victoria
    (C) Rockville, Tilbury, Quigley, Wooster, Sunnydale, York, Victoria
    (D) Quigley, Rockville, Wooster, Sunnydale, Victoria, York, Tilbury
    (E) Tilbury, Rockville, Quigley, Wooster, Sunnydale, York, Victoria

14. If the Wooster arrives at some time before the Rockville, then exactly how many different orders are there in which the seven trains could arrive?

    (A) four
    (B) five
    (C) six
    (D) seven
    (E) eight

15. Which one of the following must be true?

    (A) The first train to arrive is the Rockville.
    (B) The Quigley arrives at some time before the Sunnydale.
    (C) The Rockville arrives at some time before the Wooster.
    (D) The Victoria arrives at some time before the York.
    (E) The Wooster arrives at some time before the York.

16. Which one of the following could be true?

    (A) The Sunnydale is the next train to arrive after the Quigley.
    (B) The Rockville is the next train to arrive after the Sunnydale.
    (C) The Rockville is the next train to arrive after the Tilbury.
    (D) The Quigley is the next train to arrive after the Sunnydale.
    (E) The Quigley is the next train to arrive after the Wooster.

17. If exactly one of the trains arrives after the Wooster but before the York, then which one of the following could be true?

    (A) The sixth train to arrive is the Sunnydale.
    (B) The sixth train to arrive is the Tilbury.
    (C) The third train to arrive is the Rockville.
    (D) The second train to arrive is the Sunnydale.
    (E) The first train to arrive is the Rockville.

18. If the Quigley arrives at some time before the Rockville, then the Wooster must arrive

    (A) second
    (B) third
    (C) fourth
    (D) fifth
    (E) sixth

GO ON TO THE NEXT PAGE.

Questions 19–24

Each of exactly six doctors—Juarez, Kudrow, Longtree, Nance, Onawa, and Palermo—is at exactly one of two clinics: Souderton or Randsborough. The following conditions must be satisfied:

Kudrow is at Randsborough if Juarez is at Souderton.
Onawa is at Souderton if Juarez is at Randsborough.
If Longtree is at Souderton, then both Nance and Palermo are at Randsborough.
If Nance is at Randsborough, then so is Onawa.
If Palermo is at Randsborough, then both Kudrow and Onawa are at Souderton.

19. Which one of the following could be a complete and accurate list of the doctors that are at Souderton?

   (A)   Juarez, Kudrow, Onawa
   (B)   Juarez, Nance, Onawa, Palermo
   (C)   Kudrow, Longtree, Onawa
   (D)   Nance, Onawa
   (E)   Nance, Palermo

20. If Palermo is at Randsborough, then which one of the following must be true?

   (A)   Juarez is at Randsborough.
   (B)   Kudrow is at Randsborough.
   (C)   Longtree is at Souderton.
   (D)   Nance is at Randsborough.
   (E)   Onawa is at Randsborough.

21. What is the minimum number of doctors that could be at Souderton?

   (A)   zero
   (B)   one
   (C)   two
   (D)   three
   (E)   four

22. If Nance and Onawa are at different clinics, which one of the following must be true?

   (A)   Juarez is at Souderton.
   (B)   Kudrow is at Souderton.
   (C)   Palermo is at Randsborough.
   (D)   Four doctors are at Souderton.
   (E)   Four doctors are at Randsborough.

23. Which one of the following CANNOT be a pair of the doctors at Randsborough?

   (A)   Juarez and Kudrow
   (B)   Juarez and Palermo
   (C)   Kudrow and Onawa
   (D)   Nance and Onawa
   (E)   Nance and Palermo

24. If Kudrow is at Souderton, then which one of the following must be true?

   (A)   Juarez is at Souderton.
   (B)   Nance is at Souderton.
   (C)   Onawa is at Randsborough.
   (D)   Palermo is at Souderton.
   (E)   Palermo is at Randsborough.

S T O P

IF YOU FINISH BEFORE TIME IS CALLED, YOU MAY CHECK YOUR WORK ON THIS SECTION ONLY.
DO NOT WORK ON ANY OTHER SECTION IN THE TEST.

Acknowledgment is made to the following sources from which material has been adapted for use in this test booklet:

Larry Diamond, "The Globalization of Democracy." ©1993 by Lynne Rienner Publishers, Inc.

Otto E. Landman, "Inheritance of Acquired Characteristics." ©1993 by Scientific American, Inc.

Theophus H. Smith, *Conjuring America: Biblical Foundations of Black America*. ©1994 by Theophus H. Smith.

SIGNATURE _____   / /
                                                DATE

LSAT WRITING SAMPLE TOPIC

Faced with declining ticket sales, Funtown, a 1950s-era theme park, has decided to undertake a program of capital improvements to enhance the park's appeal. There is sufficient capital in the park's reserve fund to undertake one major construction project. The park's board of directors must choose between a proposal to revamp Futureland, one of the park's signature attractions, and a proposal to build Whirling Water, a new thrill ride that would be a cross between a roller coaster and a whirlpool. Write an essay in which you argue for one proposal over the other based on the following considerations:

- Funtown wants to increase park attendance.
- Funtown wants to exploit the latest technology to update its image.

Futureland put Funtown on the map as a tourist destination. When the park opened in 1954, Futureland quickly became its most popular attraction. Over the years, however, Futureland's vision of the future has become dated, and visitor interest in the once-novel attraction has flagged. The proposed renovation would overhaul Futureland completely, incorporating a fully interactive multimedia center featuring a virtual reality experience of life in the year 3000. The plan also calls for graphic designers to reinvent "the look of the future" depicted in Futureland's exhibit spaces. Initial marketing surveys indicate that a renovated Futureland would have strong appeal among families with younger children, although teenagers who were surveyed were somewhat less enthusiastic.

As Funtown's popularity has waned, ticket sales at a nearby water park have increased, especially among teenagers and young adults. Supporters of Whirling Water assert the need for a brand new attraction to revitalize Funtown. Whirling Water's proponents acknowledge that the water park features a full range of aquatic rides and attractions, but they believe that Whirling Water would be even more successful than the water park's newest and most popular offering. Designed to take advantage of cutting-edge engineering techniques, Whirling Water would be both bigger and faster than any attraction at the water park. However, since the ride could be frightening to young children, Whirling Water would be closed to those under the age of ten.

Directions:

1. Use the Answer Key on the next page to check your answers.

2. Use the Scoring Worksheet below to compute your raw score.

3. Use the Score Conversion Chart to convert your raw score into the 120-180 scale.

Scoring Worksheet

1. Enter the number of questions you answered correctly in each section.

	Number Correct
SECTION I.	_____
SECTION II	_____
SECTION III.	_____
SECTION IV.	_____

2. Enter the sum here: _____
   This is your Raw Score.

Conversion Chart

For Converting Raw Score to the 120-180 LSAT Scaled Score
LSAT Form 2LSS52

Reported Score	Raw Score Lowest	Raw Score Highest
180	98	101
179	97	97
178	96	96
177	95	95
176	94	94
175	93	93
174	92	92
173	91	91
172	90	90
171	89	89
170	88	88
169	87	87
168	85	86
167	84	84
166	83	83
165	81	82
164	80	80
163	78	79
162	77	77
161	75	76
160	74	74
159	72	73
158	71	71
157	69	70
156	67	68
155	66	66
154	64	65
153	62	63
152	61	61
151	59	60
150	57	58
149	55	56
148	54	54
147	52	53
146	50	51
145	48	49
144	47	47
143	45	46
142	43	44
141	42	42
140	40	41
139	38	39
138	37	37
137	35	36
136	33	34
135	32	32
134	30	31
133	29	29
132	27	28
131	26	26
130	24	25
129	23	23
128	22	22
127	20	21
126	19	19
125	18	18
124	17	17
123	15	16
122	14	14
121	—*	—*
120	0	13

*There is no raw score that will produce this scaled score for this form.

SECTION I

1.	E	8.	E	15.	E	22.	D
2.	C	9.	C	16.	B	23.	A
3.	D	10.	A	17.	D	24.	E
4.	B	11.	B	18.	C	25.	C
5.	D	12.	E	19.	D	26.	A
6.	E	13.	E	20.	C		
7.	E	14.	C	21.	D		

SECTION II

1.	A	8.	A	15.	C	22.	E
2.	E	9.	D	16.	B	23.	E
3.	E	10.	D	17.	A	24.	B
4.	C	11.	C	18.	B	25.	C
5.	B	12.	A	19.	D		
6.	B	13.	B	20.	D		
7.	A	14.	C	21.	E		

SECTION III

1.	C	8.	B	15.	D	22.	E
2.	D	9.	A	16.	E	23.	D
3.	B	10.	A	17.	D	24.	E
4.	E	11.	C	18.	E	25.	A
5.	D	12.	C	19.	B	26.	E
6.	B	13.	D	20.	A		
7.	E	14.	B	21.	C		

SECTION IV

1.	C	8.	E	15.	E	22.	A
2.	E	9.	A	16.	B	23.	E
3.	B	10.	C	17.	E	24.	B
4.	D	11.	D	18.	C		
5.	A	12.	B	19.	B		
6.	E	13.	C	20.	A		
7.	B	14.	A	21.	C		

The Official LSAT PrepTest

35

- **October 2001**
  PrepTest 35

- **Form 1LSS51**

SECTION I

Time—35 minutes

26 Questions

Directions: The questions in this section are based on the reasoning contained in brief statements or passages. For some questions, more than one of the choices could conceivably answer the question. However, you are to choose the best answer; that is, the response that most accurately and completely answers the question. You should not make assumptions that are by commonsense standards implausible, superfluous, or incompatible with the passage. After you have chosen the best answer, blacken the corresponding space on your answer sheet.

1. Some critics argue that an opera's stage directions are never reflected in its music. Many comic scenes in Mozart's operas, however, open with violin phrases that sound like the squeaking of changing scenery. Clearly Mozart intended the music to echo the sounds occurring while stage directions are carried out. Hence, a change of scenery—the most basic and frequent stage direction—can be reflected in the music, which means that other operatic stage directions can be as well.

    In the argument, the statement that many comic scenes in Mozart's operas open with violin phrases that sound like the squeaking of changing scenery is offered in support of the claim that

    (A) a change of scenery is the stage direction most frequently reflected in an opera's music
    (B) an opera's stage directions are never reflected in its music
    (C) an opera's music can have an effect on the opera's stage directions
    (D) a variety of stage directions can be reflected in an opera's music
    (E) the most frequent relation between an opera's music and its stage directions is one of musical imitation of the sounds that occur when a direction is carried out

2. Lecturer: Given our current state of knowledge and technology, we can say that the generalization that the entropy of a closed system cannot decrease for any spontaneous process has not been falsified by any of our tests of that generalization. So we conclude it to be true universally. Yet, it must be admitted that this generalization has not been conclusively verified, in the sense that it has not been tested in every corner of the universe, under every feasible condition. Nevertheless, this generalization is correctly regarded as a scientific law; indeed, it is referred to as the Second Law of Thermodynamics.

    Which one of the following principles, if valid, most justifies the lecturer's classification of the generalization described above?

    (A) Whatever is a scientific law has not been falsified.
    (B) If a generalization is confirmed only under a few circumstances, it should not be considered a scientific law.
    (C) Whatever is true universally will eventually be confirmed to the extent current science allows.
    (D) If a generalization is confirmed to the extent current science allows, then it is considered a scientific law.
    (E) Whatever is regarded as a scientific law will eventually be conclusively verified.

GO ON TO THE NEXT PAGE.

3. More women than men suffer from Alzheimer's disease—a disease that is most commonly contracted by elderly persons. This discrepancy has often been attributed to women's longer life span, but this theory may be wrong. A recent study has shown that prescribing estrogen to women after menopause, when estrogen production in the body decreases, may prevent them from developing the disease. Men's supply of testosterone may help safeguard them against Alzheimer's disease because much of it is converted by the body to estrogen, and testosterone levels stay relatively stable into old age.

Which one of the following most accurately expresses the main conclusion of the argument?

(A) A decrease in estrogen, rather than longer life span, may explain the higher occurrence of Alzheimer's disease in women relative to men.

(B) As one gets older, one's chances of developing Alzheimer's disease increase.

(C) Women who go through menopause earlier in life than do most other women have an increased risk of contracting Alzheimer's disease.

(D) The conversion of testosterone into estrogen may help safeguard men from Alzheimer's disease.

(E) Testosterone is necessary for preventing Alzheimer's disease in older men.

4. Parent P: Children will need computer skills to deal with tomorrow's world. Computers should be introduced in kindergarten, and computer languages should be required in high school.

Parent Q: That would be pointless. Technology advances so rapidly that the computers used by today's kindergartners and the computer languages taught in today's high schools would become obsolete by the time these children are adults.

Which one of the following, if true, is the strongest logical counter parent P can make to parent Q's objection?

(A) When technology is advancing rapidly, regular training is necessary to keep one's skills at a level proficient enough to deal with the society in which one lives.

(B) Throughout history people have adapted to change, and there is no reason to believe that today's children are not equally capable of adapting to technology as it advances.

(C) In the process of learning to work with any computer or computer language, children increase their ability to interact with computer technology.

(D) Automotive technology is continually advancing too, but that does not result in one's having to relearn to drive cars as the new advances are incorporated into new automobiles.

(E) Once people have graduated from high school, they have less time to learn about computers and technology than they had during their schooling years.

Questions 5–6

Proponent: Irradiation of food by gamma rays would keep it from spoiling before it reaches the consumer in food stores. The process leaves no radiation behind, and vitamin losses are comparable to those that occur in cooking, so there is no reason to reject irradiation on the grounds of nutrition or safety. Indeed, it kills harmful *Salmonella* bacteria, which in contaminated poultry have caused serious illness to consumers.

Opponent: The irradiation process has no effect on the bacteria that cause botulism, a very serious form of food poisoning, while those that cause bad odors that would warn consumers of botulism are killed. Moreover, *Salmonella* and the bacteria that cause botulism can easily be killed in poultry by using a safe chemical dip.

5. The opponent's argument proceeds by

(A) isolating an ambiguity in a crucial term in the proponent's argument

(B) showing that claims made in the proponent's argument result in a self-contradiction

(C) establishing that undesirable consequences result from the adoption of either one of two proposed remedies

(D) shifting perspective from safety with respect to consumers to safety with respect to producers

(E) pointing out an alternative way of obtaining an advantage claimed by the proponent without risking a particular disadvantage

6. Which one of the following could the opponent properly cite as indicating a flaw in the proponent's reasoning concerning vitamin losses?

(A) After irradiation, food might still spoil if kept in storage for a long time after being purchased by the consumer.

(B) Irradiated food would still need cooking, or, if eaten raw, it would not have the vitamin advantage of raw food.

(C) Vitamin loss is a separate issue from safety.

(D) Vitamins can be ingested in pill form as well as in foods.

(E) That food does not spoil before it can be offered to the consumer is primarily a benefit to the seller, not to the consumer.

GO ON TO THE NEXT PAGE.

7. Due to wider commercial availability of audio recordings of auth(_-215-_ding their own books, sales of printed books have dropped significantly.

Which one of the following conforms most closely to the principle illustrated above?

(A) Because of the rising cost of farm labor, farmers began to make more extensive use of machines.

(B) Because of the wide variety of new computer games on the market, sales of high-quality computer video screens have improved.

(C) Because a new brand of soft drink entered the market, consumers reduced their consumption of an established brand of soft drink.

(D) Because a child was forbidden to play until homework was completed, that child did much less daydreaming and focused on homework.

(E) Because neither of the two leading word processing programs has all of the features consumers want, neither has been able to dominate the market.

8. Lobsters and other crustaceans eaten by humans are more likely to contract gill diseases when sewage contaminates their water. Under a recent proposal, millions of gallons of local sewage each day would be rerouted many kilometers offshore. Although this would substantially reduce the amount of sewage in the harbor where lobsters are caught, the proposal is pointless, because hardly any lobsters live long enough to be harmed by those diseases.

Which one of the following, if true, most seriously weakens the argument?

(A) Contaminants in the harbor other than sewage are equally harmful to lobsters.

(B) Lobsters, like other crustaceans, live longer in the open ocean than in industrial harbors.

(C) Lobsters breed as readily in sewage-contaminated water as in unpolluted water.

(D) Gill diseases cannot be detected by examining the surface of the lobster.

(E) Humans often become ill as a result of eating lobsters with gill diseases.

9. Researcher: The rate of psychological problems is higher among children of divorced parents than among other children. But it would be a mistake to conclude that these problems are caused by the difficulty the children have adjusting to divorce. It is just as reasonable to infer that certain behaviors that increase the likelihood of divorce—hostility, distrust, lack of empathy—are learned by children from their parents, and that it is these learned behaviors, rather than the difficulty of adjusting to divorce, that cause the children's psychological problems.

The assertion that children of divorced parents have a higher rate of psychological problems than other children figures in the argument in which one of the following ways?

(A) It is the conclusion of the argument.

(B) It is the claim that the argument tries to refute.

(C) It is offered as evidence for the claim that divorce is harmful to the children of the divorcing parents.

(D) It is offered as evidence for the claim that certain behaviors are often responsible for divorce.

(E) It is cited as an established finding for which the argument proposes an explanation.

10. Although marathons are 26.2 miles (42.2 kilometers) long and take even world-class marathoners over 2 hours to run, athletes who train by running 90 minutes a day fare better in marathons than do those who train by running 120 minutes or more a day.

Each of the following, if true, contributes to an explanation of the difference in marathon performances described above EXCEPT:

(A) The longer the period of time that one runs daily, the greater the chances of suffering adverse health effects due to air pollution.

(B) The longer the period of time that one runs daily, the easier it is to adjust to different race lengths.

(C) The longer the run, the more frequent is the occurrence of joint injuries that significantly interfere with overall training.

(D) Runners who train over 90 minutes per day grow bored with running and become less motivated.

(E) Runners who train over 90 minutes per day deplete certain biochemical energy reserves, leaving them less energy for marathons.

GO ON TO THE NEXT PAGE.

11. Linguist: Some people have understood certain studies as showing that bilingual children have a reduced "conceptual map" because bilingualism overstresses the child's linguistic capacities. Vocabulary tests taken by bilingual children appear to show that these children tend to have a smaller vocabulary than do most children of the same age group. But these studies are deeply flawed, since the tests were given in only one language. Dual-language tests revealed that the children often expressed a given concept with a word from only one of their two languages.

The linguist's argument proceeds by

(A) offering evidence for the advantages of bilingualism over monolingualism

(B) pointing out an inconsistency in the view that bilingualism overstresses a child's linguistic capabilities

(C) offering evidence that undermines the use of any vocabulary test to provide information about a child's conceptual map

(D) providing a different explanation for the apparent advantages of bilingualism from the explanation suggested by the results of certain studies

(E) pointing out a methodological error in the technique used to obtain the purported evidence of a problem with bilingualism

12. Gene splicing can give rise to new varieties of farm animals that have only a partially understood genetic makeup. In addition to introducing the genes for whichever trait is desired, the technique can introduce genes governing the production of toxins or carcinogens, and these latter undesirable traits might not be easily discoverable.

The statements above, if true, most strongly support which one of the following?

(A) All toxin production is genetically controlled.

(B) Gene splicing to produce new varieties of farm animals should be used cautiously.

(C) Gene splicing is not effective as a way of producing new varieties of farm animals.

(D) Most new varieties of farm animals produced by gene splicing will develop cancer.

(E) Gene splicing will advance to the point where unforeseen consequences are no longer a problem.

13. Journal: In several psychological studies, subjects were given statements to read that caused them to form new beliefs. Later, the subjects were told that the original statements were false. The studies report, however, that most subjects persevered in their newly acquired beliefs, even after being told that the original statements were false. This strongly suggests that humans continue to hold onto acquired beliefs even in the absence of any credible evidence to support them.

Which one of the following, if true, most undermines the journal's argument?

(A) Regardless of the truth of what the subjects were later told, the beliefs based on the original statements were, for the most part, correct.

(B) It is unrealistic to expect people to keep track of the original basis of their beliefs, and to revise a belief when its original basis is undercut.

(C) The statements originally given to the subjects would be highly misleading even if true.

(D) Most of the subjects had acquired confirmation of their newly acquired beliefs by the time they were told that the original statements were false.

(E) Most of the subjects were initially skeptical of the statements originally given to them.

GO ON TO THE NEXT PAGE.

14. Novelists cannot become great as long as they remain in academia. Powers of observation and analysis, which schools successfully hone, are useful to the novelist, but an intuitive grasp of the emotions of everyday life can be obtained only by the kind of immersion in everyday life that is precluded by being an academic.

Which one of the following is an assumption on which the argument depends?

(A) Novelists require some impartiality to get an intuitive grasp of the emotions of everyday life.

(B) No great novelist lacks powers of observation and analysis.

(C) Participation in life, interspersed with impartial observation of life, makes novelists great.

(D) Novelists cannot be great without an intuitive grasp of the emotions of everyday life.

(E) Knowledge of the emotions of everyday life cannot be acquired by merely observing and analyzing life.

15. Statistician: A financial magazine claimed that its survey of its subscribers showed that North Americans are more concerned about their personal finances than about politics. One question was: "Which do you think about more: politics or the joy of earning money?" This question is clearly biased. Also, the readers of the magazine are a self-selecting sample. Thus, there is reason to be skeptical about the conclusion drawn in the magazine's survey.

Each of the following, if true, would strengthen the statistician's argument EXCEPT:

(A) The credibility of the magazine has been called into question on a number of occasions.

(B) The conclusions drawn in most magazine surveys have eventually been disproved.

(C) Other surveys suggest that North Americans are just as concerned about politics as they are about finances.

(D) There is reason to be skeptical about the results of surveys that are biased and unrepresentative.

(E) Other surveys suggest that North Americans are concerned not only with politics and finances, but also with social issues.

Questions 16–17

On the basis of the available evidence, Antarctica has generally been thought to have been covered by ice for at least the past 14 million years. Recently, however, three-million-year-old fossils of a kind previously found only in ocean-floor sediments were discovered under the ice sheet covering central Antarctica. About three million years ago, therefore, the Antarctic ice sheet must temporarily have melted. After all, either severe climatic warming or volcanic activity in Antarctica's mountains could have melted the ice sheet, thus raising sea levels and submerging the continent.

16. Which one of the following is the main conclusion of the argument?

(A) Antarctica is no longer generally thought to have been covered by ice for the past 14 million years.

(B) It is not the case that ancient fossils of the kind recently found in Antarctica are found only in ocean-floor sediments.

(C) The ice sheet covering Antarctica has not been continuously present throughout the past 14 million years.

(D) What caused Antarctica to be submerged under the sea was the melting of the ice sheet that had previously covered the continent.

(E) The ice sheet covering Antarctica was melted either as a result of volcanic activity in Antarctica's mountains or as a result of severe climatic warming.

17. The reasoning in the argument is most vulnerable to which one of the following criticisms?

(A) That a given position is widely believed to be true is taken to show that the position in question must, in fact, be true.

(B) That either of two things could independently have produced a given effect is taken to show that those two things could not have operated in conjunction to produce that effect.

(C) Establishing that a certain event occurred is confused with having established the cause of that event.

(D) A claim that has a very general application is based entirely on evidence from a narrowly restricted range of cases.

(E) An inconsistency that, as presented, has more than one possible resolution is treated as though only one resolution is possible.

GO ON TO THE NEXT PAGE.

18. The current pattern of human consumption of resources, in which we rely on nonrenewable resources, for example metal ore, must eventually change. Since there is only so much metal ore available, ultimately we must either do without or turn to renewable resources to take its place.

Which one of the following is an assumption required by the argument?

(A) There are renewable resource replacements for all of the nonrenewable resources currently being consumed.

(B) We cannot indefinitely replace exhausted nonrenewable resources with other nonrenewable resources.

(C) A renewable resource cannot be exhausted by human consumption.

(D) Consumption of nonrenewable resources will not continue to increase in the near future.

(E) Ultimately we cannot do without nonrenewable resources.

19. Lathyrism, a debilitating neurological disorder caused by the consumption of the legume *Lathyrus sativus*, is widespread among the domestic animals of some countries. Attempts to use rats to study lathyrism have generally failed. Rats that ingested *Lathyrus sativus* did not produce the symptoms associated with the disorder.

Which one of the following is most strongly supported by the information above?

(A) The physiology of rats is radically different from that of domestic animals.

(B) The rats did not consume as much *Lathyrus sativus* as did the domestic animals that contracted lathyrism.

(C) Not all animal species are equally susceptible to lathyrism.

(D) Most of the animals that can contract lathyrism are domestic.

(E) Laboratory conditions are not conducive to the development of lathyrism.

20. Columnist: Almost anyone can be an expert, for there are no official guidelines determining what an expert must know. Anybody who manages to convince some people of his or her qualifications in an area—whatever those may be—is an expert.

The columnist's conclusion follows logically if which one of the following is assumed?

(A) Almost anyone can convince some people of his or her qualifications in some area.

(B) Some experts convince everyone of their qualifications in almost every area.

(C) Convincing certain people that one is qualified in an area requires that one actually be qualified in that area.

(D) Every expert has convinced some people of his or her qualifications in some area.

(E) Some people manage to convince almost everyone of their qualifications in one or more areas.

GO ON TO THE NEXT PAGE.

21. A patient complained of feeling constantly fatigued. It was determined that the patient averaged only four to six hours of sleep per night, and this was determined to contribute to the patient's condition. However, the patient was not advised to sleep more.

Which one of the following, if true, most helps to resolve the apparent discrepancy in the information above?

(A) The shorter one's sleep time, the easier it is to awaken from sleeping.
(B) The first two hours of sleep do the most to alleviate fatigue.
(C) Some people require less sleep than the eight hours required by the average person.
(D) Most people who suffer from nightmares experience them in the last hour of sleep before waking.
(E) Worry about satisfying the need for sufficient sleep can make it more difficult to sleep.

22. No chordates are tracheophytes, and all members of Pteropsida are tracheophytes. So no members of Pteropsida belong to the family Hominidae.

The conclusion above follows logically if which one of the following is assumed?

(A) All members of the family Hominidae are tracheophytes.
(B) All members of the family Hominidae are chordates.
(C) All tracheophytes are members of Pteropsida.
(D) No members of the family Hominidae are chordates.
(E) No chordates are members of Pteropsida.

23. Some statisticians claim that the surest way to increase the overall correctness of the total set of one's beliefs is: never change that set, except by rejecting a belief when given adequate evidence against it. However, if this were the only rule one followed, then whenever one were presented with any kind of evidence, one would have to either reject some of one's beliefs or else leave one's beliefs unchanged. But then, over time, one could only have fewer and fewer beliefs. Since we need many beliefs in order to survive, the statisticians' claim must be mistaken.

The argument is most vulnerable to criticism on the grounds that it

(A) presumes, without providing any justification, that the surest way of increasing the overall correctness of the total set of one's beliefs must not hinder one's ability to survive
(B) neglects the possibility that even while following the statisticians' rule, one might also accept new beliefs when presented with some kinds of evidence
(C) overlooks the possibility that some large sets of beliefs are more correct overall than are some small sets of beliefs
(D) takes for granted that one should accept some beliefs related to survival even when given adequate evidence against them
(E) takes for granted that the beliefs we need in order to have many beliefs must all be correct beliefs

GO ON TO THE NEXT PAGE.

24. In every case of political unrest in a certain country, the police have discovered that some unknown person or persons organized and fomented that unrest. Clearly, therefore, behind all the cases of political unrest in that country there has been a single mastermind who organized and fomented them all.

The flawed reasoning in the argument above most closely parallels that in which one of the following?

(A) Every Chicago driver has a number on his or her license, so the number on some Chicago driver's license is the exact average of the numbers on all Chicago drivers' licenses.

(B) Every telephone number in North America has an area code, so there must be at least as many area codes as telephone numbers in North America.

(C) Every citizen of Edmonton has a social insurance number, so there must be one number that is the social insurance number for all citizens of Edmonton.

(D) Every loss of a single hair is insignificant, so no one who has a full head of hair at twenty ever becomes bald.

(E) Every moment in Vladimir's life is followed by a later moment in Vladimir's life, so Vladimir's life will never end.

25. A company that produces men's cologne had been advertising the product in general-circulation magazines for several years. Then one year the company decided to advertise its cologne exclusively in those sports magazines with a predominantly male readership. That year the company sold fewer bottles of cologne than it had in any of the three immediately preceding years.

Which one of the following, if true, best helps to explain why the sale of the company's cologne dropped that year?

(A) Television advertising reaches more people than does magazine advertising, but the company never advertised its cologne on television because of the high cost.

(B) The general-circulation magazines in which the company had placed its advertisements experienced a large rise in circulation recently.

(C) Most men do not wear cologne on a regular basis.

(D) Women often buy cologne as gifts for male friends or relatives.

(E) Successful advertisements for men's cologne often feature well-known athletes.

26. Kim: The rapidly growing world population is increasing demands on food producers in ways that threaten our natural resources. With more land needed for both food production and urban areas, less land will be available for forests and wildlife habitats.

Hampton: You are overlooking the promise of technology. I am confident that improvements in agriculture will allow us to feed the world population of ten billion predicted for 2050 without significantly increasing the percentage of the world's land now devoted to agriculture.

Kim's and Hampton's statements most strongly support the claim that both of them would agree with which one of the following?

(A) Efforts should be taken to slow the rate of human population growth and to increase the amount of land committed to agriculture.

(B) Continued research into more-efficient agricultural practices and innovative biotechnology aimed at producing more food on less land would be beneficial.

(C) Agricultural and wilderness areas need to be protected from urban encroachment by preparing urban areas for greater population density.

(D) In the next half century, human population growth will continue to erode wildlife habitats and diminish forests.

(E) The human diet needs to be modified in the next half century because of the depletion of our natural resources due to overpopulation.

S T O P

IF YOU FINISH BEFORE TIME IS CALLED, YOU MAY CHECK YOUR WORK ON THIS SECTION ONLY.
DO NOT WORK ON ANY OTHER SECTION IN THE TEST.

SECTION I I

Time—35 minutes

26 Questions

<u>Directions</u>: Each passage in this section is followed by a group of questions to be answered on the basis of what is <u>stated</u> or <u>implied</u> in the passage. For some of the questions, more than one of the choices could conceivably answer the question. However, you are to choose the <u>best</u> answer; that is, the response that most accurately and completely answers the question, and blacken the corresponding space on your answer sheet.

Of the more than one thousand people who published memoirs of the French Revolution of 1789, about eighty were women. And of these eighty women memoirists, two thirds were members of the upper
(5) class, a proportion that might be attributed solely to privilege—at the time of the Revolution, only half of all French citizens could read, and only members of the upper class were able to write easily. But there were also political reasons. Most of the memoirs were
(10) published decades after the Revolution, during the restored monarchy that came to power in 1815. Those written by royalists, who opposed the Revolution, were published under the monarchy's aegis; in contrast, republican memoirists, who supported the Revolution,
(15) risked political sanctions against their work.

Because the memoirs were written so long after the events they describe, some historians question their reliability. Certainly, memory is subject to the loss or confusion of facts and, more to the point in these
(20) partisan accounts, to the distortions of a mind intent on preserving its particular picture of the past. But other scholars have shown that close inspection of these documents resolves such doubts on two scores. First, for major public happenings, there are often multiple
(25) accounts, allowing for cross-verification. Second, regarding the truth of personal events known only to the author, more subjective guidelines must be used: Are there internal verifications within a text that suggest the author is describing a plausible sequence of
(30) events, and acting in accord with what is known of the writer's character? Or is the narrative voice so pervaded by self-justifications that it forfeits credibility?

Denis Bertholet, in a study of nineteenth-century
(35) French autobiography, states that the women memoirists of this period defined themselves "in relationship to their sex"—i.e., they conformed to socially prescribed feminine roles of the time, fulfilling obligations as daughters, wives, or mothers.
(40) Nonetheless, instances of social activism by women abounded during the Revolution. On the whole, women's memoirs during this period exhibit a variety of personalities and experiences, and describe how women participated, individually and collectively, in
(45) the events of the Revolution. For example, the imprisoned royalist Madame de La Villirouët details how she managed to liberate not only herself but her co-prisoners through an epistolary campaign, and how she subsequently saved her husband's life by pleading
(50) his case in court. In addition, in both royalist and republican camps, several women defied the ban against women serving as soldiers and bore arms for their causes. Bertholet's study attests to the credibility of these accounts on both factual and subjective
(55) grounds, making the memoirs written by women particularly significant because they embody a clearly feminist mode of discourse and experience that one would not expect to find until the French Feminist movement more than a century later.

1. Which one of the following most completely and accurately states the main idea of the passage?

(A) Despite the attempts of some historians to discredit them on factual or subjective grounds, women's memoirs of the French Revolution reflect French society's intolerance toward women's involvement in the political sphere.

(B) Even though studies have yet to draw any definitive conclusions about their factual accuracy, women's memoirs of the French Revolution appear to be at least subjectively reliable accounts of the events of the period.

(C) Although written years later, women's memoirs of the French Revolution can be regarded as factually and subjectively reliable accounts of the various ways in which women participated in the events of the period.

(D) Because of the natural tendency of memory to distort facts and of partisanship to bias accounts, it is unlikely that women's memoirs of the French Revolution can be relied upon to convey an accurate portrait of the events of the period.

(E) Regardless of their reliability, women's memoirs of the French Revolution are nevertheless a valuable resource for scholars attempting to gain insight into the impetus that led to the women's movement in France.

GO ON TO THE NEXT PAGE.

2. Based on the passage, which one of the following can most reasonably be inferred about the majority of the published memoirs of the French Revolution that were written by men?

(A) They depict women who conformed to socially prescribed roles.
(B) They depict women who participated in the Revolution.
(C) They were suppressed by political sanctions.
(D) They were written by members of the upper class.
(E) They were written by members of the lower class.

3. The passage's reference to Madame de La Villirouët is most likely intended to

(A) demonstrate that women's roles during the Revolution were partially determined by their social statuses
(B) explain why so few women published their accounts of the events of the Revolution
(C) support the claim that political partisanship inevitably biases recollections
(D) provide an example of the activism of women described in memoirs of the Revolution
(E) illustrate that royalist and republican memoirs were focused on differing themes

4. According to the passage, more of the published women's memoirs of the French Revolution were written by royalists than by republicans because

(A) royalists could publish their accounts without risking persecution
(B) royalists felt a greater urgency to relate their version of events
(C) royalists were able to afford the prohibitive expense of publication
(D) republicans had little desire to leave written accounts of their actions
(E) republicans typically belonged to professions that left them little time to write

5. Based on the passage, which one of the following views can most reasonably be attributed to the historians mentioned in line 17?

(A) Royalist memoirs of the French Revolution are more factually reliable than are republican memoirs of the same period.
(B) Republican memoirs of the French Revolution are less distorted by partisan biases than are royalist memoirs of the same period.
(C) Many memoirs of the French Revolution published during the restored monarchy likely contain factual inaccuracies.
(D) Many memoirs of the French Revolution contain accounts of events that are not skewed by the biases of their authors.
(E) Many memoirs of the French Revolution consist mostly of unverifiable accounts of certain events.

6. Based on the passage, which one of the following most accurately states a criterion that the scholars referred to in line 22 use to judge the credibility of a memoir's depiction of events known only to its author?

(A) The depiction should appear consistent with the author's personality.
(B) The depiction should contain demonstrable factual accuracies.
(C) The depiction should have been verified shortly after being written.
(D) The depiction should not be part of a partisan account.
(E) The depiction should preserve a particular picture of the past.

GO ON TO THE NEXT PAGE.

The paintings of Romare Bearden (1914–1988) represent a double triumph. At the same time that Bearden's work reflects a lifelong commitment to perfecting the innovative painting techniques he

(5) pioneered, it also reveals an artist engaged in a search for ways to explore the varieties of African-American experience.

By presenting scene, character, and atmosphere using a unique layered and fragmented style that

(10) combines elements of painting with elements of collage, Bearden suggested some of the ways in which commonplace subjects could be forced to undergo a metamorphosis when filtered through the techniques available to the resourceful artist. Bearden knew that

(15) regardless of individual painters' personal histories, tastes, or points of view, they must pay their craft the respect of approaching it through an acute awareness of the resources and limitations of the form to which they have dedicated their creative energies.

(20) But how did Bearden, so passionately dedicated to solving the more advanced problems of his painting technique, also succeed so well at portraying the realities of African-American life? During the Great Depression of the 1930s, Bearden painted scenes of the

(25) hardships of the period; the work was powerful, the scenes grim and brooding. Through his depiction of the unemployed in New York's Harlem he was able to move beyond the usual "protest painting" of the period to reveal instances of individual human suffering. His

(30) human figures, placed in abstract yet mysteriously familiar urban settings, managed to express the complex social reality lying beyond the borders of the canvas without compromising their integrity as elements in an artistic composition. Another important

(35) element of Bearden's compositions was his use of muted colors, such as dark blues and purples, to suggest moods of melancholy or despair. While functioning as part of the overall design, these colors also served as symbols of the psychological effects of

(40) debilitating social processes.

During the same period, he also painted happier scenes—depictions of religious ceremony, musical performance, and family life—and instilled them with the same vividness that he applied to his scenes of

(45) suffering. Bearden sought in his work to reveal in all its fullness a world long hidden by the clichés of sociology and rendered cloudy by the simplifications of journalism and documentary photography. Where any number of painters have tried to project the "prose" of

(50) Harlem, Bearden concentrated on releasing its poetry— its family rituals and its ceremonies of affirmation and celebration. His work insists that we truly see the African-American experience in depth, using the fresh light of his creative vision. Through an act of artistic

(55) will, he created strange visual harmonies out of the mosaic of the African-American experience, and in doing so reflected the multiple rhythms, textures, and mysteries of life.

7. Which one of the following best summarizes the main idea of the passage?

(A) Bearden was unique among chroniclers of the Great Depression in that his work depicted not just human suffering but also the happier moments that other artists tended to overlook.

(B) By combining a dedication to the perfection of his craft with a desire to portray African-American life in all its complexity, Bearden was able to produce paintings of unique vision.

(C) Without sacrificing his devotion to depicting the realities of African-American life, Bearden was able to expand the number and kind of painting techniques available to the dedicated artist.

(D) Unlike other artists of the Great Depression, who were interested mainly in sociological observation, Bearden devoted himself to the perfection of his craft.

(E) While Bearden has long been celebrated for his innovative painting techniques, he is less well known but equally notable as a compassionate chronicler of the African-American experience.

8. According to the passage, Bearden's innovative painting techniques illustrate

(A) a commitment to calling attention to human suffering

(B) a desire to instruct painters about how to approach problems of form

(C) the ability of art to transform ordinary subject matter

(D) the importance of combining the abstractions of painting with the clarity of photography

(E) the need to emphasize more prosaic elements over poetic elements in a work of art

9. As it is used in the passage, the phrase "protest painting" (line 28) appears to refer to painting that

(A) depicted general scenes of social hardship and group suffering

(B) portrayed solitary figures in abstract surroundings

(C) challenged the traditional techniques employed by painters

(D) emphasized the experiences of African Americans during the Great Depression

(E) used innovative techniques to suggest the effects of social circumstances on individuals

GO ON TO THE NEXT PAGE.

10. Based on the passage, with which one of the following statements would Bearden have been most likely to agree?

(A) To better highlight the creative technical elements of a painting an artist should choose prosaic and commonplace subjects.

(B) Technical elements such as color can be effectively used to convey social or political messages.

(C) A painter's use of technical innovations should be subservient to conveying social and political messages.

(D) A painter should focus on the positive elements of African-American life and avoid depicting suffering and injustice.

(E) The techniques of journalism and photography can bring new creative vision to painting and enrich its depiction of African-American life.

11. It can be inferred from the passage that journalistic and photographic records of Depression-era Harlem generally do not

(A) involve innovative creative techniques

(B) reveal instances of individual human suffering

(C) communicate the sociological platitudes of the period

(D) depict the richness of African-American life

(E) cloud the picture of everyday life

12. The passage gives information that helps answer all of the following questions EXCEPT:

(A) What led Bearden to choose painting as his primary means of artistic expression?

(B) What are some of Bearden's most significant contributions to art?

(C) What aspects of life during the Great Depression did Bearden depict?

(D) What specific artistic techniques lent power to Bearden's paintings of individual subjects?

(E) What did Bearden intend to convey through his use of color?

13. According to the passage, human figures in Bearden's paintings do all of the following EXCEPT:

(A) serve as particular examples of human hardship

(B) suggest circumstances outside the explicit subject of the paintings

(C) function as aspects of an artistic composition

(D) symbolize emotions or psychological states

(E) inhabit abstract but recognizable physical settings

14. The passage suggests that the author's attitude toward Bearden's innovative painting techniques is one of

(A) admiration for how they aided Bearden in communicating his rich vision of African-American life

(B) appreciation for how they transform complex social realities into simple and direct social critiques

(C) respect for how they are rooted in the rhythms and textures of African-American experience

(D) concern that they draw attention away from Bearden's social and political message

(E) strong conviction that they should be more widely utilized by African-American artists

GO ON TO THE NEXT PAGE.

Philosophers of science have long been uneasy with biology, preferring instead to focus on physics. At the heart of this preference is a mistrust of uncertainty. Science is supposed to be the study of what is true

(5) everywhere and for all times, and the phenomena of science are supposed to be repeatable, arising from universal laws, rather than historically contingent. After all, if something pops up only on occasional Tuesdays or Thursdays, it is not classified as science

(10) but as history. Philosophers of science have thus been fascinated with the fact that elephants and mice would fall at the same rate if dropped from the Tower of Pisa, but not much interested in how elephants and mice got to be such different sizes in the first place.

(15) Philosophers of science have not been alone in claiming that science must consist of universal laws. Some evolutionary biologists have also acceded to the general intellectual disdain for the merely particular and tried to emulate physicists, constructing their

(20) science as a set of universal laws. In formulating the notion of a universal "struggle for existence" that is the engine of biological history or in asserting that virtually all DNA evolves at a constant clocklike rate, they have attempted to find their own versions of the

(25) law of gravity. Recently, however, some biologists have questioned whether biological history is really the necessary unfolding of universal laws of life, and they have raised the possibility that historical contingency is an integral factor in biology.

(30) To illustrate the difference between biologists favoring universal, deterministic laws of evolutionary development and those leaving room for historical contingency, consider two favorite statements of philosophers (both of which appear, at first sight, to be

(35) universal assertions): "All planets move in ellipses" and "All swans are white." The former is truly universal because it applies not only to those planets that actually do exist, but also to those that could exist—for the shape of planetary orbits is a necessary

(40) consequence of the laws governing the motion of objects in a gravitational field.

Biological determinists would say that "All swans are white" is universal in the same way, since, if all swans were white, it would be because the laws of

(45) natural selection make it impossible for swans to be otherwise: natural selection favors those characteristics that increase the average rate of offspring production, and so traits that maximize flexibility and the ability to manipulate nature will

(50) eventually appear. Nondeterminist biologists would deny this, saying that "swans" is merely the name of a finite collection of historical objects that may happen all to be white, but not of necessity. The history of evolutionary theory has been the history of the struggle

(55) between these two views of swans.

15. Which one of the following best summarizes the main idea of the passage?

(A) Just as philosophers of science have traditionally been reluctant to deal with scientific phenomena that are not capable of being explained by known physical laws, biologists have tended to shy away from confronting philosophical questions.

(B) While science is often considered to be concerned with universal laws, the degree to which certain biological phenomena can be understood as arising from such laws is currently in dispute.

(C) Although biologists have long believed that the nature of their field called for a theoretical approach different from that taken by physicists, some biologists have recently begun to emulate the methods of physicists.

(D) Whereas physicists have achieved a far greater degree of experimental precision than has been possible in the field of biology, the two fields employ similar theoretical approaches.

(E) Since many biologists are uncomfortable with the emphasis placed by philosophers of science on the need to construct universal laws, there has been little interaction between the two disciplines.

16. The reference to the formulation of the notion of a universal "struggle for existence" (line 21) serves primarily to

(A) identify one of the driving forces of biological history

(B) illustrate one context in which the concept of uncertainty has been applied

(C) highlight the chief cause of controversy among various schools of biological thought

(D) provide an example of the type of approach employed by determinist biologists

(E) provide an example of a biological phenomenon that illustrates historical contingency

GO ON TO THE NEXT PAGE.

17. Which one of the following statements about biology is most consistent with the view held by determinist biologists, as that view is presented in the passage?

(A) The appearance of a species is the result of a combination of biological necessity and historical chance.

(B) The rate at which physiological characteristics of a species change fluctuates from generation to generation.

(C) The causes of a given evolutionary phenomenon can never be understood by biological scientists.

(D) The qualities that define a species have been developed according to some process that has not yet been identified.

(E) The chief physical characteristics of a species are inevitable consequences of the laws governing natural selection.

18. It can be inferred from the passage that philosophers of science view the laws of physics as

(A) analogous to the laws of history
(B) difficult to apply because of their uncertainty
(C) applicable to possible as well as actual situations
(D) interesting because of their particularity
(E) illustrative of the problem of historical contingency

19. It can be inferred from the passage that determinist biologists have tried to emulate physicists because these biologists believe that

(A) the methods of physicists are more easily understood by nonscientists

(B) physicists have been accorded more respect by their fellow scientists than have biologists

(C) biology can only be considered a true science if universal laws can be constructed to explain its phenomena

(D) the specific laws that have helped to explain the behavior of planets can be applied to biological phenomena

(E) all scientific endeavors benefit from intellectual exchange between various scientific disciplines

20. The passage suggests that the preference of many philosophers of science for the field of physics depends primarily upon the

(A) belief that biological laws are more difficult to discover than physical laws

(B) popular attention given to recent discoveries in physics as opposed to those in biology

(C) bias shown toward the physical sciences in the research programs of many scientific institutions

(D) teaching experiences of most philosophers of science

(E) nature of the phenomena that physicists study

GO ON TO THE NEXT PAGE.

Ronald Dworkin argues that judges are in danger of uncritically embracing an erroneous theory known as legal positivism because they think the only alternative is a theory that they (and Dworkin) see as clearly
(5) unacceptable—natural law. The latter theory holds that judges ought to interpret the law by consulting their own moral convictions, even if this means ignoring the letter of the law and the legal precedents for its interpretation. Dworkin regards this as an
(10) impermissible form of judicial activism that arrogates to judges powers properly reserved for legislators.

Legal positivism, the more popular of the two theories, holds that law and morality are wholly distinct. The meaning of the law rests on social
(15) convention in the same way as does the meaning of a word. Dworkin's view is that legal positivists regard disagreement among jurists as legitimate only if it arises over what the underlying convention is, and it is to be resolved by registering a consensus, not by
(20) deciding what is morally right. In the same way, disagreement about the meaning of a word is settled by determining how people actually use it, and not by deciding what it ought to mean. Where there is no consensus, there is no legal fact of the matter. The
(25) judge's interpretive role is limited to discerning this consensus, or the absence thereof.

According to Dworkin, this account is incompatible with the actual practice of judges and lawyers, who act as if there is a fact of the matter even
(30) in cases where there is no consensus. The theory he proposes seeks to validate this practice without falling into what Dworkin correctly sees as the error of natural law theory. It represents a kind of middle ground between the latter and legal positivism. Dworkin
(35) stresses the fact that there is an internal logic to a society's laws and the general principles they typically embody. An interpretation that conforms to these principles may be correct even if it is not supported by a consensus. Since these general principles may
(40) involve such moral concepts as justice and fairness, judges may be called upon to consult their own moral intuitions in arriving at an interpretation. But this is not to say that judges are free to impose their own morality at will, without regard to the internal logic of the laws.
(45) The positivist's mistake, as Dworkin points out, is assuming that the meaning of the law can only consist in what people think it means, whether these people be the original authors of the law or a majority of the interpreter's peers. Once we realize, as Dworkin does,
(50) that the law has an internal logic of its own that constrains interpretation, we open up the possibility of improving upon the interpretations not only of our contemporaries but of the original authors.

21. Which one of the following most accurately expresses the main point of the passage?

(A)   Dworkin regards natural law theory as a middle ground between legal positivism and judicial activism.
(B)   Dworkin holds that judicial interpretations should not be based solely on identifying a consensus or solely on moral intuition, but should be consistent with the reasoning that underlies the law.
(C)   Dworkin argues that the internal logic of the law should generally guide judges except in instances where consensus is registered or judges have strong moral intuitions.
(D)   Dworkin's theory of legal interpretation is based on borrowing equally from natural law theory and legal positivism.
(E)   Dworkin validates judges' dependence on moral intuition, reason, and the intent of the authors of a law, but only in cases where a social consensus is not present.

22. What is the main purpose of the second paragraph?

(A)   to explain why legal positivism is so popular
(B)   to evaluate the theory of legal positivism
(C)   to discuss how judicial consensus is determined
(D)   to identify the basic tenets of legal positivism
(E)   to argue in favor of the theory of legal positivism

23. Which one of the following most accurately characterizes the author's attitude toward Dworkin's theory?

(A)   confident endorsement of its central assertions
(B)   caution about its potential for justifying some forms of judicial activism
(C)   modest expectation that some of its claims will be found to be unwarranted
(D)   quiet conviction that its importance derives only from its originality
(E)   enthusiasm that it will replace legal positivism as the most popular theory of legal interpretation

GO ON TO THE NEXT PAGE.

24. According to the passage, which one of the following is a goal of Dworkin's theory of legal interpretation?

(A)   to evaluate previous legal interpretations by judges influenced by legal positivism

(B)   to dispute the notion that social consensus plays any role in legal interpretation

(C)   to provide a theoretical argument against the use of moral intuition in legal interpretation

(D)   to argue that legal decisions must be based on the principles of the original authors of the laws

(E)   to validate theoretically the method commonly used by judges in practice

25. The passage suggests that Dworkin would be most likely to agree with which one of the following statements?

(A)   Judges and lawyers too often act as though there is a fact of the matter in legal cases.

(B)   Judges should not use their moral intuition when it conflicts with the intentions of those legislators who authored the law being interpreted.

(C)   Legal positivism is a more popular theory than natural law theory because legal positivism simplifies the judge's role.

(D)   If there is consensus about how to interpret a law, then jurists should not examine the internal logic of the law being interpreted.

(E)   Legal positivists misunderstand the role of moral intuition in legal interpretation.

26. It can be inferred that legal positivists, as described in the passage, agree with which one of the following statements?

(A)   Judges sometimes ought to be allowed to use personal moral convictions as a basis for a legal interpretation.

(B)   Disagreements about the meaning of a law are never legitimate.

(C)   The ultimate standard of interpretation is the logic of the law itself, not moral intuition.

(D)   The meaning of a law derives from jurists' interpretations of that law.

(E)   There is no legal fact of the matter when jurists have differing moral convictions about an issue.

S T O P

IF YOU FINISH BEFORE TIME IS CALLED, YOU MAY CHECK YOUR WORK ON THIS SECTION ONLY.
DO NOT WORK ON ANY OTHER SECTION IN THE TEST.

SECTION III

Time—35 minutes

23 Questions

Directions: Each group of questions in this section is based on a set of conditions. In answering some of the questions, it may be useful to draw a rough diagram. Choose the response that most accurately and completely answers each question and blacken the corresponding space on your answer sheet.

Questions 1–5

From among eight candidates, four astronauts will be selected for a space flight. Four of the candidates—F, J, K, and L—are experienced astronauts and four—M, N, P, and T—are inexperienced astronauts. F, M, P, and T are geologists whereas J, K, L, and N are radiobiologists. The astronauts must be selected according to the following conditions:

Exactly two experienced astronauts and two inexperienced astronauts are selected.

Exactly two geologists and two radiobiologists are selected.

Either P or L or both are selected.

1. Which one of the following is an acceptable selection of astronauts for the space flight?

(A) F, J, N, and T
(B) F, L, M, and P
(C) F, M, N, and P
(D) J, L, M, and T
(E) K, L, N, and T

2. If F and P are selected for the space flight, the other two astronauts selected must be

(A) a radiobiologist who is an experienced astronaut and a radiobiologist who is an inexperienced astronaut
(B) a radiobiologist who is an experienced astronaut and a geologist who is an inexperienced astronaut
(C) a radiobiologist and a geologist, both of whom are experienced astronauts
(D) two radiobiologists, both of whom are experienced astronauts
(E) two radiobiologists, both of whom are inexperienced astronauts

3. If F and J are selected for the space flight, which one of the following must also be selected?

(A) K
(B) L
(C) M
(D) N
(E) T

4. If M and T are selected for the space flight, which one of the following could be, but need not be, selected for the flight?

(A) F
(B) J
(C) L
(D) N
(E) P

5. If N is selected for the space flight, which one of the following must also be selected?

(A) F
(B) J
(C) L
(D) M
(E) T

GO ON TO THE NEXT PAGE.

Questions 6–12

A showroom contains exactly six new cars—T, V, W, X, Y, and Z—each equipped with at least one of the following three options: power windows, leather interior, and sunroof. No car has any other options. The following conditions must apply:

V has power windows and a sunroof.
W has power windows and a leather interior.
W and Y have no options in common.
X has more options than W.
V and Z have exactly one option in common.
T has fewer options than Z.

6. For exactly how many of the six cars is it possible to determine exactly which options each one has?

   (A) two
   (B) three
   (C) four
   (D) five
   (E) six

7. Which one of the following must be false?

   (A) Exactly five of the six cars have leather interiors.
   (B) Exactly five of the six cars have sunroofs.
   (C) Exactly four of the six cars have leather interiors.
   (D) Exactly four of the six cars have power windows.
   (E) Exactly four of the six cars have sunroofs.

8. If all the cars that have leather interiors also have power windows, which one of the following must be false?

   (A) T has power windows.
   (B) T has a sunroof.
   (C) V has power windows.
   (D) Z has power windows.
   (E) Z has a sunroof.

9. If Z has no options in common with T but has at least one option in common with every other car, then which one of the following must be false?

   (A) T has power windows.
   (B) Z has a sunroof.
   (C) Exactly four of the six cars have power windows.
   (D) Exactly four of the six cars have leather interiors.
   (E) Exactly four of the six cars have sunroofs.

10. Suppose that no two cars have exactly the same options as one another. In that case, each of the following could be true EXCEPT:

    (A) Exactly three of the six cars have power windows.
    (B) Exactly four of the six cars have power windows.
    (C) Exactly three of the six cars have sunroofs.
    (D) Exactly four of the six cars have sunroofs.
    (E) Exactly four of the six cars have leather interiors.

11. If exactly four of the six cars have leather interiors, and exactly four of the six cars have power windows, then each of the following must be true EXCEPT:

    (A) T and V have no options in common.
    (B) T and Y have no options in common.
    (C) T and Z have exactly one option in common.
    (D) W and Z have exactly one option in common.
    (E) Y and Z have no options in common.

12. Suppose that the condition requiring that X has more options than W is replaced by a new condition requiring that X and W have exactly two options in common. If all of the other original conditions remain in effect, which one of the following must be false?

    (A) T and X have no options in common.
    (B) V and X have exactly one option in common.
    (C) V and X have exactly two options in common.
    (D) X and Z have no options in common.
    (E) X and Z have exactly two options in common.

GO ON TO THE NEXT PAGE.

Questions 13–17

Quentin, Robert, Shiro, Tony, and Umeko are the only members of the Kim family who attend an opera. Each of them sits in a separate seat in either row G or row H, and each sits in a seat numbered 1, 2, or 3. Consecutively numbered seats within each row are adjacent.

Each member of the Kim family sits in a seat adjacent to, and in the same row as, at least one other member of the family.

Tony and Umeko sit in row H.

Shiro and Umeko sit in lower numbered seats than does Tony.

Robert sits in the same row as Quentin or Shiro or both.

Robert sits in a seat numbered 2.

13. Which one of the following statements could be true?

(A) Seat G3 is empty.
(B) Seat H2 is empty.
(C) Shiro sits in a seat numbered 3.
(D) Tony sits in a seat numbered 1.
(E) Umeko sits in a seat numbered 3.

14. Which one of the following statements could be true?

(A) Robert sits in row H.
(B) Shiro sits in row H.
(C) Quentin sits in the same row as, and in a seat adjacent to, Shiro.
(D) Robert sits in the same row as, and in a seat adjacent to, Tony.
(E) Robert sits in the same row as, and in a seat adjacent to, Umeko.

15. If Tony sits in a seat numbered 2, then which one of the following statements could be false?

(A) Quentin sits in a seat numbered 3.
(B) Umeko sits in a seat numbered 1.
(C) Quentin sits in the same row as, and in a seat adjacent to, Robert.
(D) Robert sits in the same row as, and in a seat adjacent to, Shiro.
(E) Tony sits in the same row as, and in a seat adjacent to, Umeko.

16. Considering only the six seats in which members of the Kim family could sit, which one of the following is a complete and accurate list of those seats any one of which could be empty?

(A) G1, G3
(B) G3, H1
(C) H1, H3
(D) G1, G3, H1
(E) G1, G3, H1, H3

17. Which one of the following is a complete and accurate list of those members of the Kim family any one of whom could sit in seat H2?

(A) Quentin
(B) Shiro, Umeko
(C) Robert, Shiro, Umeko
(D) Tony, Shiro, Umeko
(E) Quentin, Shiro, Tony, Umeko

GO ON TO THE NEXT PAGE.

Questions 18–23

Exactly seven professors—Madison, Nilsson, Orozco, Paton, Robinson, Sarkis, and Togo—were hired in the years 1989 through 1995. Each professor has one or more specialties, and any two professors hired in the same year or in consecutive years do not have a specialty in common. The professors were hired according to the following conditions:

Madison was hired in 1993, Robinson in 1991.
There is at least one specialty that Madison, Orozco, and Togo have in common.
Nilsson shares a specialty with Robinson.
Paton and Sarkis were each hired at least one year before Madison and at least one year after Nilsson.
Orozco, who shares a specialty with Sarkis, was hired in 1990.

18. Which one of the following is a complete and accurate list of the professors who could have been hired in the years 1989 through 1991?

    (A) Nilsson, Orozco, Robinson
    (B) Orozco, Robinson, Sarkis
    (C) Nilsson, Orozco, Paton, Robinson
    (D) Nilsson, Orozco, Paton, Sarkis
    (E) Orozco, Paton, Robinson, Sarkis

19. If exactly one professor was hired in 1991, then which one of the following could be true?

    (A) Madison and Paton share a specialty.
    (B) Robinson and Sarkis share a specialty.
    (C) Paton was hired exactly one year after Orozco.
    (D) Exactly one professor was hired in 1994.
    (E) Exactly two professors were hired in 1993.

20. Which one of the following must be false?

    (A) Nilsson was hired in 1989.
    (B) Paton was hired in 1990.
    (C) Paton was hired in 1991.
    (D) Sarkis was hired in 1992.
    (E) Togo was hired in 1994.

21. Which one of the following must be true?

    (A) Orozco was hired before Paton.
    (B) Paton was hired before Sarkis.
    (C) Sarkis was hired before Robinson.
    (D) Robinson was hired before Sarkis.
    (E) Madison was hired before Sarkis.

22. If exactly two professors were hired in 1992, then which one of the following could be true?

    (A) Orozco, Paton, and Togo share a specialty.
    (B) Madison, Paton, and Togo share a specialty.
    (C) Exactly two professors were hired in 1991.
    (D) Exactly two professors were hired in 1993.
    (E) Paton was hired in 1991.

23. If Paton and Madison have a specialty in common, then which one of the following must be true?

    (A) Nilsson does not share a specialty with Paton.
    (B) Exactly one professor was hired in 1990.
    (C) Exactly one professor was hired in 1991.
    (D) Exactly two professors were hired in each of two years.
    (E) Paton was hired at least one year before Sarkis.

S T O P

IF YOU FINISH BEFORE TIME IS CALLED, YOU MAY CHECK YOUR WORK ON THIS SECTION ONLY.
DO NOT WORK ON ANY OTHER SECTION IN THE TEST.

SECTION IV
Time—35 minutes
26 Questions

Directions: The questions in this section are based on the reasoning contained in brief statements or passages. For some questions, more than one of the choices could conceivably answer the question. However, you are to choose the best answer; that is, the response that most accurately and completely answers the question. You should not make assumptions that are by commonsense standards implausible, superfluous, or incompatible with the passage. After you have chosen the best answer, blacken the corresponding space on your answer sheet.

1. The graphical illustrations mathematics teachers use enable students to learn geometry more easily by providing them with an intuitive understanding of geometric concepts, which makes it easier to acquire the ability to manipulate symbols for the purpose of calculation. Illustrating algebraic concepts graphically would be equally effective pedagogically, even though the deepest mathematical understanding is abstract, not imagistic.

   The statements above provide some support for each of the following EXCEPT:

   (A) Pictorial understanding is not the final stage of mathematical understanding.
   (B) People who are very good at manipulating symbols do not necessarily have any mathematical understanding.
   (C) Illustrating geometric concepts graphically is an effective teaching method.
   (D) Acquiring the ability to manipulate symbols is part of the process of learning geometry.
   (E) There are strategies that can be effectively employed in the teaching both of algebra and of geometry.

2. Bureaucratic mechanisms are engineered to resist change. Thus, despite growing dissatisfaction with complex bureaucratic systems, it is unlikely that bureaucracies will be simplified.

   The claim that bureaucratic mechanisms are engineered to resist change plays which one of the following roles in the argument?

   (A) It is a premise offered in support of the claim that it is unlikely that bureaucracies will be simplified.
   (B) It is a conclusion for which the only support offered is the claim that dissatisfaction with complex bureaucratic systems is growing.
   (C) It is cited as evidence that bureaucratic systems are becoming more and more complex.
   (D) It is used to weaken the claim that bureaucracies should be simplified.
   (E) It is a conclusion for which the claim that bureaucracies are unlikely to be simplified is offered as support.

3. In speech, when words or sentences are ambiguous, gesture and tone of voice are used to indicate the intended meaning. Writers, of course, cannot use gesture or tone of voice and must rely instead on style; the reader detects the writer's intention from the arrangement of words and sentences.

   Which one of the following statements is most strongly supported by the information above?

   (A) The primary function of style in writing is to augment the literal meanings of the words and sentences used.
   (B) The intended meaning of a piece of writing is indicated in part by the writer's arrangement of words and sentences.
   (C) It is easier for a listener to detect the tone of a speaker than for a reader to detect the style of a writer.
   (D) A writer's intention will always be interpreted differently by different readers.
   (E) The writer's arrangement of words and sentences completely determines the aesthetic value of his or her writing.

GO ON TO THE NEXT PAGE.

4. Last year a large firm set a goal of decreasing its workforce by 25 percent. Three divisions, totaling 25 percent of its workforce at that time, were to be eliminated and no new people hired. These divisions have since been eliminated and no new people have joined the firm, but its workforce has decreased by only 15 percent.

Which one of the following, if true, contributes most to an explanation of the difference in the planned versus the actual reduction in the workforce?

(A) The three divisions that were eliminated were well run and had the potential to earn profits.

(B) Normal attrition in the retained divisions continued to reduce staff because no new people were added to the firm.

(C) Some of the employees in the eliminated divisions were eligible for early retirement and chose that option.

(D) As the divisions were being eliminated some of their employees were assigned to other divisions.

(E) Employees in the retained divisions were forced to work faster to offset the loss of the eliminated divisions.

5. One of the advantages of *Bacillus thuringiensis* (B.t.) toxins over chemical insecticides results from their specificity for pest insects. The toxins have no known detrimental effects on mammals or birds. In addition, the limited range of activity of the toxins toward insects means that often a particular toxin will kill pest species but not affect insects that prey upon the species. This advantage makes B.t. toxins preferable to chemical insecticides for use as components of insect pest management programs.

Which one of the following statements, if true, most weakens the argument?

(A) Chemical insecticides cause harm to a greater number of insect species than do B.t. toxins.

(B) No particular B.t. toxin is effective against all insects.

(C) B.t. toxins do not harm weeds that do damage to farm crops.

(D) Insects build up resistance more readily to B.t. toxins than to chemical insecticides.

(E) Birds and rodents often do greater damage to farm crops than do insects.

6. Many people are alarmed about the population explosion. They fail to appreciate that the present rise in population has in fact been followed by equally potent economic growth. Because of this connection between an increase in population and an increase in economic activity, population control measures should not be taken.

The questionable pattern of reasoning in the argument above is most similar to that in which one of the following?

(A) Subscribers to newsmagazines are concerned that increased postage costs will be passed on to them in the form of higher subscription rates. But that is a price they have to pay for having the magazines delivered. No group of users of the postal system should be subsidized at the expense of others.

(B) Most of the salespeople are concerned with complaints about the sales manager's aggressive behavior. They need to consider that sales are currently increasing. Due to this success, no action should be taken to address the manager's behavior.

(C) Parents are concerned about their children spending too much time watching television. Those parents should consider television time as time they could spend with their children. Let the children watch television, but watch it with them.

(D) Nutritionists warn people not to eat unhealthy foods. Those foods have been in people's diets for years. Before cutting all those foods out of diets it would be wise to remember that people enjoy culinary variety.

(E) Some consumers become concerned when the price of a product increases for several years in a row, thinking that the price will continue to increase. But these consumers are mistaken since a long-term trend of price increases indicates that the price will probably decline in the future.

GO ON TO THE NEXT PAGE.

7. Attorney: I ask you to find Mr. Smith guilty of
    assaulting Mr. Jackson. Regrettably, there were no
    eyewitnesses to the crime, but Mr. Smith has a
    violent character: Ms. Lopez testified earlier that
    Mr. Smith, shouting loudly, had threatened her.
    Smith never refuted this testimony.

The attorney's argument is fallacious because it reasons
that

(A) aggressive behavior is not a sure indicator of a
     violent character
(B) Smith's testimony is unreliable since he is loud
     and aggressive
(C) since Smith never disproved the claim that he
     threatened Lopez, he did in fact threaten her
(D) Lopez's testimony is reliable since she is neither
     loud nor aggressive
(E) having a violent character is not necessarily
     associated with the commission of violent
     crimes

8. It is widely believed that by age 80, perception and
    memory are each significantly reduced from their
    functioning levels at age 30. However, a recent study
    showed no difference in the abilities of 80-year-olds and
    30-year-olds to play a card game devised to test
    perception and memory. Therefore, the belief that
    perception and memory are significantly reduced by age
    80 is false.

The reasoning above is most vulnerable to criticism on
the grounds that it fails to consider the possibility that

(A) the study's card game does not test cognitive
     abilities other than perception and memory
(B) card games are among the most difficult cognitive
     tasks one can attempt to perform
(C) perception and memory are interrelated in ways
     of which we are not currently aware
(D) the belief that 80-year-olds' perception and
     memory are reduced results from prejudice
     against senior citizens
(E) playing the study's card game perfectly requires
     fairly low levels of perception and memory

9. Moralist: Humans have a natural disposition to
    altruism—that is, to behavior that serves the needs
    of others regardless of one's own needs—but that
    very disposition prevents some acts of altruism
    from counting as moral. Reason plays an essential
    role in any moral behavior. Only behavior that is
    intended to be in accordance with a formal set of
    rules, or moral code, can be considered moral
    behavior.

Which one of the following most accurately states the
main conclusion of the moralist's argument?

(A) All moral codes prohibit selfishness.
(B) All moral behavior is motivated by altruism.
(C) Behavior must serve the needs of others in order
     to be moral behavior.
(D) Not all altruistic acts are moral behavior.
(E) Altruism develops through the use of reason.

10. A recent study suggests that Alzheimer's disease, which
     attacks the human brain, may be caused by a virus. In the
     study, blood from 11 volunteers, each of whom had the
     disease, was injected into rats. The rats eventually
     exhibited symptoms of another degenerative
     neurological disorder, Creutzfeldt-Jakob disease, which
     is caused by a virus. This led the scientist who conducted
     the study to conclude that Alzheimer's disease might be
     caused by a virus.

Which one of the following statements, if true, would
most strengthen the scientist's hypothesis that
Alzheimer's disease is caused by a virus?

(A) Alzheimer's disease in rats is not caused by a
     virus.
(B) Creutzfeldt-Jakob disease affects only motor
     nerves in rats' limbs, not their brains.
(C) The virus that causes Creutzfeldt-Jakob disease in
     rats has no effect on humans.
(D) The symptoms known, respectively, as
     Creutzfeldt-Jakob disease and Alzheimer's
     disease are different manifestations of the same
     disease.
(E) Blood from rats without Creutzfeldt-Jakob
     disease produced no symptoms of the disease
     when injected into other experimental rats.

GO ON TO THE NEXT PAGE.

11. One approach to the question of which objects discussed by a science are real is to designate as real all and only those entities posited by the most explanatorily powerful theory of the science. But since most scientific theories contain entities posited solely on theoretical grounds, this approach is flawed.

Which one of the following principles, if valid, most helps to justify the reasoning above?

(A) Any object that is posited by a scientific theory and that enhances the explanatory power of that theory should be designated as real.

(B) Objects posited for theoretical reasons only should never be designated as real.

(C) A scientific theory should not posit any entity that does not enhance the explanatory power of the theory.

(D) A scientific theory should sometimes posit entities on grounds other than theoretical ones.

(E) Only objects posited by explanatorily powerful theories should be designated as real.

12. Most doctors recommend that pregnant women eat a nutritious diet to promote the health of their babies. However, most babies who are born to women who ate nutritious diets while pregnant still develop at least one medical problem in their first year.

Which one of the following, if true, does most to resolve the apparent discrepancy in the information above?

(A) Women who regularly eat a nutritious diet while pregnant tend to eat a nutritious diet while breast-feeding.

(B) Most of the babies born to women who did not eat nutritious diets while pregnant develop no serious medical problems later in childhood.

(C) Babies of women who did not eat nutritious diets while pregnant tend to have more medical problems in their first year than do other babies.

(D) Medical problems that develop in the first year of life tend to be more serious than those that develop later in childhood.

(E) Many of the physicians who initially recommended that pregnant women consume nutritious diets have only recently reaffirmed their recommendation.

13. Mayor: The law prohibiting pedestrians from crossing against red lights serves no useful purpose. After all, in order to serve a useful purpose, a law must deter the kind of behavior it prohibits. But pedestrians who invariably violate this law are clearly not dissuaded by it; and those who comply with the law do not need it, since they would never cross against red lights even if there were no law prohibiting pedestrians from crossing against red lights.

The mayor's argument is flawed because it

(A) takes for granted that most automobile drivers will obey the law that prohibits them from driving through red lights

(B) uses the word "law" in one sense in the premises and in another sense in the conclusion

(C) ignores the possibility that a law might not serve a useful purpose even if it does deter the kind of behavior it prohibits

(D) fails to consider whether the law ever dissuades people who sometimes but not always cross against red lights

(E) provides no evidence that crossing against red lights is more dangerous than crossing on green lights

GO ON TO THE NEXT PAGE.

14. Marian Anderson, the famous contralto, did not take success for granted. We know this because Anderson had to struggle early in life, and anyone who has to struggle early in life is able to keep a good perspective on the world.

The conclusion of the argument follows logically if which one of the following is assumed?

(A) Anyone who succeeds takes success for granted.
(B) Anyone who is able to keep a good perspective on the world does not take success for granted.
(C) Anyone who is able to keep a good perspective on the world has to struggle early in life.
(D) Anyone who does not take success for granted has to struggle early in life.
(E) Anyone who does not take success for granted is able to keep a good perspective on the world.

15. Geneticist: Ethicists have fears, many of them reasonable, about the prospect of cloning human beings, that is, producing exact genetic duplicates. But the horror-movie image of a wealthy person creating an army of exact duplicates is completely unrealistic. Clones must be raised and educated, a long-term process that could never produce adults identical to the original in terms of outlook, personality, or goals. More realistic is the possibility that wealthy individuals might use clones as living "organ banks."

The claim that cloning will not produce adults with identical personalities plays which one of the following roles in the geneticist's argument?

(A) It is a reason for dismissing the various fears raised by ethicists regarding the cloning of human beings.
(B) It is evidence that genetic clones will never be produced successfully.
(C) It illustrates the claim that only wealthy people would be able to have genetic duplicates made of themselves.
(D) It is evidence for the claim that wealthy people might use genetic duplicates of themselves as sources of compatible organs for transplantation.
(E) It is a reason for discounting one possible fear concerning the cloning of human beings.

16. Publicity campaigns for endangered species are unlikely to have much impact on the most important environmental problems, for while the ease of attributing feelings to large mammals facilitates evoking sympathy for them, it is more difficult to elicit sympathy for other kinds of organisms, such as the soil microorganisms on which large ecosystems and agriculture depend.

Which one of the following is an assumption on which the argument depends?

(A) The most important environmental problems involve endangered species other than large mammals.
(B) Microorganisms cannot experience pain or have other feelings.
(C) Publicity campaigns for the environment are the most effective when they elicit sympathy for some organism.
(D) People ignore environmental problems unless they believe the problems will affect creatures with which they sympathize.
(E) An organism can be environmentally significant only if it affects large ecosystems or agriculture.

17. Politician: All nations that place a high tax on income produce thereby a negative incentive for technological innovation, and all nations in which technological innovation is hampered inevitably fall behind in the international arms race. Those nations that, through historical accident or the foolishness of their political leadership, wind up in a strategically disadvantageous position are destined to lose their voice in world affairs. So if a nation wants to maintain its value system and way of life, it must not allow its highest tax bracket to exceed 30 percent of income.

Each of the following, if true, weakens the politician's argument EXCEPT:

(A) The top level of taxation must reach 45 percent before taxation begins to deter inventors and industrialists from introducing new technologies and industries.
(B) Making a great deal of money is an insignificant factor in driving technological innovation.
(C) Falling behind in the international arms race does not necessarily lead to a strategically less advantageous position.
(D) Those nations that lose influence in the world community do not necessarily suffer from a threat to their value system or way of life.
(E) Allowing one's country to lose its technological edge, especially as concerns weaponry, would be foolish rather than merely a historical accident.

GO ON TO THE NEXT PAGE.

18. Philosopher: Scientists talk about the pursuit of truth, but, like most people, they are self-interested. Accordingly, the professional activities of most scientists are directed toward personal career enhancement, and only incidentally toward the pursuit of truth. Hence, the activities of the scientific community are largely directed toward enhancing the status of that community as a whole, and only incidentally toward the pursuit of truth.

The reasoning in the philosopher's argument is flawed because the argument

(A)   improperly infers that each and every scientist has a certain characteristic from the premise that most scientists have that characteristic

(B)   improperly draws an inference about the scientific community as a whole from a premise about individual scientists

(C)   presumes, without giving justification, that the aim of personal career enhancement never advances the pursuit of truth

(D)   illicitly takes advantage of an ambiguity in the meaning of "self-interested"

(E)   improperly draws an inference about a cause from premises about its effects

19. Several critics have claimed that any contemporary poet who writes formal poetry—poetry that is rhymed and metered—is performing a politically conservative act. This is plainly false. Consider Molly Peacock and Marilyn Hacker, two contemporary poets whose poetry is almost exclusively formal and yet who are themselves politically progressive feminists.

The conclusion drawn above follows logically if which one of the following is assumed?

(A)   No one who is a feminist is also politically conservative.

(B)   No poet who writes unrhymed or unmetered poetry is politically conservative.

(C)   No one who is politically progressive is capable of performing a politically conservative act.

(D)   Anyone who sometimes writes poetry that is not politically conservative never writes poetry that is politically conservative.

(E)   The content of a poet's work, not the work's form, is the most decisive factor in determining what political consequences, if any, the work will have.

20. Archaeologist: A skeleton of a North American mastodon that became extinct at the peak of the Ice Age was recently discovered. It contains a human-made projectile dissimilar to any found in that part of Eurasia closest to North America. Thus, since Eurasians did not settle in North America until shortly before the peak of the Ice Age, the first Eurasian settlers in North America probably came from a more distant part of Eurasia.

Which one of the following, if true, most seriously weakens the archaeologist's argument?

(A)   The projectile found in the mastodon does not resemble any that were used in Eurasia before or during the Ice Age.

(B)   The people who occupied the Eurasian area closest to North America remained nomadic throughout the Ice Age.

(C)   The skeleton of a bear from the same place and time as the mastodon skeleton contains a similar projectile.

(D)   Other North American artifacts from the peak of the Ice Age are similar to ones from the same time found in more distant parts of Eurasia.

(E)   Climatic conditions in North America just before the Ice Age were more conducive to human habitation than were those in the part of Eurasia closest to North America at that time.

GO ON TO THE NEXT PAGE.

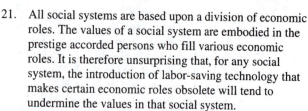
21. All social systems are based upon a division of economic roles. The values of a social system are embodied in the prestige accorded persons who fill various economic roles. It is therefore unsurprising that, for any social system, the introduction of labor-saving technology that makes certain economic roles obsolete will tend to undermine the values in that social system.

Which one of the following can most reasonably be concluded on the basis of the information above?

(A)   Social systems will have unchanging values if they are shielded from technological advancement.
(B)   No type of technology will fail to undermine the values in a social system.
(C)   A social system whose values are not susceptible to change would not be one in which technology can eliminate economic roles.
(D)   A technologically advanced society will place little value on the prestige associated with an economic role.
(E)   A technological innovation that is implemented in a social system foreign to the one in which it was developed will tend to undermine the foreign social system.

22. Multiple sclerosis is an autoimmune disease: white blood cells attack the myelin sheath that protects nerve fibers in the spinal cord and brain. Medical science now has a drug that can be used to successfully treat multiple sclerosis, but the path that led medical researchers to this drug was hardly straightforward. Initially, some scientists believed attacks characteristic of multiple sclerosis might be triggered by chronic viral infections. So in 1984 they began testing gamma interferon, one of the body's own antiviral weapons. To their horror, all the multiple sclerosis patients tested became dramatically worse. The false step proved to be instructive however.

Which one of the following is LEAST compatible with the results of the gamma interferon experiment?

(A)   Gamma interferon stops white blood cells from producing myelin-destroying compounds.
(B)   Administering gamma interferon to those without multiple sclerosis causes an increase in the number of white blood cells.
(C)   Medical researchers have discovered that the gamma interferon level in the cerebrospinal fluid skyrockets just before and during multiple sclerosis attacks.
(D)   It has now been established that most multiple sclerosis sufferers do not have chronic viral infections.
(E)   The drug now used to treat multiple sclerosis is known to inhibit the activity of gamma interferon.

23. The higher the altitude, the thinner the air. Since Mexico City's altitude is higher than that of Panama City, the air must be thinner in Mexico City than in Panama City.

Which one of the following arguments is most similar in its reasoning to the argument above?

(A)   As one gets older one gets wiser. Since Henrietta is older than her daughter, Henrietta must be wiser than her daughter.
(B)   The more egg whites used and the longer they are beaten, the fluffier the meringue. Since Lydia used more egg whites in her meringue than Joseph used in his, Lydia's meringue must be fluffier than Joseph's.
(C)   The people who run the fastest marathons these days are faster than the people who ran the fastest marathons ten years ago. Charles is a marathon runner. So Charles must run faster marathons these days than he did ten years ago.
(D)   The older a tree, the more rings it has. The tree in Lou's yard is older than the tree in Theresa's yard. Therefore, the tree in Lou's yard must have more rings than does the tree in Theresa's yard.
(E)   The bigger the vocabulary a language has, the harder it is to learn. English is harder to learn than Italian. Therefore, English must have a bigger vocabulary than Italian.

24. A recent study of 6,403 people showed that those treated with the drug pravastatin, one of the effects of which is to reduce cholesterol, had about one-third fewer nonfatal heart attacks and one-third fewer deaths from coronary disease than did those not taking the drug. This result is consistent with other studies, which show that those who have heart disease often have higher than average cholesterol levels. This shows that lowering cholesterol levels reduces the risk of heart disease.

The argument's reasoning is flawed because the argument

(A)   neglects the possibility that pravastatin may have severe side effects
(B)   fails to consider that pravastatin may reduce the risk of heart disease but not as a consequence of its lowering cholesterol levels
(C)   relies on past findings, rather than drawing its principal conclusion from the data found in the specific study cited
(D)   draws a conclusion regarding the effects of lowering cholesterol levels on heart disease, when in fact the conclusion should focus on the relation between pravastatin and cholesterol levels
(E)   fails to consider what percentage of the general population might be taking pravastatin

GO ON TO THE NEXT PAGE.

Questions 25–26

Zachary: The term "fresco" refers to paint that has been applied to wet plaster. Once dried, a fresco indelibly preserves the paint that a painter has applied in this way. Unfortunately, additions known to have been made by later painters have obscured the original fresco work done by Michelangelo in the Sistine Chapel. Therefore, in order to restore Michelangelo's Sistine Chapel paintings to the appearance that Michelangelo intended them to have, everything except the original fresco work must be stripped away.

Stephen: But it was extremely common for painters of Michelangelo's era to add painted details to their own fresco work after the frescos had dried.

25.   Stephen's response to Zachary proceeds by

(A)   calling into question an assumption on which Zachary's conclusion depends

(B)   challenging the definition of a key term in Zachary's argument

(C)   drawing a conclusion other than the one that Zachary reaches

(D)   denying the truth of one of the stated premises of Zachary's argument

(E)   demonstrating that Zachary's conclusion is not consistent with the premises he uses to support it

26.   Stephen's response to Zachary, if true, most strongly supports which one of the following?

(A)   It is impossible to distinguish the later painted additions made to Michelangelo's Sistine Chapel paintings from the original fresco work.

(B)   Stripping away everything except Michelangelo's original fresco work from the Sistine Chapel paintings would be unlikely to restore them to the appearance Michelangelo intended them to have.

(C)   The painted details that painters of Michelangelo's era added to their own fresco work were not an integral part of the completed paintings' overall design.

(D)   None of the painters of Michelangelo's era who made additions to the Sistine Chapel paintings was an important artist in his or her own right.

(E)   Michelangelo was rarely satisfied with the appearance of his finished works.

S T O P

IF YOU FINISH BEFORE TIME IS CALLED, YOU MAY CHECK YOUR WORK ON THIS SECTION ONLY.
DO NOT WORK ON ANY OTHER SECTION IN THE TEST.

SIGNATURE _____

LSAT WRITING SAMPLE TOPIC

Lexcorp, a professional services company occupying a one-story building in an outlying suburb of a large city, has outgrown its present office space. Two possible solutions are being considered. One is to enlarge the present building by adding a second story. The other is to move the company into space available in a large office building in the city. Write an essay in which you argue for one alternative over the other based on the following considerations:

- Lexcorp wants to obtain office space most suitable to its needs for the best price.
- Lexcorp wants to minimize disruptions to its employees.

Roughly 70 percent of Lexcorp's employees live within a half hour's drive of the suburb in which the company is located, roughly 20 percent commute from the city, which is about an hour's drive, and the rest come from even farther away. It would take almost a year to add a second story, during which time construction noise and debris would constitute a distraction for workers. It is estimated that the company would have to be shut down entirely for 4–5 weeks. But the addition would be tailored to the company's needs and would enable Lexcorp to continue to be housed by itself in its own building, which is desirable since the company handles confidential materials and is concerned for their security.

Space in the large office building can be had immediately and the move could be accomplished in a week or two. Lexcorp would occupy several floors of the building, at least one of which it would share with other businesses. The cost, offset by the sale of the present building, would be significantly less than that of adding a second story to that building. Property tax is also lower in the city. The city, however, imposes a 3 percent income tax, and in order to retain its employees Lexcorp would probably have to raise their salaries to compensate for this tax. There is good public transportation connecting most suburban areas with the city, but current employees living farthest from the city would face an even longer commute.

Directions:

1. Use the Answer Key on the next page to check your answers.

2. Use the Scoring Worksheet below to compute your raw score.

3. Use the Score Conversion Chart to convert your raw score into the 120-180 scale.

Scoring Worksheet

1. Enter the number of questions you answered correctly in each section.

	Number Correct
SECTION I.	_____
SECTION II	_____
SECTION III.	_____
SECTION IV.	_____

2. Enter the sum here: _____

   This is your Raw Score.

Conversion Chart

For Converting Raw Score to the 120-180 LSAT Scaled Score
LSAT Form 1LSS51

Reported Score	Raw Score	
	Lowest	Highest
180	99	101
179	98	98
178	97	97
177	96	96
176	95	95
175	—*	—*
174	94	94
173	93	93
172	91	92
171	90	90
170	89	89
169	88	88
168	86	87
167	85	85
166	84	84
165	82	83
164	80	81
163	79	79
162	77	78
161	76	76
160	74	75
159	72	73
158	71	71
157	69	70
156	67	68
155	66	66
154	64	65
153	62	63
152	61	61
151	59	60
150	57	58
149	56	56
148	54	55
147	52	53
146	51	51
145	49	50
144	47	48
143	46	46
142	44	45
141	42	43
140	41	41
139	39	40
138	38	38
137	36	37
136	35	35
135	33	34
134	32	32
133	30	31
132	29	29
131	27	28
130	26	26
129	25	25
128	24	24
127	22	23
126	21	21
125	20	20
124	19	19
123	17	18
122	16	16
121	15	15
120	0	14

*There is no raw score that will produce this scaled score for this form.

SECTION I

1.	D	8.	E	15.	E	22.	B
2.	D	9.	E	16.	C	23.	A
3.	A	10.	B	17.	E	24.	C
4.	C	11.	E	18.	B	25.	D
5.	E	12.	B	19.	C	26.	B
6.	B	13.	D	20.	A		
7.	C	14.	D	21.	E		

SECTION II

1.	C	8.	C	15.	B	22.	D
2.	D	9.	A	16.	D	23.	A
3.	D	10.	B	17.	E	24.	E
4.	A	11.	D	18.	C	25.	E
5.	C	12.	A	19.	C	26.	D
6.	A	13.	D	20.	E		
7.	B	14.	A	21.	B		

SECTION III

1.	D	8.	E	15.	C	22.	A
2.	A	9.	D	16.	E	23.	E
3.	D	10.	C	17.	E		
4.	B	11.	D	18.	C		
5.	A	12.	D	19.	A		
6.	C	13.	A	20.	E		
7.	A	14.	B	21.	D		

SECTION IV

1.	B	8.	E	15.	E	22.	A
2.	A	9.	D	16.	A	23.	D
3.	B	10.	D	17.	E	24.	B
4.	D	11.	B	18.	B	25.	A
5.	D	12.	C	19.	C	26.	B
6.	B	13.	D	20.	A		
7.	C	14.	B	21.	C		

The Official LSAT PrepTest

36

- December 2001
  PrepTest 36

- Form 1LSS50

SECTION I

Time—35 minutes

26 Questions

Directions: The questions in this section are based on the reasoning contained in brief statements or passages. For some questions, more than one of the choices could conceivably answer the question. However, you are to choose the <u>best</u> answer; that is, the response that most accurately and completely answers the question. You should not make assumptions that are by commonsense standards implausible, superfluous, or incompatible with the passage. After you have chosen the best answer, blacken the corresponding space on your answer sheet.

1. Joanna: The only way for a company to be successful, after emerging from bankruptcy, is to produce the same goods or services that it did before going bankrupt. It is futile for such a company to try to learn a whole new business.

    Ruth: Wrong. The Kelton Company was a major mining operation that went into bankruptcy. On emerging from bankruptcy, Kelton turned its mines into landfills and is presently a highly successful waste-management concern.

    Ruth uses which one of the following argumentative techniques in countering Joanna's argument?

    (A)   She presents a counterexample to a claim.
    (B)   She offers an alternative explanation for a phenomenon.
    (C)   She supports a claim by offering a developed and relevant analogy.
    (D)   She undermines a claim by showing that it rests on an ambiguity.
    (E)   She establishes a conclusion by excluding the only plausible alternative to that conclusion.

2. Nutritionist: Recently a craze has developed for home juicers, $300 machines that separate the pulp of fruits and vegetables from the juice they contain. Outrageous claims are being made about the benefits of these devices: drinking the juice they produce is said to help one lose weight or acquire a clear complexion, to aid digestion, and even to prevent cancer. But there is no indication that juice separated from the pulp of the fruit or vegetable has any properties that it does not have when unseparated. Save your money. If you want carrot juice, eat a carrot.

    Which one of the following, if true, most calls into question the nutritionist's argument?

    (A)   Most people find it much easier to consume a given quantity of nutrients in liquid form than to eat solid foods containing the same quantity of the same nutrients.
    (B)   Drinking juice from home juicers is less healthy than is eating fruits and vegetables because such juice does not contain the fiber that is eaten if one consumes the entire fruit or vegetable.
    (C)   To most people who would be tempted to buy a home juicer, $300 would not be a major expense.
    (D)   The nutritionist was a member of a panel that extensively evaluated early prototypes of home juicers.
    (E)   Vitamin pills that supposedly contain nutrients available elsewhere only in fruits and vegetables often contain a form of those compounds that cannot be as easily metabolized as the varieties found in fruits and vegetables.

GO ON TO THE NEXT PAGE.

3. Finnish author Jaakko Mikkeli was accused by Norwegian author Kirsten Halden of plagiarizing a book that she had written and that had been published 20 years before Mikkeli's. The two books, although set in different periods and regions, contain enough plot similarities to make coincidental resemblance unlikely. Mikkeli's defense rests on his argument that plagiarism was impossible in this case because Halden's book has been published only in Norwegian, a language Mikkeli does not understand, and because no reviews of Halden's book have ever been published.

The argument in Mikkeli's defense depends on the assumption that

(A) Mikkeli has never met Halden
(B) Halden's book did not become popular in Norway
(C) nobody related the plot of Halden's book in detail to Mikkeli before Mikkeli wrote his book
(D) there is a common European myth to which both authors referred subconsciously in the books in question
(E) Mikkeli is not familiar with Old Icelandic, an extinct language related to an earlier form of Norwegian

4. Most antidepressant drugs cause weight gain. While dieting can help reduce the amount of weight gained while taking such antidepressants, some weight gain is unlikely to be preventable.

The information above most strongly supports which one of the following?

(A) A physician should not prescribe any antidepressant drug for a patient if that patient is overweight.
(B) People who are trying to lose weight should not ask their doctors for an antidepressant drug.
(C) At least some patients taking antidepressant drugs gain weight as a result of taking them.
(D) The weight gain experienced by patients taking antidepressant drugs should be attributed to lack of dieting.
(E) All patients taking antidepressant drugs should diet to maintain their weight.

5. Company policy: An employee of our company must be impartial, particularly when dealing with family members. This obligation extends to all aspects of the job, including hiring and firing practices and the quality of service the employee provides customers.

Which one of the following employee behaviors most clearly violates the company policy cited above?

(A) refusing to hire any of one's five siblings, even though they are each more qualified than any other applicant
(B) receiving over a hundred complaints about the service one's office provides and sending a complimentary product to all those who complain, including one's mother
(C) never firing a family member, even though three of one's siblings work under one's supervision and authority
(D) repeatedly refusing to advance an employee, claiming that he has sometimes skipped work and that his work has been sloppy, even though no such instances have occurred for over two years
(E) promoting a family member over another employee in the company

GO ON TO THE NEXT PAGE.

Questions 6–7

It is widely believed that eating chocolate can cause acne. Indeed, many people who are susceptible to acne report that, in their own experience, eating large amounts of chocolate is invariably followed by an outbreak of that skin condition. However, it is likely that common wisdom has mistaken an effect for a cause. Several recent scientific studies indicate that hormonal changes associated with stress can cause acne and there is good evidence that people who are fond of chocolate tend to eat more chocolate when they are under stress.

6. Of the following, which one most accurately expresses the main point of the argument?

    (A)   People are mistaken who insist that whenever they eat large amounts of chocolate they invariably suffer from an outbreak of acne.

    (B)   The more chocolate a person eats, the more likely that person is to experience the hormonal changes associated with stress.

    (C)   Eating large amounts of chocolate is more likely to cause stress than it is to cause outbreaks of acne.

    (D)   It is less likely that eating large amounts of chocolate causes acne than that both the chocolate eating and the acne are caused by stress.

    (E)   The more stress a person experiences, the more likely that person is to crave chocolate.

7. The argument employs which one of the following argumentative strategies?

    (A)   It cites counterevidence that calls into question the accuracy of the evidence advanced in support of the position being challenged.

    (B)   It provides additional evidence that points to an alternative interpretation of the evidence offered in support of the position being challenged.

    (C)   It invokes the superior authority of science over common opinion in order to dismiss out of hand the relevance of evidence based on everyday experience.

    (D)   It demonstrates that the position being challenged is inconsistent with certain well-established facts.

    (E)   It provides counterexamples to show that, contrary to the assumption on which the commonly held position rests, causes do not always precede their effects.

8. It has been claimed that television networks should provide equal time for the presentation of opposing views whenever a television program concerns scientific issues—such as those raised by the claims of environmentalists—about which people disagree. However, although an obligation to provide equal time does arise in the case of any program concerning social issues, it does so because social issues almost always have important political implications and seldom can definitely be settled on the basis of available evidence. If a program concerns scientific issues, that program gives rise to no such equal time obligation.

Which one of the following, if true, most seriously weakens the argument?

    (A)   No scientific issues raised by the claims of environmentalists have important political implications.

    (B)   There are often more than two opposing views on an issue that cannot be definitely settled on the basis of available evidence.

    (C)   Some social issues could be definitely settled on the basis of evidence if the opposing sides would give all the available evidence a fair hearing.

    (D)   Many scientific issues have important political implications and cannot be definitely settled on the basis of the available evidence.

    (E)   Some television networks refuse to broadcast programs on issues that have important political implications and that cannot be definitely settled by the available evidence.

GO ON TO THE NEXT PAGE.

9. Raisins are made by drying grapes in the sun. Although some of the sugar in the grapes is caramelized in the process, nothing is added. Moreover, the only thing removed from the grapes is the water that evaporates during the drying, and water contains no calories or nutrients. The fact that raisins contain more iron per calorie than grapes do is thus puzzling.

Which one of the following, if true, most helps to explain why raisins contain more iron per calorie than do grapes?

(A) Since grapes are bigger than raisins, it takes several bunches of grapes to provide the same amount of iron as a handful of raisins does.

(B) Caramelized sugar cannot be digested, so its calories do not count toward the calorie content of raisins.

(C) The body can absorb iron and other nutrients more quickly from grapes than from raisins because of the relatively high water content of grapes.

(D) Raisins, but not grapes, are available year-round, so many people get a greater share of their yearly iron intake from raisins than from grapes.

(E) Raisins are often eaten in combination with other iron-containing foods, while grapes are usually eaten by themselves.

10. Cotrell is, at best, able to write magazine articles of average quality. The most compelling pieces of evidence for this are those few of the numerous articles submitted by Cotrell that are superior, since Cotrell, who is incapable of writing an article that is better than average, must obviously have plagiarized superior ones.

The argument is most vulnerable to criticism on which one of the following grounds?

(A) It simply ignores the existence of potential counterevidence.

(B) It generalizes from atypical occurrences.

(C) It presupposes what it seeks to establish.

(D) It relies on the judgment of experts in a matter to which their expertise is irrelevant.

(E) It infers limits on ability from a few isolated lapses in performance.

11. Any sale item that is purchased can be returned for store credit but not for a refund of the purchase price. Every home appliance and every piece of gardening equipment is on sale along with selected construction tools.

If the statements above are true, which one of the following must also be true?

(A) Any item that is not a home appliance or a piece of gardening equipment is returnable for a refund.

(B) Any item that is not on sale cannot be returned for store credit.

(C) Some construction tools are not returnable for store credit.

(D) No piece of gardening equipment is returnable for a refund.

(E) None of the things that are returnable for a refund are construction tools.

12. The consumer price index is a measure that detects monthly changes in the retail prices of goods and services. The payment of some government retirement benefits is based on the consumer price index so that those benefits reflect the change in the cost of living as the index changes. However, the consumer price index does not consider technological innovations that may drastically reduce the cost of producing some goods. Therefore, the value of government benefits is sometimes greater than is warranted by the true change in costs.

The reasoning in the argument is most vulnerable to the criticism that the argument

(A) fails to consider the possibility that there are years in which there is no change in the consumer price index

(B) fails to make explicit which goods and services are included in the consumer price index

(C) presumes, without providing warrant, that retirement benefits are not generally used to purchase unusual goods

(D) uncritically draws an inference from what has been true in the past to what will be true in the future

(E) makes an irrelevant shift from discussing retail prices to discussing production costs

GO ON TO THE NEXT PAGE.

13. When astronomers observed the comet Schwassman-Wachmann 3 becoming 1,000 times brighter in September 1995, they correctly hypothesized that its increased brightness was a result of the comet's breaking up—when comets break up, they emit large amounts of gas and dust, becoming visibly brighter as a result. However, their observations did not reveal comet Schwassman-Wachmann 3 actually breaking into pieces until November 1995, even though telescopes were trained on it throughout the entire period.

Which one of the following, if true, most helps to resolve the apparent conflict in the statements above?

(A) Comets often do not emit gas and dust until several weeks after they have begun to break up.

(B) The reason comets become brighter when they break up is that the gas and dust that they emit refract light.

(C) Gas and dust can be released by cracks in a comet even if the comet is not broken all the way through.

(D) The amount of gas and dust emitted steadily increased during the period from September through November.

(E) The comet passed close to the sun during this period and the gravitational strain caused it to break up.

14. If Slater wins the election, McGuinness will be appointed head of the planning commission. But Yerxes is more qualified to head it since she is an architect who has been on the planning commission for fifteen years. Unless the polls are grossly inaccurate, Slater will win.

Which one of the following can be properly inferred from the information above?

(A) If the polls are grossly inaccurate, someone more qualified than McGuinness will be appointed head of the planning commission.

(B) McGuinness will be appointed head of the planning commission only if the polls are a good indication of how the election will turn out.

(C) Either Slater will win the election or Yerxes will be appointed head of the planning commission.

(D) McGuinness is not an architect and has not been on the planning commission for fifteen years or more.

(E) If the polls are a good indication of how the election will turn out, someone less qualified than Yerxes will be appointed head of the planning commission.

15. In one study, engineering students who prepared for an exam by using toothpicks and string did no worse than similar students who prepared by using an expensive computer with sophisticated graphics. In another study, military personnel who trained on a costly high-tech simulator performed no better on a practical exam than did similar personnel who trained using an inexpensive cardboard model. So one should not always purchase technologically advanced educational tools.

Which one of the following principles, if valid, most helps to justify the reasoning above?

(A) One should use different educational tools to teach engineering to civilians than are used to train military personnel.

(B) High-tech solutions to modern problems are ineffective unless implemented by knowledgeable personnel.

(C) Spending large sums of money on educational tools is at least as justified for nonmilitary training as it is for military training.

(D) One should not invest in expensive teaching aids unless there are no other tools that are less expensive and at least as effective.

(E) One should always provide students with a variety of educational materials so that each student can find the materials that best suit that student's learning style.

16. A number of measures indicate the viability of a nation's economy. The level and rate of growth of aggregate output are the most significant indicators, but unemployment and inflation rates are also important. Further, Switzerland, Austria, Israel, Ireland, Denmark, and Finland all have viable economies, but none has a very large population. Switzerland and Austria each have populations of about seven million; the other populations are at least one-fourth smaller.

Which one of the following is most strongly supported by the information above?

(A) A nation's economic viability is independent of the size of its population.

(B) Having a population larger than seven million ensures that a nation will be economically viable.

(C) Economic viability does not require a population of at least seven million.

(D) A nation's population is the most significant contributor to the level and rate of growth of aggregate output.

(E) A nation's population affects the level and rate of growth of aggregate output more than it affects unemployment and inflation rates.

GO ON TO THE NEXT PAGE.

17. The best way to write a good detective story is to work backward from the crime. The writer should first decide what the crime is and who the perpetrator is, and then come up with the circumstances and clues based on those decisions.

Which one of the following illustrates a principle most similar to that illustrated by the passage?

(A) When planning a trip, some people first decide where they want to go and then plan accordingly, but, for most of us, much financial planning must be done before we can choose where we are going.

(B) In planting a vegetable garden, you should prepare the soil first, and then decide what kinds of vegetables to plant.

(C) Good architects do not extemporaneously construct their plans in the course of an afternoon; an architectural design cannot be divorced from the method of constructing the building.

(D) In solving mathematical problems, the best method is to try out as many strategies as possible in the time allotted. This is particularly effective if the number of possible strategies is fairly small.

(E) To make a great tennis shot, you should visualize where you want the shot to go. Then you can determine the position you need to be in to execute the shot properly.

18. Moderate exercise lowers the risk of blockage of the arteries due to blood clots, since anything that lowers blood cholesterol levels also lowers the risk of hardening of the arteries, which in turn lowers the risk of arterial blockage due to blood clots; and, if the data reported in a recent study are correct, moderate exercise lowers blood cholesterol levels.

The conclusion drawn above follows logically if which one of the following is assumed?

(A) The recent study investigated the relationship between exercise and blood cholesterol levels.

(B) Blockage of the arteries due to blood clots can be prevented.

(C) Lowering blood cholesterol levels lowers the risk of blockage of the arteries.

(D) The data reported in the recent study are correct.

(E) Hardening of the arteries increases the risk of blockage of the arteries due to blood clots.

19. Although it has been suggested that Arton's plays have a strong patriotic flavor, we must recall that, at the time of their composition, her country was in anything but a patriotic mood. Unemployment was high, food was costly, and crime rates were soaring. As a result, the general morale of her nation was at an especially low point. Realizing this, we see clearly that any apparent patriotism in Arton's work must have been intended ironically.

The reasoning above is questionable because it

(A) posits an unstated relationship between unemployment and crime

(B) takes for granted that straightforward patriotism is not possible for a serious writer

(C) takes for granted that Arton was attuned to the predominant national attitude of her time

(D) overlooks the fact that some citizens prosper in times of high unemployment

(E) confuses irony with a general decline in public morale

20. Editorialist: To ensure justice in the legal system, citizens must be capable of criticizing anyone involved in determining the punishment of criminals. But when the legal system's purpose is seen as deterrence, the system falls into the hands of experts whose specialty is to assess how potential lawbreakers are affected by the system's punishments. Because most citizens lack knowledge about such matters, justice is not then ensured in the legal system.

The editorialist's argument requires assuming which one of the following?

(A) Most citizens view justice as primarily concerned with the assignment of punishment to those who deserve it.

(B) In order to be just, a legal system must consider the effect that punishment will have on individual criminals.

(C) The primary concern in a legal system is to administer punishments that are just.

(D) In a legal system, a concern for punishment is incompatible with an emphasis on deterrence.

(E) Citizens without knowledge about how the legal system's punishments affect potential lawbreakers are incapable of criticizing experts in that area.

GO ON TO THE NEXT PAGE.

21. Kostman's original painting of Rosati was not a very accurate portrait. Therefore, your reproduction of Kostman's painting of Rosati will not be a very accurate reproduction of the painting.

Which one of the following is most similar in its flawed reasoning to the flawed reasoning in the argument above?

(A) George's speech was filled with half-truths and misquotes. So the tape recording made of it cannot be of good sound quality.

(B) An artist who paints a picture of an ugly scene must necessarily paint an ugly picture, unless the picture is a distorted representation of the scene.

(C) If a child's eyes resemble her mother's, then if the mother's eyes are brown the child's eyes also must be brown.

(D) Jo imitated Layne. But Jo is different from Layne, so Jo could not have imitated Layne very well.

(E) Harold's second novel is similar to his first. Therefore, his second novel must be enthralling, because his first novel won a prestigious literary prize.

22. Any writer whose purpose is personal expression sometimes uses words ambiguously. Every poet's purpose is personal expression. Thus no poetry reader's enjoyment depends on attaining a precise understanding of what the poet means.

The conclusion can be properly inferred if which one of the following is assumed?

(A) Writers who sometimes use words ambiguously have no readers who try to attain a precise understanding of what the writer means.

(B) Writers whose purpose is personal expression are unconcerned with whether anyone enjoys reading their works.

(C) No writer who ever uses words ambiguously has any reader whose enjoyment depends on attaining a precise understanding of what the writer means.

(D) Most writers whose readers' enjoyment does not depend on attaining a precise understanding of the writers' words are poets.

(E) Readers who have a precise understanding of what a writer has written derive their enjoyment from that understanding.

23. It is clear that humans during the Upper Paleolithic period used lamps for light in caves. Though lamps can be dated to the entire Upper Paleolithic, the distribution of known lamps from the period is skewed, with the greatest number being associated with the late Upper Paleolithic period, when the Magdalenian culture was dominant.

Each of the following, if true, contributes to an explanation of the skewed distribution of lamps EXCEPT:

(A) Artifacts from early in the Upper Paleolithic period are harder to identify than those that originated later in the period.

(B) More archaeological sites have been discovered from the Magdalenian culture than from earlier cultures.

(C) More efficient lamp-making techniques were developed by the Magdalenian culture than by earlier cultures.

(D) Fire pits were much more common in caves early in the Upper Paleolithic period than they were later in that period.

(E) More kinds of lamps were produced by the Magdalenian culture than by earlier cultures.

24. Columnist: George Orwell's book *1984* has exercised much influence on a great number of this newspaper's readers. One thousand readers were surveyed and asked to name the one book that had the most influence on their lives. The book chosen most often was the Bible; *1984* was second.

The answer to which one of the following questions would most help in evaluating the columnist's argument?

(A) How many books had each person surveyed read?

(B) How many people chose books other than *1984*?

(C) How many people read the columnist's newspaper?

(D) How many books by George Orwell other than *1984* were chosen?

(E) How many of those surveyed had actually read the books they chose?

GO ON TO THE NEXT PAGE.

25. A 1991 calculation was made to determine what, if any, additional health-care costs beyond the ordinary are borne by society at large for people who live a sedentary life. The figure reached was a lifetime average of $1,650. Thus people's voluntary choice not to exercise places a significant burden on society.

Which one of the following, if true and not taken into account by the calculation, most seriously weakens the argument?

(A) Many people whose employment requires physical exertion do not choose to engage in regular physical exercise when they are not at work.

(B) Exercise is a topic that is often omitted from discussion between doctor and patient during a patient's visit.

(C) Physical conditions that eventually require medical or nursing-home care often first predispose a person to adopt a sedentary life-style.

(D) Individuals vary widely in the amount and kind of exercise they choose, when they do exercise regularly.

(E) A regular program of moderate exercise tends to increase circulation, induce a feeling of well-being and energy, and decrease excess weight.

26. In the paintings by seventeenth-century Dutch artist Vermeer, we find several recurrent items: a satin jacket, a certain Turkish carpet, and wooden chairs with lion's-head finials. These reappearing objects might seem to evince a dearth of props. Yet we know that many of the props Vermeer used were expensive. Thus, while we might speculate about exactly why Vermeer worked with a small number of familiar objects, it was clearly not for lack of props that the recurrent items were used.

The conclusion follows logically if which one of the following is assumed?

(A) Vermeer often borrowed the expensive props he represented in his paintings.

(B) The props that recur in Vermeer's paintings were always available to him.

(C) The satin jacket and wooden chairs that recur in the paintings were owned by Vermeer's sister.

(D) The several recurrent items that appeared in Vermeer's paintings had special sentimental importance for him.

(E) If a dearth of props accounted for the recurrent objects in Vermeer's paintings, we would not see expensive props in any of them.

S T O P

IF YOU FINISH BEFORE TIME IS CALLED, YOU MAY CHECK YOUR WORK ON THIS SECTION ONLY.
DO NOT WORK ON ANY OTHER SECTION IN THE TEST.

SECTION II

Time—35 minutes

26 Questions

Directions: Each passage in this section is followed by a group of questions to be answered on the basis of what is <u>stated</u> or <u>implied</u> in the passage. For some of the questions, more than one of the choices could conceivably answer the question. However, you are to choose the <u>best</u> answer; that is, the response that most accurately and completely answers the question, and blacken the corresponding space on your answer sheet.

Traditionally, members of a community such as a town or neighborhood share a common location and a sense of necessary interdependence that includes, for example, mutual respect and emotional support. But as
(5) modern societies grow more technological and sometimes more alienating, people tend to spend less time in the kinds of interactions that their communities require in order to thrive. Meanwhile, technology has made it possible for individuals to interact via personal
(10) computer with others who are geographically distant. Advocates claim that these computer conferences, in which large numbers of participants communicate by typing comments that are immediately read by other participants and responding immediately to those
(15) comments they read, function as communities that can substitute for traditional interactions with neighbors.

What are the characteristics that advocates claim allow computer conferences to function as communities? For one, participants often share
(20) common interests or concerns; conferences are frequently organized around specific topics such as music or parenting. Second, because these conferences are conversations, participants have adopted certain conventions in recognition of the importance of
(25) respecting each others' sensibilities. Abbreviations are used to convey commonly expressed sentiments of courtesy such as "pardon me for cutting in" ("pmfci") or "in my humble opinion" ("imho"). Because a humorous tone can be difficult to communicate in
(30) writing, participants will often end an intentionally humorous comment with a set of characters that, when looked at sideways, resembles a smiling or winking face. Typing messages entirely in capital letters is avoided, because its tendency to demand the attention
(35) of a reader's eye is considered the computer equivalent of shouting. These conventions, advocates claim, constitute a form of etiquette, and with this etiquette as a foundation, people often form genuine, trusting relationships, even offering advice and support during
(40) personal crises such as illness or the loss of a loved one.

But while it is true that conferences can be both respectful and supportive, they nonetheless fall short of communities. For example, conferences discriminate
(45) along educational and economic lines because participation requires a basic knowledge of computers and the ability to afford access to conferences. Further, while advocates claim that a shared interest makes computer conferences similar to traditional
(50) communities—insofar as the shared interest is

analogous to a traditional community's shared location—this analogy simply does not work. Conference participants are a self-selecting group; they are drawn together by their shared interest in the topic
(55) of the conference. Actual communities, on the other hand, are "nonintentional": the people who inhabit towns or neighborhoods are thus more likely to exhibit genuine diversity—of age, career, or personal interests—than are conference participants. It might be
(60) easier to find common ground in a computer conference than in today's communities, but in so doing it would be unfortunate if conference participants cut themselves off further from valuable interactions in their own towns or neighborhoods.

1. Which one of the following most accurately expresses the central idea of the passage?

   (A) Because computer conferences attract participants who share common interests and rely on a number of mutually acceptable conventions for communicating with one another, such conferences can substitute effectively for certain interactions that have become rarer within actual communities.

   (B) Since increased participation in computer conferences threatens to replace actual communities, members of actual communities are returning to the traditional interactions that distinguish towns or neighborhoods.

   (C) Because participants in computer conferences are geographically separated and communicate only by typing, their interactions cannot be as mutually respectful and supportive as are the kinds of interactions that have become rarer within actual communities.

   (D) Although computer conferences offer some of the same benefits that actual communities do, the significant lack of diversity among conference participants makes such conferences unlike actual communities.

   (E) Even if access to computer technology is broad enough to attract a more diverse group of people to participate in computer conferences, such conferences will not be acceptable substitutes for actual communities.

GO ON TO THE NEXT PAGE.

2. Based on the passage, the author would be LEAST likely to consider which one of the following a community?

(A) a group of soldiers who serve together in the same battalion and who come from a variety of geographic regions

(B) a group of university students who belong to the same campus political organization and who come from several different socioeconomic backgrounds

(C) a group of doctors who work at a number of different hospitals and who meet at a convention to discuss issues relevant to their profession

(D) a group of teachers who work interdependently in the same school with the same students and who live in a variety of cities and neighborhoods

(E) a group of worshipers who attend and support the same religious institution and who represent a high degree of economic and cultural diversity

3. The author's statement that "conferences can be both respectful and supportive" (lines 42–43) serves primarily to

(A) counter the claim that computer conferences may discriminate along educational or economic lines

(B) introduce the argument that the conventions of computer conferences constitute a form of social etiquette

(C) counter the claim that computer conferences cannot be thought of as communities

(D) suggest that not all participants in computer conferences may be equally respectful of one another

(E) acknowledge that computer conferences can involve interactions that are similar to those in an actual community

4. Given the information in the passage, the author can most reasonably be said to use which one of the following principles to refute the advocates' claim that computer conferences can function as communities (line 15)?

(A) A group is a community only if its members are mutually respectful and supportive of one another.

(B) A group is a community only if its members adopt conventions intended to help them respect each other's sensibilities.

(C) A group is a community only if its members inhabit the same geographic location.

(D) A group is a community only if its members come from the same educational or economic background.

(E) A group is a community only if its members feel a sense of interdependence despite different economic and educational backgrounds.

5. What is the primary function of the second paragraph of the passage?

(A) to add detail to the discussion in the first paragraph of why computer conferences originated

(B) to give evidence challenging the argument of the advocates discussed in the first paragraph

(C) to develop the claim of the advocates discussed in the first paragraph

(D) to introduce an objection that will be answered in the third paragraph

(E) to anticipate the characterization of computer conferences given in the third paragraph

6. Which one of the following, if true, would most weaken one of the author's arguments in the last paragraph?

(A) Participants in computer conferences are generally more accepting of diversity than is the population at large.

(B) Computer technology is rapidly becoming more affordable and accessible to people from a variety of backgrounds.

(C) Participants in computer conferences often apply the same degree of respect and support they receive from one another to interactions in their own actual communities.

(D) Participants in computer conferences often feel more comfortable interacting on the computer because they are free to interact without revealing their identities.

(E) The conventions used to facilitate communication in computer conferences are generally more successful than those used in actual communities.

GO ON TO THE NEXT PAGE.

In *Intellectual Culture in Elizabethan and Jacobean England*, J. W. Binns asserts that the drama of Shakespeare, the verse of Marlowe, and the prose of Sidney—all of whom wrote in English—do not alone
(5) represent the high culture of Renaissance (roughly sixteenth- and seventeenth-century) England. Latin, the language of ancient Rome, continued during this period to be the dominant form of expression for English intellectuals, and works of law, theology, and science
(10) written in Latin were, according to Binns, among the highest achievements of the Renaissance. However, because many academic specializations do not overlap, many texts central to an interpretation of early modern English culture have gone unexamined. Even the most
(15) learned students of Renaissance Latin generally confine themselves to humanistic and literary writings in Latin. According to Binns, these language specialists edit and analyze poems and orations, but leave works of theology and science, law and medicine—the very
(20) works that revolutionized Western thought—to "specialists" in those fields, historians of science, for example, who lack philological training. The intellectual historian can find ample guidance when reading the Latin poetry of Milton, but little or none
(25) when confronting the more alien and difficult terminology, syntax, and content of the scientist Newton.

Intellectual historians of Renaissance England, by contrast with Latin language specialists, have surveyed
(30) in great detail the historical, cosmological, and theological battles of the day, but too often they have done so on the basis of texts written in or translated into English. Binns argues that these scholars treat the English-language writings of Renaissance England as
(35) an autonomous and coherent whole, underestimating the influence on English writers of their counterparts on the European Continent. In so doing they ignore the fact that English intellectuals were educated in schools and universities where they spoke and wrote Latin, and
(40) inhabited as adults an intellectual world in which what happened abroad and was recorded in Latin was of great importance. Writers traditionally considered characteristically English and modern were steeped in Latin literature and in the esoteric concerns of late
(45) Renaissance humanism (the rediscovery and study of ancient Latin and Greek texts), and many Latin works by Continental humanists that were not translated at the time into any modern language became the bases of classic English works of literature and scholarship.
(50) These limitations are understandable. No modern classicist is trained to deal with the range of problems posed by a difficult piece of late Renaissance science; few students of English intellectual history are trained to read the sort of Latin in which such works were
(55) written. Yet the result of each side's inability to cross boundaries has been that each presents a distorted reading of the intellectual culture of Renaissance England.

7. Which one of the following best states the main idea of the passage?

(A) Analyses of the scientific, theological, and legal writings of the Renaissance have proved to be more important to an understanding of the period than have studies of humanistic and literary works.

(B) The English works of such Renaissance writers as Shakespeare, Marlowe, and Sidney have been overemphasized at the expense of these writers' more intellectually challenging Latin works.

(C) Though traditionally recognized as the language of the educated classes of the Renaissance, Latin has until recently been studied primarily in connection with ancient Roman texts.

(D) Many Latin texts by English Renaissance writers, though analyzed in depth by literary critics and philologists, have been all but ignored by historians of science and theology.

(E) Many Latin texts by English Renaissance writers, though important to an analysis of the period, have been insufficiently understood for reasons related to academic specialization.

8. The passage contains support for which one of the following statements concerning those scholars who analyze works written in Latin during the Renaissance?

(A) These scholars tend to lack training both in language and in intellectual history, and thus base their interpretations of Renaissance culture on works translated into English.

(B) These scholars tend to lack the combination of training in both language and intellectual history that is necessary for a proper study of important and neglected Latin texts.

(C) Specialists in such literary forms as poems and orations too frequently lack training in the Latin language that was written and studied during the Renaissance.

(D) Language specialists have surveyed in too great detail important works of law and medicine, and thus have not provided a coherent interpretation of early modern English culture.

(E) Scholars who analyze important Latin works by such writers as Marlowe, Shakespeare, and Sidney too often lack the historical knowledge of Latin necessary for a proper interpretation of early modern English culture.

GO ON TO THE NEXT PAGE.

9. Which one of the following statements concerning the relationship between English and Continental writers of the Renaissance era can be inferred from the passage?

   (A) Continental writers wrote in Latin more frequently than did English writers, and thus rendered some of the most important Continental works inaccessible to English readers.

   (B) Continental writers, more intellectually advanced than their English counterparts, were on the whole responsible for familiarizing English audiences with Latin language and literature.

   (C) English and Continental writers communicated their intellectual concerns, which were for the most part different, by way of works written in Latin.

   (D) The intellectual ties between English and Continental writers were stronger than has been acknowledged by many scholars and were founded on a mutual knowledge of Latin.

   (E) The intellectual ties between English and Continental writers have been overemphasized in modern scholarship due to a lack of dialogue between language specialists and intellectual historians.

10. The author of the passage most likely cites Shakespeare, Marlowe, and Sidney in the first paragraph as examples of writers whose

    (A) nonfiction works are less well known than their imaginative works

    (B) works have unfairly been credited with revolutionizing Western thought

    (C) works have been treated as an autonomous and coherent whole

    (D) works have traditionally been seen as representing the high culture of Renaissance England

    (E) Latin writings have, according to Binns, been overlooked

11. Binns would be most likely to agree with which one of the following statements concerning the English-language writings of Renaissance England traditionally studied by intellectual historians?

    (A) These writings have unfortunately been undervalued by Latin-language specialists because of their nonliterary subject matter.

    (B) These writings, according to Latin-language specialists, had very little influence on the intellectual upheavals associated with the Renaissance.

    (C) These writings, as analyzed by intellectual historians, have formed the basis of a superficially coherent reading of the intellectual culture that produced them.

    (D) These writings have been compared unfavorably by intellectual historians with Continental works of the same period.

    (E) These writings need to be studied separately, according to intellectual historians, from Latin-language writings of the same period.

12. The information in the passage suggests which one of the following concerning late-Renaissance scientific works written in Latin?

    (A) These works are easier for modern scholars to analyze than are theological works of the same era.

    (B) These works have seldom been translated into English and thus remain inscrutable to modern scholars, despite the availability of illuminating commentaries.

    (C) These works are difficult for modern scholars to analyze both because of the concepts they develop and the language in which they are written.

    (D) These works constituted the core of an English university education during the Renaissance.

    (E) These works were written mostly by Continental writers and reached English intellectuals only in English translation.

13. The author of the passage mentions the poet Milton and the scientist Newton primarily in order to

    (A) illustrate the range of difficulty in Renaissance Latin writing, from relatively straightforward to very difficult

    (B) illustrate the differing scholarly attitudes toward Renaissance writers who wrote in Latin and those who wrote in English

    (C) illustrate the fact that the concerns of English writers of the Renaissance differed from the concerns of their Continental counterparts

    (D) contrast a writer of the Renaissance whose merit has long been recognized with one whose literary worth has only recently begun to be appreciated

    (E) contrast a writer whose Latin writings have been the subject of illuminating scholarship with one whose Latin writings have been neglected by philologists

14. The author of the passage is primarily concerned with presenting which one of the following?

    (A) an enumeration of new approaches
    (B) contrasting views of disparate theories
    (C) a summary of intellectual disputes
    (D) a discussion of a significant deficiency
    (E) a correction of an author's misconceptions

GO ON TO THE NEXT PAGE.

Discussions of how hormones influence behavior have generally been limited to the effects of gonadal hormones on reproductive behavior and have emphasized the parsimonious arrangement whereby the
(5) same hormones involved in the biology of reproduction also influence sexual behavior. It has now become clear, however, that other hormones, in addition to their recognized influence on biological functions, can affect behavior. Specifically, peptide and steroid hormones
(10) involved in maintaining the physiological balance, or homeostasis, of body fluids also appear to play an important role in the control of water and salt consumption. The phenomenon of homeostasis in animals depends on various mechanisms that promote
(15) stability within the organism despite an inconstant external environment; the homeostasis of body fluids, whereby the osmolality (the concentration of solutes) of blood plasma is closely regulated, is achieved primarily through alterations in the intake and
(20) excretion of water and sodium, the two principal components of the fluid matrix that surrounds body cells. Appropriate compensatory responses are initiated when deviations from normal are quite small, thereby maintaining plasma osmolality within relatively narrow
(25) ranges.

In the osmoregulation of body fluids, the movement of water across cell membranes permits minor fluctuations in the concentration of solutes in extracellular fluid to be buffered by corresponding
(30) changes in the relatively larger volume of cellular water. Nevertheless, the concentration of solutes in extracellular fluid may at times become elevated or reduced by more than the allowed tolerances of one or two percent. It is then that complementary
(35) physiological and behavioral responses come into play to restore plasma osmolality to normal. Thus, for example, a decrease in plasma osmolality, such as that which occurs after the consumption of water in excess of need, leads to the excretion of surplus body water in
(40) the urine by inhibiting secretion from the pituitary gland of vasopressin, a peptide hormone that promotes water conservation in the kidneys. As might be expected, thirst also is inhibited then, to prevent further dilution of body fluids. Conversely, an increase in
(45) plasma osmolality, such as that which occurs after one eats salty foods or after body water evaporates without being replaced, stimulates the release of vasopressin, increasing the conservation of water and the excretion of solutes in urine. This process is accompanied by
(50) increased thirst, with the result of making plasma osmolality more dilute through the consumption of water. The threshold for thirst appears to be slightly higher than for vasopressin secretion, so that thirst is stimulated only after vasopressin has been released in
(55) amounts sufficient to produce maximal water retention by the kidneys—that is, only after osmotic dehydration exceeds the capacity of the animal to deal with it physiologically.

15. Which one of the following best states the main idea of the passage?

(A) Both the solute concentration and the volume of an animal's blood plasma must be kept within relatively narrow ranges.

(B) Behavioral responses to changes in an animal's blood plasma can compensate for physiological malfunction, allowing the body to avoid dehydration.

(C) The effect of hormones on animal behavior and physiology has only recently been discovered.

(D) Behavioral and physiological responses to major changes in osmolality of an animal's blood plasma are hormonally influenced and complement one another.

(E) The mechanisms regulating reproduction are similar to those that regulate thirst and sodium appetite.

16. The author of the passage cites the relationship between gonadal hormones and reproductive behavior in order to

(A) review briefly the history of research into the relationships between gonadal and peptide hormones that has led to the present discussion

(B) decry the fact that previous research has concentrated on the relatively minor issue of the relationships between hormones and behavior

(C) establish the emphasis of earlier research into the connections between hormones and behavior before elaborating on the results described in the passage

(D) introduce a commonly held misconception about the relationships between hormones and behavior before refuting it with the results described in the passage

(E) summarize the main findings of recent research described in the passage before detailing the various procedures that led to those findings

GO ON TO THE NEXT PAGE.

17. It can be inferred from the passage that which one of the following is true of vasopressin?

    (A) The amount secreted depends on the level of steroid hormones in the blood.
    (B) The amount secreted is important for maintaining homeostasis in cases of both increased and decreased osmolality.
    (C) It works in conjunction with steroid hormones in increasing plasma volume.
    (D) It works in conjunction with steroid hormones in regulating sodium appetite.
    (E) It is secreted after an animal becomes thirsty, as a mechanism for diluting plasma osmolality.

18. The primary function of the passage as a whole is to

    (A) present new information
    (B) question standard assumptions
    (C) reinterpret earlier findings
    (D) advocate a novel theory
    (E) outline a new approach

19. According to the passage, all of the following typically occur in the homeostasis of blood-plasma osmolality EXCEPT:

    (A) Hunger is diminished.
    (B) Thirst is initiated.
    (C) Vasopressin is secreted.
    (D) Water is excreted.
    (E) Sodium is consumed.

20. According to the passage, the withholding of vasopressin fulfills which one of the following functions in the restoration of plasma osmolality to normal levels?

    (A) It increases thirst and stimulates sodium appetite.
    (B) It helps prevent further dilution of body fluids.
    (C) It increases the conservation of water in the kidneys.
    (D) It causes minor changes in plasma volume.
    (E) It helps stimulate the secretion of steroid hormones.

GO ON TO THE NEXT PAGE.

With the elimination of the apartheid system, South Africa now confronts the transition to a rights-based legal system in a constitutional democracy. Among lawyers and judges, exhilaration over the legal tools (5) soon to be available is tempered by uncertainty about how to use them. The changes in the legal system are significant, not just for human rights lawyers, but for all lawyers—as they will have to learn a less rule-bound and more interpretative way of looking at the (10) law. That is to say, in the past, the parliament was the supreme maker and arbiter of laws; when judges made rulings with which the parliament disagreed, the parliament simply passed new laws to counteract their rulings. Under the new system, however, a (15) constitutional court will hear arguments on all constitutional matters, including questions of whether the laws passed by the parliament are valid in light of the individual liberties set out in the constitution's bill of rights. This shift will lead to extraordinary changes, (20) for South Africa has never before had a legal system based on individual rights—one in which citizens can challenge any law or administrative decision on the basis of their constitutional rights.

South African lawyers are concerned about the (25) difficulty of fostering a rights-based culture in a multiracial society containing a wide range of political and personal beliefs simply by including a bill of rights in the constitution and establishing the means for its defense. Because the bill of rights has been drawn in (30) very general terms, the lack of precedents will make the task of determining its precise meaning a bewildering one. With this in mind, the new constitution acknowledges the need to look to other countries for guidance. But some scholars warn that (35) judges, in their rush to fill the constitutional void, may misuse foreign law—they may blindly follow the interpretations given bills of rights in other countries, not taking into account the circumstances in those countries that led to certain decisions. Nonetheless, (40) these scholars are hopeful that, with patience and judicious decisions, South Africa can use international experience in developing a body of precedent that will address the particular needs of its citizens.

South Africa must also contend with the image of (45) the law held by many of its citizens. Because the law in South Africa has long been a tool of racial oppression, many of its citizens have come to view obeying the law as implicitly sanctioning an illegitimate, brutal government. Among these South Africans the political (50) climate has thus been one of opposition, and many see it as their duty to cheat the government as much as possible, whether by not paying taxes or by disobeying parking laws. If a rights-based culture is to succeed, the government will need to show its citizens that the legal (55) system is no longer a tool of oppression but instead a way to bring about change and help further the cause of justice.

21. Which one of the following most completely and accurately states the main point of the passage?

(A) Following the elimination of the apartheid system in South Africa, lawyers, judges, and citizens will need to abandon their posture of opposition to law and design a new and fairer legal system.

(B) If the new legal system in South Africa is to succeed, lawyers, judges, and citizens must learn to challenge parliamentary decisions based on their individual rights as set out in the new constitution.

(C) Whereas in the past the parliament was both the initiator and arbiter of laws in South Africa, under the new constitution these powers will be assumed by a constitutional court.

(D) Despite the lack of relevant legal precedents and the public's antagonistic relation to the law, South Africa is moving from a legal system where the parliament is the final authority to one where the rights of citizens are protected by a constitution.

(E) While South Africa's judges will have to look initially to other countries to provide interpretations for its new bill of rights, eventually it must develop a body of precedent sensitive to the needs of its own citizens.

22. Which one of the following most accurately describes the author's primary purpose in lines 10–19?

(A) to describe the role of the parliament under South Africa's new constitution

(B) to argue for returning final legal authority to the parliament

(C) to contrast the character of legal practice under the apartheid system with that to be implemented under the new constitution

(D) to criticize the creation of a court with final authority on constitutional matters

(E) to explain why a bill of rights was included in the new constitution

23. The passage suggests that the author's attitude toward the possibility of success for a rights-based legal system in South Africa is most likely one of

(A) deep skepticism
(B) open pessimism
(C) total indifference
(D) guarded optimism
(E) complete confidence

GO ON TO THE NEXT PAGE.

24. According to the passage, under the apartheid system the rulings of judges were sometimes counteracted by

(A) decisions rendered in constitutional court
(B) challenges from concerned citizens
(C) new laws passed in the parliament
(D) provisions in the constitution's bill of rights
(E) other judges with a more rule-bound approach to the law

25. Which one of the following most accurately describes the organization of the last paragraph of the passage?

(A) A solution to a problem is identified, several methods of implementing the solution are discussed, and one of the methods is argued for.
(B) The background to a problem is presented, past methods of solving the problem are criticized, and a new solution is proposed.
(C) An analysis of a problem is presented, possible solutions to the problem are given, and one of the possible solutions is argued for.
(D) Reasons are given why a problem has existed, the current state of affairs is described, and the problem is shown to exist no longer.
(E) A problem is identified, specific manifestations of the problem are given, and an essential element in its solution is presented.

26. Based on the passage, the scholars mentioned in the second paragraph would be most likely to agree with which one of the following statements?

(A) Reliance of judges on the interpretations given bills of rights in other countries must be tempered by the recognition that such interpretations may be based on circumstances not necessarily applicable to South Africa.
(B) Basing interpretations of the South African bill of rights on interpretations given bills of rights in other countries will reinforce the climate of mistrust for authority in South Africa.
(C) The lack of precedents in South African law for interpreting a bill of rights will likely make it impossible to interpret correctly the bill of rights in the South African constitution.
(D) Reliance by judges on the interpretations given bills of rights in other countries offers an unacceptable means of attempting to interpret the South African constitution in a way that will meet the particular needs of South African citizens.
(E) Because bills of rights in other countries are written in much less general terms than the South African bill of rights, interpretations of them are unlikely to prove helpful in interpreting the South African bill of rights.

S T O P

IF YOU FINISH BEFORE TIME IS CALLED, YOU MAY CHECK YOUR WORK ON THIS SECTION ONLY.
DO NOT WORK ON ANY OTHER SECTION IN THE TEST.

SECTION III
Time—35 minutes
26 Questions

<u>Directions:</u> The questions in this section are based on the reasoning contained in brief statements or passages. For some questions, more than one of the choices could conceivably answer the question. However, you are to choose the <u>best</u> answer; that is, the response that most accurately and completely answers the question. You should not make assumptions that are by commonsense standards implausible, superfluous, or incompatible with the passage. After you have chosen the best answer, blacken the corresponding space on your answer sheet.

1. Scientists agree that ingesting lead harms young children. More lead paint remains in older apartment buildings than newer ones because the use of lead paint was common until only two decades ago. Yet these same scientists also agree that laws requiring the removal of lead paint from older apartment buildings will actually increase the amount of lead that children living in older apartment buildings ingest.

    Which one of the following, if true, most helps to resolve the apparent discrepancy in the scientists' beliefs?

    (A) Lead-free paints contain substances that make them as harmful to children as lead paint is.
    (B) The money required to finance the removal of lead paint from apartment walls could be spent in ways more likely to improve the health of children.
    (C) Other sources of lead in older apartment buildings are responsible for most of the lead that children living in these buildings ingest.
    (D) Removing lead paint from walls disperses a great deal of lead dust, which is more easily ingested by children than is paint on walls.
    (E) Many other environmental hazards pose greater threats to the health of children than does lead paint.

2. Several companies will soon offer personalized electronic news services, delivered via cable or telephone lines and displayed on a television. People using these services can view continually updated stories on those topics for which they subscribe. Since these services will provide people with the information they are looking for more quickly and efficiently than printed newspapers can, newspaper sales will decline drastically if these services become widely available.

    Which one of the following, if true, most seriously weakens the argument?

    (A) In reading newspapers, most people not only look for stories on specific topics but also like to idly browse through headlines or pictures for amusing stories on unfamiliar or unusual topics.
    (B) Companies offering personalized electronic news services will differ greatly in what they charge for access to their services, depending on how wide a range of topics they cover.
    (C) Approximately 30 percent of people have never relied on newspapers for information but instead have always relied on news programs broadcast on television and radio.
    (D) The average monthly cost of subscribing to several channels on a personalized electronic news service will approximately equal the cost of a month's subscription to a newspaper.
    (E) Most people who subscribe to personalized electronic news services will not have to pay extra costs for installation since the services will use connections installed by cable and telephone companies.

GO ON TO THE NEXT PAGE.

3. Muscular strength is a limited resource, and athletic techniques help to use this resource efficiently. Since top athletes do not differ greatly from each other in muscular strength, it follows that a requirement for an athlete to become a champion is a superior mastery of athletic techniques.

Which one of the following most accurately expresses the conclusion of the argument?

(A) Only champion athletes have a superior mastery of athletic techniques.

(B) Superior muscular strength is a requirement for an athlete to become a champion.

(C) No athlete can become a champion without a superior mastery of athletic techniques.

(D) The differences in muscular strength between top athletes are not great.

(E) Athletic techniques help athletes use limited resources efficiently.

4. Mary: Computers will make more information available to ordinary people than was ever available before, thus making it easier for them to acquire knowledge without consulting experts.

Joyce: As more knowledge became available in previous centuries, the need for specialists to synthesize and explain it to nonspecialists increased. So computers will probably create a greater dependency on experts.

The dialogue most strongly supports the claim that Mary and Joyce disagree with each other about whether

(A) computers will contribute only negligibly to the increasing dissemination of knowledge in society

(B) computers will increase the need for ordinary people seeking knowledge to turn to experts

(C) computers will make more information available to ordinary people

(D) dependency on computers will increase with the increase of knowledge

(E) synthesizing knowledge and explaining it to ordinary people can be accomplished only by computer experts

5. Solicitor: Loux named Zembaty executor of her will. Her only beneficiary was her grandson, of whom she was very fond. Prior to distributing the remainder to the beneficiary, Zembaty was legally required to choose which properties in the estate should be sold to clear the estate's heavy debts. Loux never expressed any particular desire about the Stoke Farm, which includes the only farmland in her estate. Thus, it is unlikely that Loux would have had any objection to Zembaty's having sold it rather than having transferred it to her grandson.

Which one of the following, if true, most weakens the solicitor's argument?

(A) The estate's debts could not have been cleared without selling the Stoke Farm.

(B) Loux repeatedly told her grandson that she would take care of him in her will.

(C) Loux was well aware of the legal requirements the executor of her will would have to satisfy.

(D) The Stoke Farm was the main cause of the estate's debts.

(E) Loux's grandson had repeatedly expressed his desire to own a farm.

6. Government official: A satisfactory way of eliminating chronic food shortages in our country is not easily achievable. Direct aid from other countries in the form of food shipments tends to undermine our prospects for long-term agricultural self-sufficiency. If external sources of food are delivered effectively by external institutions, local food producers and suppliers are forced out of business. On the other hand, foreign capital funneled to long-term development projects would inject so much cash into our economy that inflation would drive the price of food beyond the reach of most of our citizens.

The claim that foreign capital funneled into the economy would cause inflation plays which one of the following roles in the government official's argument?

(A) It supports the claim that the official's country must someday be agriculturally self-sufficient.

(B) It supports the claim that there is no easy solution to the problem of chronic food shortages in the official's country.

(C) It is supported by the claim that the official's country must someday be agriculturally self-sufficient.

(D) It supports the claim that donations of food from other countries will not end the chronic food shortages in the official's country.

(E) It is supported by the claim that food producers and suppliers in the official's country may be forced out of business by donations of food from other countries.

GO ON TO THE NEXT PAGE.

7. Medical doctor: Sleep deprivation is the cause of many social ills, ranging from irritability to potentially dangerous instances of impaired decision making. Most people today suffer from sleep deprivation to some degree. Therefore we should restructure the workday to allow people flexibility in scheduling their work hours.

Which one of the following, if true, would most strengthen the medical doctor's argument?

(A)   The primary cause of sleep deprivation is overwork.
(B)   Employees would get more sleep if they had greater latitude in scheduling their work hours.
(C)   Individuals vary widely in the amount of sleep they require.
(D)   More people would suffer from sleep deprivation today than did in the past if the average number of hours worked per week had not decreased.
(E)   The extent of one's sleep deprivation is proportional to the length of one's workday.

8. Essayist: Knowledge has been defined as a true belief formed by a reliable process. This definition has been criticized on the grounds that if someone had a reliable power of clairvoyance, we would not accept that person's claim to know certain things on the basis of this power. I agree that we would reject such claims, but we would do so because we really do not believe in clairvoyance as a reliable process. Were we to believe in clairvoyance, we would accept knowledge claims made on the basis of it.

Which one of the following most accurately describes the essayist's method of defending the definition against the objection?

(A)   asserting that the objection is based on a belief about the reliability of clairvoyance rather than on the nature of knowledge or its definition
(B)   asserting that the case of clairvoyance is one of knowledge even though we do not really believe in clairvoyance as a reliable process
(C)   arguing against the assumption that clairvoyance is unreliable
(D)   explaining that the definition of knowledge is a matter of personal choice
(E)   demonstrating that the case of clairvoyance is not a case of knowledge and does not fit the definition of knowledge

9. I agree that Hogan's actions resulted in grievous injury to Winters. And I do not deny that Hogan fully realized the nature of his actions and the effects that they would have. Indeed, I would not disagree if you pointed out that intentionally causing such effects is reprehensible, other things being equal. But in asking you to concur with me that Hogan's actions not be wholly condemned I emphasize again that Hogan mistakenly believed Winters to be the robber who had been terrorizing west-side apartment buildings for the past several months.

Which one of the following most accurately expresses the conclusion of the argument?

(A)   Hogan should not be considered responsible for the injuries sustained by Winters.
(B)   The robber who had been terrorizing west-side apartment buildings should be considered to be as responsible for Winters's injuries as Hogan.
(C)   The actions of Hogan that seriously injured Winters are not completely blameworthy.
(D)   Hogan thought that Winters was the person who had been terrorizing west-side apartment buildings for the last few months.
(E)   The actions of Hogan that seriously injured Winters were reprehensible, other things being equal.

GO ON TO THE NEXT PAGE.

Questions 10–11

Peter: Because the leaves of mildly drought-stressed plants are tougher in texture than the leaves of abundantly watered plants, insects prefer to feed on the leaves of abundantly watered plants. Therefore, to minimize crop damage, farmers should water crops only just enough to ensure that there is no substantial threat, from a lack of water, to either the growth or the yield of the crops.

Jennifer: Indeed. In fact, a mildly drought-stressed plant will divert a small amount of its resources from normal growth to the development of pesticidal toxins, but abundantly watered plants will not.

10. Jennifer's comment is related to Peter's argument in which one of the following ways?

(A) It offers information that supports each of the claims that Peter makes in his argument.

(B) It supports Peter's argument by supplying a premise without which Peter's conclusion cannot properly be drawn.

(C) It supports Peter's argument by offering an explanation of all of Peter's premises.

(D) It supports one of Peter's premises although it undermines Peter's conclusion.

(E) It supports the conclusion of Peter's argument by offering independent grounds for that conclusion.

11. Which one of the following, if true, most strengthens Peter's argument?

(A) The leaves of some crop plants are much larger, and therefore absorb more water, than the leaves of some other crop plants.

(B) In industrialized nations there are more crops that are abundantly watered than there are crops grown under mild drought stress.

(C) Insect damage presents a greater threat to crop plants than does mild drought stress.

(D) Farmers are not always able to control the amount of water that their crops receive when, for instance, there are rainstorms in the areas where their crops are growing.

(E) Mexican bean beetles are more likely to feed on the leaves of slightly drought-stressed soybeans than oak lace bugs are to feed on the leaves of abundantly watered soybeans.

12. Vague laws set vague limits on people's freedom, which makes it impossible for them to know for certain whether their actions are legal. Thus, under vague laws people cannot feel secure.

The conclusion follows logically if which one of the following is assumed?

(A) People can feel secure only if they know for certain whether their actions are legal.

(B) If people do not know for certain whether their actions are legal, then they might not feel secure.

(C) If people know for certain whether their actions are legal, they can feel secure.

(D) People can feel secure if they are governed by laws that are not vague.

(E) Only people who feel secure can know for certain whether their actions are legal.

13. While it was once believed that the sort of psychotherapy appropriate for the treatment of neuroses caused by environmental factors is also appropriate for schizophrenia and other psychoses, it is now known that these latter, more serious forms of mental disturbance are best treated by biochemical—that is, medicinal—means. This is conclusive evidence that psychoses, unlike neuroses, have nothing to do with environmental factors but rather are caused by some sort of purely organic condition, such as abnormal brain chemistry or brain malformations.

The argument is vulnerable to criticism because it ignores the possibility that

(A) the organic conditions that result in psychoses can be caused or exacerbated by environmental factors

(B) the symptoms of mental disturbance caused by purely organic factors can be alleviated with medicine

(C) organic illnesses that are nonpsychological in nature may be treatable without using biochemical methods

(D) the nature of any medical condition can be inferred from the nature of the treatment that cures that condition

(E) organic factors having little to do with brain chemistry may be at least partially responsible for neuroses

GO ON TO THE NEXT PAGE.

14. We learn to use most of the machines in our lives through written instructions, without knowledge of the machines' inner workings, because most machines are specifically designed for use by nonexperts. So, in general, attaining technological expertise would prepare students for tomorrow's job market no better than would a more traditional education stressing verbal and quantitative skills.

The argument depends on assuming which one of the following?

(A) Fewer people receive a traditional education stressing verbal and quantitative skills now than did 20 years ago.

(B) Facility in operating machines designed for use by nonexperts is almost never enhanced by expert knowledge of the machines' inner workings.

(C) Most jobs in tomorrow's job market will not demand the ability to operate many machines that are designed for use only by experts.

(D) Students cannot attain technological expertise and also receive an education that does not neglect verbal and quantitative skills.

(E) When learning to use a machine, technological expertise is never more important than verbal and quantitative skills.

15. Environmentalists who seek stricter governmental regulations controlling water pollution should be certain to have their facts straight. For if it turns out, for example, that water pollution is a lesser threat than they proclaimed, then there will be a backlash and the public will not listen to them even when dire threats exist.

Which one of the following best illustrates the principle illustrated by the argument above?

(A) Middle-level managers who ask their companies to hire additional employees should have strong evidence that doing so will benefit the company; otherwise, higher-level managers will refuse to follow their suggestions to hire additional employees even when doing so really would benefit the company.

(B) Politicians who defend the rights of unpopular constituencies ought to see to it that they use cool, dispassionate rhetoric in their appeals. Even if they have their facts straight, inflammatory rhetoric can cause a backlash that results in more negative reactions to these constituencies, whether or not they are deserving of more rights.

(C) People who are trying to convince others to take some sort of action should make every effort to present evidence that is emotionally compelling. Such evidence is invariably more persuasive than dry, technical data, even when the data strongly support their claims.

(D) Whoever wants to advance a political agenda ought to take the time to convince legislators that their own political careers are at stake in the matter at hand; otherwise, the agenda will simply be ignored.

(E) Activists who want to prevent excessive globalization of the economy should assign top priority to an appeal to the economic self-interest of those who would be adversely affected by it, for if they fail in such an appeal, extreme economic globalization is inevitable.

GO ON TO THE NEXT PAGE.

16. Herpetologist: Some psychologists attribute complex reasoning to reptiles, claiming that simple stimulus-response explanations of some reptiles' behaviors, such as food gathering, cannot account for the complexity of such behavior. But since experiments show that reptiles are incapable of making major alterations in their behavior, for example, when faced with significant changes in their environment, these animals must be incapable of complex reasoning.

Which one of the following is an assumption required by the herpetologist's argument?

(A) Animals could make major changes in their behavior only if they were capable of complex reasoning.

(B) Simple stimulus-response explanations can in principle account for all reptile behaviors.

(C) Reptile behavior appears more complex in the field than laboratory experiments reveal it to be.

(D) If reptiles were capable of complex reasoning, they would sometimes be able to make major changes in their behavior.

(E) Complex reasoning and responses to stimuli cannot both contribute to the same behavior.

17. The purpose of a general theory of art is to explain every aesthetic feature that is found in any of the arts. Premodern general theories of art, however, focused primarily on painting and sculpture. Every premodern general theory of art, even those that succeed as theories of painting and sculpture, fails to explain some aesthetic feature of music.

The statements above, if true, most strongly support which one of the following?

(A) Any general theory of art that explains the aesthetic features of painting also explains those of sculpture.

(B) A general theory of art that explains every aesthetic feature of music will achieve its purpose.

(C) Any theory of art that focuses primarily on sculpture and painting cannot explain every aesthetic feature of music.

(D) No premodern general theory of art achieves its purpose unless music is not art.

(E) No premodern general theory of art explains any aesthetic features of music that are not shared with painting and sculpture.

18. It is said that people should accept themselves as they are instead of being dissatisfied with their own abilities. But this is clearly a bad principle if the goal is a society whose citizens are genuinely happy, for no one can be genuinely happy if he or she is not pursuing personal excellence and is unwilling to undergo personal change of any kind.

Which one of the following is an assumption required by the argument?

(A) Those who are willing to change will probably find genuine happiness.

(B) People who are not dissatisfied with themselves are less likely than others to pursue personal excellence.

(C) Personal excellence cannot be acquired by those who lack genuine confidence in their own abilities.

(D) People are justified in feeling content with themselves when they have achieved some degree of personal excellence.

(E) Happiness is not genuine unless it is based on something that is painful to obtain.

19. My father likes turnips, but not potatoes, which he says are tasteless. So it is not true that whoever likes potatoes likes turnips.

The flawed reasoning in the argument above most closely resembles that in which one of the following?

(A) This book is not a paperback, but it is expensive. So it is not true that some paperbacks are expensive.

(B) Although this recently published work of fiction has more than 75 pages, it is not a novel. Thus, it is not the case that all novels have more than 75 pages.

(C) All ornate buildings were constructed before the twentieth century. This house is ornate, so it must be true that it was built before the twentieth century.

(D) Erica enjoys studying physics, but not pure mathematics, which she says is boring. So it is not true that whoever enjoys studying physics enjoys studying pure mathematics.

(E) People who do their own oil changes are car fanatics. My next-door neighbors are car fanatics, so it follows that they do their own oil changes.

GO ON TO THE NEXT PAGE.

20. Critic: Although some people claim it is inconsistent to support freedom of speech and also support legislation limiting the amount of violence in TV programs, it is not. We can limit TV program content because the damage done by violent programs is more harmful than the decrease in freedom of speech that would result from the limitations envisioned by the legislation.

Which one of the following principles, if valid, most helps to justify the critic's reasoning?

(A) In evaluating legislation that would impinge on a basic freedom, we should consider the consequences of not passing the legislation.

(B) One can support freedom of speech while at the same time recognizing that it can sometimes be overridden by other interests.

(C) When facing a choice between restricting freedom of speech or not, we must decide based on what would make the greatest number of people the happiest.

(D) If the exercise of a basic freedom leads to some harm, then the exercise of that freedom should be restricted.

(E) In some circumstances, we should tolerate regulations that impinge on a basic freedom.

21. Sandy: I play the Bigbucks lottery—that's the one where you pick five numbers and all the players who have picked the five numbers drawn at the end of the week share the money pot. But it's best to play only after there have been a few weeks with no winners, because the money pot increases each week that there is no winner.

Alex: No, you're more likely to win the lottery when the money pot is small, because that's when the fewest other people are playing.

Which one of the following most accurately describes a mistake in the reasoning of one of the two speakers?

(A) Sandy holds that the chances of anyone's winning are unaffected by the number of times that person plays.

(B) Alex holds that the chances of Sandy's winning are affected by the number of other people playing.

(C) Sandy holds that the chances of anyone's winning are unaffected by the size of the pot.

(D) Alex holds that the chances of Sandy's winning in a given week are unaffected by whether anyone has won the week before.

(E) Sandy holds that the chances of there being a winner go up if no one has won the lottery for quite a while.

22. The retail price of decaffeinated coffee is considerably higher than that of regular coffee. However, the process by which coffee beans are decaffeinated is fairly simple and not very costly. Therefore, the price difference cannot be accounted for by the greater cost of providing decaffeinated coffee to the consumer.

The argument relies on assuming which one of the following?

(A) Processing regular coffee costs more than processing decaffeinated coffee.

(B) Price differences between products can generally be accounted for by such factors as supply and demand, not by differences in production costs.

(C) There is little competition among companies that process decaffeinated coffee.

(D) Retail coffee-sellers do not expect that consumers are content to pay more for decaffeinated coffee than for regular coffee.

(E) The beans used for producing decaffeinated coffee do not cost much more before processing than the beans used for producing regular coffee.

GO ON TO THE NEXT PAGE.

Questions 23–24

A newspaper article on Britain's unions argued that their strength was declining. The article's evidence was the decreasing number and size of strikes, as if the reason for the unions' existence was to organize strikes. Surely, in a modern industrial society, the calling of a strike is evidence that the negotiating position of the union was too weak. Strong unions do not need to call strikes. They can concentrate their efforts on working with others in the labor market to achieve common goals, such as profitable and humane working conditions.

23. The argument criticizing the newspaper article is directed toward establishing which one of the following as its main conclusion?

(A) The negotiating position of a union is weak if the only means it has of achieving its end is a strike or the threat of a strike.

(B) Although unions represent the interests of their members, that does not preclude them from having interests in common with other participants in the labor market.

(C) There is no reason to believe, on the basis of what the newspaper article said, that union strength in Britain is declining.

(D) The reason for unions' existence is to work for goals such as profitable and humane working conditions by organizing strikes.

(E) With strong unions it is possible for a modern industrial society to achieve profitable and humane working conditions, but without them it would be impossible.

24. The argument criticizing the newspaper article employs which one of the following strategies?

(A) questioning the accuracy of the statistical evidence that the newspaper article uses

(B) detailing historical changes that make the newspaper article's analysis outdated

(C) reinterpreting evidence that the newspaper article uses as indicating the opposite of what the newspaper concludes

(D) arguing that the newspaper article's conclusion is motivated by a desire to change the role of unions

(E) pointing to common interests among unions and management which the newspaper article ignores

25. Anthropologist: All music is based on a few main systems of scale building. Clearly, if the popularity of a musical scale were a result of social conditioning, we would expect, given the diversity of social systems, a diverse mixture of diatonic and nondiatonic scales in the world's music. Yet diatonic scales have always dominated the music of most of the world. Therefore, the popularity of diatonic music can be attributed only to innate dispositions of the human mind.

The anthropologist's argument is most vulnerable to criticism on the grounds that it fails to

(A) consider the possibility that some people appreciate nondiatonic music more than they do diatonic music

(B) explain how innate dispositions increase appreciation of nondiatonic music

(C) explain the existence of diatonic scales as well as the existence of nondiatonic scales

(D) consider that innate dispositions and social conditioning could jointly affect the popularity of a type of music

(E) consider whether any appreciation of nondiatonic music is demonstrated by some nonhuman species of animals

26. Before 1986 physicists believed they could describe the universe in terms of four universal forces. Experiments then suggested, however, a fifth universal force of mutual repulsion between particles of matter. This fifth force would explain the occurrence in the experiments of a smaller measurement of the gravitational attraction between bodies than the established theory predicted.

Which one of the following, if true, most strengthens the argument that there is a fifth universal force?

(A) The extremely sophisticated equipment used for the experiments was not available to physicists before the 1970s.

(B) No previously established scientific results are incompatible with the notion of a fifth universal force.

(C) Some scientists have suggested that the alleged fifth universal force is an aspect of gravity rather than being fundamental in itself.

(D) The experiments were conducted by physicists in remote geological settings in which factors affecting the force of gravity could not be measured with any degree of precision.

(E) The fifth universal force was postulated at a time in which many other exciting and productive ideas in theoretical physics were developed.

S T O P

IF YOU FINISH BEFORE TIME IS CALLED, YOU MAY CHECK YOUR WORK ON THIS SECTION ONLY.
DO NOT WORK ON ANY OTHER SECTION IN THE TEST.

SECTION IV
Time—35 minutes
23 Questions

Directions: Each group of questions in this section is based on a set of conditions. In answering some of the questions, it may be useful to draw a rough diagram. Choose the response that most accurately and completely answers each question and blacken the corresponding space on your answer sheet.

Questions 1–6

A fruit stand carries at least one kind of the following kinds of fruit: figs, kiwis, oranges, pears, tangerines, and watermelons. The stand does not carry any other kind of fruit. The selection of fruits the stand carries is consistent with the following conditions:

If the stand carries kiwis, then it does not carry pears.
If the stand does not carry tangerines, then it carries kiwis.
If the stand carries oranges, then it carries both pears and watermelons.
If the stand carries watermelons, then it carries figs or tangerines or both.

1. Which one of the following could be a complete and accurate list of the kinds of fruit the stand carries?

   (A) oranges, pears
   (B) pears, tangerines
   (C) oranges, pears, watermelons
   (D) oranges, tangerines, watermelons
   (E) kiwis, oranges, pears, watermelons

2. Which one of the following could be the only kind of fruit the stand carries?

   (A) figs
   (B) oranges
   (C) pears
   (D) tangerines
   (E) watermelons

3. Which one of the following CANNOT be a complete and accurate list of the kinds of fruit the stand carries?

   (A) kiwis, tangerines
   (B) tangerines, watermelons
   (C) figs, kiwis, watermelons
   (D) oranges, pears, tangerines, watermelons
   (E) figs, kiwis, oranges, pears, watermelons

4. If the stand carries no watermelons, then which one of the following must be true?

   (A) The stand carries kiwis.
   (B) The stand carries at least two kinds of fruit.
   (C) The stand carries at most three kinds of fruit.
   (D) The stand carries neither oranges nor pears.
   (E) The stand carries neither oranges nor kiwis.

5. If the stand carries watermelons, then which one of the following must be false?

   (A) The stand does not carry figs.
   (B) The stand does not carry tangerines.
   (C) The stand does not carry pears.
   (D) The stand carries pears but not oranges.
   (E) The stand carries pears but not tangerines.

6. If the condition that if the fruit stand does not carry tangerines then it does carry kiwis is suspended, and all other conditions remain in effect, then which one of the following CANNOT be a complete and accurate list of the kinds of fruit the stand carries?

   (A) pears
   (B) figs, pears
   (C) oranges, pears, watermelons
   (D) figs, pears, watermelons
   (E) figs, oranges, pears, watermelons

GO ON TO THE NEXT PAGE.

Questions 7–13

A radio talk show host airs five telephone calls sequentially. The calls, one from each of Felicia, Gwen, Henry, Isaac, and Mel, are each either live or taped (but not both). Two calls are from Vancouver, two are from Seattle, and one is from Kelowna. The following conditions must apply:

Isaac's and Mel's calls are the first two calls aired, but not necessarily in that order.
The third call aired, from Kelowna, is taped.
Both Seattle calls are live.
Both Gwen's and Felicia's calls air after Henry's.
Neither Mel nor Felicia calls from Seattle.

7. Which one of the following could be an accurate list of the calls, listed in the order in which they are aired?

(A) Isaac's, Henry's, Felicia's, Mel's, Gwen's
(B) Isaac's, Mel's, Gwen's, Henry's, Felicia's
(C) Mel's, Gwen's, Henry's, Isaac's, Felicia's
(D) Mel's, Isaac's, Gwen's, Henry's, Felicia's
(E) Mel's, Isaac's, Henry's, Felicia's, Gwen's

8. Which one of the following could be true?

(A) Felicia's call airs fifth.
(B) Gwen's call airs first.
(C) Henry's call airs second.
(D) Isaac's call airs third.
(E) Mel's call airs fifth.

9. If the first call aired is from Seattle, then which one of the following could be true?

(A) Felicia's call is the next call aired after Isaac's.
(B) Henry's call is the next call aired after Felicia's.
(C) Henry's call is the next call aired after Mel's.
(D) Henry's call is the next call aired after Isaac's.
(E) Isaac's call is the next call aired after Mel's.

10. If a taped call airs first, then which one of the following CANNOT be true?

(A) Felicia's call airs fourth.
(B) Gwen's call airs fifth.
(C) A taped call airs second.
(D) A taped call airs third.
(E) A taped call airs fourth.

11. Which one of the following must be true?

(A) Gwen's call is live.
(B) Henry's call is live.
(C) Mel's call is live.
(D) Felicia's call is taped.
(E) Isaac's call is taped.

12. If no two live calls are aired consecutively and no two taped calls are aired consecutively, then in exactly how many distinct orders could the calls from the five people be aired?

(A) one
(B) two
(C) three
(D) four
(E) five

13. If a taped call airs second, then which one of the following CANNOT be true?

(A) The first call aired is from Seattle.
(B) The first call aired is from Vancouver.
(C) The fourth call aired is from Seattle.
(D) The fifth call aired is from Seattle.
(E) The fifth call aired is from Vancouver.

GO ON TO THE NEXT PAGE.

Questions 14–18

Gutierrez, Hoffman, Imamura, Kelly, Lapas, and Moore ride a bus together. Each sits facing forward in a different one of the six seats on the left side of the bus. The seats are in consecutive rows that are numbered 1, 2, and 3 from front to back. Each row has exactly two seats: a window seat and an aisle seat. The following conditions must apply:

Hoffman occupies the aisle seat immediately behind Gutierrez's aisle seat.

If Moore occupies an aisle seat, Hoffman sits in the same row as Lapas.

If Gutierrez sits in the same row as Kelly, Moore occupies the seat immediately and directly behind Imamura's seat.

If Kelly occupies a window seat, Moore sits in row 3.

If Kelly sits in row 3, Imamura sits in row 1.

14. Which one of the following could be true?

(A) Imamura sits in row 2, whereas Kelly sits in row 3.
(B) Gutierrez sits in the same row as Kelly, immediately and directly behind Moore.
(C) Gutierrez occupies a window seat in the same row as Lapas.
(D) Moore occupies an aisle seat in the same row as Lapas.
(E) Kelly and Moore both sit in row 3.

15. If Lapas and Kelly each occupy a window seat, then which one of the following could be true?

(A) Moore occupies the aisle seat in row 3.
(B) Imamura occupies the window seat in row 3.
(C) Gutierrez sits in the same row as Kelly.
(D) Gutierrez sits in the same row as Moore.
(E) Moore sits in the same row as Lapas.

16. If Moore sits in row 1, then which one of the following must be true?

(A) Hoffman sits in row 2.
(B) Imamura sits in row 2.
(C) Imamura sits in row 3.
(D) Kelly sits in row 1.
(E) Lapas sits in row 3.

17. If Kelly occupies the aisle seat in row 3, then each of the following must be true EXCEPT:

(A) Gutierrez sits in the same row as Imamura.
(B) Hoffman sits in the same row as Lapas.
(C) Lapas occupies a window seat.
(D) Moore occupies a window seat.
(E) Gutierrez sits in row 1.

18. If neither Gutierrez nor Imamura sits in row 1, then which one of the following could be true?

(A) Hoffman sits in row 2.
(B) Kelly sits in row 2.
(C) Moore sits in row 2.
(D) Imamura occupies an aisle seat.
(E) Moore occupies an aisle seat.

GO ON TO THE NEXT PAGE.

Questions 19–23

An airline has four flights from New York to Sarasota—
flights 1, 2, 3, and 4. On each flight there is exactly one pilot
and exactly one co-pilot. The pilots are Fazio, Germond, Kyle,
and Lopez; the co-pilots are Reich, Simon, Taylor, and Umlas.
Each pilot and co-pilot is assigned to exactly one flight.

The flights take off in numerical order.
Fazio's flight takes off before Germond's, and at least one
 other flight takes off between their flights.
Kyle is assigned to flight 2.
Lopez is assigned to the same flight as Umlas.

19. Which one of the following pilot and co-pilot teams
    could be assigned to flight 1?

    (A)   Fazio and Reich
    (B)   Fazio and Umlas
    (C)   Germond and Reich
    (D)   Germond and Umlas
    (E)   Lopez and Taylor

20. If Reich's flight is later than Umlas's, which one of the
    following statements cannot be true?

    (A)   Fazio's flight is earlier than Simon's.
    (B)   Kyle's flight is earlier than Reich's.
    (C)   Kyle's flight is earlier than Taylor's.
    (D)   Simon's flight is earlier than Reich's.
    (E)   Taylor's flight is earlier than Kyle's.

21. If Lopez's flight is earlier than Germond's, which one of
    the following statements could be false?

    (A)   Fazio's flight is earlier than Umlas's.
    (B)   Germond is assigned to flight 4.
    (C)   Either Reich's or Taylor's flight is earlier than
           Umlas's.
    (D)   Simon's flight is earlier than Umlas's.
    (E)   Umlas is assigned to flight 3.

22. What is the maximum possible number of different pilot
    and co-pilot teams, any one of which could be assigned
    to flight 4?

    (A)   2
    (B)   3
    (C)   4
    (D)   5
    (E)   6

23. If Simon's flight is later than Lopez's, then which one of
    the following statements could be false?

    (A)   Germond's flight is later than Reich's.
    (B)   Germond's flight is later than Taylor's.
    (C)   Lopez's flight is later than Taylor's.
    (D)   Taylor's flight is later than Reich's.
    (E)   Umlas's flight is later than Reich's.

S T O P

IF YOU FINISH BEFORE TIME IS CALLED, YOU MAY CHECK YOUR WORK ON THIS SECTION ONLY.
DO NOT WORK ON ANY OTHER SECTION IN THE TEST.

Acknowledgment is made to the following sources from which material has been adapted for use in this test booklet:

Steven Keeva, "Defending the Revolution." ©1994 Time by ABA Journal.

SIGNATURE _____   / /
                                                    DATE

LSAT WRITING SAMPLE TOPIC

The Cuthbert Foundation, a philanthropic organization promoting community renewal and redevelopment, is conducting its annual grant competition. Two finalists are competing for the award. Acting for Hope, a nonprofit organization founded by a local theater director, is seeking funding for a municipally approved school-based community theater program for urban children. The other finalist, the city of Philmont, is seeking funding to continue its municipal mural-arts program. Write an essay in which you argue for one program over the other based on the following considerations:

- The Cuthbert Foundation wants to support youth-centered programs that increase adult volunteerism within communities.
- The Cuthbert Foundation wants to reward programs that visibly improve the physical infrastructure of communities.

Through partnerships with local public schools, Acting for Hope will offer drama classes and after-school acting workshops led by volunteer working actors. Free public performances are planned. To ensure adequate staffing for these events, parents of participating students will be asked to donate their own time and recruit additional volunteers in exchange for their children's involvement with the program. The program's director plans to renovate an abandoned downtown movie theater to serve as a performance venue, but even if he wins the Cuthbert Award he will be able to renovate only the interior of the building; he will require additional funding to refurbish the exterior.

Philmont's popular mural-arts program was founded by a local artist to improve the quality of life for inner-city residents by involving urban youth and their families in the process of community revitalization. The design and execution of each mural is supervised by a volunteer artist from the community, who works with a team of local teenagers from start to finish. Murals painted by program participants now adorn a handful of abandoned buildings throughout the city, and residents living near the beautified buildings consider the murals an asset to their neighborhoods. They report that there has been noticeably less litter and graffiti on their blocks since the murals were painted.

Directions:

1. Use the Answer Key on the next page to check your answers.

2. Use the Scoring Worksheet below to compute your raw score.

3. Use the Score Conversion Chart to convert your raw score into the 120-180 scale.

Scoring Worksheet

1. Enter the number of questions you answered correctly in each section.

	Number Correct
SECTION I.	——
SECTION II	——
SECTION III.	——
SECTION IV.	——

2. Enter the sum here: ——
   This is your Raw Score.

Conversion Chart

For Converting Raw Score to the 120-180 LSAT Scaled Score
LSAT Form 1LSS50

Reported Score	Raw Score Lowest	Raw Score Highest
180	99	101
179	98	98
178	97	97
177	96	96
176	—*	—*
175	95	95
174	94	94
173	93	93
172	92	92
171	90	91
170	89	89
169	88	88
168	87	87
167	85	86
166	84	84
165	82	83
164	81	81
163	79	80
162	78	78
161	76	77
160	74	75
159	73	73
158	71	72
157	69	70
156	68	68
155	66	67
154	64	65
153	62	63
152	61	61
151	59	60
150	57	58
149	55	56
148	54	54
147	52	53
146	50	51
145	49	49
144	47	48
143	45	46
142	44	44
141	42	43
140	41	41
139	39	40
138	38	38
137	36	37
136	35	35
135	33	34
134	32	32
133	30	31
132	29	29
131	28	28
130	27	27
129	25	26
128	24	24
127	23	23
126	22	22
125	21	21
124	20	20
123	19	19
122	18	18
121	17	17
120	0	16

*There is no raw score that will produce this scaled score for this form.

SECTION I

1.	A	8.	D	15.	D	22.	C
2.	A	9.	B	16.	C	23.	E
3.	C	10.	C	17.	E	24.	B
4.	C	11.	D	18.	D	25.	C
5.	A	12.	E	19.	C	26.	E
6.	D	13.	C	20.	E		
7.	B	14.	E	21.	A		

SECTION II

1.	D	8.	B	15.	D	22.	C
2.	C	9.	D	16.	C	23.	D
3.	E	10.	D	17.	B	24.	C
4.	E	11.	C	18.	A	25.	E
5.	C	12.	C	19.	A	26.	A
6.	B	13.	E	20.	B		
7.	E	14.	D	21.	D		

SECTION III

1.	D	8.	A	15.	A	22.	E
2.	A	9.	C	16.	D	23.	C
3.	C	10.	E	17.	D	24.	C
4.	B	11.	C	18.	B	25.	D
5.	E	12.	A	19.	B	26.	B
6.	B	13.	A	20.	B		
7.	B	14.	C	21.	B		

SECTION IV

1.	B	8.	A	15.	A	22.	C
2.	D	9.	C	16.	D	23.	D
3.	E	10.	C	17.	B		
4.	C	11.	A	18.	C		
5.	E	12.	A	19.	A		
6.	C	13.	B	20.	C		
7.	E	14.	E	21.	D		

The Official LSAT PrepTest

37

- June 2002
  PrepTest 37

- Form 3LSS56

SECTION I

Time—35 minutes

26 Questions

Directions: Each passage in this section is followed by a group of questions to be answered on the basis of what is stated or implied in the passage. For some of the questions, more than one of the choices could conceivably answer the question. However, you are to choose the best answer; that is, the response that most accurately and completely answers the question, and blacken the corresponding space on your answer sheet.

The jury trial is one of the handful of democratic institutions that allow individual citizens, rather than the government, to make important societal decisions. A crucial component of the jury trial, at least in serious

(5) criminal cases, is the rule that verdicts be unanimous among the jurors (usually twelve in number). Under this requirement, dissenting jurors must either be convinced of the rightness of the prevailing opinion, or, conversely, persuade the other jurors to change their

(10) minds. In either instance, the unanimity requirement compels the jury to deliberate fully and truly before reaching its verdict. Critics of the unanimity requirement, however, see it as a costly relic that extends the deliberation process and sometimes, in a

(15) hung (i.e., deadlocked) jury, brings it to a halt at the hands of a single, recalcitrant juror, forcing the judge to order a retrial. Some of these critics recommend reducing verdict requirements to something less than unanimity, so that one or even two dissenting jurors

(20) will not be able to force a retrial.

But the material costs of hung juries do not warrant losing the benefit to society of the unanimous verdict. Statistically, jury trials are relatively rare; the vast majority of defendants do not have the option of a jury

(25) trial or elect to have a trial without a jury—or they plead guilty to the original or a reduced charge. And the incidence of hung juries is only a small fraction of the already small fraction of cases that receive a jury trial. Furthermore, that juries occasionally deadlock

(30) does not demonstrate a flaw in the criminal justice system, but rather suggests that jurors are conscientiously doing the job they have been asked to do. Hung juries usually occur when the case is very close—that is, when neither side has presented

(35) completely convincing evidence—and although the unanimity requirement may sometimes lead to inconclusive outcomes, a hung jury is certainly preferable to an unjust verdict.

Requiring unanimity provides a better chance that a

(40) trial, and thus a verdict, will be fair. Innocent people are already occasionally convicted—perhaps in some cases because jurors presume that anyone who has been brought to trial is probably guilty—and eliminating the unanimity requirement would only

(45) increase the opportunity for such mistakes. Furthermore, if a juror's dissenting opinion can easily be dismissed, an important and necessary part of the deliberation process will be lost, for effective deliberation requires that each juror's opinion be given

(50) a fair hearing. Only then can the verdict reached by the

jury be said to represent all of its members, and if even one juror has doubts that are dismissed out of hand, society's confidence that a proper verdict has been reached would be undermined.

1. Which one of the following most accurately states the main point of the passage?

(A) Because trials requiring juries are relatively rare, the usefulness of the unanimity requirement does not need to be reexamined.

(B) The unanimity requirement should be maintained because most hung juries are caused by irresponsible jurors rather than by any flaws in the requirement.

(C) The problem of hung juries is not a result of flaws in the justice system but of the less than convincing evidence presented in some cases.

(D) The unanimity requirement should be maintained, but it is only effective if jurors conscientiously do the job they have been asked to do.

(E) Because its material costs are outweighed by what it contributes to the fairness of jury trials, the unanimity requirement should not be rescinded.

GO ON TO THE NEXT PAGE.

2. Which one of the following most accurately describes the author's attitude toward the unanimity requirement?

   (A) cursory appreciation
   (B) neutral interest
   (C) cautious endorsement
   (D) firm support
   (E) unreasoned reverence

3. Which one of the following principles can most clearly be said to underlie the author's arguments in the third paragraph?

   (A) The risk of unjust verdicts is serious enough to warrant strong measures to avoid it.
   (B) Fairness in jury trials is crucial and so judges must be extremely thorough in order to ensure it.
   (C) Careful adherence to the unanimity requirement will eventually eliminate unjust verdicts.
   (D) Safeguards must be in place because not all citizens called to jury duty perform their role responsibly.
   (E) The jury system is inherently flawed and therefore unfairness cannot be eliminated but only reduced.

4. Which one of the following sentences could most logically be added to the end of the last paragraph of the passage?

   (A) It is not surprising, then, that the arguments presented by the critics of the unanimity requirement grow out of a separate tradition from that embodied in the unanimity requirement.
   (B) Similarly, if there is a public debate concerning the unanimity requirement, public faith in the requirement will be strengthened.
   (C) The opinion of each juror is as essential to the pursuit of justice as the universal vote is to the functioning of a true democracy.
   (D) Unfortunately, because some lawmakers have characterized hung juries as intolerable, the integrity of the entire legal system has been undermined.
   (E) But even without the unanimity requirement, fair trials and fair verdicts will occur more frequently as the methods of prosecutors and defense attorneys become more scientific.

5. Which one of the following could replace the term "recalcitrant" (line 16) without a substantial change in the meaning of the critics' claim?

   (A) obstinate
   (B) suspicious
   (C) careful
   (D) conscientious
   (E) naive

6. The author explicitly claims that which one of the following would be a result of allowing a juror's dissenting opinion to be dismissed?

   (A) Only verdicts in very close cases would be affected.
   (B) The responsibility felt by jurors to be respectful to one another would be lessened.
   (C) Society's confidence in the fairness of the verdicts would be undermined.
   (D) The problem of hung juries would not be solved but would surface less frequently.
   (E) An important flaw thus would be removed from the criminal justice system.

7. It can be inferred from the passage that the author would be most likely to agree with which one of the following?

   (A) Hung juries most often result from an error in judgment on the part of one juror.
   (B) Aside from the material costs of hung juries, the criminal justice system has few flaws.
   (C) The fact that jury trials are so rare renders any flaws in the jury system insignificant.
   (D) Hung juries are acceptable and usually indicate that the criminal justice system is functioning properly.
   (E) Hung juries most often occur when one juror's opinion does not receive a fair hearing.

GO ON TO THE NEXT PAGE.

Spurred by the discovery that a substance containing uranium emitted radiation, Marie Curie began studying radioactivity in 1897. She first tested gold and copper for radiation but found none. She then
(5) tested pitchblende, a mineral that was known to contain uranium, and discovered that it was more radioactive than uranium. Acting on the hypothesis that pitchblende must contain at least one other radioactive element, Curie was able to isolate a pair of previously
(10) unknown elements, polonium and radium. Turning her attention to the rate of radioactive emission, she discovered that uranium emitted radiation at a consistent rate, even if heated or dissolved. Based on these results, Curie concluded that the emission rate for
(15) a given element was constant. Furthermore, because radiation appeared to be spontaneous, with no discernible difference between radiating and nonradiating elements, she was unable to postulate a mechanism by which to explain radiation.
(20) It is now known that radiation occurs when certain isotopes (atoms of the same element that differ slightly in their atomic structure) decay, and that emission rates are not constant but decrease very slowly with time. Some critics have recently faulted Curie for not
(25) reaching these conclusions herself, but it would have been impossible for Curie to do so given the evidence available to her. While relatively light elements such as gold and copper occasionally have unstable (i.e., radioactive) isotopes, radioactive isotopes of most of
(30) these elements are not available in nature because they have largely finished decaying and so have become stable. Conversely, heavier elements such as uranium, which decay into lighter elements in a process that takes billions of years, are present in nature exclusively
(35) in radioactive form.

Furthermore, we must recall that in Curie's time the nature of the atom itself was still being debated. Physicists believed that matter could not be divided indefinitely but instead would eventually be reduced to
(40) its indivisible components. Chemists, on the other hand, observing that chemical reactions took place as if matter was composed of atomlike particles, used the atom as a foundation for conceptualizing and describing such reactions—but they were not
(45) ultimately concerned with the question of whether or not such indivisible atoms actually existed.

As a physicist, Curie conjectured that radiating substances might lose mass in the form of atoms, but this idea is very different from the explanation
(50) eventually arrived at. It was not until the 1930s that advances in quantum mechanics overthrew the earlier understanding of the atom and showed that radiation occurs because the atoms themselves lose mass—a hypothesis that Curie, committed to the indivisible
(55) atom, could not be expected to have conceived of. Moreover, not only is Curie's inability to identify the mechanism by which radiation occurs understandable, it is also important to recognize that it was Curie's investigation of radiation that paved the way for the
(60) later breakthroughs.

8. Which one of the following most accurately states the central idea of the passage?

(A) It is unlikely that quantum mechanics would have been developed without the theoretical contributions of Marie Curie toward an understanding of the nature of radioactivity.

(B) Although later shown to be incomplete and partially inaccurate, Marie Curie's investigations provided a significant step forward on the road to the eventual explanation of radioactivity.

(C) Though the scientific achievements of Marie Curie were impressive in scope, her career is blemished by her failure to determine the mechanism of radioactivity.

(D) The commitment of Marie Curie and other physicists of her time to the physicists' model of the atom prevented them from conducting fruitful investigations into radioactivity.

(E) Although today's theories have shown it to be inconclusive, Marie Curie's research into the sources and nature of radioactivity helped refute the chemists' model of the atom.

GO ON TO THE NEXT PAGE.

9. The passage suggests that the author would be most likely to agree with which one of the following statements about the contemporary critics of Curie's studies of radioactivity?

(A) The critics fail to take into account the obstacles Curie faced in dealing with the scientific community of her time.

(B) The critics do not appreciate that the eventual development of quantum mechanics depended on Curie's conjecture that radiating substances can lose atoms.

(C) The critics are unaware of the differing conceptions of the atom held by physicists and chemists.

(D) The critics fail to appreciate the importance of the historical context in which Curie's scientific conclusions were reached.

(E) The critics do not comprehend the intricate reasoning that Curie used in discovering polonium and radium.

10. The passage implies which one of the following with regard to the time at which Curie began studying radioactivity?

(A) Pitchblende was not known by scientists to contain any radioactive element besides uranium.

(B) Radioactivity was suspected by scientists to arise from the overall structure of pitchblende rather than from particular elements in it.

(C) Physicists and chemists had developed rival theories regarding the cause of radiation.

(D) Research was not being conducted in connection with the question of whether or not matter is composed of atoms.

(E) The majority of physicists believed uranium to be the sole source of radioactivity.

11. The author's primary purpose in the passage is to

(A) summarize some aspects of one scientist's work and defend it against recent criticism

(B) describe a scientific dispute and argue for the correctness of an earlier theory

(C) outline a currently accepted scientific theory and analyze the evidence that led to its acceptance

(D) explain the mechanism by which a natural phenomenon occurs and summarize the debate that gave rise to this explanation

(E) discover the antecedents of a scientific theory and argue that the theory is not a genuine advance over its forerunners

12. The primary function of the first paragraph of the passage is to

(A) narrate the progress of turn-of-the-century studies of radioactivity

(B) present a context for the conflict between physicists and chemists

(C) provide the factual background for an evaluation of Curie's work

(D) outline the structure of the author's central argument

(E) identify the error in Curie's work that undermines its usefulness

13. Which one of the following most accurately expresses the meaning of the word "mechanism" as used by the author in the last sentence of the first paragraph?

(A) the physical process that underlies a phenomenon

(B) the experimental apparatus in which a phenomenon arises

(C) the procedure scientists use to bring about the occurrence of a phenomenon

(D) the isotopes of an element needed to produce a phenomenon

(E) the scientific theory describing a phenomenon

GO ON TO THE NEXT PAGE.

Published in 1952, *Invisible Man* featured a protagonist whose activities enabled the novel's author, Ralph Ellison, to explore and to blend themes specifically tied to the history and plight of African
(5) Americans with themes, also explored by many European writers with whose works Ellison was familiar, about the fractured, evanescent quality of individual identity and character. For this thematic blend, Ellison received two related criticisms: that his
(10) allegiance to the concerns of the individual prevented him from directing his art more toward the political action that critics believed was demanded by his era's social and political state of affairs; and that his indulging in European fictional modes lessened his
(15) contribution to the development of a distinctly African American novelistic style.

Ellison found these criticisms to voice a common demand, namely that writers should censor themselves and sacrifice their individuality for supposedly more
(20) important political and cultural purposes. He replied that it demeans a people and its artists to suggest that a particular historical situation requires cultural segregation in the arts. Such a view characterizes all artists as incapable of seeing the world—with all its
(25) subtleties and complications—in unique yet expressive ways, and it makes the narrow assumption that audiences are capable of viewing the world only from their own perspectives.

Models for understanding *Invisible Man* that may
(30) be of more help than those employed by its critics can be found in Ellison's own love for and celebration of jazz. Jazz has never closed itself off from other musical forms, and some jazz musicians have been able to take the European-influenced songs of U.S. theater and
(35) transform them into musical pieces that are unique and personal but also expressive of African American culture. In like manner, Ellison avoided the mere recapitulation of existing literary forms as well as the constraints of artistic isolation by using his work to
(40) explore and express the issues of identity and character that had so interested European writers.

Further, jazz, featuring solos that, however daring, remain rooted in the band's rhythm section, provides a rich model for understanding the relationship of artist
(45) to community and parallels the ways the protagonist's voice in *Invisible Man* is set within a wider communal context. Ellison's explorations in the novel, often in the manner of loving caricature, of the ideas left him by both European and African American predecessors are
(50) a form of homage to them and thus ameliorate the sense of alienation he expresses through the protagonist. And even though *Invisible Man*'s protagonist lives alone in a basement, Ellison proves that an individual whose unique voice is the result of
(55) the transmutation of a cultural inheritance can never be completely cut off from the community.

14. It can be inferred from the passage that the author most clearly holds which one of the following views?

(A) The possibility of successfully blending different cultural forms is demonstrated by jazz's ability to incorporate European influences.

(B) The technique of blending the artistic concerns of two cultures could be an effective tool for social and political action.

(C) Due to the success of *Invisible Man*, Ellison was able to generate a renewed interest in and greater appreciation for jazz.

(D) The protagonist in *Invisible Man* illustrates the difficulty of combining the concerns of African Americans and concerns thought to be European in origin.

(E) Ellison's literary technique, though effective, is unfortunately too esoteric and complex to generate a large audience.

15. Based on the passage, Ellison's critics would most likely have responded favorably to *Invisible Man* if it had

(A) created a positive effect on the social conditions of the time

(B) provided a historical record of the plight of African Americans

(C) contained a tribute to the political contributions of African American predecessors

(D) prompted a necessary and further separation of American literature from European literary style

(E) generated a large audience made up of individuals from many cultural backgrounds

GO ON TO THE NEXT PAGE.

16. The expression "cultural segregation in the arts" (lines 22–23) most clearly refers to

(A) a general tendency within the arts whereby certain images and themes recur within the works of certain cultures

(B) an obvious separation within the art community resulting from artists' differing aesthetic principles

(C) the cultural isolation artists feel when they address issues of individual identity

(D) the cultural obstacles that affect an audience's appreciation of art

(E) an expectation placed on an artist to uphold a specific cultural agenda in the creation of art

17. The primary purpose of the third paragraph is to

(A) summarize the thematic concerns of an artist in relation to other artists within the discipline

(B) affirm the importance of two artistic disciplines in relation to cultural concerns

(C) identify the source of the thematic content of one artist's work

(D) celebrate one artistic discipline by viewing it from the perspective of an artist from another discipline

(E) introduce a context within which the work of one artist may be more fully illuminated

18. Which one of the following statements about jazz is made in the passage?

(A) It is not accessible to a wide audience.

(B) It is the most complex of modern musical forms.

(C) It embraces other forms of music.

(D) It avoids political themes.

(E) It has influenced much of contemporary literature.

19. It can be inferred from the passage that Ellison most clearly holds which one of the following views regarding an audience's relationship to works of art?

(A) Audiences respond more favorably to art that has no political content.

(B) Groundless criticism of an artist's work can hinder an audience's reception of the work.

(C) Audiences have the capacity for empathy required to appreciate unique and expressive art.

(D) The most conscientious members of any audience are those who are aware of the specific techniques employed by the artist.

(E) Most audience members are bound by their cultural upbringing to view art from that cultural perspective.

20. The primary purpose of the passage is to

(A) make a case that a certain novelist is one of the most important novelists of the twentieth century

(B) demonstrate the value of using jazz as an illustration for further understanding the novels of a certain literary trend

(C) explain the relevance of a particular work and its protagonist to the political and social issues of the time

(D) defend the work of a certain novelist against criticism that it should have addressed political and social issues

(E) distinguish clearly between the value of art for art's sake and art for purposes such as political agendas

21. The passage provides information to answer each of the following questions EXCEPT:

(A) Did Ellison himself enjoy jazz?

(B) What themes in *Invisible Man* were influenced by themes prevalent in jazz?

(C) What was Ellison's response to criticism concerning the thematic blend in *Invisible Man*?

(D) From what literary tradition did some of the ideas explored in *Invisible Man* come?

(E) What kind of music did some jazz musicians use in creating their works?

GO ON TO THE NEXT PAGE.

Recent investigations into the psychology of decision making have sparked interest among scholars seeking to understand why governments sometimes take gambles that appear theoretically unjustifiable on (5) the basis of expected costs and benefits. Researchers have demonstrated some significant discrepancies between objective measurements of possible decision outcomes and the ways in which people subjectively value such possible results. Many of these (10) discrepancies relate to the observation that a possible outcome perceived as a loss typically motivates more strongly than the prospect of an equivalent gain. Risk-taking is thus a more common strategy for those who believe they will lose what they already possess than it (15) is for those who wish to gain something they do not have.

Previously, the notion that rational decision makers prefer risk-avoiding choices was considered to apply generally, epitomized by the assumption of many (20) economists that entrepreneurs and consumers will choose a risky venture over a sure thing only when the expected measurable value of the outcome is sufficiently high to compensate the decision maker for taking the risk. What is the minimum prize that would (25) be required to make a gamble involving a 50 percent chance of losing $100 and a 50 percent chance of winning the prize acceptable? It is commonplace that the pleasure of winning a sum of money is much less intense than the pain of losing the same amount; (30) accordingly, such a gamble would typically be accepted only when the possible gain greatly exceeds the possible loss. Research subjects do, in fact, commonly judge that a 50 percent chance to lose $100 is unacceptable unless it is combined with an equal (35) chance to win more than $300. Nevertheless, the recent studies indicate that risk-accepting strategies are common when the alternative to a sure loss is a substantial chance of losing an even larger amount, coupled with some chance—even a small one—of (40) losing nothing.

Such observations are quite salient to scholars of international conflict and crisis. For example, governments typically are cautious in foreign policy initiatives that entail risk, especially the risk of armed (45) conflict. But nations also often take huge gambles to retrieve what they perceive to have been taken from them by other nations. This type of motivation, then, can lead states to take risks that far outweigh the objectively measurable value of the lost assets. For (50) example, when Britain and Argentina entered into armed conflict in 1982 over possession of the Falkland Islands—or Malvinas, as they are called in Spanish— each viewed the islands as territory that had been taken from them by the other; thus each was willing to (55) commit enormous resources—and risks—to recapturing them. In international affairs, it is vital that each actor in such a situation understand the other's subjective view of what is at stake.

22. Suppose that a country seizes a piece of territory with great mineral wealth that is claimed by a neighboring country, with a concomitant risk of failure involving moderate but easily tolerable harm in the long run. Given the information in the passage, the author would most likely say that

(A) the country's actions are consistent with previously accepted views of the psychology of risk-taking

(B) the new research findings indicate that the country from which the territory has been seized probably weighs the risk factors involved in the situation similarly to the way in which they are weighed by the aggressor nation

(C) in spite of surface appearances to the contrary, the new research findings suggest that the objective value of the potential gain is overridden by the risks

(D) the facts of the situation show that the government is motivated by factors other than objective calculation of the measurable risks and probable benefits

(E) the country's leaders most likely subjectively perceive the territory as having been taken from their country in the past

GO ON TO THE NEXT PAGE.

23. The question in lines 24–27 functions primarily as

(A) the introduction to a thought experiment whose results the author expects will vary widely among different people

(B) a rhetorical question whose assumed answer is in conflict with the previously accepted view concerning risk-taking behavior

(C) the basis for an illustration of how the previously accepted view concerning risk-taking behavior applies accurately to some types of situations

(D) a suggestion that the discrepancies between subjective and objective valuations of possible decision outcomes are more illusive than real

(E) a transitional device to smooth an otherwise abrupt switch from discussion of previous theories to discussion of some previously unaccepted research findings

24. It can most reasonably be inferred from the passage that the author would agree with which one of the following statements?

(A) When states try to regain losses through risky conflict, they generally are misled by inadequate or inaccurate information as to the risks that they run in doing so.

(B) Government decision makers subjectively evaluate the acceptability of risks involving national assets in much the same way that they would evaluate risks involving personal assets.

(C) A new method for predicting and mediating international conflict has emerged from a synthesis of the fields of economics and psychology.

(D) Truly rational decision making is a rare phenomenon in international crises and can, ironically, lead to severe consequences for those who engage in it.

(E) Contrary to previous assumptions, people are more likely to take substantial risks when their subjective assessments of expected benefits match or exceed the objectively measured costs.

25. The passage can be most accurately described as

(A) a psychological analysis of the motives involved in certain types of collective decision making in the presence of conflict

(B) a presentation of a psychological hypothesis which is then subjected to a political test case

(C) a suggestion that psychologists should incorporate the findings of political scientists into their research

(D) an examination of some new psychological considerations regarding risk and their application to another field of inquiry

(E) a summary of two possible avenues for understanding international crises and conflicts

26. The passage most clearly suggests that the author would agree with which one of the following statements?

(A) Researchers have previously been too willing to accept the claims that subjects make about their preferred choices in risk-related decision problems.

(B) There is inadequate research support for the hypothesis that except when a gamble is the only available means for averting an otherwise certain loss, people typically are averse to risk-taking.

(C) It can reasonably be argued that the risk that Britain accepted in its 1982 conflict with Argentina outweighed the potential objectively measurable benefit of that venture.

(D) The new findings suggest that because of the subjective elements involved, governmental strategies concerning risks of loss in international crises will remain incomprehensible to outside observers.

(E) Moderate risks in cases involving unavoidable losses are often taken on the basis of reasoning that diverges markedly from that which was studied in the recent investigations.

S T O P

IF YOU FINISH BEFORE TIME IS CALLED, YOU MAY CHECK YOUR WORK ON THIS SECTION ONLY.
DO NOT WORK ON ANY OTHER SECTION IN THE TEST.

SECTION II

Time—35 minutes

26 Questions

<u>Directions:</u> The questions in this section are based on the reasoning contained in brief statements or passages. For some questions, more than one of the choices could conceivably answer the question. However, you are to choose the <u>best</u> answer; that is, the response that most accurately and completely answers the question. You should not make assumptions that are by commonsense standards implausible, superfluous, or incompatible with the passage. After you have chosen the best answer, blacken the corresponding space on your answer sheet.

1. Company president: Grievance procedures should allow the grievant and the respondent to select a mediator who will attempt to work out a resolution. Grievances are costly and mediation could help to resolve many of them. However, beginning mediation fairly late in the process, as our human resources department proposes, would be relatively ineffective.

    Which one of the following, if true, most helps to justify the company president's criticism of the human resources department's proposal?

    (A)   People who file grievances are unreasonable and would resist listening to a mediator.
    (B)   Many disagreements are already being solved without the intervention of a mediator.
    (C)   Adversaries' positions tend to harden as a dispute wears on, making compromise less likely.
    (D)   Respondents tend to be supervisors who cannot give in to employees without losing authority.
    (E)   The mediation process itself is likely to cost as much in time and money as the present grievance procedures.

2. The solidity of bridge piers built on pilings depends largely on how deep the pilings are driven. Prior to 1700, pilings were driven to "refusal," that is, to the point at which they refused to go any deeper. In a 1588 inquiry into the solidity of piers for Venice's Rialto Bridge, it was determined that the bridge's builder, Antonio Da Ponte, had met the contemporary standard for refusal: he had caused the pilings to be driven until additional penetration into the ground was no greater than two inches after twenty-four hammer blows.

    Which one of the following can properly be inferred from the passage?

    (A)   The Rialto Bridge was built on unsafe pilings.
    (B)   The standard of refusal was not sufficient to ensure the safety of a bridge.
    (C)   Da Ponte's standard of refusal was less strict than that of other bridge builders of his day.
    (D)   After 1588, no bridges were built on pilings that were driven to the point of refusal.
    (E)   It is possible that the pilings of the Rialto Bridge could have been driven deeper even after the standard of refusal had been met.

3. Joan got A's on all her homework assignments, so if she had gotten an A on her term paper, she could pass the course even without doing the class presentation. Unfortunately, she did not get an A on her term paper, so it is obvious that she will have to do the class presentation to pass the course.

    The argument's reasoning is questionable because the argument

    (A)   ignores the possibility that Joan must either have an A on her term paper or do the class presentation to pass the course
    (B)   presupposes without justification that Joan's not getting an A on her term paper prevents her from passing the course without doing the class presentation
    (C)   overlooks the importance of class presentations to a student's overall course grade
    (D)   ignores the possibility that if Joan has to do the class presentation to pass the course, then she did not get an A on her term paper
    (E)   fails to take into account the possibility that some students get A's on their term papers but do not pass the course

GO ON TO THE NEXT PAGE.

4. Compared to us, people who lived a century ago had very few diversions to amuse them. Therefore, they likely read much more than we do today.

Which one of the following statements, if true, most weakens the argument?

(A) Many of the books published a century ago were of low literary quality.

(B) On average, people who lived a century ago had considerably less leisure time than we do today.

(C) The number of books sold today is larger than it was a century ago.

(D) On the average, books today cost slightly less in relation to other goods than they did a century ago.

(E) One of the popular diversions of a century ago was horse racing.

5. Although consciousness seems to arise from physical processes, physical theories can explain only why physical systems have certain physical structures and how these systems perform various physical functions. Thus, no strictly physical theory can explain consciousness.

The conclusion of the argument follows logically if which one of the following is assumed?

(A) Physical theories can explain only physical phenomena.

(B) An explanation of consciousness must encompass more than an explanation of physical structures and functions.

(C) The physical structures and functions of consciousness are currently unknown.

(D) Consciousness arises from processes that are entirely explainable by physical theories.

(E) An explanation of physical structures and functions must be formulated in strictly physical terms.

6. Advertisement: At most jewelry stores, the person assessing the diamond is the person selling it, so you can see why an assessor might say that a diamond is of higher quality than it really is. But because all diamonds sold at Gem World are certified in writing, you're assured of a fair price when purchasing a diamond from Gem World.

The reasoning in the advertisement would be most strengthened if which one of the following were true?

(A) Many jewelry stores other than Gem World also provide written certification of the quality of their diamonds.

(B) The certifications of diamonds at Gem World are written by people with years of experience in appraising gems.

(C) The diamonds sold at Gem World are generally of higher quality than those sold at other jewelry stores.

(D) The diamond market is so volatile that prices of the most expensive diamonds can change by hundreds of dollars from one day to the next.

(E) The written certifications of diamonds at Gem World are provided by an independent company of gem specialists.

7. Newtonian physics dominated science for over two centuries. It found consistently successful application, becoming one of the most highly substantiated and accepted theories in the history of science. Nevertheless, Einstein's theories came to show the fundamental limits of Newtonian physics and to surpass the Newtonian view in the early 1900s, giving rise once again to a physics that has so far enjoyed wide success.

Which one of the following logically follows from the statements above?

(A) The history of physics is characterized by a pattern of one successful theory subsequently surpassed by another.

(B) Long-standing success or substantiation of a theory of physics is no guarantee that the theory will continue to be dominant indefinitely.

(C) Every theory of physics, no matter how successful, is eventually surpassed by one that is more successful.

(D) Once a theory of physics is accepted, it will remain dominant for centuries.

(E) If a long-accepted theory of physics is surpassed, it must be surpassed by a theory that is equally successful.

GO ON TO THE NEXT PAGE.

8. Conscientiousness is high on most firms' list of traits they want in employees. Yet a recent study found that laid-off conscientious individuals are less likely to find jobs within five months than are their peers who shirked their workplace responsibilities.

Each of the following, if true, helps to resolve the apparent paradox above EXCEPT:

(A) People who shirk their workplace responsibilities are less likely to keep the jobs they have, so there are more of them looking for jobs.

(B) Conscientious people tend to have a greater than average concern with finding the job most suited to their interests and abilities.

(C) Resentment about having been laid off in spite of their conscientiousness leads some people to perform poorly in interviews.

(D) People who are inclined to shirk their workplace responsibilities are more likely to exaggerate their credentials, leading prospective employers to believe them to be highly qualified.

(E) Finding a job is less urgent for the conscientious, because they tend to have larger savings.

9. Psychologist: Although studies of young children have revealed important facts about the influence of the environment on language acquisition, it is clear that one cannot attribute such acquisition solely to environmental influences: innate mechanisms also play a role. So, the most reasonable question that ought to be studied is whether _____.

Which one of the following most logically completes the passage?

(A) language acquisition can ever be fully explained

(B) innate mechanisms are a contributing factor in language learning

(C) language acquisition is solely the product of innate mechanisms

(D) parents and peers are the most important influence on a child's learning of a language

(E) innate mechanisms play a more important role in language acquisition than a child's immediate environment

Questions 10–11

Mark: To convey an understanding of past events, a historian should try to capture what it was like to experience those events. For instance, a foot soldier in the Battle of Waterloo knew through direct experience what the battle was like, and it is this kind of knowledge that the historian must capture.

Carla: But how do you go about choosing whose perspective is the valid one? Is the foot soldier's perspective more valid than that of a general? Should it be a French or an English soldier? Your approach would generate a biased version of history, and to avoid that, historians must stick to general and objective characterizations of the past.

10. Carla does which one of the following in disputing Mark's position?

(A) contests Mark's understanding of historical events

(B) questions Mark's presupposition that one person can understand another's feelings

(C) argues that the selection involved in carrying out Mark's proposal would distort the result

(D) questions whether Mark accurately describes the kind of historical writing he deplores

(E) gives reason to believe that Mark's recommendation is motivated by his professional self-interest

11. Mark's and Carla's positions indicate that they disagree about the truth of which one of the following?

(A) The purpose of writing history is to convey an understanding of past events.

(B) The participants in a battle are capable of having an objective understanding of the ramifications of the events in which they are participating.

(C) Historians can succeed in conveying a sense of the way events in the distant past seemed to someone who lived in a past time.

(D) Historians should aim to convey past events from the perspective of participants in those events.

(E) Historians should use fictional episodes to supplement their accounts of past events if the documented record of those events is incomplete.

GO ON TO THE NEXT PAGE.

12. Rosen: One cannot prepare a good meal from bad food, produce good food from bad soil, maintain good soil without good farming, or have good farming without a culture that places value on the proper maintenance of all its natural resources so that needed supplies are always available.

Which one of the following can be properly inferred from Rosen's statement?

(A)   The creation of good meals depends on both natural and cultural conditions.

(B)   Natural resources cannot be maintained properly without good farming practices.

(C)   Good soil is a prerequisite of good farming.

(D)   Any society with good cultural values will have a good cuisine.

(E)   When food is bad, it is because of poor soil and, ultimately, bad farming practices.

13. Adam: Marking road edges with reflecting posts gives drivers a clear view of the edges, thereby enabling them to drive more safely. Therefore, marking road edges with reflecting posts will decrease the annual number of road accidents.

Aiesha: You seem to forget that drivers exceed the speed limit more frequently and drive close to the road edge more frequently on roads that are marked with reflecting posts than on similar roads without posts, and those are driving behaviors that cause road accidents.

Aiesha responds to Adam's argument by

(A)   questioning Adam's assertion that reflecting posts give drivers a clear view of road edges

(B)   presenting a possible alternative method for decreasing road accidents

(C)   raising a consideration that challenges the argument's assumption that facilitating safe driving will result in safer driving

(D)   denying that the drivers' view of the road is relevant to the number of road accidents

(E)   providing additional evidence to undermine the claim that safer driving does not necessarily reduce the number of road accidents

14. In response to office workers' worries about the health risks associated with using video display terminals (VDTs), researchers asked office workers to estimate both the amount of time they had spent using VDTs and how often they had suffered headaches over the previous year. According to the survey, frequent VDT users suffered from headaches more often than other office workers did, leading researchers to conclude that VDTs cause headaches.

Which one of the following, if true, most undermines the researchers' conclusion?

(A)   Few of the office workers surveyed participated in regular health programs during the year in question.

(B)   In their study the researchers failed to ask the workers to distinguish between severe migraine headaches and mild headaches.

(C)   Previous studies have shown that the glare from VDT screens causes some users to suffer eyestrain.

(D)   Office workers who experienced frequent headaches were more likely than other workers to overestimate how much time they spent using VDTs.

(E)   Office workers who regularly used VDTs experienced the same amount of job-related stress as workers who did not use VDTs.

GO ON TO THE NEXT PAGE.

15. Literary critic: The meaning of a literary work is not fixed but fluid, and therefore a number of equally valid interpretations of it may be offered. Interpretations primarily involve imposing meaning on a literary work rather than discovering meaning in it, so interpretations need not consider the writer's intentions. Thus, any interpretation of a literary work tells more about the critic than about the writer.

Which one of the following is an assumption required by the literary critic's argument?

(A) There are no criteria by which to distinguish the validity of different interpretations of literary works.

(B) A meaning imposed on a literary work reflects facts about the interpreter.

(C) A writer's intentions are relevant to a valid interpretation of the writer's work.

(D) The true intentions of the writer of a work of literature can never be known to a critic of that work.

(E) The deepest understanding of a literary work requires that one know the writer's history.

16. Media consultant: Electronic media are bound to bring an end to the institution of the traditional school in our culture. This is because the emergence of the traditional school, characterized by a group of students gathered with a teacher in a classroom, was facilitated by the availability of relatively inexpensive printed books. Currently, however, the function of books in communicating information is gradually being taken over by electronic media. So, it is inevitable that the traditional school will not survive in our culture.

The reasoning in the consultant's argument is flawed because it

(A) presupposes as a premise what it is trying to establish

(B) relies inappropriately on expert testimony

(C) presupposes that just because something can happen it will happen

(D) mistakes something that enables an institution to arise for something necessary to the institution

(E) confuses the value of an institution with the medium by which it operates

17. A safety report indicates that, on average, traffic fatalities decline by about 7 percent in those areas in which strict laws requiring drivers and passengers to wear seat belts have been passed. In a certain city, seat belt laws have been in effect for two years, but the city's public safety records show that the number of traffic deaths per year has remained the same.

Which one of the following, if true, does NOT help resolve the apparent discrepancy between the safety report and the city's public safety records?

(A) Two years ago speed limits in the city were increased by as much as 15 kph (9 mph).

(B) The city now includes pedestrian fatalities in its yearly total of traffic deaths, whereas two years ago it did not.

(C) In the time since the seat belt laws were passed, the city has experienced a higher than average increase in automobile traffic.

(D) Because the city's seat belt laws have been so rarely enforced, few drivers in the city have complied with them.

(E) In the last two years, most of the people killed in car accidents in the city were not wearing seat belts.

18. Some critics of space exploration programs claim that they are too costly to be justified. Moreover, there is the very real risk of a debilitating explosion—most experts say something like a 1-in-70 chance per flight. Budgetary pressures to make the programs cheaper only serve to undermine safety: one program's managers uncovered a series of manufacturing flaws that critics contend are a direct consequence of the pressure to produce results as quickly and cheaply as possible.

The passage conforms most closely to which one of the following propositions?

(A) Attempts to solve one problem can lead to the exacerbation of another problem.

(B) Safety risks are sometimes ignored in the name of scientific progress.

(C) Safety is often sacrificed in order to reach a goal as quickly as possible.

(D) Bureaucratic mistakes can lead to quality reduction and inefficiency.

(E) Space exploration is too dangerous to be continued.

GO ON TO THE NEXT PAGE.

19. Physician: Hatha yoga is a powerful tool for helping people quit smoking. In a clinical trial, those who practiced hatha yoga for 75 minutes once a week and received individual counseling reduced their smoking and cravings for tobacco as much as did those who went to traditional self-help groups once a week and had individual counseling.

Which one of the following is an assumption on which the physician's argument relies?

(A) The individual counseling received by the smokers in the clinical trial who practiced hatha yoga did not help them quit smoking.

(B) Most smokers are able to practice hatha yoga more than once a week.

(C) Traditional self-help groups are powerful tools for helping people quit smoking.

(D) People who practice hatha yoga for 75 minutes once a week are not damaging themselves physically.

(E) Other forms of yoga are less effective than hatha yoga in helping people quit smoking.

20. Antarctic seals dive to great depths and stay submerged for hours. They do not rely solely on oxygen held in their lungs, but also store extra oxygen in their blood. Indeed, some researchers hypothesize that for long dives these seals also store oxygenated blood in their spleens.

Each of the following, if true, provides some support for the researchers' hypothesis EXCEPT:

(A) Horses are known to store oxygenated blood in their spleens for use during exertion.

(B) Many species of seal can store oxygen directly in their muscle tissue.

(C) The oxygen contained in the seals' lungs and bloodstream alone would be inadequate to support the seals during their dives.

(D) The spleen is much larger in the Antarctic seal than in aquatic mammals that do not make long dives.

(E) The spleens of Antarctic seals contain greater concentrations of blood vessels than are contained in most of their other organs.

21. The studies showing that increased consumption of fruits and vegetables may help decrease the incidence of some types of cancer do not distinguish between organically grown and nonorganically grown produce; they were conducted with produce at least some of which contained pesticide residues. The studies may also be taken as showing, therefore, that there is no increased health risk associated with eating fruits and vegetables containing pesticide residues.

The pattern of flawed reasoning in which one of the following is most similar to the pattern of flawed reasoning in the argument above?

(A) Research shows that the incidence of certain major illnesses, including heart disease and cancer, is decreased in communities that have a modern power plant. The fact that this tendency is present whether the power plant is nuclear or not shows that there is no increased health risk associated with living next to a nuclear power plant.

(B) Research has shown that there is no long-term health risk associated with a diet consisting largely of foods high in saturated fat and cholesterol if such a diet is consumed by someone with a physically active lifestyle. So, exercise is a more useful strategy for achieving cardiological health than is dietary restriction.

(C) Research has shown that young people who drive motorcycles and receive one full year of extensive driving instruction are in fact less likely to become involved in accidents than those who simply pass a driving test and drive cars. This shows that there is not an inherently greater risk associated with driving a motorcycle than with driving a car.

(D) Research has shown that kitchen cutting boards retain significant numbers of microbes even after careful washing, but that after washing fewer microbes are found on wooden boards than on plastic boards. There is, therefore, no greater risk of contracting microbial illnesses associated with using wooden cutting boards than with using plastic cutting boards.

(E) Research shows that there is no greater long-term health benefit associated with taking vitamin supplements than with a moderate increase in the intake of fruits and vegetables. Clearly, then, there is no long-term health risk associated with the failure to take vitamin supplements, so long as enough fruits and vegetables are consumed.

GO ON TO THE NEXT PAGE.

22. Political theorist: Many people believe that the punishment of those who commit even the most heinous crimes should be mitigated to some extent if the crime was motivated by a sincere desire to achieve some larger good. Granted, some criminals with admirable motives deserve mitigated punishments. Nonetheless, judges should never mitigate punishment on the basis of motives, since motives are essentially a matter of conjecture and even vicious motives can easily be presented as altruistic.

Which one of the following principles, if valid, most helps to justify the political theorist's reasoning?

(A) Laws that prohibit or permit actions solely on the basis of psychological states should not be part of a legal system.

(B) It is better to err on the side of overly severe punishment than to err on the side of overly lenient punishment.

(C) The legal permissibility of actions should depend on the perceivable consequences of those actions.

(D) No law that cannot be enforced should be enacted.

(E) A legal system that, if adopted, would have disastrous consequences ought not be adopted.

Questions 23–24

Roxanne: To protect declining elephant herds from poachers seeking to obtain ivory, people concerned about such endangered species should buy no new ivory. The new ivory and old ivory markets are entirely independent, however, so purchasing antique ivory provides no incentive to poachers to obtain more new ivory. Therefore, only antique ivory—that which is at least 75 years old—can be bought in good conscience.

Salvador: Since current demand for antique ivory exceeds the supply, many people who are unconcerned about endangered species but would prefer to buy antique ivory are buying new ivory instead. People sharing your concern about endangered species, therefore, should refrain from buying any ivory at all—thereby ensuring that demand for new ivory will drop.

23. A point on which Roxanne's and Salvador's views differ is whether

(A) there are substances that can serve as satisfactory substitutes for ivory in its current uses

(B) decreased demand for antique ivory would cause a decrease in demand for new ivory

(C) people should take steps to avert a threat to the continued existence of elephant herds

(D) a widespread refusal to buy new ivory will have a substantial effect on the survival of elephants

(E) people concerned about endangered species should refuse to buy ivory objects that are less than 75 years old

24. Which one of the following principles, if established, would most help to justify Salvador's position?

(A) People concerned about endangered species should disseminate knowledge concerning potential threats to those species in order to convince others to protect the species.

(B) People concerned about endangered species should refrain from buying any products whose purchase could result in harm to those species, but only if acceptable substitutes for those products are available.

(C) People concerned about endangered species should refrain from the purchase of all manufactured objects produced from those species, except for those objects already in existence at the time the species became endangered.

(D) People concerned about endangered species should refrain from participating in trade in products produced from those species, but only if workers engaged in that trade also agree to such restraint.

(E) People concerned about endangered species should act in ways that there is reason to believe will help reduce the undesirable results of the actions performed by people who do not share that concern.

GO ON TO THE NEXT PAGE.

25. In a car accident, air bags greatly reduce the risk of serious injury. However, statistics show that cars without air bags are less likely to be involved in accidents than are cars with air bags. Thus, cars with air bags are no safer than cars without air bags.

The argument is most vulnerable to criticism on the grounds that it

(A) assumes, without providing justification, that any car with air bags will probably become involved in an accident

(B) denies the possibility that cars without air bags have other safety features that reduce the risk of serious injury at least as much as do air bags

(C) overlooks the possibility that some accidents involve both cars with air bags and cars without air bags

(D) assumes, without providing justification, that the likelihood of an accident's occurring should weigh at least as heavily as the seriousness of any resulting injury in estimates of relative safety

(E) takes for granted that all accidents would cause air bags to be deployed

26. All known deposits of the mineral tanzanite are in Tanzania. Therefore, because Ashley collects only tanzanite stones, she is unlikely ever to collect a stone not originally from Tanzania.

Which one of the following is most similar in its reasoning to the argument above?

(A) The lagoon on Scrag Island is home to many frogs. Since the owls on Scrag Island eat nothing but frogs from the island, the owls will probably never eat many frogs that live outside the lagoon.

(B) Every frog ever seen on Scrag Island lives in the lagoon. The frogs on the island are eaten only by the owls on the island, and hence the owls may never eat an animal that lives outside the lagoon.

(C) Frogs are the only animals known to live in the lagoon on Scrag Island. The diet of the owls on Scrag Island consists of nothing but frogs from the island. Therefore, the owls are unlikely ever to eat an animal that lives outside the lagoon.

(D) The only frogs yet discovered on Scrag Island live in the lagoon. The diet of all the owls on Scrag Island consists entirely of frogs on the island, so the owls will probably never eat an animal that lives outside the lagoon.

(E) Each frog on Scrag Island lives in the lagoon. No owl on Scrag Island is known to eat anything but frogs on the island. It follows that no owl on Scrag Island will eat anything that lives outside the lagoon.

S T O P

IF YOU FINISH BEFORE TIME IS CALLED, YOU MAY CHECK YOUR WORK ON THIS SECTION ONLY.
DO NOT WORK ON ANY OTHER SECTION IN THE TEST.

SECTION III

Time—35 minutes

24 Questions

Directions: Each group of questions in this section is based on a set of conditions. In answering some of the questions, it may be useful to draw a rough diagram. Choose the response that most accurately and completely answers each question and blacken the corresponding space on your answer sheet.

Questions 1–5

A school has exactly four dormitories that are to be fully occupied—Richards, Tuscarora, Veblen, and Wisteria—each consisting entirely of a North wing and a South wing. The following rules govern assignment of students to dormitory wings:

Each wing is assigned only male students or only female students.
Exactly three wings have males assigned to them.
Richards North and Tuscarora North are assigned females.
If a dormitory has males assigned to one of its wings, then its other wing is assigned females.
If males are assigned to Veblen South, then Wisteria North is assigned males.

1. If females are assigned to Veblen South and Veblen North, then which one of the following could be two other wings that are also assigned females?

   (A) Richards North and Tuscarora South
   (B) Richards South and Wisteria South
   (C) Richards South and Tuscarora North
   (D) Tuscarora North and Wisteria South
   (E) Tuscarora South and Wisteria South

2. It CANNOT be true that females are assigned to both

   (A) Richards South and Wisteria South
   (B) Richards South and Tuscarora South
   (C) Richards South and Veblen North
   (D) Tuscarora South and Wisteria South
   (E) Veblen North and Wisteria South

3. If Wisteria North is assigned females, then females must also be assigned to which one of the following?

   (A) Richards South
   (B) Wisteria South
   (C) Tuscarora South
   (D) Veblen South
   (E) Veblen North

4. If males are assigned to Veblen South, which one of the following is a complete and accurate list of the wings that CANNOT be assigned males?

   (A) Richards North, Tuscarora North
   (B) Richards North, Tuscarora North, Veblen North
   (C) Richards North, Tuscarora North, Wisteria South
   (D) Richards North, Tuscarora North, Veblen North, Wisteria South
   (E) Richards North, Richards South, Tuscarora North, Veblen North, Wisteria South

5. If Tuscarora South is assigned females, then it could be true that females are assigned to both

   (A) Richards South and Wisteria North
   (B) Richards South and Wisteria South
   (C) Veblen North and Wisteria North
   (D) Veblen South and Wisteria South
   (E) Veblen South and Veblen North

GO ON TO THE NEXT PAGE.

Questions 6–11

In a single day, exactly seven trucks—S, T, U, W, X, Y, and Z—are the only arrivals at a warehouse. No truck arrives at the same time as any other truck, and no truck arrives more than once that day. Each truck is either green or red (but not both). The following conditions apply:

No two consecutive arrivals are red.
Y arrives at some time before both T and W.
Exactly two of the trucks that arrive before Y are red.
S is the sixth arrival.
Z arrives at some time before U.

6. Which one of the following could be the order, from first to last, in which the trucks arrive?

   (A)   X, Z, U, Y, W, S, T
   (B)   X, Y, Z, U, W, S, T
   (C)   Z, W, U, T, Y, S, X
   (D)   Z, U, T, Y, W, S, X
   (E)   U, Z, Y, T, S, W, X

7. For which one of the following pairs of trucks is it the case that they CANNOT both be red?

   (A)   S and X
   (B)   T and S
   (C)   U and W
   (D)   W and T
   (E)   X and Z

8. If X is the third arrival, then which one of the following trucks must be green?

   (A)   S
   (B)   T
   (C)   U
   (D)   W
   (E)   Z

9. If exactly three of the trucks are green, then which one of the following trucks must be green?

   (A)   S
   (B)   T
   (C)   U
   (D)   W
   (E)   Z

10. For exactly how many of the seven trucks can one determine exactly how many trucks arrived before it?

    (A)   one
    (B)   two
    (C)   three
    (D)   four
    (E)   five

11. Which one of the following pairs of trucks CANNOT arrive consecutively at the warehouse?

    (A)   U and Y
    (B)   X and Y
    (C)   Y and T
    (D)   Y and W
    (E)   Y and Z

GO ON TO THE NEXT PAGE.

Questions 12–18

A total of six books occupies three small shelves—one on the first shelf, two on the second shelf, and three on the third shelf. Two of the books are grammars—one of Farsi, the other of Hausa. Two others are linguistics monographs—one on phonology, the other on semantics. The remaining two books are novels—one by Vonnegut, the other by Woolf. The books' arrangement is consistent with the following:

    There is at least one novel on the same shelf as the Farsi grammar.

    The monographs are not both on the same shelf.

    The Vonnegut novel is not on the same shelf as either monograph.

12. Which one of the following could be an accurate matching of the bookshelves to the books on each of them?

    (A)   first shelf: Hausa grammar
           second shelf: semantics monograph, Vonnegut novel
           third shelf: Farsi grammar, phonology monograph, Woolf novel

    (B)   first shelf: semantics monograph
           second shelf: Farsi grammar, Vonnegut novel
           third shelf: Hausa grammar, phonology monograph, Woolf novel

    (C)   first shelf: Vonnegut novel
           second shelf: phonology monograph, Farsi grammar
           third shelf: Hausa grammar, semantics monograph, Woolf novel

    (D)   first shelf: Woolf novel
           second shelf: phonology and semantics monographs
           third shelf: Farsi and Hausa grammars, Vonnegut novel

    (E)   first shelf: Woolf novel
           second shelf: Farsi grammar, Vonnegut novel
           third shelf: Hausa grammar, phonology and semantics monographs

13. Which one of the following CANNOT be true?

    (A)   A grammar is on the first shelf.
    (B)   A linguistics monograph is on the same shelf as the Hausa grammar.
    (C)   A novel is on the first shelf.
    (D)   The novels are on the same shelf as each other.
    (E)   Neither linguistics monograph is on the first shelf.

14. Which one of the following must be true?

    (A)   A linguistics monograph and a grammar are on the second shelf.
    (B)   A novel and a grammar are on the second shelf.
    (C)   At least one linguistics monograph and at least one grammar are on the third shelf.
    (D)   At least one novel and at least one grammar are on the third shelf.
    (E)   At least one novel and at least one linguistics monograph are on the third shelf.

15. If both grammars are on the same shelf, which one of the following could be true?

    (A)   The phonology monograph is on the third shelf.
    (B)   A novel is on the first shelf.
    (C)   Both novels are on the second shelf.
    (D)   The Farsi grammar is on the second shelf.
    (E)   The phonology monograph is on the first shelf.

16. Which one of the following must be true?

    (A)   A linguistics monograph is on the first shelf.
    (B)   No more than one novel is on each shelf.
    (C)   The Farsi grammar is not on the same shelf as the Hausa grammar.
    (D)   The semantics monograph is not on the same shelf as the Woolf novel.
    (E)   The Woolf novel is not on the first shelf.

17. If the Farsi grammar is not on the third shelf, which one of the following could be true?

    (A)   The phonology monograph is on the second shelf.
    (B)   The Hausa grammar is on the second shelf.
    (C)   The semantics monograph is on the third shelf.
    (D)   The Vonnegut novel is on the third shelf.
    (E)   The Woolf novel is on the second shelf.

18. If the Hausa grammar and the phonology monograph are on the same shelf, which one of the following must be true?

    (A)   The phonology monograph is on the third shelf.
    (B)   The Vonnegut novel is on the second shelf.
    (C)   The semantics monograph is on the second shelf.
    (D)   The semantics monograph is on the first shelf.
    (E)   The Woolf novel is on the third shelf.

GO ON TO THE NEXT PAGE.

Questions 19–24

A swim team with exactly five members—Jacobson, Kruger, Lu, Miller, Ortiz—swims a ten-lap relay race. Each team member swims exactly two of the laps: one swims laps 1 and 6, one swims laps 2 and 7, one swims laps 3 and 8, one swims laps 4 and 9, and one swims laps 5 and 10. The following conditions apply:

    Neither of Kruger's laps is immediately before either of Lu's.

    Jacobson does not swim lap 9.

    Ortiz's first lap is after (but not necessarily immediately after) Miller's.

    At least one of Jacobson's laps is immediately after one of Ortiz's laps.

19. Which one of the following could be an accurate list of the swimmers of the first five laps, in order from lap 1 through lap 5 ?

    (A)   Jacobson, Kruger, Miller, Lu, Ortiz
    (B)   Kruger, Miller, Ortiz, Jacobson, Lu
    (C)   Lu, Miller, Jacobson, Kruger, Ortiz
    (D)   Ortiz, Kruger, Miller, Lu, Jacobson
    (E)   Miller, Ortiz, Jacobson, Kruger, Lu

20. If Jacobson swims lap 8, then for exactly how many of the ten laps can one determine which team member swims the lap?

    (A)   ten
    (B)   eight
    (C)   six
    (D)   four
    (E)   two

21. If Ortiz swims lap 4, then which one of the following could be true?

    (A)   Jacobson swims lap 1.
    (B)   Jacobson swims lap 3.
    (C)   Kruger swims lap 5.
    (D)   Lu swims lap 3.
    (E)   Miller swims lap 5.

22. Which one of the following could be true?

    (A)   Jacobson swims lap 4.
    (B)   Kruger swims lap 5.
    (C)   Lu swims lap 5.
    (D)   Miller swims lap 10.
    (E)   Ortiz swims lap 6.

23. Jacobson CANNOT swim which one of the following laps?

    (A)   lap 1
    (B)   lap 2
    (C)   lap 3
    (D)   lap 6
    (E)   lap 10

24. Which one of the following could be an accurate list of the swimmers of the last five laps, in order from lap 6 through lap 10 ?

    (A)   Jacobson, Miller, Kruger, Ortiz, Lu
    (B)   Kruger, Lu, Miller, Ortiz, Jacobson
    (C)   Lu, Kruger, Miller, Ortiz, Jacobson
    (D)   Miller, Kruger, Ortiz, Jacobson, Lu
    (E)   Ortiz, Jacobson, Kruger, Miller, Lu

S T O P

IF YOU FINISH BEFORE TIME IS CALLED, YOU MAY CHECK YOUR WORK ON THIS SECTION ONLY.
DO NOT WORK ON ANY OTHER SECTION IN THE TEST.

SECTION IV
Time—35 minutes

25 Questions

<u>Directions:</u> The questions in this section are based on the reasoning contained in brief statements or passages. For some questions, more than one of the choices could conceivably answer the question. However, you are to choose the <u>best</u> answer; that is, the response that most accurately and completely answers the question. You should not make assumptions that are by commonsense standards implausible, superfluous, or incompatible with the passage. After you have chosen the best answer, blacken the corresponding space on your answer sheet.

1. Criminals often have an unusual self-image. Embezzlers often think of their actions as "only borrowing money." Many people convicted of violent crimes rationalize their actions by some sort of denial; either the victim "deserved it" and so the action was justified, or "it simply wasn't my fault." Thus, in many cases, by criminals' characterization of their situations, _____.

    Which one of the following most logically completes the passage?

    (A) they ought to be rewarded for their actions
    (B) they are perceived to be the victim of some other criminal
    (C) their actions are not truly criminal
    (D) the criminal justice system is inherently unfair
    (E) they deserve only a light sentence for their crimes

2. The vomeronasal organ (VNO) is found inside the noses of various animals. While its structural development and function are clearer in other animals, most humans have a VNO that is detectable, though only microscopically. When researchers have been able to stimulate VNO cells in humans, the subjects have reported experiencing subtle smell sensations. It seems, then, that the VNO, though not completely understood, is a functioning sensory organ in most humans.

    Which one of the following, if true, most weakens the argument?

    (A) It is not known whether the researchers succeeded in stimulating only VNO cells in the human subjects' noses.
    (B) Relative to its occurrence in certain other animals, the human VNO appears to be anatomically rudimentary and underdeveloped.
    (C) Certain chemicals that play a leading role in the way the VNO functions in animals in which it is highly developed do not appear to play a role in its functioning in humans.
    (D) Secondary anatomical structures associated with the VNO in other animals seem to be absent in humans.
    (E) For many animal species, the VNO is thought to subtly enhance the sense of smell.

3. An instructor presented two paintings to a class. She said that the first had hung in prestigious museums but the second was produced by an unknown amateur. Each student was asked which painting was better. Everyone selected the first. The instructor later presented the same two paintings in the same order to a different class. This time she said that the first was produced by an unknown amateur but the second had hung in prestigious museums. In this class, everyone said that the second painting was better.

    The statements above, if true, most strongly support which one of the following?

    (A) Most of the students would not like any work of art that they believed to have been produced by an unknown amateur.
    (B) None of the claims that the instructor made about the paintings was true.
    (C) Each of the students would like most of the paintings hanging in any prestigious museum.
    (D) In judging the paintings, some of the students were affected by what they had been told about the history of the paintings.
    (E) Had the instructor presented the paintings without telling the students anything about them, almost all of the students would have judged them to be roughly equal in artistic worth.

GO ON TO THE NEXT PAGE.

4. An overwhelming number of industry's chief executive officers who earn over $250,000 annually attended prestigious business schools. Therefore Greta Harris, who attended a prestigious business school, must be a chief executive officer who earns over $250,000 annually.

Which one of the following exhibits flawed reasoning most nearly parallel to that exhibited in the argument above?

(A) Many opera singers are high-strung. Consequently it must be true that Fred, a high-strung opera singer, will develop the health problems associated with being high-strung.

(B) The most famous opera singers practiced constantly in order to improve their voices. Therefore Franz will be more famous than will his rival Otto, who rarely practices.

(C) Many of the most popular opera singers are Italian. Thus it must be true that opera is greatly enjoyed by many Italians.

(D) Quite a few opera singers carry a bent nail onstage for good luck. Therefore George, an opera singer, must owe his good luck to the bent nail that he always carries.

(E) A great many successful opera singers studied more than one language. Hence Eileen must be a successful opera singer, since she studied more than one language.

5. After 1950, in response to record growth in worldwide food demand, farmers worldwide sharply increased fertilizer use. As a result, the productivity of farmland more than doubled by 1985. Since 1985, farmers have sought to increase farmland productivity even further. Nevertheless, worldwide fertilizer use has declined by 6 percent between 1985 and the present.

Which one of the following, if true, most helps to resolve the apparent discrepancy in the information above?

(A) Since 1985 the rate at which the world's population has increased has exceeded the rate at which new arable land has been created through irrigation and other methods.

(B) Several varieties of crop plants that have become popular recently, such as soybeans, are as responsive to fertilizer as are traditional grain crops.

(C) Between 1950 and 1985 farmers were able to increase the yield of many varieties of crop plants.

(D) After fertilizer has been added to soil for several years, adding fertilizer to the soil in subsequent years does not significantly improve crop production.

(E) Between 1975 and 1980 fertilizer prices temporarily increased because of labor disputes in several fertilizer-exporting nations, and these disputes disrupted worldwide fertilizer production.

6. In a study, infant monkeys given a choice between two surrogate mothers—a bare wire structure equipped with a milk bottle, or a soft, suede-covered wire structure equipped with a milk bottle—unhesitatingly chose the latter. When given a choice between a bare wire structure equipped with a milk bottle and a soft, suede-covered wire structure lacking a milk bottle, they unhesitatingly chose the former.

Which one of the following is most supported by the information above?

(A) Infant monkeys' desire for warmth and comfort is nearly as strong as their desire for food.

(B) For infant monkeys, suede is a less convincing substitute for their mother's touch than animal fur would be.

(C) For infant monkeys, a milk bottle is a less convincing substitute for their mother's teat than suede is for their mother's touch.

(D) For infant monkeys, a milk bottle is an equally convincing substitute for their mother's teat as suede is for their mother's touch.

(E) Infant monkeys' desire for food is stronger than their desire for warmth and comfort.

7. Hazel: Faster and more accurate order processing would help our business. To increase profits, we should process orders electronically rather than manually, because customers' orders will then go directly to all relevant parties.

Max: We would lose money if we started processing orders electronically. Most people prefer to interact with human beings when placing orders. If we switch to electronic order processing, our business will appear cold and inhuman, and we will attract fewer customers.

Hazel and Max disagree over whether

(A) electronic order processing is faster and more accurate than is manual order processing

(B) faster and more accurate order processing would be financially beneficial to their business

(C) switching to electronic order processing would be financially beneficial to their business

(D) their business has an obligation to be as profitable as possible

(E) electronic order processing would appear cold and inhuman to most of their customers

GO ON TO THE NEXT PAGE.

8. Commentator: In the new century, only nations with all the latest electronic technology will experience great economic prosperity. The people in these nations will be constantly bombarded with images of how people in other countries live. This will increase their tendency to question their own customs and traditions, leading to a dissolution of those customs and traditions. Hence, in the new century, the stability of a nation's cultural identity will likely _____.

Which one of the following most logically completes the commentator's argument?

(A) depend on a just distribution of electronic technology among all nations

(B) decrease if that nation comes to have a high level of economic wealth

(C) be ensured by laws that protect the customs and traditions of that culture

(D) be threatened only if the people of that culture fail to acquire the latest technical skills

(E) be best maintained by ensuring gradual assimilation of new technical knowledge and skills

9. Cultural historian: Universal acceptance of scientific theories that regard human beings only as natural objects subject to natural forces outside the individual's control will inevitably lead to a general decline in morality. After all, if people do not believe that they are responsible for their actions, they will feel unashamed when they act immorally, and a widespread failure of individuals to feel ashamed of their immoral actions is bound to lead to a general moral decline.

The conclusion drawn by the cultural historian follows logically if which one of the following is assumed?

(A) Science does not enable human beings to control natural forces.

(B) Human beings who regard themselves only as natural objects will as a result lose their sense of responsibility for their actions.

(C) People who have a sense of shame for their moral transgressions will feel responsible for their actions.

(D) Some scientific theories hold that human beings are not responsible for their actions.

(E) Scientific explanations that regard human beings as in some respects independent of the laws of nature will not lead to a general decline in morality.

GO ON TO THE NEXT PAGE.

Questions 10–11

Lydia: Red squirrels are known to make holes in the bark of sugar maple trees and to consume the trees' sap. Since sugar maple sap is essentially water with a small concentration of sugar, the squirrels almost certainly are after either water or sugar. Water is easily available from other sources in places where maple trees grow, so the squirrels would not go to the trouble of chewing holes in trees just to get water. Therefore, they are probably after the sugar.

Galina: It must be something other than sugar, because the concentration of sugar in the maple sap is so low that a squirrel would need to drink an enormous amount of sap to get any significant amount of sugar.

10. Lydia's argument proceeds by

(A) dismissing potentially disconfirming data

(B) citing a general rule of which the conclusion is a specific instance

(C) presenting an observed action as part of a larger pattern of behavior

(D) drawing an analogy between well-understood phenomena and an unexplained phenomenon

(E) rejecting a possible alternative explanation for an observed phenomenon

11. Which one of the following, if true, most undermines the force of Galina's attempted rebuttal of Lydia's argument?

(A) Squirrels are known to like foods that have a high concentration of sugar.

(B) Once a hole in a sugar maple trunk has provided one red squirrel with sap, other red squirrels will make additional holes in its trunk.

(C) Trees other than sugar maples, whose sap contains a lower concentration of sugar than does sugar maple sap, are less frequently tapped by red squirrels.

(D) Red squirrels leave the sugar maple sap that slowly oozes out of the holes in the tree's trunk until much of the water in the sap has evaporated.

(E) During the season when sap can be obtained from sugar maple trees, the weather often becomes cold enough to prevent sap from oozing out of the trees.

12. Pundit: People complain about how ineffectual their legislative representatives are, but this apparent ineffectuality is simply the manifestation of compromises these representatives must make when they do what they were elected to do: compete for the government's scarce funds. So, when people express dissatisfaction with their legislative representatives, we can be assured that these representatives are simply doing what they were elected to do.

The pundit's argument is flawed because it takes for granted that

(A) the apparent ineffectuality of legislative representatives is the only source of popular dissatisfaction with those representatives

(B) governmental resources that are currently scarce cannot become more abundant except by the actions of politicians

(C) constituents would continue to be dissatisfied with the effectuality of their legislative representatives if constituents were aware of the cause of this apparent ineffectuality

(D) legislative compromise inevitably results in popular dissatisfaction with politicians

(E) only elected public servants tend to elicit dissatisfaction among the public

13. When several of a dermatologist's patients complained of a rash on just one side of their faces, the dermatologist suspected that the cause was some kind of external contact. In each case it turned out that the rash occurred on the side of the face to which the telephone was held. The dermatologist concluded that the rash was caused by prolonged contact with telephones.

Each of the following, if true, provides additional support for the dermatologist's diagnosis EXCEPT:

(A) Many telephones are now manufactured using a kind of plastic to which some people are mildly allergic.

(B) Contact between other devices and the patients' faces occurred equally on both sides of their faces.

(C) Most of the patients had occupations that required them to use their telephones extensively.

(D) Telephones are used by most people in the industrialized world.

(E) The complaints occurred after an increase in the patients' use of the telephone.

GO ON TO THE NEXT PAGE.

14. The fact that politicians in a certain country are trying to reduce government spending does not by itself explain why they have voted to eliminate all government-supported scholarship programs. Government spending could have been reduced even more if instead they had cut back on military spending.

Which one of the following arguments is most similar in its reasoning to the argument above?

(A) The fact that Phyllis does not make much money at her new job does not by itself explain why she refuses to buy expensive clothing. Phyllis has always bought only inexpensive clothing even though she used to make a lot of money.

(B) The fact that Brooks has a part-time job does not by itself explain why he is doing poorly in school. Many students with part-time jobs are able to set aside enough time for study and thus maintain high grades.

(C) The fact that Sallie and Jim have different work styles does not by itself explain why they could not work together. Sallie and Jim could have resolved their differences if they had communicated more with one another when they began to work together.

(D) The fact that Roger wanted more companionship does not by itself explain why he adopted ten cats last year. He would not have adopted them all if anyone else had been willing to adopt some of them.

(E) The fact that Thelma's goal is to become famous does not by itself explain why she took up theatrical acting. It is easier to become famous through writing or directing plays than through theatrical acting.

15. Editorial: The threat of harsh punishment for a transgression usually decreases one's tendency to feel guilt or shame for committing that transgression, and the tendency to feel guilt or shame for committing a transgression reduces a person's tendency to commit transgressions. Thus, increasing the severity of the legal penalties for transgressions may amplify people's tendency to ignore the welfare of others.

Which one of the following is an assumption required by the editorial's argument?

(A) Legal penalties do not determine the morality of an action.

(B) At least some actions that involve ignoring the welfare of others are transgressions.

(C) People who are concerned about threats to their own well-being tend to be less concerned about the welfare of others.

(D) The threat of harsh punishment deters people from committing transgressions only if this threat is at least sometimes carried out.

(E) Everyone has at least some tendency to feel guilt or shame for committing extremely severe transgressions.

16. In determining the authenticity of a painting, connoisseurs claim to be guided by the emotional impact the work has on them. For example, if a painting purportedly by Rembrandt is expressive and emotionally moving in a certain way, then this is supposedly evidence that the work was created by Rembrandt himself, and not by one of his students. But the degree to which an artwork has an emotional impact differs wildly from person to person. So a connoisseur's assessment cannot be given credence.

The reasoning in the argument is most vulnerable to criticism on the grounds that the argument

(A) ignores the fact that anybody, not just a connoisseur, can give an assessment of the emotional impact of a painting

(B) is based on the consideration of the nature of just one painter's works, even though the conclusion is about paintings in general

(C) neglects the possibility that there may be widespread agreement among connoisseurs about emotional impact even when the public's assessment varies wildly

(D) presumes, without giving justification, that a painting's emotional impact is irrelevant to the determination of that painting's authenticity

(E) presumes, without offering evidence, that Rembrandt was better at conveying emotions in painting than were other painters

17. A year ago the government reduced the highway speed limit, and in the year since, there have been significantly fewer highway fatalities than there were in the previous year. Therefore, speed limit reduction can reduce traffic fatalities.

The argument is most vulnerable to the criticism that it takes for granted that

(A) highway traffic has not increased over the past year

(B) the majority of drivers obeyed the new speed limit

(C) there is a relation between driving speed and the number of automobile accidents

(D) the new speed limit was more strictly enforced than the old

(E) the number of traffic fatalities the year before the new speed limit was introduced was not abnormally high

GO ON TO THE NEXT PAGE.

18. A plausible explanation of the disappearance of the dinosaurs is what is known as the comet theory. A large enough comet colliding with Earth could have caused a cloud of dust that enshrouded the planet and cooled the climate long enough to result in the dinosaurs' demise.

Which one of the following statements, if true, most seriously weakens the argument?

(A) One of the various schools of paleontology adheres to an explanation for the disappearance of the dinosaurs that is significantly different from the comet theory.

(B) Various species of animals from the same era as the dinosaurs and similar to them in physiology and habitat did not become extinct when the dinosaurs did.

(C) It cannot be determined from a study of dinosaur skeletons whether the animals died from the effects of a dust cloud.

(D) Many other animal species from the era of the dinosaurs did not become extinct at the same time the dinosaurs did.

(E) The consequences for vegetation and animals of a comet colliding with Earth are not fully understood.

19. Large-scale government projects designed to benefit everyone—such as roads, schools, and bridges—usually benefit some small segments of society, initially at least, more than others. The more equally and widely political power is distributed among the citizenry, the less likely such projects are to receive funding. Hence, government by referendum rather than by means of elected representatives tends to diminish, not enhance, the welfare of a society.

Which one of the following is an assumption on which the argument depends?

(A) Large-scale government projects sometimes enhance the welfare of society.

(B) Large-scale projects are more likely to fulfill their intended purposes if they are not executed by the government.

(C) Government by referendum actually undermines the democratic process.

(D) The primary purpose of an equal distribution of political power is to enhance the welfare of society.

(E) Government by referendum is the only way to distribute political power equally and widely.

20. The desire for praise is the desire to obtain, as a sign that one is good, the favorable opinions of others. But because people merit praise only for those actions motivated by a desire to help others, it follows that one who aids others primarily out of a desire for praise does not deserve praise for that aid.

Which one of the following, if assumed, enables the conclusion of the argument to be properly drawn?

(A) An action that is motivated by a desire for the favorable opinion of others cannot also be motivated by a desire to help others.

(B) No action is worthy of praise if it is motivated solely by a desire for praise.

(C) People who are indifferent to the welfare of others do not deserve praise.

(D) One deserves praise for advancing one's own interests only if one also advances the interests of others.

(E) It is the motives rather than the consequences of one's actions that determine whether one deserves praise for them.

GO ON TO THE NEXT PAGE.

21. Political theorist: Newly enacted laws need a period of immunity during which they can be repealed only if circumstances are dire. This is because the short-term consequences of any statutory change are likely to be painful, since people are not accustomed to it, while its long-term benefits are initially obscure, because people require time to learn how to take advantage of it.

Which one of the following principles, if valid, most helps to justify the political theorist's argument?

(A)   Whether a law should be retained is independent of what the voters think its consequences will be.

(B)   Whether a law should be retained depends primarily on the long-term consequences of its enactment.

(C)   The repeal of a law should be at least as difficult as the passage of a law.

(D)   The short-term consequences of a law's repeal should be considered more carefully than the short-term consequences of its passage.

(E)   The long-term consequences of the enactment of a law should be more beneficial than its short-term consequences.

22. The druid stones discovered in Ireland are very, very old. But this particular druid stone was discovered in Scotland; hence, it must be of more recent vintage.

The argument is flawed because it

(A)   allows a key term to shift in meaning from one use to the next

(B)   takes the fact that most members of a group have a certain property to constitute evidence that all members of the group have that property

(C)   takes for granted the very claim that it sets out to establish

(D)   presumes without justification that what was true of the members of a group in the past will continue to be true of them in the future

(E)   takes the fact that all members of a group have a certain property to constitute evidence that the members of the group are the only things with that property

GO ON TO THE NEXT PAGE.

Questions 23–24

Robert: Speed limits on residential streets in Crownsbury are routinely ignored by drivers. People crossing those streets are endangered by speeding drivers, yet the city does not have enough police officers to patrol every street. So the city should install speed bumps and signs warning of their presence on residential streets to slow down traffic.

Sheila: That is a bad idea. People who are driving too fast can easily lose control of their vehicles when they hit a speed bump.

23. Sheila's response depends on the presupposition that

(A) problems of the kind that Robert describes are worse in Crownsbury than they are in other cities

(B) Robert's proposal is intended to address a problem that Robert does not in fact intend it to address

(C) with speed bumps and warning signs in place, there would still be drivers who would not slow down to a safe speed

(D) most of the people who are affected by the problem Robert describes would be harmed by the installation of speed bumps and warning signs

(E) problems of the kind that Robert describes do not occur on any nonresidential streets in Crownsbury

24. The relationship of Sheila's statement to Robert's argument is that Sheila's statement

(A) raises the objection that the problem with which Robert is concerned may not be as serious as he takes it to be

(B) argues that the solution Robert advocates is likely to have undesirable side effects of its own

(C) defends an alternative course of action as more desirable than the one advocated by Robert

(D) concedes that the solution advocated by Robert would be effective, but insists that the reasons for this are not those given by Robert

(E) charges that Robert's proposal would have no net effect on the problem he describes

25. In ancient Mesopotamia, prior to 2900 B.C., wheat was cultivated in considerable quantities, but after 2900 B.C. production of that grain began to decline as the production of barley increased sharply. Some historians who study ancient Mesopotamia contend that the decline in wheat production was due to excessive irrigation, lack of drainage, and the consequent accumulation of salt residues in the soil.

Which one of the following, if true, most helps to support the historians' contention concerning the reasons for the decline in wheat production in ancient Mesopotamia?

(A) The cultivation of barley requires considerably less water than does the cultivation of wheat.

(B) Barley has much greater resistance to the presence of salt in soil than does wheat.

(C) Prior to 2900 B.C., barley was cultivated along with wheat, but the amount of barley produced was far less than the amount of wheat produced.

(D) Around 2900 B.C., a series of wheat blights occurred, destroying much of the wheat crop year after year.

(E) Literary and archaeological evidence indicates that in the period following 2900 B.C., barley became the principal grain in the diet of most of the inhabitants of Mesopotamia.

S T O P

IF YOU FINISH BEFORE TIME IS CALLED, YOU MAY CHECK YOUR WORK ON THIS SECTION ONLY.
DO NOT WORK ON ANY OTHER SECTION IN THE TEST.

SIGNATURE _____ / /
DATE

LSAT WRITING SAMPLE TOPIC

The publisher of a popular how-to book on a computer graphics software product is deciding between two courses of action. The first is to order a new printing of the current edition of the book, which would otherwise probably be out of stock within three months. The second is to forgo a new printing and risk running out of copies until a revised edition of the book is ready for publication, at which point there will be no need to print more copies of the current edition. Write an argument supporting one of these courses of action over the other, using the following considerations to guide your decision:

- The publisher always tries to avoid printing more copies of a book than it can sell.
- The publisher wants to have a ready supply of some edition of the book so that customers do not instead purchase a competing publisher's book.

The particular software product that the book covers is soon to be updated, which will render the current edition of the book out of date. The revised edition of the book, which will cover only the new version of the software, can be in print within six weeks after work on the revision is begun. The company that produces the software has a history of releasing a new version every twelve months, and if the company keeps to this schedule the new version will be released within three months.

In order for a new printing of the current edition of the book to be cost-effective, the publisher must sell copies of the book at its current rate or better for at least six months. The current version of the book has been selling well and demand for the book has remained fairly steady. A source within the software company has hinted to the publisher that release of the next version of the software is likely to be delayed several months. In the past when a new version of the software was released, the majority of its users did not upgrade to the new version for months.

Directions:

1. Use the Answer Key on the next page to check your answers.

2. Use the Scoring Worksheet below to compute your raw score.

3. Use the Score Conversion Chart to convert your raw score into the 120-180 scale.

Scoring Worksheet

1. Enter the number of questions you answered correctly in each section.

	Number Correct
SECTION I	_____
SECTION II	_____
SECTION III	_____
SECTION IV	_____

2. Enter the sum here: _____

   This is your Raw Score.

Conversion Chart

For Converting Raw Score to the 120-180 LSAT Scaled Score
LSAT Form 3LSS56

Reported Score	Raw Score Lowest	Raw Score Highest
180	100	101
179	99	99
178	98	98
177	97	97
176	—*	—*
175	96	96
174	95	95
173	94	94
172	93	93
171	92	92
170	91	91
169	89	90
168	88	88
167	87	87
166	85	86
165	84	84
164	82	83
163	81	81
162	79	80
161	77	78
160	76	76
159	74	75
158	72	73
157	70	71
156	68	69
155	67	67
154	65	66
153	63	64
152	61	62
151	59	60
150	57	58
149	56	56
148	54	55
147	52	53
146	50	51
145	48	49
144	47	47
143	45	46
142	43	44
141	41	42
140	40	40
139	38	39
138	36	37
137	35	35
136	33	34
135	32	32
134	30	31
133	29	29
132	28	28
131	27	27
130	25	26
129	24	24
128	23	23
127	22	22
126	21	21
125	—*	—*
124	20	20
123	19	19
122	—*	—*
121	18	18
120	0	17

*There is no raw score that will produce this scaled score for this form.

SECTION I

1.	E	8.	B	15.	A	22.	A
2.	D	9.	D	16.	E	23.	C
3.	A	10.	A	17.	E	24.	B
4.	C	11.	A	18.	C	25.	D
5.	A	12.	C	19.	C	26.	C
6.	C	13.	A	20.	D		
7.	D	14.	A	21.	B		

SECTION II

1.	C	8.	A	15.	B	22.	B
2.	E	9.	E	16.	D	23.	B
3.	B	10.	C	17.	E	24.	E
4.	B	11.	D	18.	A	25.	D
5.	B	12.	A	19.	C	26.	D
6.	E	13.	C	20.	B		
7.	B	14.	D	21.	A		

SECTION III

1.	D	8.	C	15.	E	22.	B
2.	B	9.	A	16.	E	23.	B
3.	D	10.	B	17.	C	24.	C
4.	D	11.	E	18.	E		
5.	D	12.	B	19.	A		
6.	A	13.	A	20.	A		
7.	B	14.	D	21.	D		

SECTION IV

1.	C	8.	B	15.	B	22.	E
2.	A	9.	B	16.	C	23.	C
3.	D	10.	E	17.	E	24.	B
4.	E	11.	D	18.	B	25.	B
5.	D	12.	A	19.	A		
6.	E	13.	D	20.	A		
7.	C	14.	E	21.	B		

The Official LSAT PrepTest

38

- October 2002
  PrepTest 38

- Form 2LSS53

SECTION I

Time—35 minutes

24 Questions

Directions: The questions in this section are based on the reasoning contained in brief statements or passages. For some questions, more than one of the choices could conceivably answer the question. However, you are to choose the best answer; that is, the response that most accurately and completely answers the question. You should not make assumptions that are by commonsense standards implausible, superfluous, or incompatible with the passage. After you have chosen the best answer, blacken the corresponding space on your answer sheet.

1. Physician: In itself, exercise does not cause heart attacks; rather, a sudden increase in an exercise regimen can be a cause. When people of any physical condition suddenly increase their amount of exercise, they also increase their risk of heart attack. As a result, there will be an increased risk of heart attack among employees of this company due to the new health program.

The conclusion drawn by the physician follows logically if which one of the following is assumed?

(A)   Employees will abruptly increase their amount of exercise as a result of the new health program.

(B)   The exercises involved in the new health program are more strenuous than those in the previous health program.

(C)   The new health program will force employees of all levels of health to exercise regularly.

(D)   The new health program constitutes a sudden change in the company's policy.

(E)   All employees, no matter what their physical condition, will participate in the new health program.

2. Last month OCF, Inc., announced what it described as a unique new product: an adjustable computer workstation. Three days later ErgoTech unveiled an almost identical product. The two companies claim that the similarities are coincidental and occurred because the designers independently reached the same solution to the same problem. The similarities are too fundamental to be mere coincidence, however. The two products not only look alike, but they also work alike. Both are oddly shaped with identically placed control panels with the same types of controls. Both allow the same types of adjustments and the same types of optional enhancements.

The main point of the argument is that

(A)   the two products have many characteristics in common

(B)   ErgoTech must have copied the design of its new product from OCF's design

(C)   the similarities between the two products are not coincidental

(D)   product designers sometimes reach the same solution to a given problem without consulting each other

(E)   new products that at first appear to be unique are sometimes simply variations of other products

Questions 3–4

An anthropologist hypothesized that a certain medicinal powder contained a significant amount of the deadly toxin T. When the test she performed for the presence of toxin T was negative, the anthropologist did not report the results. A chemist who nevertheless learned about the test results charged the anthropologist with fraud. The anthropologist, however, countered that those results were invalid because the powder had inadvertently been tested in an acidic solution.

3. In the absence of the anthropologist's reply, which one of the following principles, if established, would most support the chemist's charge?

(A)   Reporting results for an experiment that was not conducted and reporting a false result for an actual experiment are both instances of scientific fraud.

(B)   Scientists can commit fraud and yet report some disconfirmations of their hypotheses.

(C)   Scientists can neglect to report some disconfirmations of their hypotheses and yet be innocent of fraud.

(D)   Scientists commit fraud whenever they report as valid any test result they know to be invalid.

(E)   Scientists who neglect to report any experiment that could be interpreted as disconfirming their hypotheses have thereby committed fraud.

4. Which one of the following, if true, most strengthens the anthropologist's counterargument?

(A)   The anthropologist had evidence from field work that the medicinal powder was typically prepared using toxin T.

(B)   The activity level of toxin T tends to decline if the powder is stored for a long time.

(C)   When it is put into an acidic solution, toxin T becomes undetectable.

(D)   A fresh batch of powder for a repeat analysis was available at the time of the test.

(E)   The type of analysis used was insensitive to very small amounts of toxin T.

GO ON TO THE NEXT PAGE.

5. Naima: The proposed new computer system, once we fully implemented it, would operate more smoothly and efficiently than the current system. So we should devote the resources necessary to accomplish the conversion as soon as possible.

   Nakai: We should keep the current system for as long as we can. The cost in time and money of converting to the new system would be greater than any predicted benefits.

   Naima and Nakai disagree with each other over whether

   (A)   the predicted benefits of the new computer system will be realized
   (B)   it is essential to have the best computer system available
   (C)   accomplishing the conversion is technically impossible
   (D)   the current computer system does not work well enough to do what it is supposed to do
   (E)   the conversion to a new computer system should be delayed

6. Every year, new reports appear concerning the health risks posed by certain substances, such as coffee and sugar. One year an article claimed that coffee is dangerous to one's health. The next year, another article argued that coffee has some benefits for one's health. From these contradictory opinions, we see that experts are useless for guiding one's decisions about one's health.

   Which one of the following most accurately describes a flaw in the argument above?

   (A)   The argument takes for granted that coffee is dangerous to one's health.
   (B)   The argument presumes, without providing warrant, that one always wants expert guidance in making decisions about one's health.
   (C)   The argument fails to consider the nature of expert opinion in areas other than health.
   (D)   The argument presumes, without providing justification, that because expert opinion is trustworthy in one case, it must therefore be trustworthy in all cases.
   (E)   The argument fails to consider that coffee may be harmful to one's health in some respects and beneficial in others.

7. Because people are generally better at detecting mistakes in others' work than in their own, a prudent principle is that one should always have one's own work checked by someone else.

   Which one of the following provides the best illustration of the principle above?

   (A)   The best elementary school math teachers are not those for whom math was always easy. Teachers who had to struggle through math themselves are better able to explain math to students.
   (B)   One must make a special effort to clearly explain one's views to someone else; people normally find it easier to understand their own views than to understand others' views.
   (C)   Juries composed of legal novices, rather than panels of lawyers, should be the final arbiters in legal proceedings. People who are not legal experts are in a better position to detect good legal arguments by lawyers than are other lawyers.
   (D)   People should always have their writing proofread by someone else. Someone who does not know in advance what is meant to be said is in a better position to spot typographical errors.
   (E)   Two people going out for dinner will have a more enjoyable meal if they order for each other. By allowing someone else to choose, one opens oneself up to new and exciting dining experiences.

8. Pundit: The only airline providing service for our town announced that because the service is unprofitable it will discontinue this service next year. Town officials have urged the community to use the airline's service more frequently so that the airline will change its decision. There is no reason to comply with their recommendation, however, for just last week these same officials drove to an out-of-town conference instead of flying.

   The pundit's reasoning is most vulnerable to criticism on the grounds that it presumes, without providing justification, that

   (A)   increasing the number of tickets sold without increasing ticket prices will be sufficient to make continued air service economically feasible
   (B)   suspending service and losing money by continuing service are the airline's only options
   (C)   the town officials paid for their trip with taxpayers' money rather than their own money
   (D)   ground transportation is usually no less expensive than airplane transportation
   (E)   if the town officials did not follow their own advice then that advice is not worth following

9. Some scientists believe that 65 million years ago an asteroid struck what is now the Yucatán Peninsula, thereby causing extinction of the dinosaurs. These scientists have established that such a strike could have hurled enough debris into the atmosphere to block sunlight and cool the atmosphere. Without adequate sunlight, food sources for herbivorous dinosaurs would have disappeared, and no dinosaurs could have survived a prolonged period of low temperatures. These same scientists, however, have also established that most debris launched by the asteroid would have settled to the ground within six months, too soon for the plants to disappear or the dinosaurs to freeze.

Which one of the following, if true, most helps to resolve the apparent discrepancy between the scientists' beliefs and the scientists' results, as described above?

(A) Loss of the herbivorous dinosaurs would have deprived the carnivorous dinosaurs of their food source.

(B) Dinosaurs inhabited most landmasses on the planet but were not especially abundant in the area of the asteroid strike.

(C) A cloud of debris capable of diminishing sunlight by 20 percent would have cooled the earth's surface by 7 to 10 degrees Celsius.

(D) The asteroid was at least 9.6 km in diameter, large enough for many dinosaurs to be killed by the strike itself and by subsequent tidal waves.

(E) Dinosaurs were susceptible to fatal respiratory problems caused by contamination of the air by asteroid debris.

10. Bernard: For which language, and thus which frequency distribution of letters and letter sequences, was the standard typewriter keyboard designed?

Cora: To ask this question, you must be making a mistaken assumption: that typing speed was to be maximized. The real danger with early typewriters was that operators would hit successive keys too quickly, thereby crashing typebars into each other, bending connecting wires, and so on. So the idea was to slow the operator down by making the most common letter sequences awkward to type.

Bernard: This is surely not right! These technological limitations have long since vanished, yet the keyboard is still as it was then.

Which one of the following, if true, could be used by Cora to counter Bernard's rejection of her explanation?

(A) Typewriters and word-processing equipment are typically sold to people who have learned to use the standard keyboard and who, therefore, demand it in equipment they buy.

(B) Typewriters have been superseded in most offices by word-processing equipment, which has inherited the standard keyboard from typewriters.

(C) The standard keyboard allows skilled operators to achieve considerable typing speeds, though it makes acquiring such skills relatively difficult.

(D) A person who has learned one keyboard layout can readily learn to use a second one in place of the first, but only with difficulty learn to use a second one alongside the first.

(E) It is now possible to construct typewriters and word-processing equipment in which a single keyboard can accommodate two or even more different keyboard layouts, each accessible to the operator at will.

GO ON TO THE NEXT PAGE.

11. Some teachers claim that students would not learn curricular content without the incentive of grades. But students with intense interest in the material would learn it without this incentive, while the behavior of students lacking all interest in the material is unaffected by such an incentive. The incentive of grades, therefore, serves no essential academic purpose.

The reasoning in the argument is flawed because the argument

(A) takes for granted that the only purpose of school is to convey a fixed body of information to students

(B) takes for granted that students who are indifferent to the grades they receive are genuinely interested in the curricular material

(C) fails to consider that the incentive of grades may serve some useful nonacademic purpose

(D) ignores the possibility that students who lack interest in the curricular material would be quite interested in it if allowed to choose their own curricular material

(E) fails to consider that some students may be neither fascinated by nor completely indifferent to the subject being taught

12. Economist: Technology now changes so rapidly that workers need periodic retraining. Such retraining can be efficient only if it allows individual companies to meet their own short-term needs. Hence, large governmental job retraining programs are no longer a viable option in the effort to retrain workers efficiently.

Which one of the following is an assumption required by the economist's argument?

(A) Workers did not need to be retrained when the pace of technological change was slower than it is currently.

(B) Large job retraining programs will be less efficient than smaller programs if the pace of technological change slows.

(C) No single type of retraining program is most efficient at retraining technological workers.

(D) Large governmental job retraining programs do not meet the short-term needs of different individual companies.

(E) Technological workers are more likely now than in the past to move in order to find work for which they are already trained.

13. Recent research indicates that increased consumption of fruits and vegetables by middle-aged people reduces their susceptibility to stroke in later years. The researchers speculate that this may be because fruits and vegetables are rich in folic acid. Low levels of folic acid are associated with high levels of homocysteine, an amino acid that contributes to blocked arteries.

Which one of the following statements is most strongly supported by the information above?

(A) An increased risk of stroke is correlated with low levels of homocysteine.

(B) A decreased risk of stroke is correlated with increased levels of folic acid.

(C) An increased propensity for blocked arteries is correlated with decreased levels of homocysteine.

(D) A decreased propensity for blocked arteries is correlated with low levels of folic acid.

(E) Stroke is prevented by ingestion of folic acid in quantities sufficient to prevent a decline in the levels of homocysteine.

14. Thirty years ago, the percentage of the British people who vacationed in foreign countries was very small compared with the large percentage of the British population who travel abroad for vacations now. Foreign travel is, and always has been, expensive from Britain. Therefore, British people must have, on average, more money to spend on vacations now than they did 30 years ago.

The argument requires assuming which one of the following?

(A) If foreign travel had been less expensive 30 years ago, British people would still not have had enough money to take vacations abroad.

(B) If travel to Britain were less expensive, more people of other countries would travel to Britain for their vacations.

(C) If the percentage of British people vacationing abroad was lower 30 years ago, then the British people of 30 years ago must have spent more money on domestic vacations.

(D) If more of the British people of 30 years ago had had enough money to vacation abroad, more would have done so.

(E) If British people are now wealthier than they were 30 years ago, then they must have more money to spend on vacations now than they did 30 years ago.

GO ON TO THE NEXT PAGE.

15. Mystery stories often feature a brilliant detective and the detective's dull companion. Clues are presented in the story, and the companion wrongly infers an inaccurate solution to the mystery using the same clues that the detective uses to deduce the correct solution. Thus, the author's strategy of including the dull companion gives readers a chance to solve the mystery while also diverting them from the correct solution.

Which one of the following is most strongly supported by the information above?

(A) Most mystery stories feature a brilliant detective who solves the mystery presented in the story.

(B) Mystery readers often solve the mystery in a story simply by spotting the mistakes in the reasoning of the detective's dull companion in that story.

(C) Some mystery stories give readers enough clues to infer the correct solution to the mystery.

(D) The actions of the brilliant detective in a mystery story rarely divert readers from the actions of the detective's dull companion.

(E) The detective's dull companion in a mystery story generally uncovers the misleading clues that divert readers from the mystery's correct solution.

16. Policy analyst: Increasing the size of a police force is only a stopgap method of crime prevention; it does not get at the root causes of crime. Therefore, city officials should not respond to rising crime rates by increasing the size of their city's police force.

The flawed reasoning in which one of the following arguments most closely resembles the flawed reasoning in the policy analyst's argument?

(A) Some people think that rules with higher standards than people can live up to, such as those enjoining total honesty, prevent some immoral behavior by giving people a guide to self-improvement. But such rules actually worsen behavior by making people cynical about rules. Thus, societies should not institute overly demanding rules.

(B) Swamps play an important role in allaying the harsh effects of floods because they absorb a great deal of water. Although dams prevent many floods, they worsen the effects of the greatest floods by drying up swamps. Thus dams should not be built.

(C) Although less effective in preventing theft than security guards, burglar alarm systems are more affordable to maintain. Because the greater loss from theft when alarms are used is outweighed by their lower cost, companies are advised always to use burglar alarm systems.

(D) Because taking this drug does not cure the disease for which it is prescribed, but only reduces the disease's most harmful effects, doctors should not continue to prescribe this drug.

(E) We will never fully understand what causes people to engage in criminal activity. Therefore, we should investigate other ways to improve society's ability to combat crime.

GO ON TO THE NEXT PAGE.

Questions 17–18

In order to determine automobile insurance premiums for a driver, insurance companies calculate various risk factors; as the risk factors increase, so does the premium. Certain factors, such as the driver's age and past accident history, play an important role in these calculations. Yet these premiums should also increase with the frequency with which a person drives. After all, a person's chance of being involved in a mishap increases in proportion to the number of times that person drives.

17. Which one of the following, if true, most undermines the argument?

    (A) People who drive infrequently are more likely to be involved in accidents that occur on small roads than in highway accidents.

    (B) People who drive infrequently are less likely to follow rules for safe driving than are people who drive frequently.

    (C) People who drive infrequently are less likely to violate local speed limits than are people who drive frequently.

    (D) People who drive frequently are more likely to make long-distance trips in the course of a year than are people who drive infrequently.

    (E) People who drive frequently are more likely to become distracted while driving than are people who drive infrequently.

18. The claim that insurance premiums should increase as the frequency with which a driver drives increases plays which one of the following roles in the argument?

    (A) a premise of the argument
    (B) the conclusion of the argument
    (C) evidence offered in support of one of the premises
    (D) an assertion phrased to preclude an anticipated objection
    (E) a clarification of a key term in the argument

19. Essayist: Only happiness is intrinsically valuable; other things are valuable only insofar as they contribute to happiness. Some philosophers argue that the fact that we do not approve of a bad person's being happy shows that we value happiness only when it is deserved. This supposedly shows that we find something besides happiness to be intrinsically valuable. But the happiness people deserve is determined by the amount of happiness they bring to others. Therefore, _____.

Which one of the following most logically completes the final sentence of the essayist's argument?

    (A) the notion that people can be deserving of happiness is ultimately incoherent

    (B) people do not actually value happiness as much as they think they do

    (C) the judgment that a person deserves to be happy is itself to be understood in terms of happiness

    (D) the only way to be assured of happiness is to bring happiness to those who have done something to deserve it

    (E) a truly bad person cannot actually be very happy

20. Sociologist: Climate and geology determine where human industry can be established. Drastic shifts in climate always result in migrations, and migrations bring about the intermingling of ideas necessary for rapid advances in civilization.

The sociologist's statements, if true, most strongly support which one of the following?

    (A) Climate is the primary cause of migration.
    (B) All shifts in climate produce a net gain in human progress.
    (C) A population remains settled only where the climate is fairly stable.
    (D) Populations settle in every place where human industry can be established.
    (E) Every migration is accompanied by rapid advances in civilization.

GO ON TO THE NEXT PAGE.

21. Some educators claim that it is best that school courses cover only basic subject matter, but cover it in depth. These educators argue that if students achieve a solid grasp of the basic concepts and investigatory techniques in a subject, they will be able to explore the breadth of that subject on their own after the course is over. But if they simply learn a lot of factual information, without truly understanding its significance, they will not be well equipped for further study on their own.

The educators' reasoning provides grounds for accepting which one of the following statements?

(A) It is easier to understand how plants and animals are classified after learning how plants and animals can be useful.

(B) It is more difficult to recall the details of a dull and complicated lecture than of a lively and interesting one.

(C) It is easier to remember new ideas explained personally by a teacher than ideas that one explores independently.

(D) It is easier to understand any Greek tragedy after one has analyzed a few of them in detail.

(E) It is easier to learn many simple ideas well than to learn a few complicated ideas well.

22. Damming the Merv River would provide irrigation for the dry land in its upstream areas; unfortunately, a dam would reduce agricultural productivity in the fertile land downstream by reducing the availability and quality of the water there. The productivity loss in the downstream area would be greater than the productivity gain upstream, so building a dam would yield no overall gain in agricultural productivity in the region as a whole.

The reasoning in the argument above most closely parallels that in which one of the following?

(A) Disease-causing bacteria in eggs can be destroyed by overcooking the eggs, but the eggs then become much less appetizing; health is more important than taste, however, so it is better to overcook eggs than not to do so.

(B) Increasing the price of transatlantic telephone calls will discourage many private individuals from making them. But since most transatlantic telephone calls are made by businesses, not by private individuals, a rate increase will not reduce telephone company profits.

(C) A new highway will allow suburban commuters to reach the city more quickly, but not without causing increased delays within the city that will more than offset any time saved on the highway. Therefore, the highway will not reduce suburban commuters' overall commuting time.

(D) Doctors can prescribe antibiotics for many minor illnesses, but antibiotics are expensive, and these illnesses can often be cured by rest alone. Therefore, it is better to rest at home than to see a doctor for these illnesses.

(E) A certain chemical will kill garden pests that damage tomatoes, but that chemical will damage certain other plants more severely than the pests damage the tomatoes, so the only gardens that will benefit from the use of the chemical are those in which only tomatoes are grown.

GO ON TO THE NEXT PAGE.

23. Activist: Food producers irradiate food in order to
    prolong its shelf life. Five animal studies were
    recently conducted to investigate whether this
    process alters food in a way that could be
    dangerous to people who eat it. The studies
    concluded that irradiated food is safe for humans
    to eat. However, because these studies were
    subsequently found by a panel of independent
    scientists to be seriously flawed in their
    methodology, it follows that irradiated food is not
    safe for human consumption.

The reasoning in the activist's argument is flawed
because that argument

(A) treats a failure to prove a claim as constituting
     proof of the denial of that claim

(B) treats methodological flaws in past studies as
     proof that it is currently not possible to devise
     methodologically adequate alternatives

(C) fails to consider the possibility that even a study
     whose methodology has no serious flaws
     nonetheless might provide only weak support for
     its conclusion

(D) fails to consider the possibility that what is safe
     for animals might not always be safe for human
     beings

(E) fails to establish that the independent scientists
     know more about food irradiation than do the
     people who produced the five studies

24. One-year-olds ordinarily prefer the taste of sweet food to
    that of salty food. Yet if one feeds a one-year-old salty
    food rather than sweet food, then over a period of about
    a year he or she will develop a taste for the salty flavor
    and choose to eat salty food rather than sweet food.
    Thus, a young child's taste preferences can be affected
    by the type of food he or she has been exposed to.

Which one of the following is an assumption required by
the argument?

(A) Two-year-olds do not naturally prefer salty food
     to sweet food.

(B) A child's taste preferences usually change
     between age one and age two.

(C) Two-year-olds do not naturally dislike salty food
     so much that they would not choose it over some
     other foods.

(D) The salty food fed to infants in order to change
     their taste preferences must taste pleasant.

(E) Sweet food is better for infant development than
     is salty food.

S T O P

IF YOU FINISH BEFORE TIME IS CALLED, YOU MAY CHECK YOUR WORK ON THIS SECTION ONLY.
DO NOT WORK ON ANY OTHER SECTION IN THE TEST.

SECTION II

Time—35 minutes

24 Questions

Directions: Each group of questions in this section is based on a set of conditions. In answering some of the questions, it may be useful to draw a rough diagram. Choose the response that most accurately and completely answers each question and blacken the corresponding space on your answer sheet.

Questions 1–7

A car drives into the center ring of a circus and exactly eight clowns—Q, R, S, T, V, W, Y, and Z—get out of the car, one clown at a time. The order in which the clowns get out of the car is consistent with the following conditions:

V gets out at some time before both Y and Q.
Q gets out at some time after Z.
T gets out at some time before V but at some time after R.
S gets out at some time after V.
R gets out at some time before W.

1. Which one of the following could be the order, from first to last, in which the clowns get out of the car?

    (A)   T, Z, V, R, W, Y, S, Q
    (B)   Z, R, W, Q, T, V, Y, S
    (C)   R, W, T, V, Q, Z, S, Y
    (D)   Z, W, R, T, V, Y, Q, S
    (E)   R, W, T, V, Z, S, Y, Q

2. Which one of the following could be true?

    (A)   Y is the second clown to get out of the car.
    (B)   R is the third clown to get out of the car.
    (C)   Q is the fourth clown to get out of the car.
    (D)   S is the fifth clown to get out of the car.
    (E)   V is the sixth clown to get out of the car.

3. If Z is the seventh clown to get out of the car, then which one of the following could be true?

    (A)   R is the second clown to get out of the car.
    (B)   T is the fourth clown to get out of the car.
    (C)   W is the fifth clown to get out of the car.
    (D)   V is the sixth clown to get out of the car.
    (E)   Y is the eighth clown to get out of the car.

4. If T is the fourth clown to get out of the car, then which one of the following must be true?

    (A)   R is the first clown to get out of the car.
    (B)   Z is the second clown to get out of the car.
    (C)   W is the third clown to get out of the car.
    (D)   V is the fifth clown to get out of the car.
    (E)   Y is the seventh clown to get out of the car.

5. If Q is the fifth clown to get out of the car, then each of the following could be true EXCEPT:

    (A)   Z is the first clown to get out of the car.
    (B)   T is the second clown to get out of the car.
    (C)   V is the third clown to get out of the car.
    (D)   W is the fourth clown to get out of the car.
    (E)   Y is the sixth clown to get out of the car.

6. If R is the second clown to get out of the car, which one of the following must be true?

    (A)   S gets out of the car at some time before T does.
    (B)   T gets out of the car at some time before W does.
    (C)   W gets out of the car at some time before V does.
    (D)   Y gets out of the car at some time before Q does.
    (E)   Z gets out of the car at some time before W does.

7. If V gets out of the car at some time before Z does, then which one of the following could be true?

    (A)   R is the second clown to get out of the car.
    (B)   T is the fourth clown to get out of the car.
    (C)   Q is the fourth clown to get out of the car.
    (D)   V is the fifth clown to get out of the car.
    (E)   Z is the sixth clown to get out of the car.

GO ON TO THE NEXT PAGE.

Questions 8–13

Each of six tasks—harvesting, milling, plowing, spinning, threshing, and weaving—will be demonstrated exactly once at a farm exhibition. No two tasks will be demonstrated concurrently. Three volunteers—Frank, Gladys, and Leslie—will each demonstrate exactly two of the tasks. The tasks must be demonstrated in accordance with the following conditions:

Frank demonstrates exactly one task before Gladys demonstrates any of the tasks.
Frank performs neither the first nor the last demonstration.
Gladys demonstrates neither harvesting nor milling.
Leslie demonstrates neither harvesting nor threshing.
Milling is the next task demonstrated after threshing is demonstrated.

8. Which one of the following is an acceptable list of the volunteers and the tasks each demonstrates, in order from the first to the last demonstration?

   (A)   Frank: weaving; Gladys: threshing;
         Leslie: milling; Leslie: spinning;
         Frank: harvesting; Gladys: plowing
   (B)   Leslie: plowing; Frank: harvesting;
         Frank: threshing; Leslie: milling;
         Gladys: spinning; Gladys: weaving
   (C)   Leslie: plowing; Frank: spinning;
         Gladys: threshing; Leslie: milling;
         Frank: harvesting; Gladys: weaving
   (D)   Leslie: spinning; Leslie: weaving;
         Frank: plowing; Gladys: harvesting;
         Frank: threshing; Gladys: milling
   (E)   Leslie: weaving; Frank: threshing;
         Gladys: spinning; Leslie: milling;
         Frank: harvesting; Gladys: plowing

9. Which one of the following must be true?

   (A)   Frank demonstrates harvesting.
   (B)   Frank demonstrates milling.
   (C)   Frank demonstrates threshing.
   (D)   Gladys demonstrates plowing.
   (E)   Gladys demonstrates weaving.

10. If Leslie performs the fourth demonstration, then harvesting could be the demonstration performed

    (A)   first
    (B)   second
    (C)   third
    (D)   fourth
    (E)   sixth

11. If Gladys demonstrates plowing immediately before Frank demonstrates threshing, which one of the following must be true?

    (A)   Frank demonstrates harvesting for the second demonstration.
    (B)   Gladys demonstrates spinning for the fifth demonstration.
    (C)   Leslie demonstrates weaving for the first demonstration.
    (D)   Gladys performs the fourth demonstration.
    (E)   Leslie performs the sixth demonstration.

12. Which one of the following must be true?

    (A)   Frank performs the second demonstration.
    (B)   Gladys performs the fourth demonstration.
    (C)   Gladys performs the sixth demonstration.
    (D)   Leslie performs the first demonstration.
    (E)   Leslie performs the second demonstration.

13. Which one of the following could be true?

    (A)   Harvesting is demonstrated first.
    (B)   Milling is demonstrated second.
    (C)   Threshing is demonstrated first.
    (D)   Threshing is demonstrated last.
    (E)   Weaving is demonstrated first.

GO ON TO THE NEXT PAGE.

Questions 14–19

Seven job applicants—Feng, Garcia, Herrera, Ilias, Weiss, Xavier, and Yates—are hired to fill seven new positions at Chroma, Inc. One position is in the management department, three are in the production department, and three are in the sales department. The following conditions must apply:

Herrera is hired for a position in the same department as Yates.

Feng is hired for a position in a different department from Garcia.

If Xavier is hired for a sales position, then Weiss is hired for a production position.

Feng is hired for a production position.

14. Which one of the following could be a complete and accurate matching of the applicants with the departments in which they were hired?

(A) management: Weiss
production: Feng, Herrera, Yates
sales: Garcia, Ilias, Xavier

(B) management: Weiss
production: Garcia, Ilias, Xavier
sales: Feng, Herrera, Yates

(C) management: Xavier
production: Feng, Garcia, Herrera
sales: Ilias, Yates, Weiss

(D) management: Xavier
production: Feng, Herrera, Ilias
sales: Garcia, Weiss, Yates

(E) management: Xavier
production: Feng, Ilias, Weiss
sales: Garcia, Herrera, Yates

15. Which one of the following is a complete and accurate list of the applicants, each of whom CANNOT be hired for a production position?

(A) Feng, Ilias, Xavier
(B) Garcia, Herrera, Yates
(C) Herrera, Yates
(D) Garcia
(E) Ilias

16. It can be determined in which department each of the seven applicants is hired if which one of the following statements is true?

(A) Feng and Weiss are both hired for production positions.
(B) Garcia and Yates are both hired for sales positions.
(C) Ilias and Weiss are both hired for sales positions.
(D) Ilias and Weiss are both hired for production positions.
(E) Ilias and Xavier are both hired for production positions.

17. Each of the following could be an accurate partial list of the applicants hired for sales positions EXCEPT:

(A) Garcia, Ilias
(B) Garcia, Xavier
(C) Garcia, Yates
(D) Herrera, Weiss
(E) Herrera, Xavier

18. If Feng is hired for a position in the same department as Xavier, then each of the following could be true EXCEPT:

(A) Garcia is hired for a sales position.
(B) Herrera is hired for a production position.
(C) Ilias is hired for a sales position.
(D) Weiss is hired for the management position.
(E) Weiss is hired for a production position.

19. If Xavier is not hired for one of the production positions, then which one of the following could be true?

(A) Feng and Herrera are both hired for sales positions.
(B) Herrera and Weiss are both hired for sales positions.
(C) Feng and Yates are both hired for production positions.
(D) Garcia and Weiss are both hired for production positions.
(E) Herrera and Weiss are both hired for production positions.

GO ON TO THE NEXT PAGE.

Questions 20–24

Musicians perform each of exactly five pieces—Nexus, Onyx, Synchrony, Tailwind, and Virtual—once, and one at a time; the pieces are performed successively (though not necessarily in that order). Each piece is performed with exactly two instruments: Nexus with fiddle and lute, Onyx with harp and mandolin, Synchrony with guitar and harp, Tailwind with fiddle and guitar, and Virtual with lute and mandolin. The following conditions must apply:

Each piece shares one instrument with the piece performed immediately before it or after it (or both).
Either Nexus or Tailwind is performed second.

20. Which one of the following could be the order, from first to last, in which the pieces are performed?

   (A)   Nexus, Synchrony, Onyx, Virtual, Tailwind
   (B)   Synchrony, Tailwind, Onyx, Nexus, Virtual
   (C)   Tailwind, Nexus, Onyx, Virtual, Synchrony
   (D)   Tailwind, Nexus, Synchrony, Onyx, Virtual
   (E)   Virtual, Nexus, Synchrony, Onyx, Tailwind

21. Which one of the following instruments CANNOT be shared by the third and fourth pieces performed?

   (A)   fiddle
   (B)   guitar
   (C)   harp
   (D)   lute
   (E)   mandolin

22. If each piece (except the fifth) shares one instrument with the piece performed immediately after it, then which one of the following could be true?

   (A)   Virtual is performed first.
   (B)   Synchrony is performed second.
   (C)   Onyx is performed third.
   (D)   Nexus is performed fourth.
   (E)   Tailwind is performed fifth.

23. Each of the following could be the piece performed first EXCEPT:

   (A)   Nexus
   (B)   Onyx
   (C)   Synchrony
   (D)   Tailwind
   (E)   Virtual

24. If Synchrony is performed fifth, then which one of the following could be true?

   (A)   Nexus is performed third.
   (B)   Onyx is performed third.
   (C)   Tailwind is performed fourth.
   (D)   Virtual is performed first.
   (E)   Virtual is performed second.

S T O P

IF YOU FINISH BEFORE TIME IS CALLED, YOU MAY CHECK YOUR WORK ON THIS SECTION ONLY.
DO NOT WORK ON ANY OTHER SECTION IN THE TEST.

3 **3** **3** **3**

SECTION III
Time—35 minutes
27 Questions

Directions: Each passage in this section is followed by a group of questions to be answered on the basis of what is stated or implied in the passage. For some of the questions, more than one of the choices could conceivably answer the question. However, you are to choose the best answer; that is, the response that most accurately and completely answers the question, and blacken the corresponding space on your answer sheet.

The myth persists that in 1492 the Western Hemisphere was an untamed wilderness and that it was European settlers who harnessed and transformed its ecosystems. But scholarship shows that forests, in
(5) particular, had been altered to varying degrees well before the arrival of Europeans. Native populations had converted much of the forests to successfully cultivated stands, especially by means of burning. Nevertheless, some researchers have maintained that the extent,
(10) frequency, and impact of such burning was minimal. One geographer claims that climatic change could have accounted for some of the changes in forest composition; another argues that burning by native populations was done only sporadically, to augment the
(15) effects of natural fires.

However, a large body of evidence for the routine practice of burning exists in the geographical record. One group of researchers found, for example, that sedimentary charcoal accumulations in what is now the
(20) northeastern United States are greatest where known native American settlements were greatest. Other evidence shows that, while the characteristics and impact of fires set by native populations varied regionally according to population size, extent of
(25) resource management techniques, and environment, all such fires had markedly different effects on vegetation patterns than did natural fires. Controlled burning created grassy openings such as meadows and glades. Burning also promoted a mosaic quality to North and
(30) South American ecosystems, creating forests in many different stages of ecological development. Much of the mature forestland was characterized by open, herbaceous undergrowth, another result of the clearing brought about by burning.

(35) In North America, controlled burning created conditions favorable to berries and other fire-tolerant and sun-loving foods. Burning also converted mixed stands of trees to homogeneous forest, for example the longleaf, slash pine, and scrub oak forests of the
(40) southeastern U.S. Natural fires do account for some of this vegetation, but regular burning clearly extended and maintained it. Burning also influenced forest composition in the tropics, where natural fires are rare. An example is the pine-dominant forests of Nicaragua,
(45) where warm temperatures and heavy rainfall naturally favor mixed tropical or rain forests. While there are extensive pine forests in Guatemala and Mexico, these primarily grow in cooler, drier, higher elevations, regions where such vegetation is in large part natural
(50) and even prehuman. Today, the Nicaraguan pines

occur where there has been clearing followed by regular burning, and the same is likely to have occurred in the past: such forests were present when Europeans arrived and were found only in areas where native
(55) settlements were substantial; when these settlements were abandoned, the land returned to mixed hardwoods. This succession is also evident elsewhere in similar low tropical elevations in the Caribbean and Mexico.

1. Which one of the following most accurately expresses the main idea of the passage?

(A) Despite extensive evidence that native populations had been burning North and South American forests extensively before 1492, some scholars persist in claiming that such burning was either infrequent or the result of natural causes.

(B) In opposition to the widespread belief that in 1492 the Western Hemisphere was uncultivated, scholars unanimously agree that native populations were substantially altering North and South American forests well before the arrival of Europeans.

(C) Although some scholars minimize the scope and importance of the burning of forests engaged in by native populations of North and South America before 1492, evidence of the frequency and impact of such burning is actually quite extensive.

(D) Where scholars had once believed that North and South American forests remained uncultivated until the arrival of Europeans, there is now general agreement that native populations had been cultivating the forests since well before 1492.

(E) While scholars have acknowledged that North and South American forests were being burned well before 1492, there is still disagreement over whether such burning was the result of natural causes or of the deliberate actions of native populations.

GO ON TO THE NEXT PAGE.

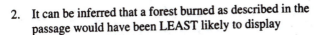
2. It can be inferred that a forest burned as described in the passage would have been LEAST likely to display

    (A) numerous types of hardwood trees
    (B) extensive herbaceous undergrowth
    (C) a variety of fire-tolerant plants
    (D) various stages of ecological maturity
    (E) grassy openings such as meadows or glades

3. Which one of the following is a type of forest identified by the author as a product of controlled burning in recent times?

    (A) scrub oak forests in the southeastern U.S.
    (B) slash pine forests in the southeastern U.S.
    (C) pine forests in Guatemala at high elevations
    (D) pine forests in Mexico at high elevations
    (E) pine forests in Nicaragua at low elevations

4. Which one of the following is presented by the author as evidence of controlled burning in the tropics before the arrival of Europeans?

    (A) extensive homogeneous forests at high elevation
    (B) extensive homogeneous forests at low elevation
    (C) extensive heterogeneous forests at high elevation
    (D) extensive heterogeneous forests at low elevation
    (E) extensive sedimentary charcoal accumulations at high elevation

5. With which one of the following would the author be most likely to agree?

    (A) The long-term effects of controlled burning could just as easily have been caused by natural fires.
    (B) Herbaceous undergrowth prevents many forests from reaching full maturity.
    (C) European settlers had little impact on the composition of the ecosystems in North and South America.
    (D) Certain species of plants may not have been as widespread in North America without controlled burning.
    (E) Nicaraguan pine forests could have been created either by natural fires or by controlled burning.

6. As evidence for the routine practice of forest burning by native populations before the arrival of Europeans, the author cites all of the following EXCEPT:

    (A) the similar characteristics of fires in different regions
    (B) the simultaneous presence of forests at varying stages of maturity
    (C) the existence of herbaceous undergrowth in certain forests
    (D) the heavy accumulation of charcoal near populous settlements
    (E) the presence of meadows and glades in certain forests

7. The "succession" mentioned in line 57 refers to

    (A) forest clearing followed by controlled burning of forests
    (B) tropical rain forest followed by pine forest
    (C) European settlement followed by abandonment of land
    (D) homogeneous pine forest followed by mixed hardwoods
    (E) pine forests followed by established settlements

8. The primary purpose of the passage is to

    (A) refute certain researchers' views
    (B) support a common belief
    (C) counter certain evidence
    (D) synthesize two viewpoints
    (E) correct the geographical record

GO ON TO THE NEXT PAGE.

Intellectual authority is defined as the authority of arguments that prevail by virtue of good reasoning and do not depend on coercion or convention. A contrasting notion, institutional authority, refers to the power of
(5) social institutions to enforce acceptance of arguments that may or may not possess intellectual authority. The authority wielded by legal systems is especially interesting because such systems are institutions that nonetheless aspire to a purely intellectual authority.
(10) One judge goes so far as to claim that courts are merely passive vehicles for applying the intellectual authority of the law and possess no coercive powers of their own.

In contrast, some critics maintain that whatever
(15) authority judicial pronouncements have is exclusively institutional. Some of these critics go further, claiming that intellectual authority does not really exist—i.e., it reduces to institutional authority. But it can be countered that these claims break down when a
(20) sufficiently broad historical perspective is taken: Not all arguments accepted by institutions withstand the test of time, and some well-reasoned arguments never receive institutional imprimatur. The reasonable argument that goes unrecognized in its own time
(25) because it challenges institutional beliefs is common in intellectual history; intellectual authority and institutional consensus are not the same thing.

But, the critics might respond, intellectual authority is only recognized as such because of institutional
(30) consensus. For example, if a musicologist were to claim that an alleged musical genius who, after several decades, had not gained respect and recognition for his or her compositions is probably not a genius, the critics might say that basing a judgment on a unit of time—
(35) "several decades"—is an institutional rather than an intellectual construct. What, the critics might ask, makes a particular number of decades reasonable evidence by which to judge genius? The answer, of course, is nothing, except for the fact that such
(40) institutional procedures have proved useful to musicologists in making such distinctions in the past.

The analogous legal concept is the doctrine of precedent, i.e., a judge's merely deciding a case a certain way becoming a basis for deciding later cases
(45) the same way—a pure example of institutional authority. But the critics miss the crucial distinction that when a judicial decision is badly reasoned, or simply no longer applies in the face of evolving social standards or practices, the notion of intellectual
(50) authority is introduced: judges reconsider, revise, or in some cases throw out the decision. The conflict between intellectual and institutional authority in legal systems is thus played out in the reconsideration of decisions, leading one to draw the conclusion that legal
(55) systems contain a significant degree of intellectual authority even if the thrust of their power is predominantly institutional.

9. Which one of the following most accurately states the main idea of the passage?

(A) Although some argue that the authority of legal systems is purely intellectual, these systems possess a degree of institutional authority due to their ability to enforce acceptance of badly reasoned or socially inappropriate judicial decisions.

(B) Although some argue that the authority of legal systems is purely institutional, these systems are more correctly seen as vehicles for applying the intellectual authority of the law while possessing no coercive power of their own.

(C) Although some argue that the authority of legal systems is purely intellectual, these systems in fact wield institutional authority by virtue of the fact that intellectual authority reduces to institutional authority.

(D) Although some argue that the authority of legal systems is purely institutional, these systems possess a degree of intellectual authority due to their ability to reconsider badly reasoned or socially inappropriate judicial decisions.

(E) Although some argue that the authority of legal systems is purely intellectual, these systems in fact wield exclusively institutional authority in that they possess the power to enforce acceptance of badly reasoned or socially inappropriate judicial decisions.

10. That some arguments "never receive institutional imprimatur" (lines 22–23) most likely means that these arguments

(A) fail to gain institutional consensus
(B) fail to challenge institutional beliefs
(C) fail to conform to the example of precedent
(D) fail to convince by virtue of good reasoning
(E) fail to gain acceptance except by coercion

GO ON TO THE NEXT PAGE.

11. Which one of the following, if true, most challenges the author's contention that legal systems contain a significant degree of intellectual authority?

(A) Judges often act under time constraints and occasionally render a badly reasoned or socially inappropriate decision.

(B) In some legal systems, the percentage of judicial decisions that contain faulty reasoning is far higher than it is in other legal systems.

(C) Many socially inappropriate legal decisions are thrown out by judges only after citizens begin to voice opposition to them.

(D) In some legal systems, the percentage of judicial decisions that are reconsidered and revised is far higher than it is in other legal systems.

(E) Judges are rarely willing to rectify the examples of faulty reasoning they discover when reviewing previous legal decisions.

12. Given the information in the passage, the author is LEAST likely to believe which one of the following?

(A) Institutional authority may depend on coercion; intellectual authority never does.

(B) Intellectual authority may accept well-reasoned arguments; institutional authority never does.

(C) Institutional authority may depend on convention; intellectual authority never does.

(D) Intellectual authority sometimes challenges institutional beliefs; institutional authority never does.

(E) Intellectual authority sometimes conflicts with precedent; institutional authority never does.

13. The author discusses the example from musicology primarily in order to

(A) distinguish the notion of institutional authority from that of intellectual authority

(B) give an example of an argument possessing intellectual authority that did not prevail in its own time

(C) identify an example in which the ascription of musical genius did not withstand the test of time

(D) illustrate the claim that assessing intellectual authority requires an appeal to institutional authority

(E) demonstrate that the authority wielded by the arbiters of musical genius is entirely institutional

14. Based on the passage, the author would be most likely to hold which one of the following views about the doctrine of precedent?

(A) It is the only tool judges should use if they wish to achieve a purely intellectual authority.

(B) It is a useful tool in theory but in practice it invariably conflicts with the demands of intellectual authority.

(C) It is a useful tool but lacks intellectual authority unless it is combined with the reconsidering of decisions.

(D) It is often an unreliable tool because it prevents judges from reconsidering the intellectual authority of past decisions.

(E) It is an unreliable tool that should be abandoned because it lacks intellectual authority.

GO ON TO THE NEXT PAGE.

In explaining the foundations of the discipline known as historical sociology—the examination of history using the methods of sociology—historical sociologist Philip Abrams argues that, while people are
(5) made by society as much as society is made by people, sociologists' approach to the subject is usually to focus on only one of these forms of influence to the exclusion of the other. Abrams insists on the necessity for sociologists to move beyond these one-sided
(10) approaches to understand society as an entity constructed by individuals who are at the same time constructed by their society. Abrams refers to this continuous process as "structuring."

Abrams also sees history as the result of
(15) structuring. People, both individually and as members of collectives, make history. But our making of history is itself formed and informed not only by the historical conditions we inherit from the past, but also by the prior formation of our own identities and capacities,
(20) which are shaped by what Abrams calls "contingencies"—social phenomena over which we have varying degrees of control. Contingencies include such things as the social conditions under which we come of age, the condition of our household's
(25) economy, the ideologies available to help us make sense of our situation, and accidental circumstances. The ways in which contingencies affect our individual or group identities create a structure of forces within which we are able to act, and that partially determines
(30) the sorts of actions we are able to perform.

In Abrams's analysis, historical structuring, like social structuring, is manifold and unremitting. To understand it, historical sociologists must extract from it certain significant episodes, or events, that their
(35) methodology can then analyze and interpret. According to Abrams, these events are points at which action and contingency meet, points that represent a cross section of the specific social and individual forces in play at a given time. At such moments, individuals stand forth
(40) as agents of history not simply because they possess a unique ability to act, but also because in them we see the force of the specific social conditions that allowed their actions to come forth. Individuals can "make their mark" on history, yet in individuals one also finds the
(45) convergence of wider social forces. In order to capture the various facets of this mutual interaction, Abrams recommends a fourfold structure to which he believes the investigations of historical sociologists should conform: first, description of the event itself; second,
(50) discussion of the social context that helped bring the event about and gave it significance; third, summary of the life history of the individual agent in the event; and fourth, analysis of the consequences of the event both for history and for the individual.

15. Which one of the following most accurately states the central idea of the passage?

(A) Abrams argues that historical sociology rejects the claims of sociologists who assert that the sociological concept of structuring cannot be applied to the interactions between individuals and history.

(B) Abrams argues that historical sociology assumes that, despite the views of sociologists to the contrary, history influences the social contingencies that affect individuals.

(C) Abrams argues that historical sociology demonstrates that, despite the views of sociologists to the contrary, social structures both influence and are influenced by the events of history.

(D) Abrams describes historical sociology as a discipline that unites two approaches taken by sociologists to studying the formation of societies and applies the resulting combined approach to the study of history.

(E) Abrams describes historical sociology as an attempt to compensate for the shortcomings of traditional historical methods by applying the methods established in sociology.

16. Given the passage's argument, which one of the following sentences most logically completes the last paragraph?

(A) Only if they adhere to this structure, Abrams believes, can historical sociologists conclude with any certainty that the events that constitute the historical record are influenced by the actions of individuals.

(B) Only if they adhere to this structure, Abrams believes, will historical sociologists be able to counter the standard sociological assumption that there is very little connection between history and individual agency.

(C) Unless they can agree to adhere to this structure, Abrams believes, historical sociologists risk having their discipline treated as little more than an interesting but ultimately indefensible adjunct to history and sociology.

(D) By adhering to this structure, Abrams believes, historical sociologists can shed light on issues that traditional sociologists have chosen to ignore in their one-sided approaches to the formation of societies.

(E) By adhering to this structure, Abrams believes, historical sociologists will be able to better portray the complex connections between human agency and history.

GO ON TO THE NEXT PAGE.

17. The passage states that a contingency could be each of the following EXCEPT:

    (A) a social phenomenon
    (B) a form of historical structuring
    (C) an accidental circumstance
    (D) a condition controllable to some extent by an individual
    (E) a partial determinant of an individual's actions

18. Which one of the following is most analogous to the ideal work of a historical sociologist as outlined by Abrams?

    (A) In a report on the enactment of a bill into law, a journalist explains why the need for the bill arose, sketches the biography of the principal legislator who wrote the bill, and ponders the effect that the bill's enactment will have both on society and on the legislator's career.
    (B) In a consultation with a patient, a doctor reviews the patient's medical history, suggests possible reasons for the patient's current condition, and recommends steps that the patient should take in the future to ensure that the condition improves or at least does not get any worse.
    (C) In an analysis of a historical novel, a critic provides information to support the claim that details of the work's setting are accurate, explains why the subject of the novel was of particular interest to the author, and compares the novel with some of the author's other books set in the same period.
    (D) In a presentation to stockholders, a corporation's chief executive officer describes the corporation's most profitable activities during the past year, introduces the vice president largely responsible for those activities, and discusses new projects the vice president will initiate in the coming year.
    (E) In developing a film based on a historical event, a filmmaker conducts interviews with participants in the event, bases part of the film's screenplay on the interviews, and concludes the screenplay with a sequence of scenes speculating on the outcome of the event had certain details been different.

19. The primary function of the first paragraph of the passage is to

    (A) outline the merits of Abrams's conception of historical sociology
    (B) convey the details of Abrams's conception of historical sociology
    (C) anticipate challenges to Abrams's conception of historical sociology
    (D) examine the roles of key terms used in Abrams's conception of historical sociology
    (E) identify the basis of Abrams's conception of historical sociology

20. Based on the passage, which one of the following is the LEAST illustrative example of the effect of a contingency upon an individual?

    (A) the effect of the fact that a person experienced political injustice on that person's decision to work for political reform
    (B) the effect of the fact that a person was raised in an agricultural region on that person's decision to pursue a career in agriculture
    (C) the effect of the fact that a person lives in a particular community on that person's decision to visit friends in another community
    (D) the effect of the fact that a person's parents practiced a particular religion on that person's decision to practice that religion
    (E) the effect of the fact that a person grew up in financial hardship on that person's decision to help others in financial hardship

GO ON TO THE NEXT PAGE.

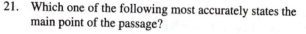
One of the greatest challenges facing medical students today, apart from absorbing volumes of technical information and learning habits of scientific thought, is that of remaining empathetic to the needs of
(5) patients in the face of all this rigorous training. Requiring students to immerse themselves completely in medical coursework risks disconnecting them from the personal and ethical aspects of doctoring, and such strictly scientific thinking is insufficient for grappling
(10) with modern ethical dilemmas. For these reasons, aspiring physicians need to develop new ways of thinking about and interacting with patients. Training in ethics that takes narrative literature as its primary subject is one method of accomplishing this.
(15) Although training in ethics is currently provided by medical schools, this training relies heavily on an abstract, philosophical view of ethics. Although the conceptual clarity provided by a traditional ethics course can be valuable, theorizing about ethics
(20) contributes little to the understanding of everyday human experience or to preparing medical students for the multifarious ethical dilemmas they will face as physicians. A true foundation in ethics must be predicated on an understanding of human behavior that
(25) reflects a wide array of relationships and readily adapts to various perspectives, for this is what is required to develop empathy. Ethics courses drawing on narrative literature can better help students prepare for ethical dilemmas precisely because such literature attaches its
(30) readers so forcefully to the concrete and varied world of human events.

The act of reading narrative literature is uniquely suited to the development of what might be called flexible ethical thinking. To grasp the development of
(35) characters, to tangle with heightening moral crises, and to engage oneself with the story not as one's own but nevertheless as something recognizable and worthy of attention, readers must use their moral imagination. Giving oneself over to the ethical conflicts in a story
(40) requires the abandonment of strictly absolute, inviolate sets of moral principles. Reading literature also demands that the reader adopt another person's point of view—that of the narrator or a character in a story— and thus requires the ability to depart from one's
(45) personal ethical stance and examine moral issues from new perspectives.

It does not follow that readers, including medical professionals, must relinquish all moral principles, as is the case with situational ethics, in which decisions
(50) about ethical choices are made on the basis of intuition and are entirely relative to the circumstances in which they arise. Such an extremely relativistic stance would have as little benefit for the patient or physician as would a dogmatically absolutist one. Fortunately, the
(55) incorporation of narrative literature into the study of ethics, while serving as a corrective to the latter stance, need not lead to the former. But it can give us something that is lacking in the traditional philosophical study of ethics—namely, a deeper
(60) understanding of human nature that can serve as a foundation for ethical reasoning and allow greater flexibility in the application of moral principles.

21. Which one of the following most accurately states the main point of the passage?

(A) Training in ethics that incorporates narrative literature would better cultivate flexible ethical thinking and increase medical students' capacity for empathetic patient care as compared with the traditional approach of medical schools to such training.

(B) Traditional abstract ethical training, because it is too heavily focused on theoretical reasoning, tends to decrease or impair the medical student's sensitivity to modern ethical dilemmas.

(C) Only a properly designed curriculum that balances situational, abstract, and narrative approaches to ethics will adequately prepare the medical student for complex ethical confrontations involving actual patients.

(D) Narrative-based instruction in ethics is becoming increasingly popular in medical schools because it requires students to develop a capacity for empathy by examining complex moral issues from a variety of perspectives.

(E) The study of narrative literature in medical schools would nurture moral intuition, enabling the future doctor to make ethical decisions without appeal to general principles.

22. Which one of the following most accurately represents the author's use of the term "moral imagination" in line 38?

(A) a sense of curiosity, aroused by reading, that leads one to follow actively the development of problems involving the characters depicted in narratives

(B) a faculty of seeking out and recognizing the ethical controversies involved in human relationships and identifying oneself with one side or another in such controversies

(C) a capacity to understand the complexities of various ethical dilemmas and to fashion creative and innovative solutions to them

(D) an ability to understand personal aspects of ethically significant situations even if one is not a direct participant and to empathize with those involved in them

(E) an ability to act upon ethical principles different from one's own for the sake of variety

GO ON TO THE NEXT PAGE.

23. It can be inferred from the passage that the author would most likely agree with which one of the following statements?

    (A) The heavy load of technical coursework in today's medical schools often keeps them from giving adequate emphasis to courses in medical ethics.

    (B) Students learn more about ethics through the use of fiction than through the use of nonfictional readings.

    (C) The traditional method of ethical training in medical schools should be supplemented or replaced by more direct practical experience with real-life patients in ethically difficult situations.

    (D) The failings of an abstract, philosophical training in ethics can be remedied only by replacing it with a purely narrative-based approach.

    (E) Neither scientific training nor traditional philosophical ethics adequately prepares doctors to deal with the emotional dimension of patients' needs.

24. Which one of the following is most likely the author's overall purpose in the passage?

    (A) to advise medical schools on how to implement a narrative-based approach to ethics in their curricula

    (B) to argue that the current methods of ethics education are counterproductive to the formation of empathetic doctor-patient relationships

    (C) to argue that the ethical content of narrative literature foreshadows the pitfalls of situational ethics

    (D) to propose an approach to ethical training in medical school that will preserve the human dimension of medicine

    (E) to demonstrate the value of a well-designed ethics education for medical students

25. The passage ascribes each of the following characteristics to the use of narrative literature in ethical education EXCEPT:

    (A) It tends to avoid the extreme relativism of situational ethics.

    (B) It connects students to varied types of human events.

    (C) It can help lead medical students to develop new ways of dealing with patients.

    (D) It requires students to examine moral issues from new perspectives.

    (E) It can help insulate future doctors from the shock of the ethical dilemmas they will confront.

26. With regard to ethical dilemmas, the passage explicitly states each of the following EXCEPT:

    (A) Doctors face a variety of such dilemmas.

    (B) Purely scientific thinking is inadequate for dealing with modern ethical dilemmas.

    (C) Such dilemmas are more prevalent today as a result of scientific and technological advances in medicine.

    (D) Theorizing about ethics does little to prepare students to face such dilemmas.

    (E) Narrative literature can help make medical students ready to face such dilemmas.

27. The author's attitude regarding the traditional method of teaching ethics in medical school can most accurately be described as

    (A) unqualified disapproval of the method and disapproval of all of its effects

    (B) reserved judgment regarding the method and disapproval of all of its effects

    (C) partial disapproval of the method and clinical indifference toward its effects

    (D) partial approval of the method and disapproval of all of its effects

    (E) partial disapproval of the method and approval of some of its effects

S T O P

IF YOU FINISH BEFORE TIME IS CALLED, YOU MAY CHECK YOUR WORK ON THIS SECTION ONLY.
DO NOT WORK ON ANY OTHER SECTION IN THE TEST.

SECTION IV

Time—35 minutes

26 Questions

Directions: The questions in this section are based on the reasoning contained in brief statements or passages. For some questions, more than one of the choices could conceivably answer the question. However, you are to choose the best answer; that is, the response that most accurately and completely answers the question. You should not make assumptions that are by commonsense standards implausible, superfluous, or incompatible with the passage. After you have chosen the best answer, blacken the corresponding space on your answer sheet.

Questions 1–2

Ms. Smith: I am upset that my son's entire class lost two days of recess because some of the children were throwing raisins in the cafeteria. He was not throwing raisins, and it was clear to everyone just who the culprits were.

Principal: I'm sorry you're upset, Ms. Smith, but your son's situation is like being caught in a traffic jam caused by an accident. People who aren't involved in the accident nevertheless have to suffer by sitting there in the middle of it.

1. If the principal is speaking sincerely, then it can be inferred from what the principal says that the principal believes that

   (A)   many children were throwing raisins in the cafeteria
   (B)   Ms. Smith's son might not have thrown raisins in the cafeteria
   (C)   after an accident the resulting traffic jams are generally caused by police activity
   (D)   Ms. Smith's son knows who it was that threw raisins in the cafeteria
   (E)   losing two days of recess will deter future disruptions

2. The principal's response to Ms. Smith's complaint is most vulnerable to criticism on which one of the following grounds?

   (A)   It makes a generalization about all the children in the class which is not justified by the facts.
   (B)   It suggests that throwing raisins in the cafeteria produces as much inconvenience as does being caught in a traffic jam.
   (C)   It does not acknowledge the fact that a traffic jam following an accident is unavoidable while the mass punishment was avoidable.
   (D)   It assumes that Ms. Smith's son is guilty when there is evidence to the contrary which the principal has disregarded.
   (E)   It attempts to confuse the point at issue by introducing irrelevant facts about the incident.

3. Journalist: Obviously, though some animals are purely carnivorous, none would survive without plants. But the dependence is mutual. Many plant species would never have come to be had there been no animals to pollinate, fertilize, and broadcast their seeds. Also, plants' photosynthetic activity would deplete the carbon dioxide in Earth's atmosphere were it not constantly being replenished by the exhalation of animals, engine fumes, and smoke from fires, many set by human beings.

Which one of the following most accurately expresses the main conclusion of the journalist's argument?

   (A)   The photosynthetic activity of plants is necessary for animal life, but animal life is also necessary for the occurrence of photosynthesis in plants.
   (B)   Some purely carnivorous animals would not survive without plants.
   (C)   The chemical composition of Earth and its atmosphere depends, at least to some extent, on the existence and activities of the animals that populate Earth.
   (D)   Human activity is part of what prevents plants from depleting the oxygen in Earth's atmosphere on which plants and animals alike depend.
   (E)   Just as animals are dependent on plants for their survival, plants are dependent on animals for theirs.

GO ON TO THE NEXT PAGE.

4. The government-owned gas company has begun selling stoves and other gas appliances to create a larger market for its gas. Merchants who sell such products complain that the competition will hurt their businesses. That may well be; however, the government-owned gas company is within its rights. After all, the owner of a private gas company might well decide to sell such appliances and surely there would be nothing wrong with that.

Which one of the following principles, if valid, most helps to justify the reasoning above?

(A) Government-owned companies have the right to do whatever private businesses have the right to do.

(B) A government should always take seriously the complaints of merchants.

(C) Private businesses have no right to compete with government monopolies.

(D) There is nothing wrong with a government-owned company selling products so long as owners of private companies do not complain.

(E) There is nothing wrong with private companies competing against each other.

5. Toxicologist: A survey of oil-refinery workers who work with MBTE, an ingredient currently used in some smog-reducing gasolines, found an alarming incidence of complaints about headaches, fatigue, and shortness of breath. Since gasoline containing MBTE will soon be widely used, we can expect an increased incidence of headaches, fatigue, and shortness of breath.

Each of the following, if true, strengthens the toxicologist's argument EXCEPT:

(A) Most oil-refinery workers who do not work with MBTE do not have serious health problems involving headaches, fatigue, and shortness of breath.

(B) Headaches, fatigue, and shortness of breath are among the symptoms of several medical conditions that are potentially serious threats to public health.

(C) Since the time when gasoline containing MBTE was first introduced in a few metropolitan areas, those areas reported an increase in the number of complaints about headaches, fatigue, and shortness of breath.

(D) Regions in which only gasoline containing MBTE is used have a much greater incidence of headaches, fatigue, and shortness of breath than do similar regions in which only MBTE-free gasoline is used.

(E) The oil-refinery workers surveyed were carefully selected to be representative of the broader population in their medical histories prior to exposure to MBTE, as well as in other relevant respects.

6. In any field, experience is required for a proficient person to become an expert. Through experience, a proficient person gradually develops a repertory of model situations that allows an immediate, intuitive response to each new situation. This is the hallmark of expertise, and for this reason computerized "expert systems" cannot be as good as human experts. Although computers have the ability to store millions of bits of information, the knowledge of human experts, who benefit from the experience of thousands of situations, is not stored within their brains in the form of rules and facts.

The argument requires the assumption of which one of the following?

(A) Computers can show no more originality in responding to a situation than that built into them by their designers.

(B) The knowledge of human experts cannot be adequately rendered into the type of information that a computer can store.

(C) Human experts rely on information that can be expressed by rules and facts when they respond to new situations.

(D) Future advances in computer technology will not render computers capable of sorting through greater amounts of information.

(E) Human experts rely heavily on intuition while they are developing a repertory of model situations.

7. When drivers are deprived of sleep there are definite behavioral changes, such as slower responses to stimuli and a reduced ability to concentrate, but people's self-awareness of these changes is poor. Most drivers think they can tell when they are about to fall asleep, but they cannot.

Each of the following illustrates the principle that the passage illustrates EXCEPT:

(A) People who have been drinking alcohol are not good judges of whether they are too drunk to drive.

(B) Elementary school students who dislike arithmetic are not good judges of whether multiplication tables should be included in the school's curriculum.

(C) Industrial workers who have just been exposed to noxious fumes are not good judges of whether they should keep working.

(D) People who have just donated blood and have become faint are not good judges of whether they are ready to walk out of the facility.

(E) People who are being treated for schizophrenia are not good judges of whether they should continue their medical treatments.

GO ON TO THE NEXT PAGE.

8. Politician: My opponent says our zoning laws too strongly promote suburban single-family dwellings and should be changed to encourage other forms of housing like apartment buildings. Yet he lives in a house in the country. His lifestyle contradicts his own argument, which should therefore not be taken seriously.

The politician's reasoning is most vulnerable to criticism on the grounds that

(A) its characterization of the opponent's lifestyle reveals the politician's own prejudice against constructing apartment buildings

(B) it neglects the fact that apartment buildings can be built in the suburbs just as easily as in the center of the city

(C) it fails to mention the politician's own living situation

(D) its discussion of the opponent's lifestyle is irrelevant to the merits of the opponent's argument

(E) it ignores the possibility that the opponent may have previously lived in an apartment building

9. Consumers are deeply concerned about the quantity of plastic packaging on the market and have spurred manufacturers to find ways to recycle plastic materials. Despite their efforts, however, only 6.5 percent of plastic is now being recycled, as compared to 33 percent of container glass.

Each of the following, if true, helps to explain the relatively low rate of plastic recycling EXCEPT:

(A) Many factories are set up to accept and make economical use of recycled glass, whereas there are few factories that make products out of recycled plastic.

(B) Many plastic products are incompatible and cannot be recycled together, whereas most containers made of glass are compatible.

(C) The manufacture of new plastic depletes oil reserves, whereas the manufacture of new glass uses renewable resources.

(D) Unlike glass, which can be heated to thousands of degrees during the recycling process to burn off contaminants, recycled plastic cannot be heated enough to sterilize it.

(E) Plastic polymers tend to break down during the recycling process and weaken the resulting product, whereas glass does not break down.

10. Technological progress makes economic growth and widespread prosperity possible; it also makes a worker's particular skills less crucial to production. Yet workers' satisfaction in their work depends on their believing that their work is difficult and requires uncommon skills. Clearly, then, technological progress _____.

Which one of the following most logically completes the argument?

(A) decreases the quality of most products

(B) provides benefits only to those whose work is not directly affected by it

(C) is generally opposed by the workers whose work will be directly affected by it

(D) causes workers to feel less satisfaction in their work

(E) eliminates many workers' jobs

11. Environmentalist: The complex ecosystem of the North American prairie has largely been destroyed to produce cattle feed. But the prairie ecosystem once supported 30 to 70 million bison, whereas North American agriculture now supports about 50 million cattle. Since bison yield as much meat as cattle, and the natural prairie required neither pesticides, machinery, nor government subsidies, returning as much land as possible to an uncultivated state could restore biodiversity without a major decrease in meat production.

Which one of the following most accurately expresses the environmentalist's main conclusion?

(A) If earlier North American agricultural techniques were reintroduced, meat production would decrease only slightly.

(B) Protecting the habitat of wild animals so that we can utilize these animals as a food source is more cost effective than raising domesticated animals.

(C) The biodiversity of the North American prairie ecosystem should not be restored if doing so will have intolerable economic consequences.

(D) Preservation of the remaining North American bison would be a sensible policy.

(E) The devastation of the North American prairie ecosystem could be largely reversed without significantly decreasing meat production.

GO ON TO THE NEXT PAGE.

12.

Item Removed From Scoring

13. A recent study reveals that television advertising does not significantly affect children's preferences for breakfast cereals. The study compared two groups of children. One group had watched no television, and the other group had watched average amounts of television and its advertising. Both groups strongly preferred the sugary cereals heavily advertised on television.

Which one of the following statements, if true, most weakens the argument?

(A) The preferences of children who do not watch television advertising are influenced by the preferences of children who watch the advertising.

(B) The preference for sweets is not a universal trait in humans, and can be influenced by environmental factors such as television advertising.

(C) Most of the children in the group that had watched television were already familiar with the advertisements for these cereals.

(D) Both groups rejected cereals low in sugar even when these cereals were heavily advertised on television.

(E) Cereal preferences of adults who watch television are known to be significantly different from the cereal preferences of adults who do not watch television.

14. Reducing speed limits neither saves lives nor protects the environment. This is because the more slowly a car is driven, the more time it spends on the road spewing exhaust into the air and running the risk of colliding with other vehicles.

The argument's reasoning is flawed because the argument

(A) neglects the fact that some motorists completely ignore speed limits

(B) ignores the possibility of benefits from lowering speed limits other than environmental and safety benefits

(C) fails to consider that if speed limits are reduced, increased driving times will increase the number of cars on the road at any given time

(D) presumes, without providing justification, that total emissions for a given automobile trip are determined primarily by the amount of time the trip takes

(E) presumes, without providing justification, that drivers run a significant risk of collision only if they spend a lot of time on the road

15. Loggerhead turtles live and breed in distinct groups, of which some are in the Pacific Ocean and some are in the Atlantic. New evidence suggests that juvenile Pacific loggerheads that feed near the Baja peninsula hatch in Japanese waters 10,000 kilometers away. Ninety-five percent of the DNA samples taken from the Baja turtles match those taken from turtles at the Japanese nesting sites.

Which one of the following, if true, most seriously weakens the reasoning above?

(A) Nesting sites of loggerhead turtles have been found off the Pacific coast of North America several thousand kilometers north of the Baja peninsula.

(B) The distance between nesting sites and feeding sites of Atlantic loggerhead turtles is less than 5,000 kilometers.

(C) Loggerhead hatchlings in Japanese waters have been declining in number for the last decade while the number of nesting sites near the Baja peninsula has remained constant.

(D) Ninety-five percent of the DNA samples taken from the Baja turtles match those taken from Atlantic loggerhead turtles.

(E) Commercial aquariums have been successfully breeding Atlantic loggerheads with Pacific loggerheads for the last five years.

GO ON TO THE NEXT PAGE.

16. People who do not believe that others distrust them are confident in their own abilities, so people who tend to trust others think of a difficult task as a challenge rather than a threat, since this is precisely how people who are confident in their own abilities regard such tasks.

   The conclusion above follows logically if which one of the following is assumed?

   (A) People who believe that others distrust them tend to trust others.
   (B) Confidence in one's own abilities gives one confidence in the trustworthiness of others.
   (C) People who tend to trust others do not believe that others distrust them.
   (D) People who are not threatened by difficult tasks tend to find such tasks challenging.
   (E) People tend to distrust those who they believe lack self-confidence.

17. Mullen has proposed to raise taxes on the rich, who made so much money during the past decade. Yet Mullen's tax records show heavy investment in business during that time and large profits; so Mullen's proposal does not deserve our consideration.

   The flawed reasoning in the argument above is most similar to the flawed reasoning in which one of the following?

   (A) Do not vote for Smith's proposed legislation to subsidize child care for working parents; Smith is a working parent.
   (B) Do not put any credence in Dr. Han's recent proposal to ban smoking in all public places; Dr. Han is a heavy smoker.
   (C) The previous witness's testimony ought to be ignored; he has been convicted of both forgery and mail fraud.
   (D) Board member Timm's proposal to raise the salaries of the company's middle managers does not deserve to be considered; Timm's daughter is a middle manager at the company's headquarters.
   (E) Dr. Wasow's analysis of the design of this bridge should not be taken seriously; after all, Dr. Wasow has previously only designed factory buildings.

Questions 18–19

Anders: The physical structure of the brain plays an important role in thinking. So researchers developing "thinking machines"—computers that can make decisions based on both common sense and factual knowledge—should closely model those machines on the structure of the brain.

Yang: Important does not mean essential. After all, no flying machine closely modeled on birds has worked; workable aircraft are structurally very different from birds. So thinking machines closely modeled on the brain are also likely to fail. In developing a workable thinking machine, researchers would therefore increase their chances of success if they focus on the brain's function and simply ignore its physical structure.

18. The statement "thinking machines closely modeled on the brain are also likely to fail" serves which one of the following roles in Yang's argument?

   (A) the main conclusion of the argument
   (B) a subsidiary conclusion used in support of the main conclusion
   (C) a principle of research invoked in support of the conclusion
   (D) a particular example illustrating a general claim
   (E) background information providing a context for the argument

19. In evaluating Yang's argument it would be most helpful to know whether

   (A) studies of the physical structure of birds provided information crucial to the development of workable aircraft
   (B) researchers currently working on thinking machines take all thinking to involve both common sense and factual knowledge
   (C) as much time has been spent trying to develop a workable thinking machine as had been spent in developing the first workable aircraft
   (D) researchers who specialize in the structure of the brain are among those who are trying to develop thinking machines
   (E) some flying machines that were not closely modeled on birds failed to work

GO ON TO THE NEXT PAGE.

20. Shy adolescents often devote themselves totally to a hobby to help distract them from the loneliness brought on by their shyness. Sometimes they are able to become friends with others who share their hobby. But if they lose interest in that hobby, their loneliness may be exacerbated. So developing an all-consuming hobby is not a successful strategy for overcoming adolescent loneliness.

Which one of the following assumptions does the argument depend on?

(A) Eventually, shy adolescents are going to want a wider circle of friends than is provided by their hobby.

(B) No successful strategy for overcoming adolescent loneliness ever intensifies that loneliness.

(C) Shy adolescents will lose interest in their hobbies if they do not make friends through their engagement in those hobbies.

(D) Some other strategy for overcoming adolescent loneliness is generally more successful than is developing an all-consuming hobby.

(E) Shy adolescents devote themselves to hobbies mainly because they want to make friends.

21. Political scientist: As a political system, democracy does not promote political freedom. There are historical examples of democracies that ultimately resulted in some of the most oppressive societies. Likewise, there have been enlightened despotisms and oligarchies that have provided a remarkable level of political freedom to their subjects.

The reasoning in the political scientist's argument is flawed because it

(A) confuses the conditions necessary for political freedom with the conditions sufficient to bring it about

(B) fails to consider that a substantial increase in the level of political freedom might cause a society to become more democratic

(C) appeals to historical examples that are irrelevant to the causal claim being made

(D) overlooks the possibility that democracy promotes political freedom without being necessary or sufficient by itself to produce it

(E) bases its historical case on a personal point of view

22. In humans, ingested protein is broken down into amino acids, all of which must compete to enter the brain. Subsequent ingestion of sugars leads to the production of insulin, a hormone that breaks down the sugars and also rids the bloodstream of residual amino acids, except for tryptophan. Tryptophan then slips into the brain uncontested and is transformed into the chemical serotonin, increasing the brain's serotonin level. Thus, sugars can play a major role in mood elevation, helping one to feel relaxed and anxiety-free.

Which one of the following is an assumption on which the argument depends?

(A) Elevation of mood and freedom from anxiety require increasing the level of serotonin in the brain.

(B) Failure to consume foods rich in sugars results in anxiety and a lowering of mood.

(C) Serotonin can be produced naturally only if tryptophan is present in the bloodstream.

(D) Increasing the level of serotonin in the brain promotes relaxation and freedom from anxiety.

(E) The consumption of protein-rich foods results in anxiety and a lowering of mood.

GO ON TO THE NEXT PAGE.

23. If an act of civil disobedience—willfully breaking a specific law in order to bring about legal reform—is done out of self-interest alone and not out of a concern for others, it cannot be justified. But one is justified in performing an act of civil disobedience if one's conscience requires one to do so.

Which one of the following judgments most closely conforms to the principles stated above?

(A) Keisha's protest against what she perceived to be a brutal and repressive dictatorship in another country was an act of justified civil disobedience, because in organizing an illegal but peaceful demonstration calling for a return to democratic leadership in that country, she acted purely out of concern for the people of that country.

(B) Janice's protest against a law that forbade labor strikes was motivated solely by a desire to help local mine workers obtain fair wages. But her conscience did not require her to protest this law, so Janice did not perform an act of justified civil disobedience.

(C) In organizing an illegal protest against the practice in her country of having prison inmates work eighteen hours per day, Georgette performed an act of justified civil disobedience: she acted out of concern for her fellow inmates rather than out of concern for herself.

(D) Maria's deliberate violation of a law requiring prepublication government approval of all printed materials was an act of justified civil disobedience: though her interest as an owner of a publishing company would be served by repeal of the law, she violated the law because her conscience required doing so on behalf of all publishers.

(E) In organizing a parade of motorcyclists riding without helmets through the capital city, Louise's act was not one of justified civil disobedience: she was willfully challenging a specific law requiring motorcyclists to wear helmets, but her conscience did not require her to organize the parade.

24. Most land-dwelling vertebrates have rotating limbs terminating in digits, a characteristic useful for land movement. Biologists who assume that this characteristic evolved only after animals abandoned aquatic environments must consider the *Acanthostega*, a newly discovered ancestor of all land vertebrates. It possessed rotating limbs terminating in digits, but its skeleton was too feeble for land movement. It also breathed using only internal gills, indicating that it and its predecessors were exclusively aquatic.

The statements above, if true, most strongly support which one of the following?

(A) Many anatomical characteristics common to most land animals represent a disadvantage for survival underwater.

(B) None of the anatomical characteristics common to most aquatic animals represent an advantage for survival on land.

(C) *Acanthostega* originated as a land-dwelling species, but evolved gills only after moving to an underwater environment.

(D) All anatomical characteristics not useful for land movement but common to most land animals represent an advantage for survival underwater.

(E) Certain anatomical characteristics common to some aquatic animals represent an advantage for survival on land.

GO ON TO THE NEXT PAGE.

25. One reason why European music has had such a strong influence throughout the world, and why it is a sophisticated achievement, is that over time the original function of the music—whether ritual, dance, or worship—gradually became an aspect of its style, not its defining force. Dance music could stand independent of dance, for example, and sacred music independent of religious worship, because each composition has so much internal coherence that the music ultimately depends on nothing but itself.

The claims made above are compatible with each of the following EXCEPT:

(A) African music has had a more powerful impact on the world than European music has had.

(B) European military and economic expansionism partially explains the global influence of European music.

(C) original functions of many types of Chinese music are no longer their defining forces.

unintelligible when it is presented of its original function tends to be ated music.

e their appeal when they are function other than their

26. Tony: A short story is little more than a novelist's sketch pad. Only novels have narrative structures that allow writers to depict human lives accurately by portraying characters whose personalities gradually develop through life experience.

Raoul: Life consists not of a linear process of personality development, but rather of a series of completely disjointed vignettes, from many of which the discerning observer may catch glimpses of character. Thus, the short story depicts human lives more faithfully than does the novel.

The dialogue most supports the claim that Tony and Raoul disagree about whether

(A) human lives are best understood as series of completely disjointed vignettes

(B) novels and short stories employ the same strategies to depict human lives

(C) novels usually depict gradual changes in characters' personalities

(D) only short stories are used as novelists' sketch pads

(E) short stories provide glimpses of facets of character that are usually kept hidden

S T O P

IF YOU FINISH BEFORE TIME IS CALLED, YOU MAY CHECK YOUR WORK ON THIS SECTION ONLY.
DO NOT WORK ON ANY OTHER SECTION IN THE TEST.

SIGNATURE _____ ___/___/___
                                                    DATE

LSAT WRITING SAMPLE TOPIC

Due to declining student enrollment, the school board of the Winterdale School District has decided to close either Brookhaven Elementary or Oakwood Elementary. The district will need to renovate the school it leaves open. Write an essay in favor of closing one school over the other based on the following considerations:

- The school board wants to minimize renovation costs.
- The school board wants to minimize the impact of a school closing on students and staff.

Brookhaven was built in 1925, and although it is a solid building, its plumbing and heating systems are outdated, and its classroom layout will need to be reconfigured to accord with current trends in school design. The renovations required to bring Brookhaven up to date will be extensive, and architects estimate that the project will take a year to complete. The contractors chosen for the Brookhaven renovation will be able to do the most disruptive work over the summer, however. They anticipate that all classrooms will be available by the start of the school year. Only half of the administrative offices will be available, so administrators plan to share these offices until the rest can be finished. After Brookhaven is renovated, the 209 students enrolled at Oakwood will be bused to Brookhaven. All but a handful of them already take the bus to school.

Oakwood was built in the 1950s but underwent limited renovation in the 1990s. Because the plumbing and heating systems do not now require replacement, architects estimate that renovations will consist mainly of reconfiguring the administrative offices and updating the building's facade. These renovations are expected to take six months. Due to an irresolvable scheduling conflict, the contractors chosen for the Oakwood renovation will have to do all of the work while school is in session. During construction, Oakwood's administrative offices will be housed in trailers located on the school's athletic fields, which will consequently be unavailable for student use. After Oakwood is renovated, the 215 students enrolled at Brookhaven will be bused to Oakwood. About half of them currently live close enough to Brookhaven to walk to school.

Directions:

1. Use the Answer Key on the next page to check your answers.

2. Use the Scoring Worksheet below to compute your raw score.

3. Use the Score Conversion Chart to convert your raw score into the 120-180 scale.

Scoring Worksheet

1. Enter the number of questions you answered correctly in each section.

	Number Correct
SECTION I.	_____
SECTION II	_____
SECTION III.	_____
SECTION IV.	_____

2. Enter the sum here: _____

This is your Raw Score.

Conversion Chart

For Converting Raw Score to the 120-180 LSAT Scaled Score
LSAT Form 2LSS53

Reported Score	Raw Score	
	Lowest	Highest
180	98	100
179	97	97
178	96	96
177	95	95
176	94	94
175	93	93
174	92	92
173	91	91
172	90	90
171	89	89
170	88	88
169	87	87
168	86	86
167	84	85
166	83	83
165	82	82
164	80	81
163	79	79
162	77	78
161	75	76
160	74	74
159	72	73
158	71	71
157	69	70
156	67	68
155	66	66
154	64	65
153	62	63
152	60	61
151	59	59
150	57	58
149	55	56
148	54	54
147	52	53
146	50	51
145	48	49
144	47	47
143	45	46
142	44	44
141	42	43
140	40	41
139	39	39
138	37	38
137	36	36
136	34	35
135	33	33
134	31	32
133	30	30
132	29	29
131	27	28
130	26	26
129	25	25
128	23	24
127	22	22
126	21	21
125	20	20
124	18	19
123	17	17
122	16	16
121	15	15
120	0	14

SECTION I

1.	A	8.	E	15.	C	22.	C
2.	C	9.	E	16.	D	23.	A
3.	E	10.	A	17.	B	24.	A
4.	C	11.	E	18.	B		
5.	E	12.	D	19.	C		
6.	E	13.	B	20.	C		
7.	D	14.	D	21.	D		

SECTION II

1.	E	8.	C	15.	D	22.	A
2.	D	9.	A	16.	C	23.	B
3.	C	10.	B	17.	B	24.	D
4.	D	11.	A	18.	B		
5.	D	12.	D	19.	C		
6.	E	13.	E	20.	D		
7.	E	14.	E	21.	A		

SECTION III

1.	C	8.	A	15.	D	22.	D
2.	A	9.	D	16.	E	23.	E
3.	E	10.	A	17.	B	24.	D
4.	B	11.	E	18.	A	25.	E
5.	D	12.	B	19.	E	26.	C
6.	A	13.	D	20.	C	27.	E
7.	D	14.	C	21.	A		

SECTION IV

1.	B	8.	D	15.	D	22.	D
2.	C	9.	C	16.	C	23.	D
3.	E	10.	D	17.	B	24.	E
4.	A	11.	E	18.	B	25.	D
5.	B	12.	*	19.	A	26.	A
6.	B	13.	A	20.	B		
7.	B	14.	D	21.	D		

*Item removed from scoring.

Introducing . . . The Champion of LSAT Preparation™

The Official LSAT SuperPrep™

$28

The Official LSAT SuperPrep™

The Champion of LSAT Preparation™

A Publication of the Law School Admission Council,
The Producers of the LSAT®

Contains three previously administered LSATs with three full
sets of item explanations, answer keys, writing samples, and
score-conversion tables.

"The Most Noted Authority in Legal Publications."—Choice

• Practice on Genuine LSAT Questions • Review Explanations
for Right and Wrong Answers • Target Specific Categories for
Intensive Review • Simulate Actual LSAT Timing

SuperPrep is the newest, most comprehensive test preparation book by LSAC, the organization that administers the test. No other LSAT prep book has the official LSAT logic guide— an extensive guide to the critical reasoning skills measured by the test. In addition to the logic guide, this book contains three actual, previously undisclosed LSATs with explanations for every answer for every question in all three tests. You can use the exams to practice timing, and you can use the answer rationales and the logic guide to master all of the item types on the LSAT. Only LSAC offers official LSAT *PrepTests*®, and only the *Official LSAT SuperPrep* offers the most comprehensive LSAT preparation you can find in one book, all for only $28.

Visit our website: www.LSAC.org or call: 215.968.1001

General Directions for the LSAT Answer Sheet

The actual testing time for this portion of the test will be 2 hours 55 minutes. There are five sections, each with a time limit of 35 minutes. The supervisor will tell you when to begin and end each section. If you finish a section before time is called, you may check your work on that section <u>only</u>; do not turn to any other section of the test book and do not work on any other section either in the test book or on the answer sheet.

There are several different types of questions on the test, and each question type has its own directions. <u>Be sure you understand the directions for each question type before attempting to answer any questions in that section.</u>

Not everyone will finish all the questions in the time allowed. Do not hurry, but work steadily and as quickly as you can without sacrificing accuracy. You are advised to use your time effectively. If a question seems too difficult, go on to the next one and return to the difficult question after completing the section. MARK THE BEST ANSWER YOU CAN FOR EVERY QUESTION. NO DEDUCTIONS WILL BE MADE FOR WRONG ANSWERS. YOUR SCORE WILL BE BASED ONLY ON THE NUMBER OF QUESTIONS YOU ANSWER CORRECTLY.

ALL YOUR ANSWERS MUST BE MARKED ON THE ANSWER SHEET. Answer spaces for each question are lettered to correspond with the letters of the potential answers to each question in the test book. After you have decided which of the answers is correct, blacken the corresponding space on the answer sheet. BE SURE THAT EACH MARK IS BLACK AND COMPLETELY FILLS THE ANSWER SPACE. Give only one answer to each question. If you change an answer, be sure that all previous marks are <u>erased completely</u>. Since the answer sheet is machine scored, incomplete erasures may be interpreted as intended answers. ANSWERS RECORDED IN THE TEST BOOK WILL NOT BE SCORED.

There may be more questions noted on this answer sheet than there are questions in a section. Do not be concerned but be certain that the section and number of the question you are answering matches the answer sheet section and question number. Additional answer spaces in any answer sheet section should be left blank. Begin your next section in the number one answer space for that section.

LSAC takes various steps to ensure that answer sheets are returned from test centers in a timely manner for processing. In the unlikely event that an answer sheet(s) is not received, LSAC will permit the examinee to either retest at no additional fee or to receive a refund of his or her LSAT fee. THESE REMEDIES ARE THE EXCLUSIVE REMEDIES AVAILABLE IN THE UNLIKELY EVENT THAT AN ANSWER SHEET IS NOT RECEIVED BY LSAC.

Score Cancellation

Complete this section only if you are absolutely certain you want to cancel your score. A CANCELLATION REQUEST CANNOT BE RESCINDED. IF YOU ARE AT ALL UNCERTAIN, YOU SHOULD NOT COMPLETE THIS SECTION; INSTEAD, YOU SHOULD CONSIDER SUBMITTING A SIGNED SCORE CANCELLATION FORM, WHICH MUST BE RECEIVED AT LSAC WITHIN 9 CALENDAR DAYS OF THE TEST.

To cancel your score from this administration, you **must**:

A. fill in both ovals here ..... ◯ ◯
    AND

B. read the following statement. Then sign your name and enter the date. **YOUR SIGNATURE ALONE IS NOT SUFFICIENT FOR SCORE CANCELLATION. BOTH OVALS ABOVE MUST BE FILLED IN FOR SCANNING EQUIPMENT TO RECOGNIZE YOUR REQUEST FOR SCORE CANCELLATION.**

I certify that I wish to cancel my test score from this administration. I understand that my request is irreversible and that my score will not be sent to me or to the law schools to which I apply.

_____
Sign your name in full

_____
Date

FOR LSAC USE ONLY ●

HOW DID YOU PREPARE FOR THE LSAT?
(Select all that apply.)

Responses to this item are voluntary and will be used for statistical research purposes only.

◯ By studying the sample questions in the *LSAT Registration and Information Book*.
◯ By taking the free sample LSAT in the *LSAT Registration and Information Book*.
◯ By working through *The Official LSAT Prep Test(s) and/or TriplePrep*.
◯ By using a book on how to prepare for the LSAT **not** published by LSAC.
◯ By attending a commercial test preparation or coaching course.
◯ By attending a test preparation or coaching course offered through an undergraduate institution.
◯ Self study.
◯ Other preparation.
◯ No preparation.

CERTIFYING STATEMENT

Please write (DO NOT PRINT) the following statement. Sign and date.

I certify that I am the examinee whose name appears on this answer sheet and that I am here to take the LSAT for the sole purpose of being considered for admission to law school. I further certify that I will neither assist nor receive assistance from any other candidate, and I agree not to copy or retain examination questions or to transmit them in any form to any other person.

_____
_____
_____
_____
_____
_____
_____
_____
_____

SIGNATURE: _____ TODAY'S DATE: ___/___/___
                                                      MONTH DAY YEAR

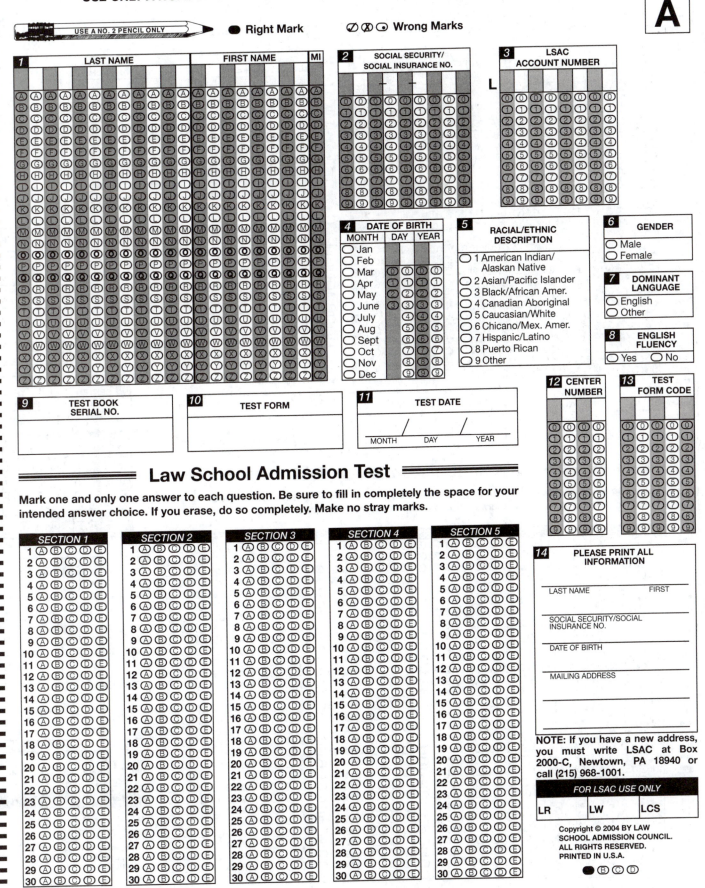

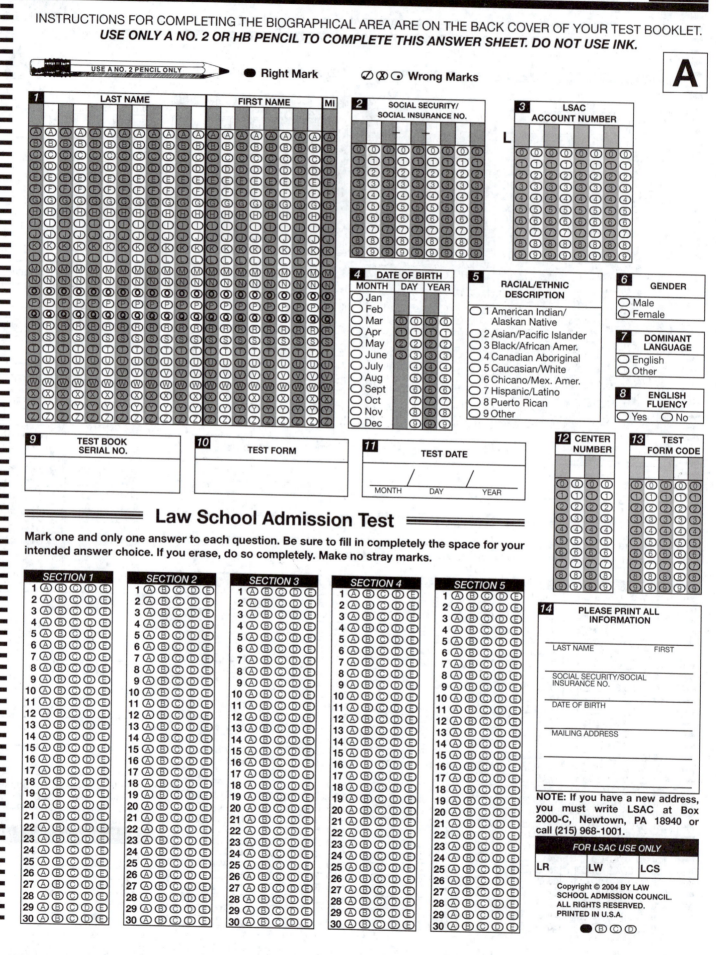

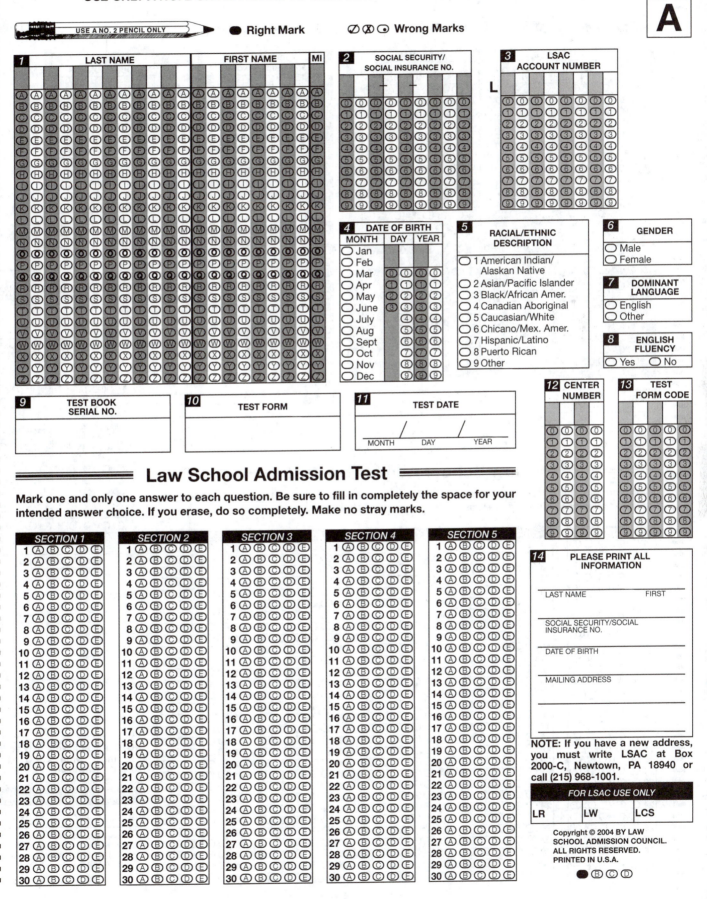

EliteView™ forms by NCS Pearson EM-250133-3:654321 Printed in U.S.A. SIDE 1

INSTRUCTIONS FOR COMPLETING THE BIOGRAPHICAL AREA ARE ON THE BACK COVER OF YOUR TEST BOOKLET.

USE ONLY A NO. 2 OR HB PENCIL TO COMPLETE THIS ANSWER SHEET. DO NOT USE INK.

USE A NO. 2 PENCIL ONLY

● Right Mark ⊘ ⊗ ⊙ Wrong Marks

A

1 LAST NAME | FIRST NAME | MI

2 SOCIAL SECURITY/ SOCIAL INSURANCE NO.

3 LSAC ACCOUNT NUMBER

L

4 DATE OF BIRTH

MONTH | DAY | YEAR

Jan, Feb, Mar, Apr, May, June, July, Aug, Sept, Oct, Nov, Dec

5 RACIAL/ETHNIC DESCRIPTION

- 1 American Indian/ Alaskan Native
- 2 Asian/Pacific Islander
- 3 Black/African Amer.
- 4 Canadian Aboriginal
- 5 Caucasian/White
- 6 Chicano/Mex. Amer.
- 7 Hispanic/Latino
- 8 Puerto Rican
- 9 Other

6 GENDER

- Male
- Female

7 DOMINANT LANGUAGE

- English
- Other

8 ENGLISH FLUENCY

- Yes
- No

9 TEST BOOK SERIAL NO.

10 TEST FORM

11 TEST DATE

MONTH / DAY / YEAR

12 CENTER NUMBER

13 TEST FORM CODE

Law School Admission Test

Mark one and only one answer to each question. Be sure to fill in completely the space for your intended answer choice. If you erase, do so completely. Make no stray marks.

	SECTION 1	SECTION 2	SECTION 3	SECTION 4	SECTION 5
1	A B C D E	A B C D E	A B C D E	A B C D E	A B C D E
2	A B C D E	A B C D E	A B C D E	A B C D E	A B C D E
3	A B C D E	A B C D E	A B C D E	A B C D E	A B C D E
4	A B C D E	A B C D E	A B C D E	A B C D E	A B C D E
5	A B C D E	A B C D E	A B C D E	A B C D E	A B C D E
6	A B C D E	A B C D E	A B C D E	A B C D E	A B C D E
7	A B C D E	A B C D E	A B C D E	A B C D E	A B C D E
8	A B C D E	A B C D E	A B C D E	A B C D E	A B C D E
9	A B C D E	A B C D E	A B C D E	A B C D E	A B C D E
10	A B C D E	A B C D E	A B C D E	A B C D E	A B C D E
11	A B C D E	A B C D E	A B C D E	A B C D E	A B C D E
12	A B C D E	A B C D E	A B C D E	A B C D E	A B C D E
13	A B C D E	A B C D E	A B C D E	A B C D E	A B C D E
14	A B C D E	A B C D E	A B C D E	A B C D E	A B C D E
15	A B C D E	A B C D E	A B C D E	A B C D E	A B C D E
16	A B C D E	A B C D E	A B C D E	A B C D E	A B C D E
17	A B C D E	A B C D E	A B C D E	A B C D E	A B C D E
18	A B C D E	A B C D E	A B C D E	A B C D E	A B C D E
19	A B C D E	A B C D E	A B C D E	A B C D E	A B C D E
20	A B C D E	A B C D E	A B C D E	A B C D E	A B C D E
21	A B C D E	A B C D E	A B C D E	A B C D E	A B C D E
22	A B C D E	A B C D E	A B C D E	A B C D E	A B C D E
23	A B C D E	A B C D E	A B C D E	A B C D E	A B C D E
24	A B C D E	A B C D E	A B C D E	A B C D E	A B C D E
25	A B C D E	A B C D E	A B C D E	A B C D E	A B C D E
26	A B C D E	A B C D E	A B C D E	A B C D E	A B C D E
27	A B C D E	A B C D E	A B C D E	A B C D E	A B C D E
28	A B C D E	A B C D E	A B C D E	A B C D E	A B C D E
29	A B C D E	A B C D E	A B C D E	A B C D E	A B C D E
30	A B C D E	A B C D E	A B C D E	A B C D E	A B C D E

14 PLEASE PRINT ALL INFORMATION

LAST NAME FIRST

SOCIAL SECURITY/SOCIAL INSURANCE NO.

DATE OF BIRTH

MAILING ADDRESS

NOTE: If you have a new address, you must write LSAC at Box 2000-C, Newtown, PA 18940 or call (215) 968-1001.

FOR LSAC USE ONLY

LR	LW	LCS

● B C D

INSTRUCTIONS FOR COMPLETING THE BIOGRAPHICAL AREA ARE ON THE BACK COVER OF YOUR TEST BOOKLET.
USE ONLY A NO. 2 OR HB PENCIL TO COMPLETE THIS ANSWER SHEET. DO NOT USE INK.

A

USE A NO. 2 PENCIL ONLY   ● **Right Mark**   ⊘⊗⊙ **Wrong Marks**

1 LAST NAME   FIRST NAME   MI

2 SOCIAL SECURITY/ SOCIAL INSURANCE NO.

3 LSAC ACCOUNT NUMBER

L

4 DATE OF BIRTH

MONTH	DAY	YEAR
Jan		
Feb		
Mar		
Apr		
May		
June		
July		
Aug		
Sept		
Oct		
Nov		
Dec		

5 RACIAL/ETHNIC DESCRIPTION

- 1 American Indian/ Alaskan Native
- 2 Asian/Pacific Islander
- 3 Black/African Amer.
- 4 Canadian Aboriginal
- 5 Caucasian/White
- 6 Chicano/Mex. Amer.
- 7 Hispanic/Latino
- 8 Puerto Rican
- 9 Other

6 GENDER
- Male
- Female

7 DOMINANT LANGUAGE
- English
- Other

8 ENGLISH FLUENCY
- Yes   No

9 TEST BOOK SERIAL NO.

10 TEST FORM

11 TEST DATE

MONTH   DAY   YEAR

12 CENTER NUMBER

13 TEST FORM CODE

Law School Admission Test

Mark one and only one answer to each question. Be sure to fill in completely the space for your intended answer choice. If you erase, do so completely. Make no stray marks.

SECTION 1 — 1–30 (A B C D E)

SECTION 2 — 1–30 (A B C D E)

SECTION 3 — 1–30 (A B C D E)

SECTION 4 — 1–30 (A B C D E)

SECTION 5 — 1–30 (A B C D E)

14 PLEASE PRINT ALL INFORMATION

LAST NAME   FIRST

SOCIAL SECURITY/SOCIAL INSURANCE NO.

DATE OF BIRTH

MAILING ADDRESS

NOTE: If you have a new address, you must write LSAC at Box 2000-C, Newtown, PA 18940 or call (215) 968-1001.

FOR LSAC USE ONLY		
LR	LW	LCS

● Ⓑ Ⓒ Ⓓ

INSTRUCTIONS FOR COMPLETING THE BIOGRAPHICAL AREA ARE ON THE BACK COVER OF YOUR TEST BOOKLET.
USE ONLY A NO. 2 OR HB PENCIL TO COMPLETE THIS ANSWER SHEET. DO NOT USE INK.

A

USE A NO. 2 PENCIL ONLY   ● **Right Mark**   ⊘ⓧ⊙ **Wrong Marks**

1 LAST NAME   FIRST NAME   MI

2 SOCIAL SECURITY/ SOCIAL INSURANCE NO.

3 LSAC ACCOUNT NUMBER

L

4 DATE OF BIRTH

MONTH	DAY	YEAR
○ Jan		
○ Feb		
○ Mar		
○ Apr		
○ May		
○ June		
○ July		
○ Aug		
○ Sept		
○ Oct		
○ Nov		
○ Dec		

5 RACIAL/ETHNIC DESCRIPTION

- ○ 1 American Indian/ Alaskan Native
- ○ 2 Asian/Pacific Islander
- ○ 3 Black/African Amer.
- ○ 4 Canadian Aboriginal
- ○ 5 Caucasian/White
- ○ 6 Chicano/Mex. Amer.
- ○ 7 Hispanic/Latino
- ○ 8 Puerto Rican
- ○ 9 Other

6 GENDER
- ○ Male
- ○ Female

7 DOMINANT LANGUAGE
- ○ English
- ○ Other

8 ENGLISH FLUENCY
- ○ Yes   ○ No

9 TEST BOOK SERIAL NO.

10 TEST FORM

11 TEST DATE

MONTH / DAY / YEAR

12 CENTER NUMBER

13 TEST FORM CODE

Law School Admission Test

Mark one and only one answer to each question. Be sure to fill in completely the space for your intended answer choice. If you erase, do so completely. Make no stray marks.

SECTION 1
1 Ⓐ Ⓑ Ⓒ Ⓓ Ⓔ
2 Ⓐ Ⓑ Ⓒ Ⓓ Ⓔ
3 Ⓐ Ⓑ Ⓒ Ⓓ Ⓔ
4 Ⓐ Ⓑ Ⓒ Ⓓ Ⓔ
5 Ⓐ Ⓑ Ⓒ Ⓓ Ⓔ
6 Ⓐ Ⓑ Ⓒ Ⓓ Ⓔ
7 Ⓐ Ⓑ Ⓒ Ⓓ Ⓔ
8 Ⓐ Ⓑ Ⓒ Ⓓ Ⓔ
9 Ⓐ Ⓑ Ⓒ Ⓓ Ⓔ
10 Ⓐ Ⓑ Ⓒ Ⓓ Ⓔ
11 Ⓐ Ⓑ Ⓒ Ⓓ Ⓔ
12 Ⓐ Ⓑ Ⓒ Ⓓ Ⓔ
13 Ⓐ Ⓑ Ⓒ Ⓓ Ⓔ
14 Ⓐ Ⓑ Ⓒ Ⓓ Ⓔ
15 Ⓐ Ⓑ Ⓒ Ⓓ Ⓔ
16 Ⓐ Ⓑ Ⓒ Ⓓ Ⓔ
17 Ⓐ Ⓑ Ⓒ Ⓓ Ⓔ
18 Ⓐ Ⓑ Ⓒ Ⓓ Ⓔ
19 Ⓐ Ⓑ Ⓒ Ⓓ Ⓔ
20 Ⓐ Ⓑ Ⓒ Ⓓ Ⓔ
21 Ⓐ Ⓑ Ⓒ Ⓓ Ⓔ
22 Ⓐ Ⓑ Ⓒ Ⓓ Ⓔ
23 Ⓐ Ⓑ Ⓒ Ⓓ Ⓔ
24 Ⓐ Ⓑ Ⓒ Ⓓ Ⓔ
25 Ⓐ Ⓑ Ⓒ Ⓓ Ⓔ
26 Ⓐ Ⓑ Ⓒ Ⓓ Ⓔ
27 Ⓐ Ⓑ Ⓒ Ⓓ Ⓔ
28 Ⓐ Ⓑ Ⓒ Ⓓ Ⓔ
29 Ⓐ Ⓑ Ⓒ Ⓓ Ⓔ
30 Ⓐ Ⓑ Ⓒ Ⓓ Ⓔ

SECTION 2
1 Ⓐ Ⓑ Ⓒ Ⓓ Ⓔ
2 Ⓐ Ⓑ Ⓒ Ⓓ Ⓔ
3 Ⓐ Ⓑ Ⓒ Ⓓ Ⓔ
4 Ⓐ Ⓑ Ⓒ Ⓓ Ⓔ
5 Ⓐ Ⓑ Ⓒ Ⓓ Ⓔ
6 Ⓐ Ⓑ Ⓒ Ⓓ Ⓔ
7 Ⓐ Ⓑ Ⓒ Ⓓ Ⓔ
8 Ⓐ Ⓑ Ⓒ Ⓓ Ⓔ
9 Ⓐ Ⓑ Ⓒ Ⓓ Ⓔ
10 Ⓐ Ⓑ Ⓒ Ⓓ Ⓔ
11 Ⓐ Ⓑ Ⓒ Ⓓ Ⓔ
12 Ⓐ Ⓑ Ⓒ Ⓓ Ⓔ
13 Ⓐ Ⓑ Ⓒ Ⓓ Ⓔ
14 Ⓐ Ⓑ Ⓒ Ⓓ Ⓔ
15 Ⓐ Ⓑ Ⓒ Ⓓ Ⓔ
16 Ⓐ Ⓑ Ⓒ Ⓓ Ⓔ
17 Ⓐ Ⓑ Ⓒ Ⓓ Ⓔ
18 Ⓐ Ⓑ Ⓒ Ⓓ Ⓔ
19 Ⓐ Ⓑ Ⓒ Ⓓ Ⓔ
20 Ⓐ Ⓑ Ⓒ Ⓓ Ⓔ
21 Ⓐ Ⓑ Ⓒ Ⓓ Ⓔ
22 Ⓐ Ⓑ Ⓒ Ⓓ Ⓔ
23 Ⓐ Ⓑ Ⓒ Ⓓ Ⓔ
24 Ⓐ Ⓑ Ⓒ Ⓓ Ⓔ
25 Ⓐ Ⓑ Ⓒ Ⓓ Ⓔ
26 Ⓐ Ⓑ Ⓒ Ⓓ Ⓔ
27 Ⓐ Ⓑ Ⓒ Ⓓ Ⓔ
28 Ⓐ Ⓑ Ⓒ Ⓓ Ⓔ
29 Ⓐ Ⓑ Ⓒ Ⓓ Ⓔ
30 Ⓐ Ⓑ Ⓒ Ⓓ Ⓔ

SECTION 3
1 Ⓐ Ⓑ Ⓒ Ⓓ Ⓔ
2 Ⓐ Ⓑ Ⓒ Ⓓ Ⓔ
3 Ⓐ Ⓑ Ⓒ Ⓓ Ⓔ
4 Ⓐ Ⓑ Ⓒ Ⓓ Ⓔ
5 Ⓐ Ⓑ Ⓒ Ⓓ Ⓔ
6 Ⓐ Ⓑ Ⓒ Ⓓ Ⓔ
7 Ⓐ Ⓑ Ⓒ Ⓓ Ⓔ
8 Ⓐ Ⓑ Ⓒ Ⓓ Ⓔ
9 Ⓐ Ⓑ Ⓒ Ⓓ Ⓔ
10 Ⓐ Ⓑ Ⓒ Ⓓ Ⓔ
11 Ⓐ Ⓑ Ⓒ Ⓓ Ⓔ
12 Ⓐ Ⓑ Ⓒ Ⓓ Ⓔ
13 Ⓐ Ⓑ Ⓒ Ⓓ Ⓔ
14 Ⓐ Ⓑ Ⓒ Ⓓ Ⓔ
15 Ⓐ Ⓑ Ⓒ Ⓓ Ⓔ
16 Ⓐ Ⓑ Ⓒ Ⓓ Ⓔ
17 Ⓐ Ⓑ Ⓒ Ⓓ Ⓔ
18 Ⓐ Ⓑ Ⓒ Ⓓ Ⓔ
19 Ⓐ Ⓑ Ⓒ Ⓓ Ⓔ
20 Ⓐ Ⓑ Ⓒ Ⓓ Ⓔ
21 Ⓐ Ⓑ Ⓒ Ⓓ Ⓔ
22 Ⓐ Ⓑ Ⓒ Ⓓ Ⓔ
23 Ⓐ Ⓑ Ⓒ Ⓓ Ⓔ
24 Ⓐ Ⓑ Ⓒ Ⓓ Ⓔ
25 Ⓐ Ⓑ Ⓒ Ⓓ Ⓔ
26 Ⓐ Ⓑ Ⓒ Ⓓ Ⓔ
27 Ⓐ Ⓑ Ⓒ Ⓓ Ⓔ
28 Ⓐ Ⓑ Ⓒ Ⓓ Ⓔ
29 Ⓐ Ⓑ Ⓒ Ⓓ Ⓔ
30 Ⓐ Ⓑ Ⓒ Ⓓ Ⓔ

SECTION 4
1 Ⓐ Ⓑ Ⓒ Ⓓ Ⓔ
2 Ⓐ Ⓑ Ⓒ Ⓓ Ⓔ
3 Ⓐ Ⓑ Ⓒ Ⓓ Ⓔ
4 Ⓐ Ⓑ Ⓒ Ⓓ Ⓔ
5 Ⓐ Ⓑ Ⓒ Ⓓ Ⓔ
6 Ⓐ Ⓑ Ⓒ Ⓓ Ⓔ
7 Ⓐ Ⓑ Ⓒ Ⓓ Ⓔ
8 Ⓐ Ⓑ Ⓒ Ⓓ Ⓔ
9 Ⓐ Ⓑ Ⓒ Ⓓ Ⓔ
10 Ⓐ Ⓑ Ⓒ Ⓓ Ⓔ
11 Ⓐ Ⓑ Ⓒ Ⓓ Ⓔ
12 Ⓐ Ⓑ Ⓒ Ⓓ Ⓔ
13 Ⓐ Ⓑ Ⓒ Ⓓ Ⓔ
14 Ⓐ Ⓑ Ⓒ Ⓓ Ⓔ
15 Ⓐ Ⓑ Ⓒ Ⓓ Ⓔ
16 Ⓐ Ⓑ Ⓒ Ⓓ Ⓔ
17 Ⓐ Ⓑ Ⓒ Ⓓ Ⓔ
18 Ⓐ Ⓑ Ⓒ Ⓓ Ⓔ
19 Ⓐ Ⓑ Ⓒ Ⓓ Ⓔ
20 Ⓐ Ⓑ Ⓒ Ⓓ Ⓔ
21 Ⓐ Ⓑ Ⓒ Ⓓ Ⓔ
22 Ⓐ Ⓑ Ⓒ Ⓓ Ⓔ
23 Ⓐ Ⓑ Ⓒ Ⓓ Ⓔ
24 Ⓐ Ⓑ Ⓒ Ⓓ Ⓔ
25 Ⓐ Ⓑ Ⓒ Ⓓ Ⓔ
26 Ⓐ Ⓑ Ⓒ Ⓓ Ⓔ
27 Ⓐ Ⓑ Ⓒ Ⓓ Ⓔ
28 Ⓐ Ⓑ Ⓒ Ⓓ Ⓔ
29 Ⓐ Ⓑ Ⓒ Ⓓ Ⓔ
30 Ⓐ Ⓑ Ⓒ Ⓓ Ⓔ

SECTION 5
1 Ⓐ Ⓑ Ⓒ Ⓓ Ⓔ
2 Ⓐ Ⓑ Ⓒ Ⓓ Ⓔ
3 Ⓐ Ⓑ Ⓒ Ⓓ Ⓔ
4 Ⓐ Ⓑ Ⓒ Ⓓ Ⓔ
5 Ⓐ Ⓑ Ⓒ Ⓓ Ⓔ
6 Ⓐ Ⓑ Ⓒ Ⓓ Ⓔ
7 Ⓐ Ⓑ Ⓒ Ⓓ Ⓔ
8 Ⓐ Ⓑ Ⓒ Ⓓ Ⓔ
9 Ⓐ Ⓑ Ⓒ Ⓓ Ⓔ
10 Ⓐ Ⓑ Ⓒ Ⓓ Ⓔ
11 Ⓐ Ⓑ Ⓒ Ⓓ Ⓔ
12 Ⓐ Ⓑ Ⓒ Ⓓ Ⓔ
13 Ⓐ Ⓑ Ⓒ Ⓓ Ⓔ
14 Ⓐ Ⓑ Ⓒ Ⓓ Ⓔ
15 Ⓐ Ⓑ Ⓒ Ⓓ Ⓔ
16 Ⓐ Ⓑ Ⓒ Ⓓ Ⓔ
17 Ⓐ Ⓑ Ⓒ Ⓓ Ⓔ
18 Ⓐ Ⓑ Ⓒ Ⓓ Ⓔ
19 Ⓐ Ⓑ Ⓒ Ⓓ Ⓔ
20 Ⓐ Ⓑ Ⓒ Ⓓ Ⓔ
21 Ⓐ Ⓑ Ⓒ Ⓓ Ⓔ
22 Ⓐ Ⓑ Ⓒ Ⓓ Ⓔ
23 Ⓐ Ⓑ Ⓒ Ⓓ Ⓔ
24 Ⓐ Ⓑ Ⓒ Ⓓ Ⓔ
25 Ⓐ Ⓑ Ⓒ Ⓓ Ⓔ
26 Ⓐ Ⓑ Ⓒ Ⓓ Ⓔ
27 Ⓐ Ⓑ Ⓒ Ⓓ Ⓔ
28 Ⓐ Ⓑ Ⓒ Ⓓ Ⓔ
29 Ⓐ Ⓑ Ⓒ Ⓓ Ⓔ
30 Ⓐ Ⓑ Ⓒ Ⓓ Ⓔ

14 PLEASE PRINT ALL INFORMATION

LAST NAME   FIRST

SOCIAL SECURITY/SOCIAL INSURANCE NO.

DATE OF BIRTH

MAILING ADDRESS

NOTE: If you have a new address, you must write LSAC at Box 2000-C, Newtown, PA 18940 or call (215) 968-1001.

FOR LSAC USE ONLY		
LR	LW	LCS

● Ⓑ Ⓒ Ⓓ

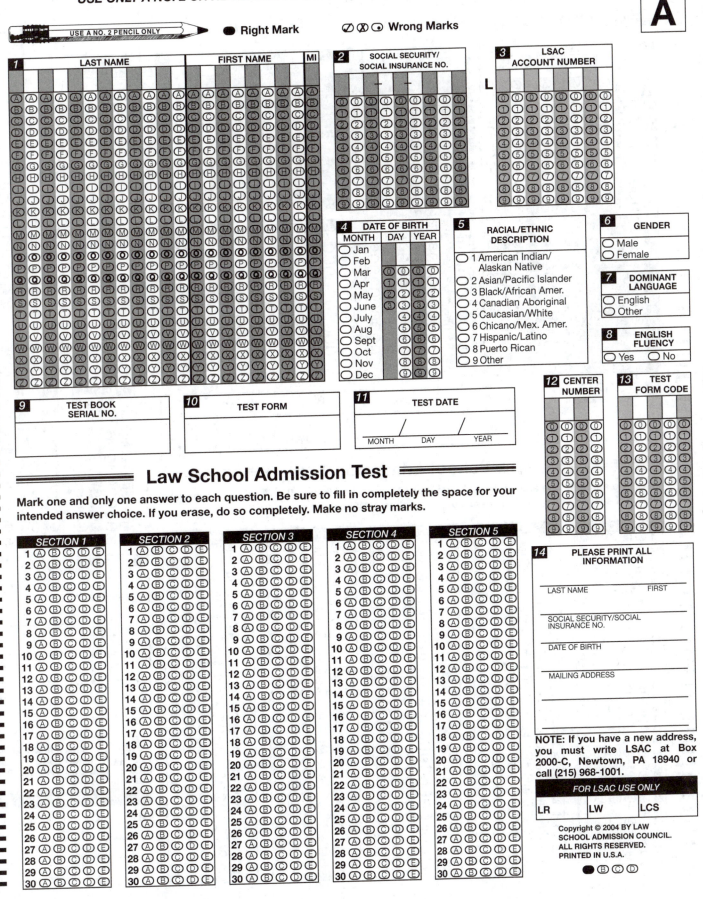

EliteView™ forms by NCS Pearson EM-250133-3:654321   Printed in U.S.A.

SIDE 1

INSTRUCTIONS FOR COMPLETING THE BIOGRAPHICAL AREA ARE ON THE BACK COVER OF YOUR TEST BOOKLET.
USE ONLY A NO. 2 OR HB PENCIL TO COMPLETE THIS ANSWER SHEET. DO NOT USE INK.

USE A NO. 2 PENCIL ONLY   ● Right Mark   ⊘ ⊗ ⊙ Wrong Marks

A

1 LAST NAME   FIRST NAME   MI

2 SOCIAL SECURITY/ SOCIAL INSURANCE NO.

3 LSAC ACCOUNT NUMBER

L

4 DATE OF BIRTH

MONTH	DAY	YEAR
○ Jan		
○ Feb		
○ Mar		
○ Apr		
○ May		
○ June		
○ July		
○ Aug		
○ Sept		
○ Oct		
○ Nov		
○ Dec		

5 RACIAL/ETHNIC DESCRIPTION

- ○ 1 American Indian/ Alaskan Native
- ○ 2 Asian/Pacific Islander
- ○ 3 Black/African Amer.
- ○ 4 Canadian Aboriginal
- ○ 5 Caucasian/White
- ○ 6 Chicano/Mex. Amer.
- ○ 7 Hispanic/Latino
- ○ 8 Puerto Rican
- ○ 9 Other

6 GENDER
- ○ Male
- ○ Female

7 DOMINANT LANGUAGE
- ○ English
- ○ Other

8 ENGLISH FLUENCY
- ○ Yes   ○ No

9 TEST BOOK SERIAL NO.

10 TEST FORM

11 TEST DATE

MONTH   DAY   YEAR

12 CENTER NUMBER

13 TEST FORM CODE

Law School Admission Test

Mark one and only one answer to each question. Be sure to fill in completely the space for your intended answer choice. If you erase, do so completely. Make no stray marks.

SECTION 1

1 ⒶⒷⒸⒹⒺ
2 ⒶⒷⒸⒹⒺ
3 ⒶⒷⒸⒹⒺ
4 ⒶⒷⒸⒹⒺ
5 ⒶⒷⒸⒹⒺ
6 ⒶⒷⒸⒹⒺ
7 ⒶⒷⒸⒹⒺ
8 ⒶⒷⒸⒹⒺ
9 ⒶⒷⒸⒹⒺ
10 ⒶⒷⒸⒹⒺ
11 ⒶⒷⒸⒹⒺ
12 ⒶⒷⒸⒹⒺ
13 ⒶⒷⒸⒹⒺ
14 ⒶⒷⒸⒹⒺ
15 ⒶⒷⒸⒹⒺ
16 ⒶⒷⒸⒹⒺ
17 ⒶⒷⒸⒹⒺ
18 ⒶⒷⒸⒹⒺ
19 ⒶⒷⒸⒹⒺ
20 ⒶⒷⒸⒹⒺ
21 ⒶⒷⒸⒹⒺ
22 ⒶⒷⒸⒹⒺ
23 ⒶⒷⒸⒹⒺ
24 ⒶⒷⒸⒹⒺ
25 ⒶⒷⒸⒹⒺ
26 ⒶⒷⒸⒹⒺ
27 ⒶⒷⒸⒹⒺ
28 ⒶⒷⒸⒹⒺ
29 ⒶⒷⒸⒹⒺ
30 ⒶⒷⒸⒹⒺ

SECTION 2

1 ⒶⒷⒸⒹⒺ
2 ⒶⒷⒸⒹⒺ
3 ⒶⒷⒸⒹⒺ
4 ⒶⒷⒸⒹⒺ
5 ⒶⒷⒸⒹⒺ
6 ⒶⒷⒸⒹⒺ
7 ⒶⒷⒸⒹⒺ
8 ⒶⒷⒸⒹⒺ
9 ⒶⒷⒸⒹⒺ
10 ⒶⒷⒸⒹⒺ
11 ⒶⒷⒸⒹⒺ
12 ⒶⒷⒸⒹⒺ
13 ⒶⒷⒸⒹⒺ
14 ⒶⒷⒸⒹⒺ
15 ⒶⒷⒸⒹⒺ
16 ⒶⒷⒸⒹⒺ
17 ⒶⒷⒸⒹⒺ
18 ⒶⒷⒸⒹⒺ
19 ⒶⒷⒸⒹⒺ
20 ⒶⒷⒸⒹⒺ
21 ⒶⒷⒸⒹⒺ
22 ⒶⒷⒸⒹⒺ
23 ⒶⒷⒸⒹⒺ
24 ⒶⒷⒸⒹⒺ
25 ⒶⒷⒸⒹⒺ
26 ⒶⒷⒸⒹⒺ
27 ⒶⒷⒸⒹⒺ
28 ⒶⒷⒸⒹⒺ
29 ⒶⒷⒸⒹⒺ
30 ⒶⒷⒸⒹⒺ

SECTION 3

1 ⒶⒷⒸⒹⒺ
2 ⒶⒷⒸⒹⒺ
3 ⒶⒷⒸⒹⒺ
4 ⒶⒷⒸⒹⒺ
5 ⒶⒷⒸⒹⒺ
6 ⒶⒷⒸⒹⒺ
7 ⒶⒷⒸⒹⒺ
8 ⒶⒷⒸⒹⒺ
9 ⒶⒷⒸⒹⒺ
10 ⒶⒷⒸⒹⒺ
11 ⒶⒷⒸⒹⒺ
12 ⒶⒷⒸⒹⒺ
13 ⒶⒷⒸⒹⒺ
14 ⒶⒷⒸⒹⒺ
15 ⒶⒷⒸⒹⒺ
16 ⒶⒷⒸⒹⒺ
17 ⒶⒷⒸⒹⒺ
18 ⒶⒷⒸⒹⒺ
19 ⒶⒷⒸⒹⒺ
20 ⒶⒷⒸⒹⒺ
21 ⒶⒷⒸⒹⒺ
22 ⒶⒷⒸⒹⒺ
23 ⒶⒷⒸⒹⒺ
24 ⒶⒷⒸⒹⒺ
25 ⒶⒷⒸⒹⒺ
26 ⒶⒷⒸⒹⒺ
27 ⒶⒷⒸⒹⒺ
28 ⒶⒷⒸⒹⒺ
29 ⒶⒷⒸⒹⒺ
30 ⒶⒷⒸⒹⒺ

SECTION 4

1 ⒶⒷⒸⒹⒺ
2 ⒶⒷⒸⒹⒺ
3 ⒶⒷⒸⒹⒺ
4 ⒶⒷⒸⒹⒺ
5 ⒶⒷⒸⒹⒺ
6 ⒶⒷⒸⒹⒺ
7 ⒶⒷⒸⒹⒺ
8 ⒶⒷⒸⒹⒺ
9 ⒶⒷⒸⒹⒺ
10 ⒶⒷⒸⒹⒺ
11 ⒶⒷⒸⒹⒺ
12 ⒶⒷⒸⒹⒺ
13 ⒶⒷⒸⒹⒺ
14 ⒶⒷⒸⒹⒺ
15 ⒶⒷⒸⒹⒺ
16 ⒶⒷⒸⒹⒺ
17 ⒶⒷⒸⒹⒺ
18 ⒶⒷⒸⒹⒺ
19 ⒶⒷⒸⒹⒺ
20 ⒶⒷⒸⒹⒺ
21 ⒶⒷⒸⒹⒺ
22 ⒶⒷⒸⒹⒺ
23 ⒶⒷⒸⒹⒺ
24 ⒶⒷⒸⒹⒺ
25 ⒶⒷⒸⒹⒺ
26 ⒶⒷⒸⒹⒺ
27 ⒶⒷⒸⒹⒺ
28 ⒶⒷⒸⒹⒺ
29 ⒶⒷⒸⒹⒺ
30 ⒶⒷⒸⒹⒺ

SECTION 5

1 ⒶⒷⒸⒹⒺ
2 ⒶⒷⒸⒹⒺ
3 ⒶⒷⒸⒹⒺ
4 ⒶⒷⒸⒹⒺ
5 ⒶⒷⒸⒹⒺ
6 ⒶⒷⒸⒹⒺ
7 ⒶⒷⒸⒹⒺ
8 ⒶⒷⒸⒹⒺ
9 ⒶⒷⒸⒹⒺ
10 ⒶⒷⒸⒹⒺ
11 ⒶⒷⒸⒹⒺ
12 ⒶⒷⒸⒹⒺ
13 ⒶⒷⒸⒹⒺ
14 ⒶⒷⒸⒹⒺ
15 ⒶⒷⒸⒹⒺ
16 ⒶⒷⒸⒹⒺ
17 ⒶⒷⒸⒹⒺ
18 ⒶⒷⒸⒹⒺ
19 ⒶⒷⒸⒹⒺ
20 ⒶⒷⒸⒹⒺ
21 ⒶⒷⒸⒹⒺ
22 ⒶⒷⒸⒹⒺ
23 ⒶⒷⒸⒹⒺ
24 ⒶⒷⒸⒹⒺ
25 ⒶⒷⒸⒹⒺ
26 ⒶⒷⒸⒹⒺ
27 ⒶⒷⒸⒹⒺ
28 ⒶⒷⒸⒹⒺ
29 ⒶⒷⒸⒹⒺ
30 ⒶⒷⒸⒹⒺ

14 PLEASE PRINT ALL INFORMATION

LAST NAME   FIRST

SOCIAL SECURITY/SOCIAL INSURANCE NO.

DATE OF BIRTH

MAILING ADDRESS

NOTE: If you have a new address, you must write LSAC at Box 2000-C, Newtown, PA 18940 or call (215) 968-1001.

FOR LSAC USE ONLY		
LR	LW	LCS

INSTRUCTIONS FOR COMPLETING THE BIOGRAPHICAL AREA ARE ON THE BACK COVER OF YOUR TEST BOOKLET.
USE ONLY A NO. 2 OR HB PENCIL TO COMPLETE THIS ANSWER SHEET. DO NOT USE INK.

A

USE A NO. 2 PENCIL ONLY　　● **Right Mark**　　⊘ⓧ⊙ **Wrong Marks**

1 LAST NAME　　FIRST NAME　　MI

2 SOCIAL SECURITY/ SOCIAL INSURANCE NO.

3 LSAC ACCOUNT NUMBER

4 DATE OF BIRTH

MONTH	DAY	YEAR
Jan		
Feb		
Mar		
Apr		
May		
June		
July		
Aug		
Sept		
Oct		
Nov		
Dec		

5 RACIAL/ETHNIC DESCRIPTION
- 1 American Indian/ Alaskan Native
- 2 Asian/Pacific Islander
- 3 Black/African Amer.
- 4 Canadian Aboriginal
- 5 Caucasian/White
- 6 Chicano/Mex. Amer.
- 7 Hispanic/Latino
- 8 Puerto Rican
- 9 Other

6 GENDER
- Male
- Female

7 DOMINANT LANGUAGE
- English
- Other

8 ENGLISH FLUENCY
- Yes　- No

9 TEST BOOK SERIAL NO.

10 TEST FORM

11 TEST DATE
MONTH / DAY / YEAR

12 CENTER NUMBER

13 TEST FORM CODE

Law School Admission Test

Mark one and only one answer to each question. Be sure to fill in completely the space for your intended answer choice. If you erase, do so completely. Make no stray marks.

SECTION 1 (1–30, A B C D E)
SECTION 2 (1–30, A B C D E)
SECTION 3 (1–30, A B C D E)
SECTION 4 (1–30, A B C D E)
SECTION 5 (1–30, A B C D E)

14 PLEASE PRINT ALL INFORMATION

LAST NAME　　FIRST

SOCIAL SECURITY/SOCIAL INSURANCE NO.

DATE OF BIRTH

MAILING ADDRESS

NOTE: If you have a new address, you must write LSAC at Box 2000-C, Newtown, PA 18940 or call (215) 968-1001.

FOR LSAC USE ONLY		
LR	LW	LCS

● Ⓑ Ⓒ Ⓓ

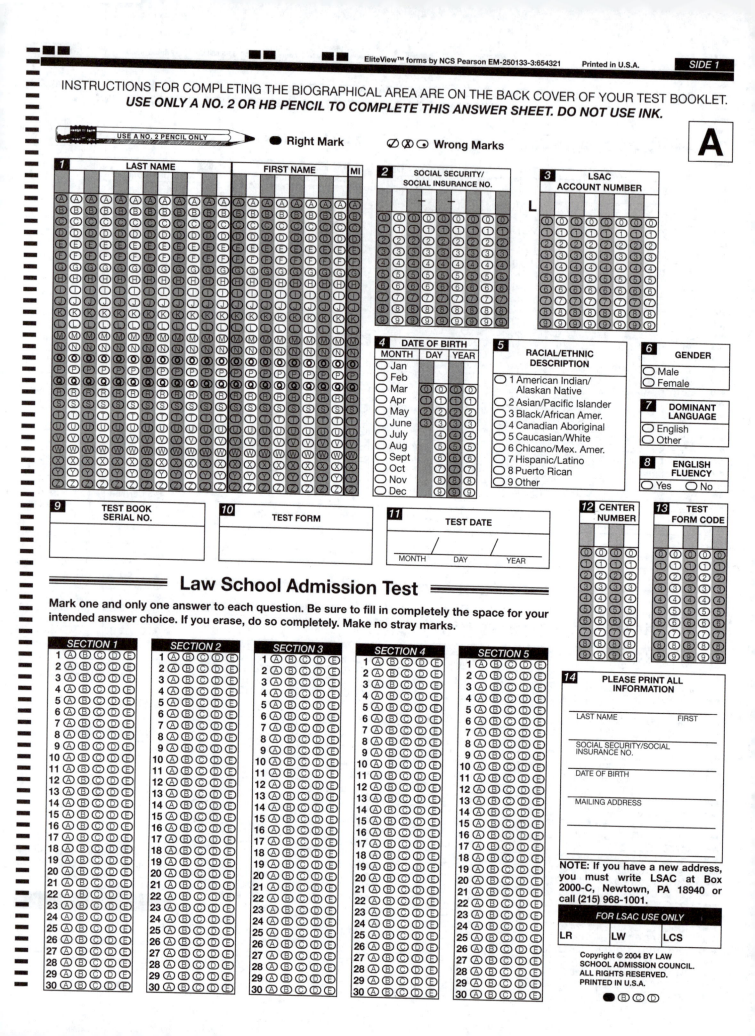

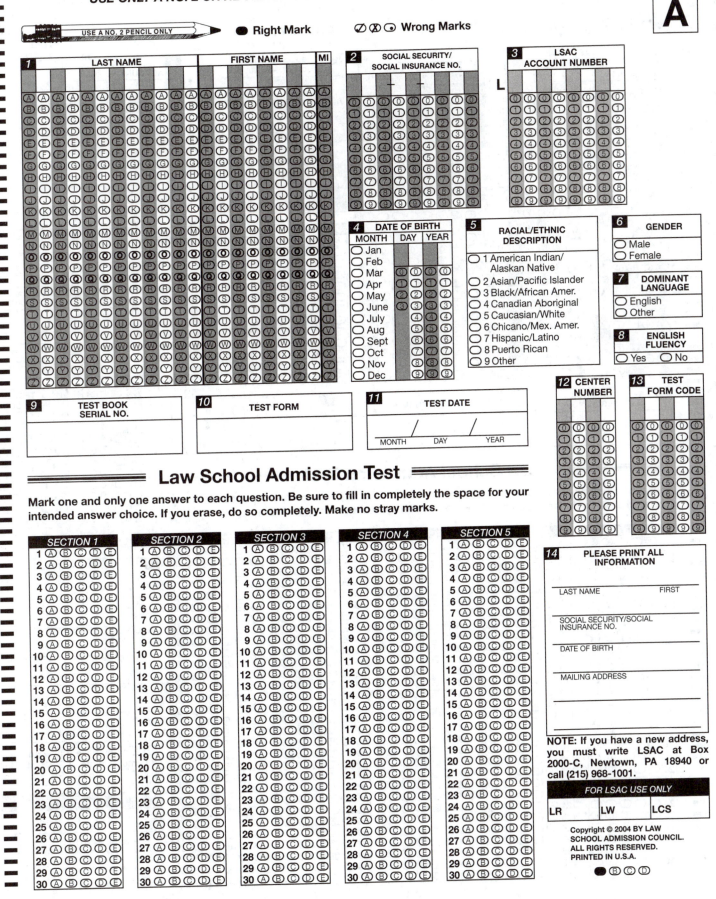

EliteView™ forms by NCS Pearson EM-250133-3:654321   Printed in U.S.A.   SIDE 1

INSTRUCTIONS FOR COMPLETING THE BIOGRAPHICAL AREA ARE ON THE BACK COVER OF YOUR TEST BOOKLET.
USE ONLY A NO. 2 OR HB PENCIL TO COMPLETE THIS ANSWER SHEET. DO NOT USE INK.

USE A NO. 2 PENCIL ONLY   ● Right Mark   ⊘ ⊗ ⊙ Wrong Marks

A

1 LAST NAME / FIRST NAME / MI

2 SOCIAL SECURITY/ SOCIAL INSURANCE NO.

3 LSAC ACCOUNT NUMBER

L

4 DATE OF BIRTH

MONTH	DAY	YEAR
○ Jan		
○ Feb		
○ Mar		
○ Apr		
○ May		
○ June		
○ July		
○ Aug		
○ Sept		
○ Oct		
○ Nov		
○ Dec		

5 RACIAL/ETHNIC DESCRIPTION

○ 1 American Indian/ Alaskan Native
○ 2 Asian/Pacific Islander
○ 3 Black/African Amer.
○ 4 Canadian Aboriginal
○ 5 Caucasian/White
○ 6 Chicano/Mex. Amer.
○ 7 Hispanic/Latino
○ 8 Puerto Rican
○ 9 Other

6 GENDER
○ Male
○ Female

7 DOMINANT LANGUAGE
○ English
○ Other

8 ENGLISH FLUENCY
○ Yes   ○ No

9 TEST BOOK SERIAL NO.

10 TEST FORM

11 TEST DATE
MONTH / DAY / YEAR

12 CENTER NUMBER

13 TEST FORM CODE

Law School Admission Test

Mark one and only one answer to each question. Be sure to fill in completely the space for your intended answer choice. If you erase, do so completely. Make no stray marks.

SECTION 1 — questions 1–30, choices A B C D E
SECTION 2 — questions 1–30, choices A B C D E
SECTION 3 — questions 1–30, choices A B C D E
SECTION 4 — questions 1–30, choices A B C D E
SECTION 5 — questions 1–30, choices A B C D E

14 PLEASE PRINT ALL INFORMATION

LAST NAME   FIRST

SOCIAL SECURITY/SOCIAL INSURANCE NO.

DATE OF BIRTH

MAILING ADDRESS

NOTE: If you have a new address, you must write LSAC at Box 2000-C, Newtown, PA 18940 or call (215) 968-1001.

FOR LSAC USE ONLY		
LR	LW	LCS

INSTRUCTIONS FOR COMPLETING THE BIOGRAPHICAL AREA ARE ON THE BACK COVER OF YOUR TEST BOOKLET.
USE ONLY A NO. 2 OR HB PENCIL TO COMPLETE THIS ANSWER SHEET. DO NOT USE INK.

A

USE A NO. 2 PENCIL ONLY   ● **Right Mark**   ⊘⊗⊙ **Wrong Marks**

1 LAST NAME   FIRST NAME   MI

2 SOCIAL SECURITY/ SOCIAL INSURANCE NO.

3 LSAC ACCOUNT NUMBER

L

4 DATE OF BIRTH

MONTH	DAY	YEAR
Jan		
Feb		
Mar		
Apr		
May		
June		
July		
Aug		
Sept		
Oct		
Nov		
Dec		

5 RACIAL/ETHNIC DESCRIPTION

1 American Indian/ Alaskan Native
2 Asian/Pacific Islander
3 Black/African Amer.
4 Canadian Aboriginal
5 Caucasian/White
6 Chicano/Mex. Amer.
7 Hispanic/Latino
8 Puerto Rican
9 Other

6 GENDER
○ Male
○ Female

7 DOMINANT LANGUAGE
○ English
○ Other

8 ENGLISH FLUENCY
○ Yes   ○ No

12 CENTER NUMBER

13 TEST FORM CODE

9 TEST BOOK SERIAL NO.

10 TEST FORM

11 TEST DATE

MONTH   DAY   YEAR

Law School Admission Test

Mark one and only one answer to each question. Be sure to fill in completely the space for your intended answer choice. If you erase, do so completely. Make no stray marks.

SECTION 1 (1–30, A B C D E)
SECTION 2 (1–30, A B C D E)
SECTION 3 (1–30, A B C D E)
SECTION 4 (1–30, A B C D E)
SECTION 5 (1–30, A B C D E)

14 PLEASE PRINT ALL INFORMATION

LAST NAME   FIRST

SOCIAL SECURITY/SOCIAL INSURANCE NO.

DATE OF BIRTH

MAILING ADDRESS

NOTE: If you have a new address, you must write LSAC at Box 2000-C, Newtown, PA 18940 or call (215) 968-1001.

FOR LSAC USE ONLY		
LR	LW	LCS

● Ⓑ Ⓒ Ⓓ

EliteView™ forms by NCS Pearson EM-250133-3:654321   Printed in U.S.A.   **SIDE 1**

INSTRUCTIONS FOR COMPLETING THE BIOGRAPHICAL AREA ARE ON THE BACK COVER OF YOUR TEST BOOKLET.
USE ONLY A NO. 2 OR HB PENCIL TO COMPLETE THIS ANSWER SHEET. DO NOT USE INK.

USE A NO. 2 PENCIL ONLY   ● Right Mark   ⊘⊗⊙ Wrong Marks

A

1 LAST NAME   FIRST NAME   MI

2 SOCIAL SECURITY / SOCIAL INSURANCE NO.

3 LSAC ACCOUNT NUMBER   L

4 DATE OF BIRTH

MONTH	DAY	YEAR
○ Jan		
○ Feb		
○ Mar		
○ Apr		
○ May		
○ June		
○ July		
○ Aug		
○ Sept		
○ Oct		
○ Nov		
○ Dec		

5 RACIAL/ETHNIC DESCRIPTION

- ○ 1 American Indian/ Alaskan Native
- ○ 2 Asian/Pacific Islander
- ○ 3 Black/African Amer.
- ○ 4 Canadian Aboriginal
- ○ 5 Caucasian/White
- ○ 6 Chicano/Mex. Amer.
- ○ 7 Hispanic/Latino
- ○ 8 Puerto Rican
- ○ 9 Other

6 GENDER
- ○ Male
- ○ Female

7 DOMINANT LANGUAGE
- ○ English
- ○ Other

8 ENGLISH FLUENCY
- ○ Yes   ○ No

9 TEST BOOK SERIAL NO.

10 TEST FORM

11 TEST DATE
MONTH / DAY / YEAR

12 CENTER NUMBER

13 TEST FORM CODE

Law School Admission Test

Mark one and only one answer to each question. Be sure to fill in completely the space for your intended answer choice. If you erase, do so completely. Make no stray marks.

SECTION 1 — **SECTION 2** — **SECTION 3** — **SECTION 4** — **SECTION 5**

(Each section: questions 1–30, answer choices A B C D E)

14 PLEASE PRINT ALL INFORMATION

LAST NAME   FIRST

SOCIAL SECURITY/SOCIAL INSURANCE NO.

DATE OF BIRTH

MAILING ADDRESS

NOTE: If you have a new address, you must write LSAC at Box 2000-C, Newtown, PA 18940 or call (215) 968-1001.

FOR LSAC USE ONLY		
LR	LW	LCS

● Ⓐ Ⓑ Ⓒ Ⓓ

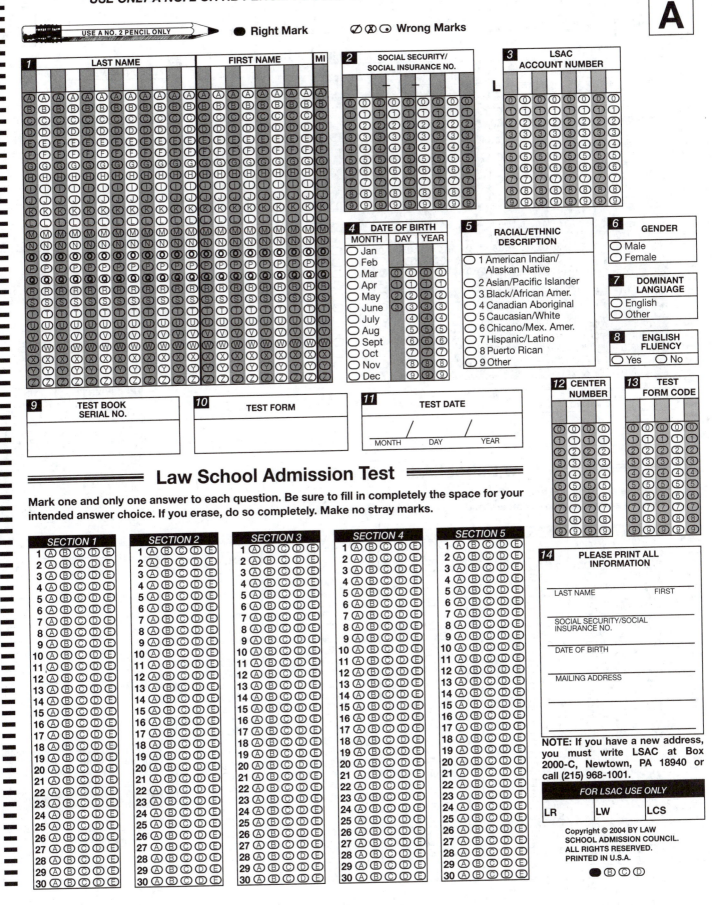

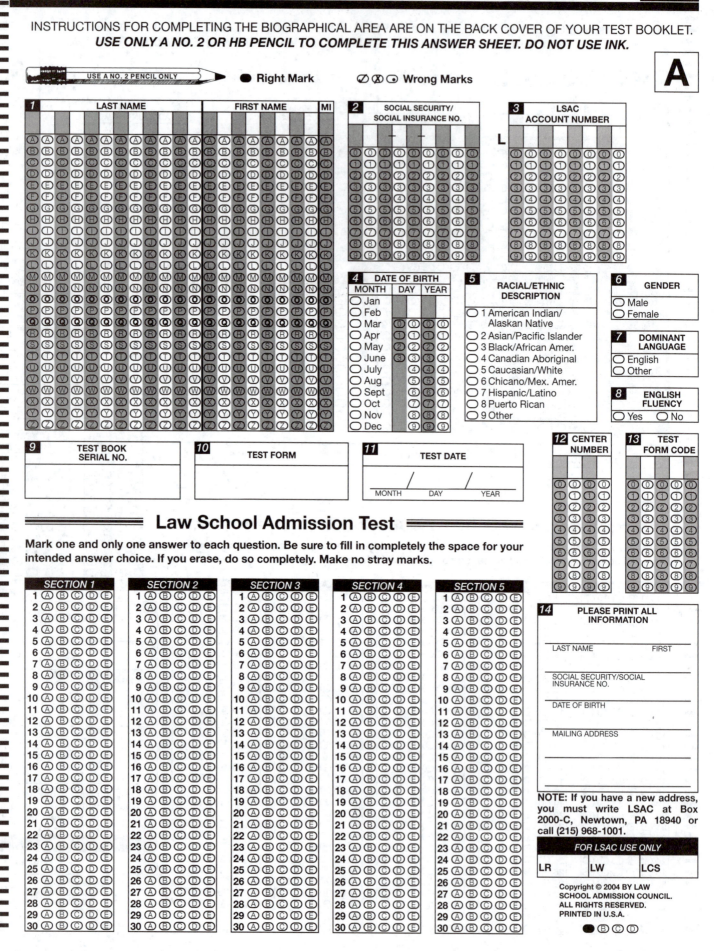